Seated *in the* Heavenly Realms

Seated *in the* Heavenly Realms

Covenant and Eschatology

YOUNG JAE SONG

Foreword by Jeong Koo Jeon

WIPF & STOCK · Eugene, Oregon

SEATED IN THE HEAVENLY REALMS
Covenant and Eschatology

Copyright © 2022 Young Jae Song. All rights reserved. Except for brief quotations in critical publications or reviews, no part of this book may be reproduced in any manner without prior written permission from the publisher. Write: Permissions, Wipf and Stock Publishers, 199 W. 8th Ave., Suite 3, Eugene, OR 97401.

Wipf & Stock
An Imprint of Wipf and Stock Publishers
199 W. 8th Ave., Suite 3
Eugene, OR 97401

www.wipfandstock.com

Except where otherwise noted, all biblical quotations are from the Holy Bible, New International Version® (NIV®), copyright © 1973, 1978, 1984, 2011 by Biblica, Inc.™ Used by permission. All rights reserved worldwide.

PAPERBACK ISBN: 978-1-6667-3868-1
HARDCOVER ISBN: 978-1-6667-9970-5
EBOOK ISBN: 978-1-6667-9971-2

JULY 25, 2022 9:14 AM

For my students

Contents

Foreword Jeong Koo Jeon | ix

Preface | xi

Chapter 1	Theology and Eschatology	1
Chapter 2	God and Eschatology	43
Chapter 3	Man and Eschatology	74
Chapter 4	Christ and Eschatology	115
Chapter 5	Redemption and Eschatology	163
Chapter 6	Spirit and Eschatology	188
Chapter 7	Kingdom and Eschatology	215
Chapter 8	Worldview and Eschatology	236

Bibliography | 259

Foreword

GEERHARDUS VOS (1862–1949) WAS A PIONEER of biblical theology. As a brilliant Dutch American linguist and biblical theologian, Vos encountered the destructive power of liberal theology while a PhD student in Germany. After returning to American soil, he began to develop his harmonious and organic integration of biblical theology and systematic theology as a seminary professor at Calvin Theological Seminary (1888–1892) and then at Princeton Theological Seminary (1892–1932). In a sense, Vos marked a gigantic but silent telos of the Old Princeton. Moreover, he was able to effectively respond to the classical liberalism of his day, as represented by German liberal scholars in the nineteenth century. For example, Albrecht Ritschl abandoned the authority of the Bible and reduced the biblical doctrine of the kingdom of God to a mere moralistic kingdom of God, highlighting the exemplary life of Jesus Christ in his public life. Capturing the core principles of *Pauline eschatology*, Vos mapped out the eschatological kingdom of God in light of the "already but not yet." Remarkably, he reenvisioned the eschatological kingdom of God from a two-age perspective: the present age and the age to come. Furthermore, he shed new light on the arena of eschatology, succinctly summarized by the phrase "eschatology precedes soteriology."

Inspired by the biblical and theological insights of Vos, his former professor, John Murray (1898–1975) endeavored to develop a biblical-systematic theology in his teaching and writing career at Westminster Theological Seminary (1930–1966), founded by the leadership of Gresham Machen in 1929. In doing so, he sought to clear the arena of systematic theology of all philosophical speculation. Murray ably expounded on the rich gold mines of biblical-systematic theology, countering the backdrop of existential liberal theology represented by Karl Barth and Rudolf Bultmann in his own historical and theological context. Nevertheless, Murray rejected Reformed covenant theology, which distinguished between the Covenant of Works and the Covenant of Grace along with the intra-Trinitarian Covenant of Redemption (*Pactum Salutis*). Murray maintained that the concept of covenant in the Bible did not appear until Genesis 6:18 at the time of Noah. Because of this, he preferred the term "Adamic administration" rather than Covenant of Works, although preserving much of the theological content of the latter.

Dr. Song is a Korean-American missionary, pastor, and theologian. He was fully aware of Vos's biblical theological ideas since his training under the tutelage of Vosian

Foreword

scholars at Westminster Theological Seminary in Philadelphia. He subsequently reintroduced the remarkable value of Vos's biblical theology while teaching underground church leaders in China suffering under harsh persecution. Based upon Reformed covenant theology, he restructured systematic theology in light of eschatology, inspired by Vos's famous phrase, "eschatology precedes soteriology." In that sense, Dr. Song's book may be read as a compendium of eschatological systematic theology with its persuasive paradigm shift toward systematic theology. Furthermore, Dr. Song's footstep toward eschatological systematic theology may consummate Murray's unfulfilled vision of biblical systematic theology because he stands on the shoulders of Reformed covenant theology. At the same time, he refutes the radical reinterpretation of the biblical doctrines by the exponents of the New Perspective on Paul, notably James D. G. Dunn, E. P. Sanders, and N. T. Wright.

Dr. Song's *Seated in the Heavenly Realms* is simply a gift from heaven as it expounds on the glorious and invisible realm where God the Father has already seated believers in Christ Jesus through the works of the Holy Spirit. I highly recommend that laypeople, missionaries, pastors, seminarians, and theologians alike read through this precious book several times. Especially, it will be heavenly manna for those who are scattered and persecuted as the pilgrims of the New Covenant diaspora in the global mission field. In addition, it will be a profound cornerstone to building an eschatological biblical worldview and will be a godly crescent in the present age to advance the Great Commission before the glorious and spectacular arrival of the age to come.

Dr. Jeong Koo Jeon
Professor of Biblical and Systematic Theology
Faith Theological Seminary

Preface

THIS BOOK EXPLAINS KEY DOCTRINES in theology from the perspective of biblical eschatology. Eschatology first appears in Genesis rather than in Revelation, for it is about the chief end of man and God's creation. It is placed in the beginning rather than at the end of theology as the central and foundational motif. "The chief end of man" in Westminster Catechism, for instance, is an eschatological concept in nature as well as in redemption. Eschatology precedes redemption, but the *eschatology of nature* is fulfilled through the *eschatology of redemption* in Jesus Christ. In this book, the "Golden Chain" of God's plan of salvation and the progress of redemptive history are interpreted through the lenses of eschatology and Christology. The theological stance of this book is the historical Reformed tradition and it owes to such theologians as Geerhardus Vos, Herman Ridderbos, and Richard B. Gaffin Jr. Their works on biblical theology and systematic theology inspired a fresh perspective to interpret biblical revelations from the point of view of the *Historia Salutis* as well as the *Ordo Salutis*. The writings of Geerhardus Johannes Vos (1862–1949) on eschatology, in particular, have had a significant influence on the present work. The pioneering achievements of Vos in the field of eschatology (*The Eschatology of the Old Testament*, *The Pauline Eschatology*) are the foundation of this book. The book stands on the shoulders of these theological giants in a modest attempt to reorganize the traditional approach to doctrines into an eschatology-based order and substance. Eschatology has traditionally remained at the tail end of theology as the doctrine of the last things rather than at the beginning as the foundational motif of all doctrines. In this work, it will be placed at the *protos* rather than at the *eschatos* of theology as the backbone of other teachings in the Scriptures. It not only precedes them in logical order but also fans them into flame as the tonic of theology and spiritual life. Eschatology is a theology of the supernatural that breathes *ruach* (wind) into the "valley of dry bones" (Ezek 37:1–14).

The basic premise of eschatology is that it existed in nature preceding redemption. The eschatology of nature, however, was to be consummated through another means, redemption in Jesus Christ. It was the eschatology of redemption, then, that fulfilled the eschatology of nature. It is the final order of affairs in the supernatural realms of redemptive heaven already given to believers in Christ, but not yet consummated until the Parousia. The heavenly realms, or the age to come, is not an unfamiliar reality postponed to a distant future, but has arrived at the closing of this age through the incarnation, death, and resurrection of the Messiah. The kingdom of God is the new schema of the age to come, a "spatial" transformation into the heavenly realms, where believers are seated with the risen Christ. Redemptive eschatology precedes the Golden Chain of the *Ordo Salutis* and the subjective application of salvation takes place as part of the new schema: "Set your minds on things above, not on earthly things" (Col 3:2). The apostle sees believers as being seated in heaven with Christ but they must continue to put to death the remaining members of "the earthly nature." Rebirth in the Spirit is not just a subjective change in the believer but a shift of ages in the objective sphere. For Vos, one of the key ideas in the eschatological concept of the Spirit is the "spatial, atmospheric character" of his work that produces "a new world-order," or "a new system of reality." The Parousia notwithstanding, the kingdom of God as the new pattern of the heavenly realms is a gift of the Spirit at present. The Spirit is resurrection life itself, a new order of life even while believers live in the last days of this age that is passing away. The appearance of the Messiah and the outpouring of the Spirit, then, mark the closing of this age, and the inauguration of the age to come. In this sense, redemption is not only the soteric rectitude of sin but the eschatological fulfillment of nature. There is more to redemption than a personal *Ordo Salutis* as these historical events decisively transformed time and history into the new and higher order of affairs in Christ. History is not defined merely in the horizontal passing of time toward the end but in terms of the vertical union of heaven and earth in Christ as the previous age became full. While the church awaits Christ's return at the Parousia, it is also seated in heaven with a foretaste of the final victory. The current state of redemption is not incomplete, as to be completed in the future, but a foretaste of the perfect redemption at the Parousia. As Vos put it, the eschatological priority of redemption is the primary rather than secondary perspective: believers are saved now because they will be saved in the future. In this sense, it is positively framed as *already* but *not yet* in that our troubles on earth will be "light and momentary" compared to "the eternal glory that far outweighs them all." As the kingdom of priests reigning with the risen Christ, the church wages war against the spiritual forces of darkness in personal sanctification but also in the holy of war of Great Commission in the age of mission.

The emphasis of soteric rectitude from sin as a central motif does not necessarily give due attention to the aeonic aspect of Christ's work and the outpouring of the Spirit. The order of movement has often been from the soteric to the eschatological rather than the reverse. The believers of all ages since the fall have been saved by the same means of justification by faith alone and imputation of Christ's righteousness. The Covenant of Grace remains the same in substance whether in the Old or the New Testament as stated by Westminster Confession of Faith: "The justification of believers under the Old Testament was, in all these respects, one and the same with the justification of believers under the New Testament." The soteric aspect of atonement, however, is somewhat linear in scope and does not necessarily take into account the organic progress of revelation toward the fulfillment in Christ. In other words, the eschatological outlook is a strand of revelation distinct from the soteric interest that requires an analysis into the vertical and spatial plane of heaven and earth. In Christ, believers have already arrived in "Mount Zion, the heavenly Jerusalem, and the city of God" as "citizens of heaven." In the meantime, they are pilgrims on the earthly journey where there is no "enduring city, looking for the city that is to come." The eschatology of redemption, said Vos, is the fulfillment of the eschatology of nature with "a soteric plus." The progress of redemption includes both aspects in that the vertical plane of eschatology firmly secures the indicative of life in God but also provides a powerful impetus to the imperative of ethics in the earthly pilgrimage.

Biblical revelation unfolds in the order of a probation in the garden of Eden, the preeschatological types in the Old Covenant, the semi-eschatological fulfillment of the New Covenant, and the final consummation of the kingdom of God in the new heaven and new earth. The provisional kingdom of Christ will be handed over to the Father in the eschatological kingdom at the Parousia, which makes any post-Parousia millennial kingdom redundant. The Christology and eschatology of the New Testament will not allow for repetition of another intermediate kingdom after the Parousia. The eschatology of redemption in Christ resulted in the closing of the New Testament canon and completion of the apostolic foundation in revelation. Since that time, the Scriptures are "God-breathed and is useful for teaching, rebuking, correcting and training in righteousness" (2 Tim 3:16). A unified system of biblical teachings is based on the closing and the consequent unity of revelations in the Son "so that the man of God may be complete, equipped for every good work" (2 Tim 3:17).

Eschatology, Christology, and soteriology are not independent or unrelated topics but mutually dependent, constituting the backbone of other doctrines in theology. They function as the broad strokes of a paint brush that outline God's vision for his creation from Eden to new Eden through the redemptive work of Christ. Its origin lies in the Counsel of Peace between the Father and the Son whose pact the Spirit applies in the new schema of the age of mission. In the New Testament, union with Christ by the Spirit represents the first endowment of the final victory in resurrection. It is a sweet foretaste of the wedding already consummated in principle and of the banquet in the new garden of God. The movement of redemption, then, is more from the end to the beginning than from the beginning to the end. Eschatology understood this way may not have been a part of regular diet of the Christian faith in church history. It has often been synonymous with the last things to be transpired at the end of history as the crown of soteriology. Such sentiment may be attributed to a delay of the Parousia, and the gradual growth of indifference to the heavenly realms as a present reality in preference to the more urgent things below. As the wait was further prolonged, the church gradually lost sight of the things above and started to look for ways to build a kingdom on earth. The earlier eschatological vision gradually gave way to interim theologies seeking ways to justify an extended stay in this world. In regions of the world where believers are faced with harsh persecution, however, the yearning is growing for the heavenly sanctuary which is "the anchor for the soul, firm and secure" (Heb 6:19). They pray, "Your kingdom come . . . on earth as it is in heaven" (Matt 6:10). The hostility against God and the church is often the greatest catalyst for believers to nurture a faith that is otherworldly in outlook. They are in the world but not of the world just like the kingdom of Christ.

The two extreme views of the kingdom of God are either a purely heavenly (future) or a purely earthly (present) kingdom. In view of redemptive eschatology, the reign of God is neither purely in the future nor purely at present: "In putting everything under him, God left nothing that is not subject to him. Yet at present we do not see everything subject to him" (Heb 2:8). The close interaction between eschatology and redemption at present is unmistakable, however. The modern atheistic culture on the one hand seeks reason, scientific inquiry, and human fulfillment in the natural world, yet on the other hand seeks an escape from reason into the mystical and supernatural realms. The eschatology of the kingdom of God in the New Testament establishes the preeminence of nature but also understands that "this world in its present form is passing away" (1 Cor 7:31).

There are many outstanding works on eschatology but they seldom explain in detail how eschatology is integrated with the loci in systematic theology. This book is a modest attempt to implement Vosian eschatology to this task as the nucleus and driving force of the *Ordo Salutis* in particular and the loci of theology in general. Eschatology is not only "curative" but "tonic,"[1] that it should breath supernatural life and energy from the heavenly places into all other teachings of the Scriptures. The eschatology of Vos, the Christology of high priesthood in particular, greatly influenced my views while I was serving an underground seminary in China. I was familiar with his works during my earlier years in seminary but rediscovered them in the later stage of my calling in a hostile environment under the government crackdown of churches. I am deeply indebted to the persecuted church in China for the contents of this work, as much as I am indebted to all my teachers in seminary for the knowledge they have taught me. In any case, I was motivated by a sense of dissatisfaction with the traditional approach to theology, which seemed piecemeal and mechanical. It seemed to be fixated on a logical order and coherence of the loci, which the eschatological approach could complement from above. Vos's watershed insight that eschatology precedes soteriology does not weaken the latter but actually establishes it. It provided some corrective measures to the linear model of progress in time by the vertical growth from this age to the age to come at the closing of time. The new order resulted in the two-age structure of the subsequent history until the Parousia in which all forms of interim theologies can be neither sufficient nor permanent.

In recent times, a collection of theological writings of Geerhardus Vos has been put together into a book (*Reformed Dogmatics*). This is an immensely valuable supplement to his previous works, yet it feels more like a collection of his thoughts rather than

---

1. Vos, *Eschatology of Old Testament*, 74.

an organized system of thought. It is a useful resource but leaves much to be desired in terms of how eschatology is permeated into the rest of his doctrinal formulations. I thought the present work in honor of him would be beneficial to and timely for the next generation of students who wish to build on his legacy. This book is written with the hope that the brilliance of this genius may be brought out of the closet and be utilized for further edification of the church. Systematic theology in the modern era should be put in a larger perspective of the *Historia Salutis* as more studies are being done in the areas of the kingdom of God, a close correlate of redemptive eschatology. For instance, Vos briefly discusses how in the four areas of resurrection, justification, salvation, and the conception of the Spirit there is a close interaction between eschatology and soteriology. How the new *schema* of the age to come, as a product of the eschatology of redemption, should be lived out in the practice of faith, ethics, and mission is a great challenge for the church still faced with many earthly troubles. The historical gap between the eschatological faith of the early church and the faith of the modern church seems to be ever widening. The modern church often displays a fading hope in the imminent return of Christ, and is entrenched in the earthly realms for a long-haul journey. In this regard, I consider it an immeasurable blessing and a great challenge personally to have lived and taught in China. Like the New Testament times, the church in China nourishes an intense thirst for the heavenly places and insatiable appetite for the spiritual bread of the risen Christ. There is little to be hoped for in this world, hence they naturally turn to the other world and set their minds on things above. Their voluntary self-denial and cross-bearing in the midst of persecution is the proactive manifestation of their eternal rest in heaven. As Vos aptly pointed out, eschatology is not opposed to realism; it is only against materialism of this age.

It has been a pleasant surprise to me to discover that believers in that part of the world responded to eschatological theology with unforeseen levels of enthusiasm. This work was born out of the church, though under persecution is filled with so much eschatological hope and untiring energy supplied from above where their Lord is seated with them. This book is written in honor of and gratitude to those with whom I have had the privilege of sharing joy and tears together in Christ.

Chapter 1

Theology and Eschatology

1.1 Heaven and Earth

The anticipation of life eternal appears before redemptive history in the Scriptures as demonstrated by the tree of life eternal in creation (Gen 2:9; 3:24). Geerhardus Vos captured this critical piece of revelation and laid a foundational principle in theology that "eschatology precedes soteriology."[1] In creation prior to redemption, therefore, a vision of the eschatological world and life eternal for man already appeared. This means that an eschatology of creation existed from the beginning that would be postponed to the end of history by the fall of man and creation. Thus, the salvific work of God in redemptive history is not the end in itself but has a higher and everlasting goal in the eschatological purpose of nature. Since the Covenant of Grace began in the promise of the seed of woman, the upward as well as the forward progress toward life eternal was put in motion. The last things of eschatology are not merely a matter of the end in chronology but properly a matter of the telos in theology. The final purpose of redemptive eschatology is the consummation of man and creation through redemption in Christ. Therefore, redemptive grace does not stop at deliverance of believers from sin but immediately brings them before God in the heavenly realms (Eph 2:6; Col 3:1). In this sense, redemption in Christ includes the spatial ascension to the heavenly realms of the age to come. The atonement of sin is a soteric part of that vertical change from the earthly to the heavenly regions in union with the risen Christ. The glorification of believers at the Parousia is the harvest and fruition of their present foretaste of the final redemption. The redemptive heaven in Christ, therefore, is the fulfillment of the eschatology of creation with an "added soteric force."[2]

In traditional theology, the subject of eschatology was not considered an integral element of the present experience of salvation but relevant to events at the Parousia. The doctrine of the last things primarily concerned the second coming of Christ and had no direct bearing on the present state of believers or their earthly pilgrimage. The anticipation of the end of history was mostly defined in terms of the horizontal

---

1. Vos, *Pauline Eschatology*, 45, 60.
2. Vos, *Eschatology of the Old Testament*, 74.

perspective of time. The present and the future state of believers were seen as two distinct entities separated by time rather than one and the same entity unfolding in two successive stages. In Paul's conception of salvation, however, a new element was added that brought a fundamental shift in how the new birth in the Spirit would be understood.[3] The new birth of the believer, beside personal regeneration, also involved the objective, vertical, and spatial elevation to heaven in the Spirit. A change in the schema (pattern) of the age is involved in the rebirth of the believer. The believer is raised and seated with Christ in the heavenly places, not figuratively, but truly and objectively in fulfillment of the covenant between the Father and the Son (John 17:21–24). The apostle Paul is thought to be the first of biblical writers to correlate the schema of the age to come with personal rebirth, broadening the scope of Christ's work to the union of heaven and earth subsequent to the closing of this age (Eph 1:10).[4] The personal and the spatial aspects are inseparable in that redemption is now defined within the larger scope of eschatology and *Historia Salutis*. On account of union with Christ, the rebirth of the Spirit is contemporaneous with the vertical ascension to heaven.[5] The resurrection of the Messiah as "firstfruit" has opened up "redemptive heaven" and believers have joined him in their rebirth through the Spirit who guarantees the final harvest (1 Cor 15:20, 45–48). The work of the Spirit is both soteric and eschatological, rendering baptism into the death and resurrection of Christ (Rom 6:5). The personal rebirth and the new schema of the age to come ("atmospheric character of the Spirit's working"[6]) take place contemporaneously. The rest of the book is an attempt to delineate the theological and practical import of this expansion in scope by the eschatology of redemption in Christ.

Horizontal and Vertical Perspective

In the rebirth of regeneration the believer is raised with Christ and brought before God in the new schema of the heavenly realms. In union with Christ, believers are "buried with him in baptism and raised with him" to the place where he is seated (Col 2:12). The overlaying of the two ages in the lower and the upper regions, sandwiched between the two comings of Christ, forms the "last days" in redemptive eschatology (Acts 2:17). It is the last days of the this age and the first days of the age to come since believers have joined the firstfruit of resurrection in Christ. This "semi-eschatological"[7] period of the kingdom of Christ is sometimes called the "already-but-not-yet" kingdom—the period between D-Day and the V-Day of redemption. The "semi" does not mean that half of salvation is fulfilled now and the other half will be fulfilled later, but

---

3. Vos, *Pauline Eschatology*, 42–61.
4. Vos, *Pauline Eschatology*, 42–61
5. Vos, *Pauline Eschatology*, 45.
6. Vos, *Pauline Eschatology*, 59.
7. Vos, *Pauline Eschatology*, 258.

the redemption accomplished will unfold in two successive stages. Believers are saved now because they will be saved later; at present is a foretaste of the perfect salvation rather than its part. The believer is already seated in the heavenly realms with Christ through the rebirth in the Spirit, only his bodily resurrection awaits (Col 3:1; 1 Cor 15:24). The two successive stages correspond to the vertical fulfillment in resurrection and the horizontal progress toward the Parousia.

The ascension to heaven in Christ shows that nature had a higher purpose than the natural life in Eden and that vision is not altered by sin (Gen 2:9, 17). God "set eternity in the human heart" in creation because man was never meant to be satisfied solely with natural life but desired the supernatural world (Eccl 3:11). The tree of life and the tree of knowledge reminded Adam that he was created as the image-bearer of God for that supernatural life. Nature was but probationary and looked forward to the consummation of God's rest on the seventh day (Gen 2:1–3). Adam lost more than natural life in the fall, for his chief end is to glorify and enjoy God, for which purpose he had been given the image of God (Rom 3:23). Even in nature, union and communion with God was the final goal in the eschatology of creation toward the supernatural state. The life eternal would have been a covenant reward for man in nature, and the tree of knowledge was a good reminder that the reward is conditioned upon keeping the covenant (Hos 6:7). The probationary state was an evidence that life eternal has yet to be reached in nature and the earthly man was yet to be transformed into the heavenly man (1 Cor 15:45–48).

Eschatology precedes soteriology but it does not bypass it. Nature was typical of redemption in regard to the chief end of man, and God achieved it through redemption in Christ. The priority of eschatology does not mean soteriology is of secondary importance but only means that the chief end of man remains the glory and enjoyment of God. Eschatology is related to creation rather than redemption at first, for the "correlate of eschatology is creation" and redemption only appeared later.[8] Eden was an excellent creation of God, and it will be transformed into the new Eden in Christ as the fulfillment of the former.[9] It is one thing to cure the disease of sin, but another thing to restore the vitality of life and make it everlasting. It would not be enough to restore the fallen creation from decay to its original form but it must be recreated so that the chief end is achieved. Hence, redemption in Christ does not stop at restoration of nature but proceeds to its recreation and consummation by way of the soteric grace. The great mystery is that God used the soteric means to achieve a far better end than nature through the redemption of Christ. The chief end is the same but the means were different in nature and in redemption. Adam was created in God's image to walk uprightly in the presence of God, to glorify and enjoy him. God achieved the same end but this time through the redemptive means: "They will come and bind

---

8. Vos, *Eschatology of the Old Testament*, 1.
9. Vos, *Redemptive History*, 243.

themselves to the LORD in an everlasting covenant that will not be forgotten" (Jer 50:5).

The union of God and man in redemption means a union of heaven and earth—the eschatological vision from the outset in nature but with a superior outcome (Eph 1:10).[10] In the fallen world the union could only be achieved through the redemptive work of the obedience of the Second Adam, who is *Immanuel*—God with us (Matt 1:23). This title of Jesus is important because he came not only to rectify sin but also to fulfill the covenant whose chief end is to render man holy and blameless before God. In Christ, life will not just be restored to its presoteric form, but will be recreated to the highest order of resurrection.[11] Hence, redemption taken as a whole is greater than atonement as it envisages the consummation of life: "One God and Father of all, who is over all and through all and in all" (Eph 4:6). All things in heaven and on earth will be unified through Christ for the glory of God, for *soli Deo gloria* as the chief end of man (Rom 11:36; 1 Cor 15:28).[12] A thousand years on earth will still be in vain compared to eternity in the presence of God and never again to be separated from the love of the Father (Rom 8:39): "A man may have a hundred children and live many years; yet no matter how long he lives, if he cannot enjoy . . . I say that a stillborn child is better than he" (Eccl 6:3).

Eschatology in Salvation

The focus of eschatology is the chief end of man in relation to God, whereas the focus of soteriology itself is rectitude from sin and liberation of man from the bondage of sin. The two are not mutually exclusive but the emphasis and scope are different. The preeminence of nature is the logical and theological ground of redemption and eschatology. The soteric goal is in order that the fallen man might return to his chief end, only with a superior Adam (Rom 5:1–3, 12–18). In the traditional approach, the two topics were not often treated together and the soteric has been the main focus in part due to the role of justification in theology. But even justification is for the praise of the glory of God and fellowship with him just as Adam walked with God in the garden (Gen 3:8). It is not a surprise, again, that Paul defines sin in terms of falling short of the glory of God rather than merely a fall from the state of innocence: "[For] all have sinned and fall short of the glory of God" (Rom 3:23). Sin is a fall from the chief end of God's glory rather than merely a fall from the innocence of nature. It is a loss of enjoyment of God more than it is breaking the law of God, and the greater tragedy is not a descent to hell, but descent from the height of God's glory. The former concerns the soterics whereas the latter concerns the eschatological goal of covenant: "I and you will have fellowship through this covenant. The condition of this covenant

---

10. Calvin, *Sermons on Ephesians*, 62.
11. Calvin, *Sermons on Ephesians*, 62.
12. Bavinck, *Reformed Dogmatics*, 1:360.

is obedience. If you obey me and keep the covenant, I will give you the blessings of the eternal life and complete happiness."[13]

C. S. Lewis's insight that there are two kinds of "nearness" to God helps us to make the distinction between forensic justification and consummate union with God. The first is nearness in *likeness* (created in God's image) and the second is nearness in *approach* (seated next to God).[14] Man is near to God in likeness, but he is not necessarily near God in approach because he has sinned against God. Adam and Eve were banned from God and Eden subsequent to the fall because they were moral and religious beings created in God's image. Hence, they must first be legally justified by God before they can begin to approach God again. "He who has great love is 'near' God. However, it is a 'nearness of similarity' in the sense of resemblance, and does not itself create 'nearness of approach.'"[15] The nearness in likeness is the reason that remedy from sin is necessary (the soteric) before nearness in approach can be allowed (the eschatological). Nearness in likeness does not automatically guarantee nearness in approach precisely because the likeness is of moral and religious nature: Adam was to obey the law of God and to walk with him in the garden. It was the eschatological nature of the chief end of man that necessitated the soteric need for legal justification. The order is that the chief end of man as the image-bearer of God precedes the soteric justification and reconciliation of man with God. Nevertheless, nature did not a priori guarantee satisfaction of the ethical and religious ends of man but was to be confirmed by the covenant. God's dealings with man is built on the two pillars of nature and redemption, and it is in the eschatology of redemption nature is perfected to its original vision. Nearness to God in likeness and approach will be sealed through the Last Adam in whom believers are seated next to God (Eph 2:6; Col 2:12; Heb 4:16). They behold God's glory and walk with him in the new garden of God (Rev 2:7).[16] The soteric addition to the eschatology of nature was accidental but superior to the latter because of the Last Adam. Eternal nearness to God now has to pass through Christ; nature has been upgraded to redemption in Christ in whom man will never again be separated from the love of God (Rom 8:39).

The redemptive eschatology in Christ is typified by the eschatology of nature in that all things exist for the glory of God (Rom 11:36). The soteric emphasis on the rectitude of sin tends to overlook the theological significance of nature and how that fits into redemption. In soteriology, holiness is against sin but in the eschatology of creation is the fulfillment of nature: "And God blessed the seventh day and made it holy, because on it he rested from all the work of creating that he had done" (Gen 2:3). Here, the notion of holiness is associated with the seventh day, when God rested from the six days of work. The particular holiness expressed here is an eschatological vision

---

13. Dunahoo, *Making Kingdom Disciples*, 108.
14. Lewis, *Four Loves*, 15.
15. Lewis, *Four Loves*, 19.
16. Lewis, *Four Loves*, 19.

in distinction from the natural order of work. It is borne out of creation rather than out of redemption. God made the seventh day holy in contrast to the six days of work prior to any mention of entrance of sin into the world. Adam was to fulfill God's purpose in creation and had proper internal and external conditions to assist him as the vice-regent of God for six days a week but God reserved the seventh day as holy for the Sabbath rest. As a sculptor appreciates his masterpiece, God expressed great joy for the work of creation during the six days. On the sixth day, the level of excitement had reached the peak when God saw the created world and exclaimed "very good!" (Gen 1:31). Good is not the same as holy, however, and the seventh day was particularly reserved as the Sabbath of God and the eschatological goal of creation. The potential of man to rebel against God was not due to any deficiencies in nature but only reflected the moral nature of man's being (Gen 2:9, 17). Adam was prophet, priest, and king bearing God's image to rule and care for the garden and the whole creation for that matter (Gen 1:26–28; 2:15).[17] But the natural world was not an end in itself and Adam would have entered the seventh day of God's rest with no further possibility of death had he kept the covenant (Gen 2:17; 3:22; Eccl 3:11). The probationary state was cut short by temptation and man's fall into sin, which necessitated a soteric means of achieving the eschatological vision of nature that never got cancelled (Gen 6:3; Hos 6:7). Adam and Eve missed the chance to turn Eden into eternal paradise filled with the glory of God and the beauty of the natural world (Gen 1:26–28; Ps 19:1). The theology of nature and its correlate eschatology not only precede redemption but provide the very foundation of it.

The trees at the center of the garden hinted that creation was not an end in itself but a process toward the higher state of life.[18] In due course, the six days would have been transformed into the seventh day, heaven and earth would have been united in some ways, and mankind would have remained forever in the garden of God. The ethical and religious aspects of man's relation to God were built into the natural order of creation rather than produced later in the fallen state for redemptive needs.[19] The ethical and religious needs of man originated from creation with a vision toward consummation. While the soteric addition later may have intensified them further, it did not produce them. The Sabbath in creation precedes the Sabbath in redemption specified later in Sinai: "Remember the Sabbath day by keeping it holy" (Gen 2:1–3; Exod 20:8). The natural order of six days were good but temporal, blessed but unrested: "There remains, then, a Sabbath-rest for the people of God; for anyone who enters God's rest also rests from their works, just as God did from his" (Heb 4:9–10). The final shift from the natural to the supernatural will only be completed in the redemptive work of Christ with the closure of time in this age (Mark 1:15). In the new order of

---

17. Gentry and Wellum, *Kingdom through Covenant*, 594.
18. Gentry and Wellum, *Kingdom through Covenant*, 592.
19. In the first chapter of *Progress of Redemption*, VanGemeren stresses the eschatological and christological import of the creation narrative in Genesis.

time, rebirth is equal to ascension to redemptive heaven: "Since, then, you have been raised with Christ, set your hearts on things above, where Christ is seated at the right hand of God. Set your minds on things above, not on earthly things" (Col 3:1–2).[20] In Pauline eschatology, Vos called this movement an "interaction between eschatology and soteriology."[21] The key distinction in the pre-fall state of man was not righteousness versus unrighteousness, but the natural versus supernatural (Gen 3:22).[22] In the eschatology of nature, the antithesis of death was not natural life but the supernatural life in God, hence Paul defined sin as falling short of God's glory rather than falling short of natural life (Rom 3:23).[23] In this sense, the prohibition in the garden was not so much a test of the obedience of the creature (which he owes God anyway) but a covenantal arrangement to reward man.[24]

The probationary state of Adam in the Covenant of Works plays a significant role in the nature of redemption in Christ. The traditional approach with a greater soteric emphasis does not necessarily give due attention to the probationary state of Adam as part of the natural eschatology. The pre-fall state of Adam seems almost redundant in the traditional view, whose focus largely remains on the fall itself, which requires a remedy. In this regard, the Lutheran view differs from the Reformed view, whose covenant doctrine focuses on the chief end of man rather than liberation of man.[25] The upward view toward heaven will put soteriology in a better perspective. Redemption is not merely penal but covenantal, and believers must "bind themselves to the Lord," "love the name of the Lord," and to "hold fast to my covenant" (Isa 56:6). The superiority of the New Covenant and the necessity of the Old Covenant are maintained by the vertical as well as horizontal progress in redemptive history. The doctrine of justification itself may not need to consider the vertical view since its focus lies in the soteric aspect. But the work of *eschatos* Adam mirrors that of *protos* Adam not only in a substitutionary sense but also in a covenantal sense as an image-bearer of God. Paul never diverges from the eschatological vision in Christ's redemptive work even in his discourse on the salvific rectitude from sin. The eschatology of nature was a possibility for Adam in Eden: "If his obedience is ratified, he would have been recognized as holy. He would've moved from a state of 'able not to sin (*posse non peccare*)' to a state of 'not able to sin (*non posse peccare*).'"[26] The goal of redemption is not only to secure the ability not to sin but to guarantee the inability to sin. In redemption, the integrity of nature is upgraded rather than degraded as heaven and earth are united through resurrection. Eschatology is not against naturalism but only against materialism for it

20. Vos, *Pauline Eschatology*, 42–61.
21. Vos, *Pauline Eschatology*, 42.
22. Vos, "Doctrine of Covenant," in *Redemptive History*, 243.
23. Hodge, *Confession of Faith*, 107.
24. Vos, *Redemptive History*, 243–44.
25. Vos, *Redemptive History*, 243–44.
26. Berkhof, *History of Christian Doctrines*, 134.

seeks the union of all things in God: "To be put into effect when the times reach their fulfillment—to bring unity to all things in heaven and on earth under Christ" (Eph 1:10). Paul never pits redemption against nature but brings them into unity through Christ: "And through him to reconcile to himself all things, whether things on earth or things in heaven, by making peace through his blood, shed on the cross" (Col 1:20).

Redemptive History

The progress of redemption ought to be viewed within the twofold purposes of recreation and consummation. Salvation presupposes antithesis of sin and grace, but consummation seeks the unity of heaven and earth recreated in redemption. The forward progress in time is led by the upward progress toward heaven, both reaching their climax in Christ. The historical process alone does not fully explain the eschatological events of the Messiah in the vertical plane of the age to come. Other than the fulfillment of types and figures, there is little to speak of in terms of the new order of the world ushered in by Christ (Luke 24:44; John 19:30). The soteric means remains identical throughout redemptive history under the Covenant of Grace but this does not explain the historical and theological distinction between the orders of Aaron and Melchizedek (Heb 5:9–19; 7:11). The progress must transcend the historical fulfillment of the prophecies in order to explain the two priestly orders. The order of Melchizedek is of the vertical direction since Christ entered the inner sanctuary of heaven after resurrection: "We have this hope as an anchor of the soul, firm and secure. It enters the inner sanctuary behind the curtain, where Jesus, who went before us, has entered on our behalf. He has become a high priest forever, in the order of Melchizedek" (Heb 6:19–20). On the other hand, the order of Aaron was imperfect in that it was only a type of the heavenly priesthood and Israel could not be made perfect in it (Heb 11:40). Under its weak order, even Moses and Aaron failed to trust God and enter the promises land (Num 20:12). Those who did enter failed to keep the covenant and could not receive "God's rest," eventually being expelled from the land into exile in Babylon (Heb 4:8): "If perfection could have been attained through the Levitical priesthood (for on the basis of it the law was given to the people), why was there still need for another priest to come—one in the order of Melchizedek, not in the order of Aaron?" (Heb 7:11).

The formal arrival of the kingdom of God coincides with the ascension of Christ into the heavenly realms subsequent to "the fullness of time" (Mark 1:15; Acts 2:17; Gal 4:4; Eph 1:10). The personal salvation of believers and the priestly kingdom of heaven have finally converged in Christ to a degree unseen previously. Israel was to be a priestly kingdom in the order of Aaron but was not perfected until the eternal high priesthood of Christ in the order of Melchizedek (Exod 19:5–6). In the New Testament, the rebirth of believers in the Spirit means entrance into the kingdom of heaven from where they can never again be expelled or separated from God (John

3:3; Rom 8:31–39). They are reborn into the kingdom: "The Law and the Prophets were proclaimed until John. Since that time, the good news of the kingdom of God is being preached, and everyone is forcing his way into it" (Luke 16:16). The Covenant of Grace has always been "curative and medical" in the horizontal order of Aaron but became "tonic, supernatural" in the vertical order of Melchizedek.[27] With the added dimension of heaven, redemption does not only cure the disease of sin, but rejuvenates the vitality of life as believers approach the throne of grace in the heavenly sanctuary. Christ covers guilt and shame, but now also restores goodness and glory in the new schema of heaven, infusing eschatological joy into the soul. In Ezekiel's prophecy, the dry bones of the valley were not just restored to a living soul, but were given the Spirit (*pneuma*) (Gen 2:7; Ezek 37:5; 1 Cor 15:44). They were given the supernatural life of the Spirit beyond restoration to natural life. The order of Melchizedek meant not only removal of guilt but also transformation to the heavenly order of affairs. The order of Aaron had a purpose but could not be perfected: Israel was to be a kingdom of priests and a holy nation in the pagan world but failed to keep the covenant (Exod 19:5–6). God's purpose in deliverance of Israel out of Egypt was not merely personal salvation but a priestly kingdom in the war of holiness (1 Cor 6:9–11). Israel did not inherit an everlasting kingdom under the order of Aaron because it did not conform to the standards of a theocratic kingdom (Lev 18:5).

In the order of Melchizedek, the new Israel will not fail like their predecessors for their High Priest is Christ. Nonetheless, the principle of holiness for the kingdom of priests remains unchanged: "Do you not know that the wicked will not inherit the kingdom of God?" (1 Cor 6:9). The difference lies in the weakness or the strength of the two orders but the requirement of God remains unchanged: that whatever (whoever) does not conform to the kingdom of God will not be allowed in it. In the New Testament, therefore, redemption does not stop with Christ's earthly work of atonement but proceeds to his heavenly work of appearance before God: "For Christ did not enter a sanctuary made with human hands that was only a copy of the true one; he entered heaven itself, now to appear for us in God's presence" (Heb 9:24). The High Priest in the order of Melchizedek was resurrected to the heavenly sanctuary to draw near God so that believers may draw near God in him without delay: "If we have been united with him like this in his death, we will certainly also be united with him in his resurrection" (Rom 6:5). Forensic justification by faith universally applies to all believers in history, but union with Christ is the vertical entrance into the age to come that was absent in the Old Testament: "What we received through the second Adam is not limited to what was lost through the first Adam: It's what the first Adam would have received if he had not fallen."[28] Eternal life in the *pneuma*, which Adam did not receive, believers received through the resurrection of the Second Adam (1 Cor 15:45).

---

27. Vos, *Eschatology of Old Testament*, 74.
28. Calvin, *Commentary on Ephesians*, 62.

Some argue that the gospel restores creation and the traditional approach overlooked the importance of nature, giving preference to saving souls.[29] This criticism is valid to a certain degree but regaining creation should be qualified by the eschatology of redemption and new creation. It is true that the progress in redemption is predicated on the eschatological kingdom of God that will consummate nature. But the goal of redemption is not restoration but recreation of the world through Christ. After the fall, nature was cursed to destruction and has been decaying ever since. Christ created a new order of heaven and earth in "the last days" of "this evil world" so that nature might be consummated, not abrogated (Gal 1:4; Heb 1:1–3; 9:26). The new order of the coming age is the immutable foundation of soteriology, "an anchor for the soul, firm and secure" (Heb 6:19). The world in its present form (*schema*) will pass away, but in the vertical direction the new world from the coming age has already arrived in Christ (1 Cor 7:31; Eph 2:6). The eschatological vision in Revelation will be the final outcome of this new order already set in motion: "Then I saw a new heaven and a new earth, for the first heaven and the first earth had passed away, and there was no longer any sea" (Rev 21:1). The probationary state of creation will not be necessary in this new order of creation for the old order has entered its "last days" (Joel 2:3; Ezek 31:18). The last days of this world means the first days (D-Day) of the new world in Christ (John 19:30; 1 Cor 11:25). The semi-eschatological kingdom of Christ is provisional until handed over to the Father but believers already live in it (1 Cor 15:24): "In putting everything under him, God left nothing that is not subject to him. Yet at present we do not see everything subject to him" (Heb 2:8).

The New Testament seems far more interested in the eschatological world of Christ than in the present form of the world that is passing away. That response is due to the interim nature of the present world produced by the gap between Christ's resurrection and the Parousia (Luke 17:21; 1 Cor 15:24).[30] The scope of redemption is far-reaching and wider than personal justification, yet the full extent of its public manifestation awaits consummation. The clash of the two worlds in these last days was actually anticipated long ago in the proto-gospel (Gen 3:15; Matt 11:12). The kingdom of Christ offers a foretaste of heaven but will also provoke violent reaction by the kingdom of darkness that knows the end is near (Mark 4:26–29). The seed of the kingdom will grow invisibly and gradually, but will be harvested abruptly when the time arrives: "As soon as the grain is ripe, he puts the sickle to it, because the harvest has come" (v. 29). Regardless, the kingdom has arrived because the King has arrived and the clash of the two worlds will be ever more fierce.[31] During the interim state, believers must carry their cross, following their Servant-King, which is the true mark of their union with him: "Now I rejoice in what was suffered for you, and I fill up in my flesh what is still lacking in regard to Christ's afflictions, for the sake his body, which

---

29. Wolters, *Creation Regained*, 63.
30. Hoekema, *Saved by Grace*, 17.
31. Semel, "Geerhardus Vos and Eschatology," 25–40.

is the church" (Col 1:24). Since the King is already enthroned, however, it will only be a matter of time before he returns as the Judge.[32] The only gap that exists between believers then and now is the length of time but the heavenly state of all believers is the same seen from the vertical union with the risen Lord. The believers in the New Testament expected a speedy return of the exalted Christ since time has already entered its last days. Regardless of the time on earth, however, believers then and now share in the same union with Christ seated together next to the Father. The vertical schema of heaven takes precedence over the horizontal flow of time, and provides the supernatural foundation and energy to its earthly life .

The incarnation of the Son of God is particularly significant in the new order of the world, for the Person of Christ is the ground of both the soteric remedy and the inaugurated kingdom. All believers in history, before or after Christ, are justified by faith alone as part of the Covenant of Grace (Rom 4:1–2). But the central difference lies in the incarnation of the Son of God in person because "perfection" could not have been attained through the Levitical priesthood (Heb 7:11). The soteric means of grace in both administrations remains unchanged but that perfection can only be achieved through Christ in person. The pre-Christ period, therefore, can be seen as preeschatological while the post-Christ era is semi-eschatological. The eschatology of redemption has been accomplished in the bodily incarnation, resurrection, and ascension of the Messiah and the everlasting union of God and man has been sealed (Isa 7:14; Matt 1:23). God's appearance in humanity is essential to substitutionary work of atonement but also necessary for the final union of God and man (Eph 1:10). Traditionally, incarnation was largely understood in terms of vicarious atonement, but in the redemptive eschatology the final use of it is to bring believers before God (Heb 4:16; 9:24). Implied in "God with us" is the chief end of man that transcends all other ends. In the ethical and religious sense, man as the image-bearer of God is perfected in "God with us." Christ is the Last Man who approaches God so that those in him might also be able to do the same. The Spirit was poured out that believers might be seated next to God with him (Acts 2:33). The rebirth in the Spirit is rebirth into a new man, but also rebirth into a new order of man in the Last Man (Eph 2:15). In redemption, believers transcended the original righteousness of Adam to the eschatological righteousness of Christ.

The nearness to God is a central theme in eschatology, i.e., the temple of God. The Spirit of God in redemptive history has always represented either the presence or departure of God (1 Sam 16:14; Ps 51:11; Eph 1:13–14). During the Aaronic order of figures and types, the Spirit could temporarily depart since the work of its mediators could not be perfect, and even prayers reflected this: "Do not cast me from your presence or take your Holy Spirit from me" (Ps 51:11). At Pentecost, however, the Spirit was poured out and will never again depart from believers for whom God is Father (Rom 8:9, 15, 39). The Spirit cannot depart them any more than he can depart Christ

---

32. Semel, "Geerhardus Vos and Eschatology," 25–40.

since they are united. The bond between the Spirit and believers is as secure as the bond between the Spirit and Christ. The Spirit gives the rebirth to each believer but the rebirth involves adoption into the sonship of the Father. It is significant that Christ retained humanity in resurrection, for it secures the adoption and the everlasting filial status. The child of God will never be chased out of the city of God in heaven like Israel was chased out of the city of God in Canaan (Heb 12:22). The vertical entrance into the inner sanctuary of heaven, Vos noted, represents the "final and proper" use of Christ's humanity besides the substitutionary atonement of sin for union of God and man: "We have this hope as an anchor for the soul, firm and secure. It enters the inner sanctuary behind the curtain" (Heb 6:19).

Present Reign of Christ

In this new order, believers are given a foretaste of heaven as they have already arrived in the heavenly Jerusalem and dwell in the eternal temple: "But you have come to Mount Zion, to the heavenly Jerusalem, the city of the living God" (Heb 12:22). The earthly church, then, is the reverse image of the heavenly Jerusalem and the outcome of the vertical ascension in Christ. In Christ, the church does not wait on earth to go to heaven but waits in heaven to finish its earthly pilgrimage. In one sense, they are already home in Christ, hence more than eager to "return" there once the earthly mission is completed (Phil 1:22–24). The horizontal wait of believers is led by the vertical reality of their union with Christ so that "to live is Christ and to die is gain" (v. 21). The doxology and theology of believers on earth flows down from the eschatology in heaven. Christ's prayer was not that the disciples be taken out of the world but that they be protected in the world until mission is completed (John 17:15). The focus of his prayer was union, between the Son and the Father and between all believers and themselves (John 17:21). The chief end of redemption is nothing less than union with the three Persons of the blessed God. This union is also the chief end in eschatology: "On that day you will realize that I am in my Father, and you are in me, and I am in you" (John 14:20). In this sense, redemption is eschatological first and soteriological second: the "Golden Chain"[33] of the *Ordo Salutis* is the application of that union rather than its cause. The soteric remedy is not an end in itself but a fruition of drawing near God himself.

The provisional union of heaven and earth in Christ gave rise to the semi-eschatological structure of the kingdom of God. The dual existence of the upper and the lower ages enables the eternal life of heaven to flow into the believer, but evokes a fierce reaction by the spiritual forces of evil (Matt 11:12). Having entered its last days, this world stands condemned already:

---

33. Muller, "Perkins' *A Golden Chaine*," 69–81.

Theology and Eschatology

> But I tell you the truth: It is for your good that I am going away. Unless I go away, the Counselor will not come to you; but if I go, I will send him to you. When he comes, he will convict the world of guilt in regard to sin and righteousness and judgment . . . because the prince of this world now stands condemned. (John 16:7–8, 11)

The new order of heaven is the outcome of the entrance of Christ into the inner sanctuary "behind the curtain," where he is seated (Heb 6:19; 9:26).[34] In the order of Aaron, the people of Israel stood outside of the tabernacle while the high priest stood in the inner sanctuary praying for them because they could not have imagined sitting before God. But in the order of Melchizedek, believers are brought into the inner sanctuary of heaven behind the curtain with the eternal high priest interceding for them. Christ is not merely a progress in redemption but the completion of it in the vertical order of Melchizedek.[35] The eschatological union of God and believers is achieved through union with the eternal high priest. What is crucified on the cross is not just the old man, but the old order of the world to which the old man is crucified (2 Cor 5:17; Gal 1:4; 6:14). The redemptive-eschatological significance of the cross is evident: "Then Christ would have had to suffer many times since the creation of the world. But now he has appeared once for all at the end of the ages to do away with sin by the sacrifice of himself" (Heb 9:26). The church is victorious in heaven but militant on earth in the spiritual war that is expanded from personal holiness to the kingdom of God. But the church has already gained the vertical perspective and panoramic view of heaven and earth so that they may pray, "Your kingdom come, your will be done, on earth as it is in heaven" (Matt 6:10).

If the two natures of divinity and humanity can be united in the Person of Christ, it is not surprising that heaven and earth can be united through him.[36] Eschatology provides a total view of the cosmos in redemption, but it also provides otherworldly life and energy for the Christian life.[37] The opening words of the Lord's Prayer are that God's will be done on earth as it is in heaven: "The event of the resurrection of Christ in history is the protrusion of the resurrection of the dead into time."[38] In redemption the reality of heaven has intruded from the future into the present, making the believer's hope authentic and unashamed (1 Cor 15:19; Col 3:1–4). The believer does not hate the world, nor is he pitied by it despite the cross-bearing in this world for his hope is sustained by corresponding reality of heaven (Eph 1:3; Col 2:12). Christ's crucifixion and resurrection took place in public so the Christian faith ought to be a public profession of Christ and his kingdom: "All worldviews, including that of Christianity,

---

34. Ridderbos, *Paul*, 14.
35. Wright, *Paul and Faithfulness of God*, 1473.
36. Calvin, *Ephesians*, 63.
37. Vos, *Pauline Eschatology*, 37.
38. Campbell, *Paul and Union with Christ*, 411.

are in principle public statements."³⁹ While the Christian faith is intensely personal, it is public by nature because faith is ultimately about "God and His world."⁴⁰ The undue spiritualizing of the Christian faith is like the Gnosticism of the early church, especially in its prejudice against the physical world.⁴¹ In the Gnostic view of the world, nature is denied, much less is there a recreation of nature into a new heaven and earth (Rev 21:1). But true eschatology affirms the glory and splendor of nature, which God created and will consummate (1 Cor 15:28; Rom 11:36): "The heavens are yours, and yours also the earth; you founded the world and all that is in it" (Ps 89:11).

1.2 Divine Covenant

Covenant is one of the central themes in the Scriptures essential to understanding eschatology and soteriology. The Covenant of Grace progresses in the horizontal direction toward Christ and in the vertical direction to the inner sanctuary of heaven (Heb 6:19–20). The Covenant of Grace is not unrelated to the Covenant of Works for both seek the chief end of man as the final goal. The Counsel of Peace between the Father and the Son is completed, rendering the chosen in Christ holy and blameless before God (Eph 1:4). It is also the fulfillment of the Davidic covenant by the resurrection of Jesus, who is declared to be the Lord and the Messiah (Acts 2:17, 31–36). The prophecy of Jeremiah about union of God and Israel by the eternal covenant is fulfilled through Christ (Jer 50:5). The redemptive-eschatological history is a covenant history of Adam, Noah, Abraham, Moses, David, and finally Christ, who fulfilled all previous covenants and entered the heavenly sanctuary, where he is seated next to the Father.

Covenant and Eschatology

Eschatology flows out of the Divine Being, who is the Alpha and the Omega of all things, and worthy of man's praise and adoration (Rom 11:36). God's dealings with man in a covenant form is rooted in the image of God, which is of an ethical and religious nature. Thus, the origin of the covenant is the image of the three Persons of the blessed God, who exist in mutual glory, love, and knowledge (John 17:21–24). Accordingly, the ultimate purpose of God's covenant with man is to produce the eschatological man in whom the image of God is perfected for fulfillment of the chief end of man (1 Cor 15:47; 2 Cor 4:4). In this sense, it may be noted that the doctrine of justification itself does not necessarily deal with the image of God, but is mostly concerned with deliverance of man from unrighteousness. The ethical and religious nature of man imbedded in covenant is not in conflict with the sovereign grace rooted in predestination (Eph 1:3–4). Historically, covenant theology has focused largely on

---

39. Wright, *New Testament and People of God*, 135.
40. Wright, *New Testament and People of God*, 135.
41. Wright, *New Testament and People of God*, 135.

the horizontal development of the covenants in the Scriptures to the exclusion of the vertical consideration of the *Pactum Salutis*. The covenant viewed as a bilateral treaty places strong emphasis on ethics that appears to be in conflict with unilateral predestination. The doctrine of predestination, for instance, is seen to be at the opposite end of the doctrine of covenant. But the false dichotomy is quickly resolved by the purpose of predestination, which is to produce holy and blameless children of God (Eph 1:4). The covenant is the means by which the purpose of election in Christ is achieved in the consciousness of believers through faith and repentance. As a result, the image of God in truth, righteousness, and holiness is recreated in the regenerate man through union with Christ (Eph 4:24).

Predestination and covenant do not clash and are not mutually exclusive as they are connected through the Golden Chain of God's redemptive plan (Rom 8:29–30). The covenant is gracious yet recreative of man fulfilling the ultimate purpose of the eternal election for the children of God. The probation of Adam had the same purpose of confirmation in the image of God through obedience in the covenant visually reminded by the tree of knowledge.[42] The first Adam broke the covenant, but the second Adam came to restore and consummate the original purpose. In this sense, the Person of Christ takes logical priority over the work of Christ who is the perfect image of God (2 Cor 4:4). As Calvin said, there can be no benefit in the work of Christ apart from union with the Person of Christ.[43] It is clear that Covenant of Grace cannot be in conflict with predestination because it is the historical means of fulfilling the eternal purpose. The doctrine of covenant, whether of works or grace, originates from the very image of the Trinitarian God and the creation of man in "their" likeness (Gen 1:26). The fulfillment of covenant in the form of "God with us" thus manifests the particular nuance of religious and personal fellowship of man with God. Union with Christ is more than soteric for it means consummation of the covenant that includes imputation of his righteousness and recreation of his image (Rom 8:29; 1 Cor 1:30; Eph 4:24; Col 3:10). The covenant reveals that man's desire for eternity is rooted in his longing for God and a return to his ontological origin. Therefore, the final destination of believers is not so much a particular place as much as a particular being, namely, the Divine Being himself (John 17:21–24).

Understandably, soteriology by definition deals more with *iustitia Dei* (justice of God) than with *imago Dei* (image of God). The soterics deals with the "curative" of sin whereas eschatology concerns the "tonic" of the eternal life and intimacy with God.[44] In this sense, the acts of Adam and Christ are covenantal in that they involve the image of their persons rather than mere outward performances (Rom 5:12, 19). The point of comparison between the two men was more than bare disobedience or obedience but the image of person that resulted in those acts. The exhortation to conform to

---

42. Vos, "Doctrine of Covenant," 243.
43. Horton, *Covenant and Salvation*, 183.
44. Vos, *Eschatology of Old Testament*, 74.

Christ's image likewise underscores the centrality of the personhood in the covenant that Christ fulfilled (Rom 8:29). Vos summarizes the fundamental problem of legalism despite its sincerity: "Legalism lacks the supreme sense of worship. It obeys but it does not adore." The purpose of redemption is recreation of God's image whose substance is truth, righteousness and holiness in order that the believer may adore God as well as obey him (Eph 4:24). The covenant love of *Hesed* always precedes the obedience of Israel whom God redeemed out of Egypt by his covenantal grace and faithfulness (Exod 24:7; 34:6). Yahweh is a God who keeps the covenant of love and faithfulness and expects to be loved back: "Know therefore that the Lord your God is God; he is the faithful God, keeping his covenant of love to a thousand generations of those who love him and keep his commandments" (Deut 7:9). In the language of the New Testament, they were chosen in Christ so that they might conform to Jesus: "For those God foreknew he also predestined to be conformed to the image of his Son, that he might be the firstborn among many brothers and sisters" (Rom 8:29).

This federal union in covenant reaches deeper than substitution though vicarious atonement is absolutely necessary for reconciliation with the righteous God (Rom 5:18–19). The union renders God's children not only forgiven and justified, but also seated in the heavenly realms with Christ to "participate in the divine nature, having escaped the corruption in the world caused by evil desires" (Eph 4:24; 2 Pet 1:4). The union of the divine and the human natures in Christ is not irrelevant to the federal union of believers with Christ. The Chalcedonian Creed found that the two natures of Christ are united "without confusion, without change, without division, without separation."[45] The image of Christ cannot be detached from the work of Christ, and this image is recreated in believers immediately upon being united with him. In this sense, Christology is not only for eschatology but is eschatology. The beginning of the end or the last things of the age to come starts in the first coming of Christ rather than his second coming. The latter is but the harvest of the first or the end of the end. It also explains the typological covenant marriage of Yahweh and Israel, later fulfilled by the covenant union of Christ and Church (Eph 5:23). The Word became flesh not only to reconcile church with God but also to accept her as his glorious Bride (John 1:14). For this, he learned to obey the Father in suffering, declared by the Spirit as righteous through resurrection so that believers might draw near God with him (1 Tim 3:16; Heb 5:8–10; 1 Pet 3:18). The transaction first took place within the Godhead before the foundation of the world, and only then it is later transferred to Christ and believers through their mystical union (Heb 4:14–16).

---

45. Council of Chalcedon (451 AD).

Covenant Love

Man's innate desire to be with God yet his total inability to draw near him is the outcome of the broken covenant in Eden. The nearness of likeness to God can actually work against the nearness of approach because a "justification" to approach is required. Man's natural instinct to worship, adore, and obey God is the mark of covenantal being, and will seek a substitute in the absence of God's presence. Idolatry is the flipside of the innate need of man to be near God and adore him. They will "devote unconditional loyalty worthy of God alone, to man's love, and at that moment, they turn into gods. They become demons."[46] God "condescends" himself and makes covenant with Adam with reward and curses because man is the image-bearer of God (Gen 2:17, 3:15–24).[47] The elements of God's image were truth, righteousness, holiness that were necessary for the office of the vice-gerent appointed to care for the world as king, priest and prophet (Gen 1:26–28, 2:15; Eph 4:24). These traits are essential to man's being for the purpose of covenantal duty caring for God's creation, and the enjoyment of the divine company in the temple of paradise.

In the redemptive side of history, the ethical and religious traits of man are eternally restored when Christ died and resurrected. "Who then is the one who condemns? No one. Christ Jesus who died—more than that, who was raised to life—is at the right hand of God and is also interceding for us. Who shall separate us from the love of Christ?" (Rom 8:34–35). The intercession is taking place next to the Father where God's *Hesed* (covenant love) will never again be taken away from believers (v. 39). God's covenant faithfulness in all of its ethical and religious aspects is now given to believers as their eternal inheritance: "Now if we are children, then we are heirs—heirs of God and co-heirs with Christ, if indeed we share in his sufferings in order that we may also share in his glory" (v. 17). The work given to the Son in the Counsel of Peace by the Father has been executed by the Son through the means of covenant (Eph 1:3–14). Covenant of Redemption (*Pactum Salutis*) has been fulfilled in history through Covenant of Grace and believers may now share in the glory and love of the Father and the Son (John 14:20; 17:21–24). Christ is the fulfillment of the Counsel of Peace[48] in history and believers now may join in the Trinitarian fellowship upon their rebirth without a delay: "Now this is the eternal life: that they may know you, the only true God, and Jesus Christ, whom you have sent" (John 17:3, 21). They could then draw near God at the throne of grace in time of need and receive grace by their union with the high priest who kept his end of the Counsel (Heb 4:16).

---

46. Lewis, *Four Loves*, 19–20.

47. Lewis, *Four Loves*, 21.

48. Zech 6:13 (ESV): "It is he who shall build the temple of the Lord and shall bear royal honor, and shall sit and rule on his throne. And there shall be a priest on his throne, and the counsel of peace shall be between them both."

The foretaste of covenant love of the Father, is not postponed to the end of the world but available now to those who are united to Christ through the Spirit. Thus, he prayed "I have made you known to them, and will continue to make you known in order that the love you have for me may be in them and that I myself may be in them" (John 17:26). This is eschatology now rather than eschatology later in that God's love is made available immediately in the heavenly realms. The chief end of man to "glorify God and to enjoy him forever" given in paradise is no longer postponed to the future as believers may at once approach the throne of grace (Heb 4:16). The covenant of love is rooted in the image of God and has been the chief end of man since the creation of the world.[49] It has not been suspended or altered by the entrance of sin but has been further established in the redemptive eschatology: "And he passed in front of Moses, proclaiming, 'The LORD, the LORD, the compassionate and gracious God, slow to anger, abounding in love and faithfulness'" (Exod 34:6). In Greek New Testament, *agape, phileo* or *eros* all denote love, but agape in particular denotes covenant love comparable to *Hesed* (John 21:15–17).[50] Central to agape love is covenant: God in Christ wants to make his children holy and blameless just as the Son is holy and blameless (Eph 1:4). The culmination of this covenant love has been witnessed at Pentecost subsequent to the resurrection of Christ:[51] "Having believed, you were marked in him with a seal, the promised Holy Spirit, who is a deposit guaranteeing our inheritance until the redemption of those who are God's possession—to the praise of his glory" (Eph 1:13b-14). The covenant love of agape is loving faithfulness between two parties as shown in the metaphor of marriage between Yahweh and Israel.[52] "God's love is at the heart of the biblical story,"[53] and Paul refers to it as the foundation of election in Christ and the guarantee of adoption to sonship (Eph1:3–4; Rom 8:39).

To drive a wedge between predestination or covenant, therefore, is a false dichotomy nowhere found or sanctioned in the Scriptures. The predestination in the form of Covenant of Redemption was conceived "in love" and its purpose was to produce holy and blameless children of God. The Golden Chain of the *Ordo Salutis* is of great significance in this regard for it covers the whole ground from one side of eternity to the other (Rom. 8:30): "For he chose us in him before the creation of the world to be holy and blameless in his sight. In love he predestined us for adoption to sonship through Jesus Christ . . ." (Eph 1:4). The covenant is indeed gracious, yet demands holiness and obedience as essential parts of the inter-Trinitarian relationship, and God's children are expected to conform to the image of the firstborn in God's family (Rom 8:29). There is no greater motive than conformation to Christ that explains the eschatological goal of creation and redemption. God created the world *ex nihilo* for no

---

49. Frame, *Doctrine of God*, 437.
50. Frame, *Doctrine of God*, 415.
51. Frame, *Doctrine of God*, 415.
52. Frame, *Doctrine of God*, 415.
53. Frame, *Doctrine of God*, 414.

greater reason than man's conformation to the image of the Son whom he loves and is well pleased with (Luke 3:22). The ability to sin (*posse peccare*) was not a sign of inherent defect in creation, or a dualism of the spiritual and the material, but a reflection of covenantal being created in God's image: "The non-redemptive strand explains the preeminence of the natural (physical) element in biblical eschatology."[54] The thought process of biblical authors was such that the ethical and religious nature of man does not contradict the eternal election in Christ. In their minds, "the first-cause" of God's eternal will did not negate "the secondary cause" of man's liberty and covenantal duty (Gal 5:6). The biblical dictum that faith expresses itself through love is true regardless of perspective—the first or the second cause.[55] Again, covenant conjoins truth and love that "speaking the truth in love, we will grow to become in every respect the mature body of him who is the head, that is, Christ" (Eph 4:15). In the same vein, the love of God and neighbor is the central principle of the law and the substance of covenant, "Jesus replied: Love the Lord your God with all your heart and with all your soul and with all your mind. This is the first and greatest commandment. And the second is like it: Love your neighbor as yourself" (Matt 22:37–39). The election in Christ does not contradict the ethics of covenant in the logic of biblical authors, especially the Apostle Paul.[56] Eschatology, explained Vos, manifested on a personal level is nothing other than "faith expressing itself through love." New Covenant not only fulfills Old Covenant in the horizontal plane of history, but accomplishes the eternal decree in the vertical plane of the Golden Chain.

In short, the relationship between predestination and covenant is directly proportional (mutually corroborating) rather than inversely proportional. The sovereign election of believers by God undergirds and strengthens the integrity of covenant: "What is the point of the covenant? It is to establish oneness between God and his people . . . 'I shall be your God and you shall be my people,' functioning as the central unifying theme of the covenant, underscores the role of oneness as the essence of the goal of the covenant."[57] In this bond of oneness, ideally speaking, one party does not unilaterally possess the other, but the two parties mutually and fully share themselves as covenant partners. It is a most stunning pronouncement of Yahweh that he offers himself as the husband to Israel, who will be his treasured possession (Exod 19:5). A union of two parties through a human intermediary cannot be a perfect union for it would still be an *indirect* union. For this reason, the law was written on tablets of stone rather than on the heart, and the Old Covenant was insufficient to consummate that marriage union (Jer 31:31–34). But the bond between God and man through Christ is a *direct* union because the mediator in the order of Melchizedek is God himself (Gal 3:20). The law can now be written directly in the heart for there is no longer need

---

54. Vos, *Eschatology of Old Testament*, 74.
55. Gentry and Wellum, *Kingdom through Covenant*, 585.
56. Gentry and Wellum, *Kingdom through Covenant*, 585.
57. Robertson, *Christ of Covenants*, 302.

for human mediators or the veil over Moses' face to hide the fading radiance (2 Cor 3:13). The weakness of the Old Covenant lies in the weakness of the union: "So long as the administration of God's covenant transpires through a system of intermediaries, covenant oneness essentially has been negated."[58] The direct union, on the other hand, requires an intra-Trinitarian covenant where one of the Persons of the Godhead unites himself with man in the bilateral covenant: "A mediator, however, implies more than one party; but God is one" (Gal 3:20). The mystery of that union is so profound that God used the union of man and woman as the metaphor of covenant between God and man, Christ and church (Gen 2:24; Eph 5:31–32). The union of God and believers through Christ is immediate and unmediated, especially in view of their vertical ascension to be seated next to the Father. The joy of this union and fellowship is unparalleled by anything on earth: "Though you have not seen him, you love him; and even though you do not see him now, you believe in him and are filled with an inexpressible and glorious joy . . ." (1 Pet 1:8). The feeling is mutual as God rejoices in them as much as they rejoice in him: "The Lord your God is with you, he is mighty to save. He will take great delight in you, he will quiet you with his love, he will rejoice over you with singing" (Zeph 3:17).

Divine Law

The bilateral union and fellowship in covenant is modelled after the eternal covenant of the *Pactum Salutis* in the Trinity, from which the image of God in man is derived. The use of the law in the prelapsarian state of Eden was not given much consideration in Lutheran theology because its view of the primary function of the law was to convict and penalize the sinner. In covenant theology, on the other hand, the law primarily reflects God's image and the divine attributes shared by the Persons of the Trinity (John 17:21–26). Accordingly, the positive purpose of the law is traced back to creation, for all that man does in covenant with God reveals the divine attributes. The term "covenant" to denote the original state of man thus meant a special arrangement rather than a mere test of obedience.[59] God has voluntarily "condescended" himself to make a covenant with Adam to bless and reward him with life eternal upon obedience.[60] Reformed theology viewed the relationship as a covenant—not as a mere test of obedience—because it was a means of blessing and reward by God upon the consummation of his image shared by the creature (Gen 2:17).[61] It was a means by which man would have reached the highest state of the *imago Dei* and be granted the gift of the eternal life. This prelapsarian arrangement has been replaced by the Covenant of Grace after the fall, but the nature of covenant itself remains unchanged: "If you keep

---

58. Robertson, *Christ of Covenants*, 302.
59. Vos, "Doctrine of Covenant," 244.
60. Westminster Confession of Faith, 7.
61. Vos, "Doctrine of Covenant," 243.

my commands, you will remain in my love, just as I have kept my Father's commands and remain in his love" (John 15:10). In all of this, the law thus serves a positive purpose of the covenant rather than just being a means of remedy for sin. God expects man to be a certain kind of being and to live a certain way of life regardless of whether or not he has the ability to do so: "He has shown you, O mortal, what is good. And what does the Lord require of you? To act justly and to love mercy and to walk humbly with your God" (Mic 6:8). The law is not a legal condition of the Covenant of Grace but a moral principle of the image of God. Since the covenant first began between the Father and the Son, voluntary obedience rather than bare rituals is expected of anyone who enters it: "But Samuel replied, 'Does the Lord delight in burnt offerings and sacrifices as much as in obeying the Lord? To obey is better than sacrifice, and to heed is better than the fat of rams'" (1 Sam 15:22). The covenantal nature of the law demands not only repentance of sin but loving God with all of one's heart, soul, mind, and strength as the fulfillment of the *imago Dei*.

In the Old Testament, a covenant (*berit*) is said to be cut (*karat*) between two parties making a treaty (Gen 15:17–18). Similarly, a check is "cut" today as the guarantee of payment between two parties. Hence, God cut up a sacrificial animal carcass into pieces as a metaphor that a covenant was "cut" with Abraham with life and death on the line. As God passed through the bloody carcass he visually demonstrated a covenant vow that involves his own life or death. It was a solemn but gracious oath on God's part that the promise would be kept at all costs. For Abraham, it was meant to be a promise of blessing as well as a solemn warning that if broken it would require the penalty of death. The gruesome metaphor signified the seriousness of the oath, its consequences, and the means of redemption if and when broken. The message was clear that the covenant union is not meant to be broken, and if broken there would be no remedy without shedding of blood: "In fact, the law requires that nearly everything be cleansed with blood, and without shedding of blood there is no forgiveness" (Heb 9:22). In any case, the nature and requirement of the covenant remain the same at all times before or after the fall, although the persons who fulfill it have been changed from Adam to the Second Adam (Gen 2:17, Rom 5:11). The covenantal arrangement is provided to no other creatures except for man; God has entered into covenant with no other creature, including angels. As it turns out, the covenant with Abraham has been kept as God "bought" the church "with his own blood" (Acts 20:28; Eph 5:22–33). The broken covenant, as promised, was redeemed by the piercing nails that cut through the body of Christ and by the blood he shed on the cross (Hos 6:7; Rom 5:12–21; Col 2:11–12). The union of the Son and the Father was cut off on the cross in exchange for the eternal union of believers with the Father from whose love they will never again be separated (Rom 8:39). In this sense, the New Covenant fulfills the Old Covenant in the horizontal direction but also moves from the earthly to the heavenly in the vertical direction (Heb 9:12). The law written on the stone tablets is now written in the heart of believers, "who with unveiled faces all reflect the Lord's glory, are being transformed into his likeness with ever-increasing glory, which comes from the Lord, who is the Spirit" (2 Cor 3:18).

New Covenant

The New Covenant is also the eternal covenant when sealed by the crucifixion and resurrection of Christ, who is the eternal high priest in the order of Melchizedek (Heb 13:20). The vertical perfection is added to the horizontal fulfillment in the New Covenant that instantly secures the everlasting union of believers with God in the inner sanctuary of heaven (Heb 4:16; 6:19–20). The New Covenant has thus inaugurated the coming of the kingdom of heaven with the new schema of the coming age—also the last days of this age (Mark 1:15; Acts 2:17). The prophecy of Jeremiah concerning the eternal union of God and man has been fulfilled: "They will ask the way to Zion and turn their faces toward it. They will come and bind themselves to the Lord in an everlasting covenant that will not be forgotten" (Jer 50:5). The shedding of blood on the cross that ratified the eternal covenant produced the new kind of repentance in believers that is called the "circumcision of the heart" (Deut 10:16):

> When the people heard this, they were *cut*[62] to the heart and said to Peter and the other Apostles, "Brothers, what shall we do?" Peter replied, "Repent and be baptized, every one of you, in the name of Jesus Christ for the forgiveness of your sins. And you will receive the gift of the Holy Spirit." (Acts 2:37–38)

The "cut to the heart" reminds us of the cutting (*karat*) of the covenant made with Abraham, and also the cut to the sacrificial animal, now ratified by the piercing of Christ's body and shedding of his blood on the cross. The following words are significant in this regard: "In him you were also circumcised, in the putting off of the sinful nature, not with a circumcision done by the hands of men but with the circumcision done by Christ, having been buried with him in baptism and raised with him through your faith in the power of God, who raised him from the dead" (Col 2:11). At Pentecost, the Spirit has sealed Christ to believers and their hearts were *cut* open by the piercing "sword of the Spirit" just as the bloody carcass of the Abrahamic covenant (Eph 6:17). Repentance in the New Covenant is a covenantal remorse of the heart that results in the putting to death of the earthly nature (Col 3:5). The earthly nature can be put to death for no greater reason than that believers are crucified and raised with Christ to the heavenly regions. The ability to put our minds on things above rather than on earthly things is rooted in the objective reality of having been raised with Christ once and for all (Col 3:1).

The eschatology of nature is that there was more to creation than its temporal existence. The covenant of the first man was non-salvific yet eschatological in that the earthly image of man was to be transformed into the heavenly image. Every chosen

---

62. Italics added.

person in Christ will be saved at some point in the course of redemptive history but the arrival of the last days of this age is introduced in the New Covenant era (Heb 1:2). Therefore, the New Covenant could not have been arbitrarily called the eternal covenant; it is not only new but eternal (Heb 13:20). The multiple covenants of the past are eventually merged into one eternal covenant in Christ that united things in heaven and things on earth. It is true that the provisional distinction of soteriology and eschatology will be redundant in the new heaven and earth but still relevant in the present order of things. Unlike the Old Covenant, the union of God and man in the New Covenant is perfect as believers participate in the finished work of Christ (Jer 31:33; John 19:30; Heb 11:39–40). In union with Christ, the spatial movement from earth to heaven takes place contemporaneous with the rebirth in the Spirit. Eschatology now possess a "redemptive plus" for it is far better than the eschatology of nature which the first Adam failed to experience.[63] The eschatology of nature is at work in tandem with a soteric purpose in the Person and work of Christ with a far better outcome than the first. In redemption, therefore, believers receive far more than deliverance from sin because grace does more than take us back to the probationary state of paradise: "But where sin increased, grace increased all the more, so that, just as sin reigned in death, so also grace might reign through righteousness to bring the eternal life through Jesus Christ our Lord" (Rom 5:20b-21). The prelapsarian state of "normal" would certainly be better than the fallen state but redemptive grace produces a far better state of "supernormal" in Christ.[64] Redemption is not a return back to temporal paradise, but an ascension to the eternal paradise of God (Rev 2:8): to "this original eschatology is now added a soteric force."[65]

The New Covenant transformed the notion of heaven from impersonal location into covenantal relation of "God with us." The invitation of Yahweh to Israel to be united with him through the eternal covenant is at last accomplished by the one called *Immanuel* (Jer 50:5; Matt 1:23). The substance of life eternal is the knowledge of God, and the final *destination* of salvation is first and foremost God himself rather than an utopian location (John 17:3, 21). The covenant union of God and man is modelled after the fellowship of the Father and the Son. After all, man is created in God's image and likeness, having been given certain commutable attributes of God (Gen 1:26). The Promised Land was never really the true and final destination of Israel proven by the fact that they could not enter "God's rest" even in Canaan (Heb 4:8). The true reward of the covenant is the uninhibited presence of Yahweh himself in the heavenly sanctuary of which the earthly sanctuary was but a shadow. In the inner sanctuary of heaven, the covenant marriage between Yahweh and his bride is consummated through Christ (Isa 54:5; Heb 6:19, 8:5). After the golden calf incident at Sinai God refused to go with Israel to Canaan, but Moses prayed:

63. Vos, *Eschatology of Old Testament*, 77.
64. Vos, *Eschatology of Old Testament*, 73–76.
65. Vos, *Eschatology of Old Testament*, 73–76.

> If your Presence does not go with us, do not send us up from here. How will anyone know that you are pleased with me and with your people unless you go with us? What else will distinguish me and your people from all the other people on the face of the earth? (Exod 33:15–16)

Even the land flowing with milk and honey would be a curse, much less heaven, if God's presence does not go with them. Moses regarded the presence of God as the only worthy sign of the priestly kingdom, a holy nation, and Yahweh's treasured possession among nations (Exod 19:5–6).

The New Covenant begins with the incarnation of the Word, who is the true and eternal temple (Mark 14:58). Theophany began in the first paradise where God walked with man and it will be fully manifested in the new and eternal paradise (Gen 3:8; Rev 2:8). The Word became flesh to dwell—literally, "pitch tabernacle"—among man so that the unfulfilled covenant union in Eden at last may be consummated (John 1:12–14). The High-Priestly Prayer of Jesus for union of believers with the Father is particularly meaningful in this regard (John 17:21). The full glory of heaven has yet to be revealed, but believers will no more be in God than they already are in Christ. The covenant union is the consummation of the chief end of man and the two pillars of eschatology in the covenant are ethics (obedience to God) and religion (intimacy with God).[66] The New Covenant envisions the heavenly temple, the garden of God, where Christ has entered with believers. In the garden of God, the law is not legalistic but covenantal as expressed by the command, "Love the LORD your God with all your heart and with all your soul and with your strength" (Deut 6:5). To this end the elect are foreordained, called, regenerated, justified, sanctified, and glorified in Christ (Rom 8:30). New Covenant of Christ thus is comprehensive in scope and consummative in purpose as the means of fulfilling eternal plan of redemption (Eph 1:4). The New Covenant is the eternal covenant since Christ is the "end of the law" in both horizontal and vertical senses of redemptive history (Rom 13:8–10).

History of Covenant

Biblical history is led by the vertical goal of union of heaven and earth, yet administered in diverse ways through horizontal history culminating in Christ. The covenants in biblical history essentially move from the first to the Last Man despite the variety in between. After the broken covenant of Adam in Eden, the covenants of Noah, Abraham, Moses, and David, and finally the New Covenant of Christ constitute Covenant of Grace. The final progress of biblical history is the progress of covenant from earth to heaven, or the natural to the supernatural.[67] The valley of dry bones in the prophecy of Ezekiel epitomizes this as the dry bones were resurrected by the breath of the Spirit

---

66. Vos, *Eschatology of Old Testament*, 75.
67. Vos, *Eschatology of Old Testament*, 74.

in distinction from the breath of biological life (Gen 2:7). Hence, union with Christ leads to putting off the old self and putting on the new self (Eph 4:22–24), of which the latter corresponds to the eschatological life in the Spirit. The vivification of life is manifested in varying degrees proportional to particular phases of biblical history as revelation becomes larger and clearer. The spiritual maturity of God's people in the vertical sense corresponds to the volume and clarity of revelation in each corresponding period. The pre-Christ and post-Christ phases of history could not have equally perceived and experienced mortification of sin and vivification of life (Heb 11:39–40). The height and depth of God's covenant with his people will depend on nearness to Christ as the order of Aaron is about to be substituted by the order of Melchizedek. God's people looked forward and upward in eager anticipation of Christ and his entrance into the heavenly tabernacle (John 8:56; Heb 6:19–20). The goal of covenant is the chief end of man's being: "For we are God's handiwork [*poiema*], created in Christ Jesus to do good works, which God prepared in advance for us to do" (Eph 2:10). The new creation produces God's poem (*poiema*) in believers, his masterpiece as the chief end of redemption. In biblical history, therefore, the last days does not only refer to the end of history in time, but the fulfillment of God's purpose in his dealings with man through Christ. The forensic justification is universal to all God's people regardless of time, but the covenant purpose of God's masterpiece is particular to the New Covenant. The biblical authors do not see the unilateral grace of election and the bilateral response of man in covenant as mutually exclusive—i.e., the so-called Calvinist versus Federalist theory.[68] The Covenant of Grace is constituted by the diverse covenants in history with the bilateral elements of holiness and obedience that are consummated in New Covenant. The vertical unity within the horizontal diversity is what truly unifies redemptive history:

> They serve at a sanctuary that is a copy and shadow of what is in heaven . . . It was necessary, then, for the copies of the heavenly things to be purified with these sacrifices, but the heavenly things themselves with better sacrifices than these. For Christ did not enter a man-made sanctuary that was only a copy of the true one; he entered heaven itself, now to appear for us in God's presence. (Heb 8:5, 9:23–24)

The overarching covenant formula throughout redemptive history is "I will be your God and you will be my people." This marriage metaphor indicates a unifying motif in biblical history that supersedes the diversity in the forms of various covenants (Jer 50:5). In view of this, the theory that predestination and covenant are mutually exclusive (unilateral/bilateral) systems of theology is speculative and does not conform to biblical revelation. The covenant by nature is unilateral and bilateral, and predestination does not soften the demand of ethics and holiness essential to covenant; instead, it corroborates and strengthens the latter (Eph 1:4, 2:10).

---

68. Song, *Theology and Piety*, 1–21.

The comprehensive view of biblical covenants thus requires both vertical and horizontal perspectives of history such as found in Hebrews (Heb 8:5).[69] In particular, the heaven and earth contrast is very conspicuous in the heavenly priesthood of Christ subsequent to the finished work on earth. The redemptive-historical process is brought to its final telos when the two directions in biblical history meet in Christ seated next to the Father (Col 2:2). The Old Covenant is not only a *type* of the New Covenant in the horizontal direction but an *antitype* of heaven in the vertical direction.[70] First, there was the vertical descension from heaven to earth in the form of copy and shadow, then the forward progress from the Old to the New Covenant. But it does not end there, as Christ the eternal high priest in the order of Melchizedek enters the inner sanctuary of heaven subsequent to his atoning work on the cross. Thus, Christ in his ascension to heaven completes the full circle (triangle) of biblical history in both directions. At the same time, it also completes the history of revelation as the canon of the Scriptures is closed for provisions of all necessary doctrines and teachings (2 Tim 3:15–17).[71] The history of revelation is completed simultaneously with the history of redemption in Christ. Thus, the metaphors of a *line* (progressive) and a *circle* (unified) make sense when considered in both directions in the growth of revelation.[72] The linear progress in revelation turns into the circular unity of all teachings in the last days when God finally speaks through his Son (Heb 1:1–2). With the full revelation in Christ, a systematic and unified organization of biblical doctrines is made possible and necessary "so that the servant of God may be thoroughly equipped for every good work" (2 Tim 3:17).[73]

In this sense, eschatology is indispensable not only to biblical theology but to systematic theology. The saving revelation has entered its final phase in the Son and unity in knowledge is coextensive with unity of heaven and earth (Eph 1:10; Col 2:3; Heb 1:2–3). In Christ, believers have reached to the heavenly heights previously unknown to Old Covenant saints such that they are able to make conclusive statements on all biblical doctrines.[74] One of the most significant moments in the Old Covenant was when God's people began to call him by the name of "Lord" (Exod 6:3); the most significant moment in the New Covenant was when believers began to call Jesus by the name of "Lord and Messiah" (Acts 2:36; Rom 10:9; 1 Cor 12:3; Phil 2:11). The authority of Jesus is now made equal to that of Yahweh and God now speaks through him, who is the "radiance of God's glory and the exact representation of his being"

---

69. Song, *Theology and Piety*, 19–21.

70. Vos, *Pauline Eschatology*, 61. Vos uses these phrases to call attention to the heavenly archetype that precedes the earthly type, and the heaven-earth structure provides a "philosophy of history" in Hebrews.

71. See the "Introduction" of Vos's *Biblical Theology* for the explanation on the difference between biblical and systematic theology.

72. Vos, *Biblical Theology*, "Introduction."

73. Vos, *Biblical Theology*, "Introduction."

74. Horton, *Covenant and Eschatology*, 1.

(Heb 1:3).[75] He is none other than the God who bound himself with Israel in the covenant of Sinai, and now the incarnate Word who dwells among his people (Matt 26:28; John 1:14; 1 Cor 11:25).[76] It is Jesus who now speaks to his bride, "I will be your God, and you will be my people," and in reply they confess, "My Lord and my God!" (John 20:28).

1.3 Already but Not Yet

Last Days

The provisional kingdom of Christ in the New Covenant is often characterized as being the already-but-not-yet kingdom which is in the world but not of the world (John 18:36). It would be the third or second to the last stage in the sequence of historical shifts toward the new heaven and earth. The sequence in broad strokes is often narrated as creation, fall, redemption, and consummation. The current state of the New Testament is also called a semi-eschatological period for believers are risen and seated with Christ in heaven with the Spirit "as a deposit" of the final resurrection (2 Cor 5:5). The provisional ascension of believers to heaven with Christ is the most unique feature of salvation in the New Covenant era. A common thread that runs through the New Testament is the reference to the last days signifying the perfection of Christ's finished work (Acts 2:17; Heb 1:2; 1 Pet 1:20). These are the last days of this age, but the beginning of the coming age, marked by the final pronouncements of blessings and curses through the cross. The end has arrived in a real sense and personal salvation could not any longer be told apart from this new eschatological reality. The doctrine of forensic justification, or any other segment of the *Ordo Salutis* for that matter, cannot be properly explained apart from the sense of finality in Christ's crucifixion and resurrection. He is the final and greatest revelation of God: "Whoever believes in him is not condemned, but whoever does not believe stands condemned already because he has not believed in the name of God's one and only Son" (John 3:18). Rebirth, justification, adoption, sanctification, perseverance, and glorification are not many separate gifts but the one and final gift in Christ (1 Cor 1:30). Salvation is not granted half now and half later, but given in its entirety to believers in union with Christ except the kingdom of heaven is already, but not yet. "Justification, now tied to resurrection of Christ, brought the declaration of innocence at the last day to the present."[77]

As the subjective experience of believers is incorporated into the objective reality of new creation and the kingdom, the new order breeds life into them (Eph 2:5–10). The exalted Christ is not only the Savior of the soul, but the Head of church and the Lord of all creation (Col 1:16–20). In the well-known analogy, Oscar Cullman

---

75. Frame, *Doctrine of God*, 651.
76. Frame, *Doctrine of God*, 650.
77. Campbell, *Paul and Union*, 411.

compared the new structure of history to D-Day and V-Day.[78] His insights propelled further studies into the eschatological nature of Christ's work and the distinction between *Historia* and the *Ordo Salutis*.[79] Despite the chronological postponement of Christ's return, the New Testament believers persevered amid severe persecution because they knew the D-Day of God's victory over evil had already been achieved.[80] Christ's crucifixion and resurrection permanently modified the structure of history because the kingdom of heaven has intruded the earthly time and space. They were turned upside down with the convergence of *kairos* and *chronos*, an overthrow of time, not just a progress of it.[81] A radical change in history took place, so much so that things in heaven and on earth are unified in Christ (Eph 1:10; Col 1:20). The end of this evil age is only a matter of time in the horizontal direction since the new order is set in motion in the vertical direction. For this reason, believers are called "more than conquerors" and nothing can separate them from the love of God in Christ (Rom 8:31–39). The New Testament view of the world is such that the earthly existence in the horizontal delay does not contradict or weaken the existence in the upper stratum produced by the vertical ascension of Christ. A new order of creation has been set in motion, and built into personal salvation is the birth of a new order of humanity (2 Cor 5:14–17).

As the semi-eschatological state of the age to come provides a larger historical structure to personal salvation, two common mischaracterizations with regard to the end times ought to be avoided.[82] The realized D-Day of ascension with Christ in the Spirit and the postponement of V-Day in the Parousia should be kept in proper balance. The tension between the two events must be held together as the tension between the cross and the resurrection. The realized eschatology is incomplete without Christ's return in history, but conversely, the anticipation of the Parousia should not also diminish the present significance of Christ's finished work.[83] A proper tension between the two eschatological events is the key to understanding the New Testament view of salvation and the end times.[84] The soteric aspects cannot be detached from the two-age structure of the end times already set in motion. The beginning of the end and the end of the end are separated by the two comings of Christ. At times, it may by possible and even preferable to place more accent on one over the other as need be but the overarching structure cannot be ignored at any point in time. Sometimes the vertical *already* should be called upon to reassure and invigorate believers, but at other

---

78. Cullman, *Christ and Time*, 141.

79. Ridderbos, *Paul*, 42.

80. Ridderbos, *Paul*, 43.

81. Cullman, *Christ and Time*, 141.

82. Cullman, *Christ and Time*, 41.

83. Cullman, *Christ and Time*, 41. A case in point for a timeless view of eschatology is C. H. Dodd's "realized eschatology."

84. Cullman, *Christ and Time*, 43.

times the horizontal *not yet* should be invoked for obedience and faithfulness to the end. Depending on the context, believers need to hear more about their present state in heaven or their struggle against this evil age. As pilgrims in the earthly journey, believers often need more of the heavenly Sabbath rest already made available and accessible in Christ.[85] They are not only forgiven of their sins but brought near God: "For Christ also suffered once for sins, the righteous for the unrighteous, to bring you to God" (1 Pet 3:18). At other times in tribulation, however, nothing else but the great anticipation of the return of Christ in glory might be sufficient to console them. The early church did not expect a prolonged delay of Christ's return since the vertical ascension had already taken place, which was the beginning of the end. They took great comfort in the finality of work of Christ, and were assured that their earthly journey would be guided by the decisive victory achieved by the cross and resurrection: "He did not enter by means of the blood of goats and calves; but he entered the Most Holy Place once for all by his own blood, thus obtaining eternal redemption" (Heb 9:12). The cross to them represented more than a substitutionary death for the atonement of sin but was the means of the eternal covenant so that man can be united with God (Heb 9:24).

Semi-Eschatological Kingdom

In the New Testament, redemption has become both personal and cosmic in the nature of the case (Eph 1:22–23). The personal aspect of salvation should not overlook the cosmic changes brought about by Christ's work but ought to be placed within its larger scope. Furthermore, the cosmic shift that took place with regard to the heavenly realms cannot be postponed to the end of history in the horizontal sense. Apart from the *Historia Salutis,* personal salvation at present will be reduced to purely a matter of subjective decisions and experiences. There is a great risk of legalism or antinomianism in this because individual believers are left to themselves to work out their own salvation on earth. Such a view nullifies the qualitative difference between the Old and the New Covenants, but more signficantly it overlooks the arrival and nearness of the kingdom of heaven so emphasized in the Gospels (Heb 11:39–40; Luke 16:17). Beside the fulfillment of types, there is little to speak of in the way of superiority of the New Covenant in Christ, let alone the coming of the kingdom on earth. These latter aspects can only be explained as the eschatological fulfillment in the progress of redemptive history that culminated with "the closing of the ages" (1 Cor 10:11). The primary mission of the Spirit in this new order of history is the application of the finished work of Christ to individual believers, who subjectively appropriate it (John 19:30).[86] In the Spirit, the last days of this evil age and the old man have turned into the first days of the coming age and the new man (Eph 4:23–24). The heavenly realm

85. Cullman, *Christ and Time*, 14.
86. Gaffin, *By Faith Not by Sight*, 25–26.

is now open to believers by faith through ascension with Christ in their union with his death and resurrection (Col 2:12).[87] The opening words of Jesus' public ministry are significant in this regard: "'The time has come,' he said. 'The kingdom of God has come near. Repent and believe the good news!'" (Mark 1:15). In the new order of the kingdom of God, every spiritual blessing in the heavenly realms is at once appropriated by believers in union with Christ (Eph 1:3). The Golden Chain of salvation, from election to glorification, is a logical order rather than a chronological order, and the present salvation is a foretaste of the final one or the firstfruit of the final harvest (1 Cor 15:23; 2 Pet 3:13).

In the nature of the case, the kingdom of heaven consummates creation as well as redeems man. The arrival of the Messiah and his kingdom meant the beginning of the end has begun simultaneously with personal salvation of believers by faith and repentance (Acts 2:36). Theology is literally *logos* of *Theos*, hence the chief end of all things is God and his glory (Rom 11:36). This suggests that there is a maturing process of history itself toward the eschatological kingdom of God above and beyond personal redemption from sin (Matt1:23; Luke 17:21). Ever since the fall from paradise, history has been marching forward to recreation of all things in the Last Adam toward the new heaven and new earth (Rev 21:1–2). The gradual and accumulative progress of revelation and redemption is foretold from the start, and history would lose significance if it persisted merely as a postponement of the final judgment. Redemptive history is not only "a delay of postponement but a delay of gestation,"[88] building tension toward the incarnation of Christ, who consummates history. Old Covenant revelation and history are still necessary for this purpose as the copy and shadow of the things in heaven (Heb 8:5). If it were nothing more than serving as a shadow of the New Covenant, it might as well be discarded altogether when the latter arrived. But the gestation is more than the horizontal passing of time just as a person's growth from infancy to adulthood is more than outward changes in time; it is revelatory and accumulative. God's redemption and revelation gradually developed through biblical history until they arrive at a new and final order in Christ (Heb 1:2; Gal 1:4; 2 Cor 5:17). "Since that time, the good news of the kingdom of God is being preached, and everyone is forcing their way into it," whereas prior to Christ the good news was preached only through types and shadows of what was to come (Luke 16:16). The soteric aspect of salvation now must be understood in tandem with the eschatological kingdom in which believers have become a holy nation under the reign of Christ (1 Pet 2:9). In the latter perspective, grace and nature are both upheld in view of the new creation in Christ. In the consummative vision, the creation is not merely an object of curse doomed to destruction, much less a source of evil. Man and nature fell short of God's glory due to sin but have been regained in redemption with a plus: "Yours, O Lord, is the greatness and the power and the glory and the majesty and the

---

87. Gaffin, *By Faith Not by Sight*, 18.
88 Kline, *Structure of Biblical Authority*, 155; Jeon, *Biblical Theology*, 227.

splendor, for everything in heaven and earth is yours. Yours, O Lord, is the kingdom; you are exalted as head over all" (1 Chr 29:11). Hence, the knowledge and glory of God revealed in nature and man reach their fullness in the revelation of the Son of God (John 17:3, 24). Again, Christ as the Last Adam fulfilled the chief end of man: "Q: What is the chief end of man? A: The chief end of man is to glorify God and to enjoy him forever."[89] In eschatology, the bar is raised so much higher that the knowledge of the Son includes the consummation of nature as well as the redemption of man.

The coming of the kingdom of God from above is expressed by the unique sense of time in the New Testament, which includes a spatial concept. Expressions such as "the time has come," "when the set time had fully come," and "when the times reach their fulfillment" allude to a special time concept with the arrival of the kingdom from above (Mark 1:15; Gal 4:4; Eph 1:10). These special markers of the kingdom of heaven are synonymous with the New Testament notion of a new creation in Christ.[90] In view of the heavenly realms where believers are seated, Paul calls on them to "put on the new-self created to be like God" because they have become a new order of humanity (Eph 2:15; 4:24).[91] The new birth and the new order of creation are not two different events but one and the same act of God in Christ. Christ not only died for us but is also in us; the flow of thought moves from Christ *for* me to Christ *in* me (2 Cor 5:14–17). Christ will not be for us without being in us, and cannot be in us without first being for us. The kingdom of God is eschatological not only in the sense of the end in time, but the end in purpose so that believers already begin to live in the new life.[92] The last days of this evil age have begun, hence the first days of the new order of life have also begun in Christ. This evil age has essentially run its course at the cross, where the old self is crucified (Gal 1:4): "May I never boast except in the cross of our Lord Jesus Christ, through which the world has been crucified to me, and I to the world" (6:14). The kingdom of God in the Gospels is essentially synonymous with the new creation in Paul seen from the eschatological perspective: "Therefore, if anyone is in Christ, he is a new creation; The old has gone, the new has come!" (2 Cor 5:17). The ascension of Christ and believers together to be seated in the heavenly realms in particular signal this historical shift.

In Vosian language, the cross is the "cure" of sin but the resurrection is the "tonic" of life eternal signaling a transition from the earthly to the heavenly image of man (1 Cor 15:48). "Heaven" in the New Testament points to a bigger reality than personal salvation as it is the new order of reality believers enter into by their union with Christ.[93] Salvation in this new era is understood within the higher life of heaven in contrast to a largely curative view of atonement or national character of God's

---

89. *Westminster Shorter Catechism*, 1.
90. Beale, "Eschatological Conception" 12; Gaffin, *By Faith Not by Sight*, 28.
91. Gaffin, *By Faith Not by Sight*, 28.
92. Gaffin, *By Faith Not by Sight*, 28.
93. Wright, *Paul and Faithfulness of God*, 1046.

kingdom in the pre-Christ period. Sometimes called the *Historia Salutis* in contrast to the *Ordo Salutis*, this view of redemption expands the scope of the message of Jesus as he called it "the Gospel of the kingdom of heaven" (Luke 16:16). The kingdom aspect of the Covenant of Grace has been a part of the priestly call of Israel among nations but is now revealed in full force and expanded to all believers: "Now if you obey me fully and keep my covenant, then out of all nations you will be my treasured possession. Although the whole earth is mine, you will be for me a kingdom of priests and a holy nation . . ." (Exod 19:5–6). The Old Testament vision of a priestly kingdom has reached its final stage and finds fulfillment in the Messiah: "The coming of the kingdom is not something that can be observed, nor will people say, 'Here it is,' or 'There it is,' because the kingdom of God is in your midst" (Luke 17:21). The biblical view of salvation has always been salvation of a chosen people, not merely individuals by themselves. They are now seated above with Christ as a holy nation that is not of this world, though not yet seen by sight but seen only by faith (2 Cor. 5:7; 1 Pet 2:9).

Two Ages

Prior to the coming of Christ, the present age below and the coming age above remained detached while believers put their faith in the promised Messiah by way of prophecies, types, and the law (Heb 8:5; 10:1). With respect to personal justification and righteousness, Abraham was justified by faith alone just as Paul would be justified by faith alone, but they belong to two distinct administrations of the Covenant of Grace (Rom 4:1–25). During the law administration of the Covenant of Grace, the age to come remained as a promise, anticipated only through the scarce glimpses of the messianic age (Eph 1:21). The "upper strata" of heaven was yet to be vertically unified with the "lower strata"[94] of earth in the premessianic periods. During this time, a believer may have been left with personal faith and the Old Covenant sacraments to pass through his earthly journey hoping for heaven from a distance (Heb 11:16). Heaven was yet to be united with earth and remained a future hope: "When the foundations are being destroyed, what can the righteous do?" (Ps 11:3). Though justified by faith as righteous, they were without the foundation from above, being on their own to deal with earthly troubles until the foundation was laid in the future as the psalmist explains what it is: "The LORD is in his holy temple; the LORD is on his heavenly throne. He observes the sons of men; his eyes examine them" (v. 4). The last days when heaven and earth would be turned upside down by the enthroned Messiah were still at a distance away as a promise (Acts 2:36; Eph 1:10; Heb 11:39–40). They could only have a small foretaste of heaven through the limited sacraments of grace rather than the actual Person of the Messiah.

---

94 Vos, *Pauline Eschatology*, 297.

Again, the difference is one of the *Historia Salutis* rather than atonement or justification. It has been said that one of the major differences between the Reformers and their successors is that of the *Historia Salutis* rather than the *Ordo Salutis*.[95] Post-Reformation theology gradually moved away from the *Historia Salutis* nature of Christ's finished work; instead, it shifted its attention to the *Ordo Salutis* itself, i.e., the means of salvation. But, the question at hand is not about the means of obtaining personal salvation, which is universally applicable to all periods and all believers within the same Covenant of Grace. The question at hand, the uniqueness of the New Testament history, however, is one of the *Historia Salutis* or the convergence of two ages by the death and resurrection of the Messiah. The significance of the historical events surrounding Christ exceeds the benefits of salvation, and the Reformers such as Luther and Calvin carefully observed the important difference between the two. They were more interested in the finished work of redemption than in the means of redemption. The doctrines of saving grace and justification by faith alone were stressed, but not without the redemptive-historical significance Christ's death and resurrection in the inauguration of the kingdom of heaven. In the daily practice of faith and piety, believers need the latter to sustain the assurance of faith and perseverance despite tribulations. They need the eternal foundation of heaven as a present reality that will transcend the realm of personal moralism, pietism, mysticism, or antinomianism, for that matter. So long as heaven and earth remain detached, believers could only strive to do their best on earth in the hope that their efforts might be good enough to arrive in heaven. As long as the objective reality of heaven remains in the distance future, one can only rely on personal resources to deal with the earthly issues. Thus, it cannot be overstressed that the Covenant of Grace fulfilled by Christ's death and resurrection is eschatological as well as soteric. The symptom of a soteriology detached from eschatology is often an undue emphasis on personal means of safeguarding one's faith and piety, which tends to incline toward legalism or antinomianism. As mentioned, however, the only way to guarantee and sustain personal faith, piety, and ethics is not found in ourselves but in Christ, who united heaven and earth through his death and resurrection (Col 1:20).

1.4 Crucifixion and Resurrection

Significance of Resurrection

Eschatology is built into soteriology in Paul's theology because the entire system of his thought, "the gospel I preached to you," is rooted in the inseparability of the cross and resurrection (1 Cor 15:1–4). The death and resurrection of Christ are not two separate events but one event in two phases. These epochal events as a single unit (even including his exaltation) fulfilled the prophecies of the Old Covenant in the horizontal plane

---

95. Ridderbos, *Paul*, 14.

and unified heaven and earth in the vertical plane (Luke 24:44; Eph 1:10). The new creation in Christ involves believers' participation in both the death and resurrection of Christ as though they are a single event (Rom 6:4–5; Col 2:12; 3:1). If the only goal of the Covenant of Grace is the atonement of sin, a speedy resurrection of Christ in three days, at least in theory, would not have been an essential factor. The shedding of blood on the cross would have been sufficient for the atonement of sin. The resurrection in three days, however, took place "according to the Scriptures" and is essential because God intended the new creation of believers to be a present gift rather than just a future consummation. The resurrection and ascension of Christ, in particular, poses an important question with regard to the current state of believers despite the postponement of his return. This question is theological as well as practical for the believers in their post-salvation journey on earth toward the new heaven and earth. Christ's crucifixion and resurrection together brought the relevance of heaven in this present age, which Old Covenant believers could not have known or experienced (Acts 2:1–47; Heb 11:39–40). For the most part, Old Covenant history remained within the boundaries of personal atonement or a national kingdom without the definitive vertical element. The latter fulfillment had to wait until the incarnation of the Son of God in the Person of Jesus. In the absence of the latter, heaven would have been explained purely as a postmortem experience for believers and the kingdom of God would have remained within the national boundaries of Israel. Apart from the resurrection of Christ in particular, heaven and earth would have remained ununited until the end of the horizontal plane of time. The present salvation and the future resurrection of believers, then, would have remained merely as two separate events separated by time. But thanks be to God that Christ's death and resurrection in three days renders the two as a single redemption unfolded in two successive stages.

God's Word is not a quick manual of how to obtain salvation and its benefits but the record of the progressive history of God's revelation and redemption toward the consummation of all things. It is an organic process cumulative in content and clarity toward the birth of Christ, through whom God intended to speak "in these last days" (Heb 1:1–2). The progress and accumulation of revelation ends with the fulfillment of all previous types, symbols, and prophecies: "Everything must be fulfilled that is written about me in the Law of Moses, the Prophets and the Psalms" (Luke 24:44). Besides the horizontal fulfillment of the Old Covenant, there is now the vertical perfection of the purpose of God in the Counsel of Peace: "It is finished [*tetelestai*]" (John 19:30). The first is relevant to the covenant history of the Old and the New Testament; the second is relevant to the covenant union of heaven and earth, God and man. The incarnation of Christ was to fulfill and finish the covenant in both directions, and his bodily exaltation to the heavenly sanctuary as the eternal High Priest completes the eternal union of God and man (Jer 50:5; Ezek 16:60; Heb 13:20). For this reason the apostles preached the cross and the resurrection *together* as the culmination of all previous revelations and history (Acts 2:14–42). They could not have preached the cross without the resurrection, or vice versa, for their preaching was specifically set in the context of the last days (Acts 2:17). The content of their preaching was eschatological as well as redemptive: "I will show wonders in the heaven above and signs on the earth below, blood and fire and billows of smoke. The sun will be turned to darkness and the moon to blood before the coming of the great and glorious day of the Lord. And everyone who calls on the name of the Lord will be saved" (Acts 2:19–21). The difference between the two priestly orders of Aaron and Melchizedek cannot be overlooked though both are of the same substance in the Covenant of Grace:

> We have this hope as an anchor for the soul, firm and secure. It enters the inner sanctuary behind the curtain, where our forerunner, Jesus, has entered on our behalf. He has become a high priest forever, in the order of Melchizedek. (Heb 6:19–20)

> These were all commanded for their faith, yet none of them received what had been promised. God had planned something better for us so that only together with us would they be made perfect. (Heb 11:39–40)

As to their personal faith and piety, believers in the Aaronic order were highly praised as models of strong faith, but for the entrance into the inner sanctuary of heaven in the Melchizedek order they were still at a distance from the telos of the ages. Despite the similarities, a clear distinction exists between the believers of the two orders of high priesthood and this had to do with Christ's exaltation into heaven. For the perfection of the Melchizedek order and its benefits for the believers of the new order, Christ's resurrection should have been relatively immediate (in three days) after his death. It is no accident, therefore, that a unified knowledge of the biblical revelations by the closure of the canon coincides with the completion of this heavenly act: "All Scripture is God-breathed and is useful for teaching, rebuking, correcting and training in righteousness so that the man of God may be thoroughly equipped for every good work" (2 Tim 3:16–17). The unity of the Scriptures and their sufficiency to train up a man of God in the proper doctrine and life are thus rooted in the work of Christ both on earth and in heaven. Those in Christ are "thoroughly equipped for every good work" because they conform to the image of Christ, who himself was equipped to do so and "learned obedience from what he suffered" (Rom 8:29; Heb 5:8). Such good works are genuinely the fruit of the Spirit rather than personal morality. The immediate resurrection and ascension of Christ brings every believer before the Father, whose presence and company is greater than any earthly possessions. Israel's final destination was not the Promised Land, but the presence of God, and the Sabbath rest could not be found in the land but in God alone (Exod 33:15; Heb 4:8–10). When God's presence left them, however, it was the land that needed rest from them; the order and the outcome were reversed (1 Chr 36:21). The promise of "God's rest" in "another day" other than the Sabbath in the Promised Land is fulfilled in Jesus, who invites everyone weary or burdened to come and receive that rest by being in Christ and being seated in the heavenly realms (Matt 11:28–30).

Union with Christ

Union with Christ in his death and resurrection brings present fellowship with God in addition to the future glorification. This will have radically positive implications for the earthly journey of believers today as well as their future resurrection. It immediately brings ethical and religious significance as believers do not only receive the benefits of work of Christ, but enjoy the presence of the person. They live on earth but simultaneously are seated in heaven, so the Lord's Prayer that "Thy will be done on earth as it is in heaven" is made possible. The proper understanding of Christ's work on both sides of eternity and what they bring to history, as well as to individuals, will affect how one interprets and makes use of God's Word. It will widen the horizon of biblical interpretations that include both the *Ordo Salutis* and *Historia Salutis* that Christ indeed turned this world upside down and established a new order to history (Gal 1:4; 6:14; Col 1:13). If the age to come is viewed solely as a remote destination in the future, it means believers are still part of this evil age, and the quality of their current salvation will be significantly diminished. Notwithstanding the anticipation of his return, the foretaste of heaven is so present that believers are asked to seek the things above (Col 3:1–4).

The significance of Christ's resurrection, in contrast to the cross, has not received due attention in the traditional method of theology. Perhaps due to the soteriological debate on atonement and justification, interest in the resurrection has been usually associated with the bodily resurrection and glorification of believers in the Parousia. Eschatology seen as a prologue rather than an epilogue of theology is relatively a recent shift that began to see believer's regeneration and resurrection as a single event acted out in two successive stages rather than as two independent events (Eph 2:6). It means that Christ not only forgives sin and imputes righteousness on believers but he also accompanies them into the heavenly temple to approach God and be forever near him (Heb 9:23–24). In this sense, even the crucifixion of Christ at the cross reaches beyond atonement of sin to the crucifixion of this world (age) to the cross (Gal 6:14–15). The cross is used to denote the crossroad between this evil age and the age to come (John 19:30; Gal 1:4). In this, believers experience their own death, resurrection, and ascension with Christ in a true and authentic way (Eph 1:21; 2:5–10). The last days of this world have truly arrived from above so that the resurrection of believers can no longer be seen solely from a chronological sense of time; a spatial element has been added to it since the resurrection and exaltation of Christ. If this is true, the idea that the cross is necessary for *now* but the resurrection is necessary *later* in time would not be an accurate description of the true state of believers. In the mind of the New Testament authors, Christ died and rose after three days; the two are inseparable, a synecdoche usually uttered in the same sentence.

Christ's finished work may be understood as unfolding in two stages—the earthly part of perfect obedience and sacrificial death, and the heavenly part of intercession seated next to the Father (Rom 8:31–39; Eph 1:3). Leviticus 16 and Hebrews 9 form a close parallel to tell us of the two distinct phases of Christ's work on earth and in heaven. On the Day of Atonement (Lev 16:1–34), the work of the high priest begins at the altar outside of the tabernacle to prepare for the sacrificial lamb but is not finished until he enters the inner sanctuary with the blood of sacrifice (Heb 6:19–20; 9:11–12). Christ's entrance into the inner sanctuary of heaven, then, is likened to the high priest's entrance into the inner room of the tabernacle where the Ark of the Covenant is located. The entrance into the inner sanctuary was to ratify the sacrifice prepared outside in the very presence of God separated by the curtain and protected by the cherubim. The ascension of Christ, then, represents the final ratification of the eternal sacrifice he himself prepared at the cross. The order of Melchizedek is of the heavenly tabernacle typified by the earthly copy and shadow in the Aaronic order at Sinai (Heb 8:5). In short, the work of the high priest is not done until he enters the inner sanctuary where he stands before God, who will declare that the sins of Israel are forgiven. In the same way, the work of Christ on earth is only effective if and when Christ enters the inner sanctuary of heaven and intercedes for believers. The altar outside is effective and useful only in conjunction with the inner sanctuary of the tabernacle. Hence, the cross of Jesus is the eternal altar and his resurrection is the entrance through the curtain into the inner sanctuary of heaven, where he is seated next to the Father.

Although the *Ordo Salutis* is composed of many stages, the *Historia Salutis* is accomplished once for all (*ephapax*) (Heb 10:10). Because Christ died and rose once for all, redemption is applied to believers at once rather than given in many installments. The whole is greater than sum of its parts and redemption as a whole lies in the perfection of the Person and work of Christ (1 Pet 3:18). Just as the Person of Christ cannot be divided, his works cannot be divided in fragments or applied to believers in piecemeal fashion. The preparation of sacrifice at the altar and entrance into the inner sanctuary of heaven are the work of the same High Priest who lives in believers. The only proper distinction necessary is the redemption accomplished and applied by way of the logical order of salvation. When Christ is given to believers, the whole redemption is given to them; his works can no more be divided than he can be divided (1 Cor 1:30).[96] The integrity and assurance of salvation, therefore, is guaranteed by the vertical union with the Person of Christ as it holds together faith and obedience of believers through their earthly journey. They cannot be dead to sin (cross) without being alive to God (resurrection):

---

96. Ridderbos, *Paul*, 54.

> For if we have been united with him like this in his death, we will certainly also be united with him in his resurrection . . . The death he died, he died to sin once for all; but the life he lives, he lives to God. In the same way, count yourselves dead to sin but alive to God in Christ Jesus. (Rom 6:5, 10–11)

In this baptism into Christ, the temporal gap between the present and the future is superseded at once by the ascension with him to the throne of grace (Heb 4:16). It is called a "mystical union" by the Holy Spirit that unites the One in heaven and those on earth. The sequence of events that take place in the heavenly realms subsequent to Christ's ascension leading to the outpouring of the Spirit illustrate the centrality of resurrection (Acts 2:33; Eph 1:3–14). The outpouring of the Spirit takes place in the last days as prophesied by Joel, and Peter in his Pentecost sermon understands faith and repentance as part of the marks of the last days:

> "'In the last days, God says, I will pour out my Spirit on all people' . . . Repent and be baptized every one of you, in the name of Jesus Christ for the forgiveness of your sins. And you will receive the gift of the Holy Spirit." (Acts 2:17, 38)

At first glance, the significance of the resurrection for the present may not seem practically relevant, especially if the work of Christ is viewed primarily as curative of sin. This is misleading, however, because the covenant in the Scriptures was never understood solely as a cure but also as a tonic of the new and the eternal life. Christ who died *for* them is also *in* them; both substitution and renewal (2 Cor 5:14–17). For this reason Christ told his disciples not to be dismayed and that he will not leave them behind as orphans but will soon take them with him to the Father in heaven: "But I tell you the truth: It is for your good that I am going away. Unless I go away, the Counselor will not come to you; but if I go, I will send him to you" (John 16:7). The undelayed resurrection of Christ renders effective the imputation of righteousness and the forensic justification of believers as the declaration is made when Christ intercedes for them in heaven next to the Father (Rom 8:31–39). Hence, the declaration of justification for believers and their coming near to God are contemporaneous with Christ being seated next to the Father as the Mediator. This means the exaltation of the risen Christ, as well as the cross, is absolutely indispensable for the justification of believers. At the throne of grace, the atonement of the cross will be effective, the imputation of Christ's righteousness will be complete, and believers will never again be separated from the love of God. This scene in the heavenly realms is something we would expect to witness in the future at the final judgment but is unfolding before our eyes in the present tense (Rom 8:31–39). For now, the heavenly scene is seen through the eyes of faith but will be seen by sight in the future (1 Cor 15:24; 2 Cor 5:7). Believers are forgiven, justified, adopted, and sanctified at once in the invisible realms of heaven through Christ, although progressive sanctification and perseverance take place on earth until their glorification.

Christ's resurrection also makes possible the immediate adoption of believers to sonship to be coheirs with the firstborn of God's family (Rom 8:29). They are so thoroughly identified with Christ that they are crucified because he is crucified, raised because he is raised, seated above because he is seated next to God (Eph 2:6; Col 2:12; Heb 10:12). They are in the same sitting posture, at the same location of the throne of God, with the same goal of adoption to sonship for inheritance as coheirs of God: "Praise be to the God and Father of our Lord Jesus Christ, who has blessed us in the heavenly realms with every spiritual blessing in Christ" (Eph 1:3). Christ's resurrection does more than serve as an illustration of the future bodily resurrection of believers, though it certainly does that. No doubt his is the firstfruit and theirs is the harvest of the bodily resurrection. An illustration, however, is not the same as identification, and moreover, if it were a mere illustration, then the time of resurrection would not be of the essence. One might ask, "Did Christ need to resurrect in three days?" But as we have seen above, immediacy is of the essence for the declaration of justification and the sanctification in God's love for his adopted children. An indefinite time of resurrection, on the other hand, could mean uncertainty in these matters. Moreover, believers can be certain of their bodily resurrection in the future precisely because they have been resurrected and seated with Christ in the Spirit. A marriage is not consummated if the union between man and woman is postponed indefinitely. The authenticity of the union with Christ is corroborated by the believer's baptism and the spiritual journey on earth is guided by that union (Rom 6:1–23). In this sense, baptism is more than a mark of justification by faith, but the sign and seal of union into the Person of Christ. The faith that embraces Christ is not an instrument of any single stage in the Golden Chain of salvation but an instrument of receiving every blessing in Christ (Rom 8:32). Hence, believers are not baptized into his death at present and then baptized into his resurrection in the future, but simultaneously baptized into both in the present.[97]

By definition, resurrection is an eschatological event of the last days (*eschatai hemerai*). But the last days of the present age have been brought near us from the future into the present. In the New Testament, the phrase "the last days" denotes the end of this age rather than the end of history (Isa 2:2; Acts 2:17; Heb 1:2). The definition of the term "is restricted and never means the future era," but "refers to the closing era of the first world-period (i.e., present development)."[98] In the Old Testament, it referred to the "final era in time," but in the New Testament "it is spoken of as an eternity in distinction from time."[99] "The last days," then, signals the intrusion of heaven on earth, eternity into time, from the time of Christ's resurrection to the time of the final judgment. The important contrast is no longer between the earlier and the latter days in the horizontal passing of time, but between the upper and the lower strata of the

---

97. Gentry and Wellum, *Kingdom through Covenants*, 597.
98. Vos, *Eschatology of Old Testament*, 4.
99. Vos, *Eschatology of Old Testament*, 4.

two ages. Eternal life has intruded into those who believe in him: "I tell you the truth, he who believes has everlasting life. I am the bread of life . . . But here is the bread that comes down from heaven, which a man may eat and not die" (John 6:47–50). The present age and the age to come coexist, in the upper and the lower levels, during the last days in which believers will experience both: "Therefore, we do not lose heart. Though outwardly we are wasting away, yet inwardly we are being renewed day by day" (2 Cor 4:16). The New Testament authors were keenly aware that they had entered a most unique period in history called the last days. Aside from personal justification by faith, history had progressed to a new height where believers see themselves as seated in heaven while passing through life on earth. They realized that anyone in Christ belongs to a new order of creation regardless of the outward decay (2 Cor 5:17). The provisional kingdom of Christ fits the provisional resurrection in the Spirit (1 Cor 15:24). This means that not only is their future resurrection guaranteed, but they may begin to live and foretaste resurrection life here and now through the Spirit (2 Cor 5:5). Such a vertical dimension could not have been anticipated in the prophecies of the Old Testament concerning the "latter days" but it is clearly revealed in "the last days."[100]

Hope Not Pitied

In the Epistle to the Hebrews, faith is particularly marked by the eschatological hope above and beyond the soteric remedy of sin (Heb 11:1–2). This hope is a vertical sight vaguely expressed in the typological era of the Old Testament but is now fulfilled, brought clearly to light in the life of the New Testament believers. Their participation in the death and resurrection of Christ and the spatial transition from earth to heaven radically altered their worldview. This reversal of the upper and the lower strata is reflected in these words of Paul: "If only for this life we have hope in Christ, we are of all people most to be pitied" (1 Cor 15:19). The certainty of hope expressed here is not rooted in this age, but in the age to come, the heavenly realms, where believers are already seated with him. In Christ, it has now become a "living hope" and their "inheritance is kept in heaven" on account of the resurrection with him (1 Pet 1:3). This living hope is out of heaven for believers do not merely wish for the new and eternal life but already belong to it. If that were not the case, Paul argues, they would be most pitied because then they would be living for an uncertain future. In the uncertainty of the future, he argues, it would be better to enjoy the pleasures of the present. On the other hand, believers in their earthly pilgrimage have a reason to be "filled with inexpressible and glorious joy" of heaven despite self-denial and cross-bearing, because of their present state of union with the exalted Christ (1 Pet 1:8). They are far from being pitied because their hope, out of heaven, is true and authentic.

The demarcation line between heaven and earth is all but indistinguishable in Christ by this otherworldly nature of hope. The hope is of such nature that "whether by

---

100. Vos, *Eschatology of Old Testament*, 5.

life or by death" the apostle desires to honor Christ, and in all circumstances "to live is Christ, and to die is gain" (Phil 1:21). The ground of this eschatological hope is nothing less than the union of God and man in Christ, who brought the eternal into the temporal through his death and resurrection. With the promise of a great blessing also comes a great warning, as is always the case in biblical covenants: "How shall we escape if we ignore such great a salvation?" In so far as the redemption of God reached its climax in Christ, it also warns against the unbelief and rejection of the good news (Heb 2:3). This is how Hebrews understands the order of Melchizedek in contrast to the order of Aaron: "See to it that you do not refuse him who speaks. If they did not escape when they refused him who warned them on earth, how much less will we, if we turn away from him who warns us from heaven?" (Heb 12:25). The eschatological hope in the order of Melchizedek now accessible by the New Testament believers is simply too great to be neglected or taken lightly, and its consequence is spelled out in no uncertain terms by the author.[101] In any case, the vertical hope is irrespective of the horizontal postponement of the Parousia, thus equally available to all believers since the time of Christ. In this vertical reality of being seated in the heavenly realms, one's faith and assurance will be protected by the eschatological foundation from above (Col 3:1–4). In this way, the original goal of creation is not subsumed under the soteric cure, but guides it from above: "In sum, the original goal remains regulative for the redemptive development of eschatology by aiming to rectify the results of sin (remedial) and uphold, in connection with this, the realization of the original goal as that which transcends the state of rectitude (i.e., rising beyond the possibility of death in life eternal)."[102]

In this new order of time and history, faith must embrace the whole reality of earth and heaven, the visible and the invisible. In particular, faith cannot be separated from the kind of hope we just talked about. In a sense, it may be said that faith and hope still remained separate in the pre-Christ era as heaven and earth remained detached. But they are now inseparable in Christ since hope is grounded in the present reality of heaven and faith embraces the totality of heaven and earth. As Vos argued, the concept of hope may have been the most prominent motif in Paul's thought due to his understanding of Christ's work as eschatological in nature. In his thought, the hope of the *Historia Salutis* guides the faith of the *Ordo Salutis*. Jesus revealed the final destination of his redemptive work to be the Trinitarian union and fellowship marked by mutual glory, love, and knowledge (John 17:21–24). It was summarized in one sentence: "Now this is eternal life: that they may know you, the only true God, and Jesus Christ, whom you have sent" (John 17:3). Redemptive eschatology must go beyond the "state of rectitude" into the state of eternal union and fellowship of the Trinitarian God. Wright argued that the core of Paul's gospel does not lie in soteriology but in eschatology[103] and in this he seems to be in agreement with Vos. Horton added that eschatology is not a novel idea discovered

---

101. Wright, *Paul and Faithfulness of God*, 1047.
102. Vos, *Eschatology of Old Testament*, 74. Also see Wright, *Paul and Faithfulness of God*, 14.
103. Wright, *Paul and Faithfulness of God*, 1047.

recently, but had already existed long ago in covenant theology reaped from redemptive-historical interpretations of the Scriptures.[104] The difference, however, is that covenant theology did not have to rely on a "New Perspective on Paul" to discover or understand eschatology. "My kingdom is not of this world," said Jesus, which means those who follow him are not of this world but of another world (John 18:36). As said earlier, if redemption and resurrection remain as two separate events, a logical contradiction is unavoidable that believers are redeemed out of this world yet remain of this world. This creates a theological problem that believers who are said to be "in" Christ yet remain "of" this world. The living hope that is not of this world is only possible if and when both the cross and resurrection of Christ are part of the present being and state of believers.

In conclusion, the *Historia Salutis* with its eschatological ramifications will safeguard the *Ordo Salutis* from being reduced to unduly subjective, private, and spiritualized experiences. It will keep the vertical and horizontal perspectives in balance so that believers should not have to muster up private resources to navigate through earthly pilgrimage detached from the eternal foundation (Ps 11:3). It also means that believers are spatially transported from one dominion to another through union with the risen Lord, enabling them to tap into the heavenly life and energy while passing through this world: "For he has rescued us from the dominion of darkness and brought us into the kingdom of the Son . . ." (Col 1:13). The death and resurrection of Jesus are so closely intertwined in the New Testament as a synecdoche that one is always predicated in the other. Through the cross believers are said to be crucified to and rescued from this evil age—with the implication that they are taken to the coming age or the kingdom of heaven (Gal 1:4; 6:14). The "rescue" may be taken as a theological equivalent of resurrection from death into the new life; Christ died and rose in order "to bring us to God" (1 Pet 3:13). The covenant, rooted in the *Pactum Salutis*, has always envisioned the chief end of man to draw near God for doxology and intimacy. So much so that the thought flows naturally without any sense of gap in between from soteriology to eschatology, and vice versa. Sometimes it does not even matter whether a New Testament author is looking at the reality of heaven and earth from below or from above because he is so much part of this new order (Col 3:1–4). The cross is where the two ages divide, and the resurrection is the transition from one to the other, where death no longer exists or is even possible (John 3:5; 11:25–26). There was never a moment in their mind that the cross was considered apart from the resurrection just as atonement was never detached from everlasting life (John 3:16; Eph 2:15; 2 Cor 5:17). The final victory over death is yet to come, but we are already "more than conquerors" over death: "Where, O death, is your victory? Where, O death, is your sting? . . . But thanks be to God! He gives us the victory through our Lord Jesus Christ" (1 Cor 15:55, 57).

---

104. Horton, *Covenant and Salvation*, 7.

Chapter 2

God and Eschatology

2.1 God's Attributes

Divine Being

THE TRACES OF THE DIVINE glory are found in man's greatest joy and achievements in all facets of the human existence and culture—family, the arts, science, literature, and music. These traits of the divine attributes are so deeply ingrained in the human heart that their manifestations are often profoundly inspiring and boundlessly vast. We are at times amazed by the sheer brilliance of mankind's creativity and ingenuity in the imitation of the Creator. The greatest irony, by the same token, is that man's willful suppression of the knowledge of God in him led to the sad and tragic consequences of this fallen world (Gen 3:15–24; Rom 1:18–23). The apostle Paul particularly brings our attention to the idolatry of mankind: "They exchanged the truth about God for a lie, and worshiped and served created things rather than the Creator—who is forever praised. Amen" (Rom 1:25). The excellence of God's creation has turned into vanity and the possibility of life eternal for man was lost, resulting in all man falling short of the glory of God (Rom 3:23). The vanity of man is poetically expressed as follows: "For, 'All men are like grass, and all their glory is like the flowers of the field; the grass withers and the flowers fall, but the word of the Lord stands forever.' And this is the word that was preached to you" (1 Pet 1:24; Isa 40:7). Despite the tragedy of the human existence caused by sinful rebellion, nevertheless, the original paradise of God is proof that man is created with the traces of divine glory and attributes (Gen 1:26; 3:8).

Eschatology is a study of *eschatos* (the last things) but paradoxically also a study of *protos* (the first things). Theology, in the nature of the case, is theocentric because God is the Alpha and the Omega of all things and eschatology begins with God (Rev 1:8). Eschatology is protology of "God's fundamental purpose for humanity," which in theological language is "the chief end of man." Eschatology is rooted in theology proper, and the chief end of man to "glorify God and to enjoy him forever" is derived from the theological foundation: "For from him and through him and to him are all things. To him be the glory forever! Amen" (Rom 11:36). The divine attributes are generally distinguished into two general categories of the communicable (shared) and the incommunicable (unshared). The shared attributes are such as love, joy, hope, wisdom, knowledge, justice, righteousness, and faithfulness. The fruit of the Spirit, for instance, may help us to visualize the communicable attributes of God (Gal 5:22–23). The unshared attributes are such as eternity, self-existence, immutability, omniscience, omnipotence, and omnipresence (Exod 3:14; Ps 89:34).

These two categories, however, are not to be taken as an absolute distinction, although practically useful and appropriate. In some cases, the categories do overlap to some extent and a particular attribute of God may said to be true of both categories. For instance, when an attribute is said to be shared by God and man, they are never identical (of equal quality). Love is considered a communicable attribute of God but it's quality is never the same in God as in man. Conversely, an incommunicable attribute does not mean that there is nothing in common between God and man in that regard. God is eternal and man is not, but man's final destiny is eternal and there is a sense of communicated attribute in this regard. Grudem thinks the communicable attributes are better called the "more shared," and the incommunicable better called the "less shared." Some of God's attributes are shared more with man while others are shared less, but in all cases an absolute gulf exists between the Creator and the creature. The theological significance of the two categories lies in the question of how the Divine Being is similar and dissimilar to man, who is created in his image. The absolute distance between the Creator and the creature makes the shared divine attributes a great mystery yet a glorious blessing: "The secret things belong to the LORD our God, but the things revealed belong to us and to our children forever, that we may follow all the words of this law" (Deut 29:29). God is completely unknown to man in the secret category of heaven, but is known in the revealed category of history. Man's innate knowledge of God in the natural state before the fall constitutes the natural revelation (Rom 1:19–20; 2:14–15). The "eschatology of nature" was rooted in the natural revelation through which Adam had intimate fellowship with God: "Highest life is characterized by the most intimate connection with God. Paradise is spoken of as a garden of God (cf. Isa 51:3; Gen 3:8)."[1]

Eschatology flows out God since he is properly the foundation of all things and the doctrine of God makes possible all other teachings of the Scriptures. He is the Alpha and the Omega of all things, and everything exists for his glory and will return to him (Rom 11:36). The Westminster Confession of Faith, therefore, starts with God[2] and then proceeds to discuss the eternal decrees, creation, providence, and redemption. The details of the latter topics all flow out of a particular view of God, who possess certain known and unknown attributes. Its view of God logically leads to a particular view of man and the world from creation to redemption, and from redemption to

---

1. Vos, *Eschatology of Old Testament*, 75.
2. Westminster Confession of Faith, 2.

consummation. The character and process of the entire history originates from the very character of God, who has planned, created, redeemed, and will perfect it (Rom 11:36). The consummation (eschatology) of the world is of particular importance here since it underlies the purpose of the eternal decrees and provides the ultimate goal of creation. One of the attributes of God related to eschatology is that he "rested" on the seventh day of creation (Gen 2:1–3). The history of redemption is a temporal history toward the eternal life (consummation) symbolized by the Sabbath rest of God (Heb 4:1–11). The seventh day, then, would have been the confirmed state of Adam for the eternal union and fellowship with God in paradise. It would have meant the end of probation and a transition from the natural order of *works* to the eschatological order of *rest*. Man is created after the image of God and takes after the attribute of God working and resting:

> The Sabbath finds its prototype in the life and works of God. Thus, it means fulfillment; not cessation and weariness, but consummation. This rest of consummation was introduced into the life of man in order to show him his goal. Even in unfallen man the Sabbath was an eschatological sign because its meaning lies in the relation of man and God.[3]

The Covenant of Works was made in order that man might work according to the image of his Creator, and eventually enter into his rest, into the everlasting state of union and fellowship with him. The shared attributes between God and man are meaningful for they must have been central to the perfection of this final union (Jer 50:5). The work-rest pattern was the natural order that preceded redemption: "The Lord God took the man and put him in the Garden of Eden to work it and take care of it" (Gen 2:15). This provides an important foundation to redemption that man is saved in order that he may arrive at this chief end left unfinished by Adam. Man was created in the image of God with certain communicable attributes of God to glorify and enjoy him forever, first through works but eventually through union with him. The purpose of God for man has never been altered but will continue and be perfected: "we know that in all things God works for the good of those who love him, who have been called according to his purpose" (Rom 8:28). The tree of life in paradise was a reminder to Adam that he is created for life eternal and that there will be God's rest following the works in the natural order. The communicable attributes of God must have played a central role in the *communication* between the Creator and the creature in the garden. God is supernaturally transcendent but also personally immanent: he condescended to be with man in order to execute the eternal will for the world he created. These attributes of God are known to man from creation "since what may be known about God is plain to them, because God has made it plain to them" (Gen 1:26; Rom 1:19). They are like signposts that say Adam and Eve were covenantal beings accountable to God, created to imitate, glorify, and enjoy his presence. But in the fallen

---

3. Vos, *Eschatology of Old Testament*, 75.

state, mankind swings back and forth between rationalism ("they claim to be wise") and irrationalism ("their thinking became futile"), unable to communicate with God, much less enjoy him (Rom 1:21–22). These attributes of God made it possible for man to function as the vice-regent of the Creator to serve in the capacities of prophet, priest, and king as Adam faithfully did until the temptation. Man's chief end, in short, is to participate in the divine nature through the covenant in order that he may walk before God and be blameless (Gen 17:1; 1 Pet 1:4). Along with the image of God, the communicable attributes were given to aid man achieve his ethical and religious end in paradise.

Knowledge of God

The intimate covenant knowledge of God is the chief end of man and is itself the "eternal life" (John 17:3). All creation in one voice declares the splendor of the divine knowledge: "The heavens declare the glory of God; the skies proclaim the work of his hands" (Ps 19:1). In the original state of paradise, the eschatology of nature is rooted in the natural knowledge of God. The special knowledge of curative redemption is an added gift subsequent to the fall. The natural revelation and the natural law written in man's heart were thus meant to serve the higher purpose of the supernatural life (Rom 1:19–20; 2:14–15). The creation was not an end in itself but envisions its consummation: "Whether one feels capable of conceiving it or accepting it depends ultimately on his concept of God. A God who cannot create cannot consummate things because he is conditioned by something outside himself..."[4] All the creeds and confessions in the history of the church begin with the knowledge of God that precedes every other teaching in the Scriptures. God is the Alpha and the Omega of all things—the eschatological foundation of the universe—so that "God does not exist because of man, but man exists because of God."[5] In this sense, the history of redemption is a process of collective maturity in the knowledge of God until God's children finally arrive in the union and fellowship of the Trinity (John 17:3, 21–24). In the macroscopic perspective, eschatology is all about God himself for all things start from, move toward, and end in God for his glory (Rom 11:36). A theology is essentially an eschatology, and vice versa, because it is a consistent application and outworking of its view of God in all areas of faith and life on both sides of the eternity. Thus, from theology flows doxology that "God may be all in all" (1 Cor 15:28); even sin is defined as falling short of God's glory (Rom 3:23). In this particular definition of sin, the apostle measures it against nothing short of the glory of God because sin offends God before it destroys man. The loss of the original righteousness of man requires a soteric rectitude but the loss of God's glory demands sanctification and glorification. The reversal of the broken covenant in paradise, therefore, is more than a restoration of the natural order

---

4. Vos, *Eschatology of Old Testament*, 1.
5. Vos, *Redemptive History*, 242.

but recreation to the supernatural order (2 Cor 5:17). The new order will include reconciliation and ethical restoration but also the highest form of life—union and intimacy with God in the new paradise (Gen 3:8; Isa 51:3; Rev 2:7). Redemption in the Son is more than justification in the ethical sense, for it is the covenant knowledge of God like that between the Father and the Son (John 17:3). The Father knows the Son and the Son knows the Father, and believers are to join this knowledge of God (vv. 21–26): "Let us acknowledge the Lord; let us press on to acknowledge him. As surely as the sun rises, he will appear; he will come to us like the winter rains, like the spring rains that water the earth" (Hos 6:3).

The paradise of Eden was a temple where the two primary elements of eschatology, ethics and religion, would have received confirmation had Adam kept the covenant. The disobedience of Adam in breaking the covenant was not only unethical before God but also unfaithful to God (Hos 6:7). It was not only the disobedience of God's law but the profanation of God's temple that rendered Adam's act serious and consequential. Just as an adultery is a sacrilege of the sanctity of marriage, the breaking of the covenant was morally and religiously offensive to God. Hence, the redemptive work of Christ and the everlasting life Christ gained for believers is both soteric and covenantal in nature (John 17:3). To know God, in the covenantal sense, is eternal life: "They will neither harm nor destroy on all my holy mountains, for the earth will be filled with the knowledge of the Lord as the waters cover the sea" (Isa 11:9). The eschatology of nature in paradise is called "primeval eschatology,"[6] and is the basis of the new and eternal covenant Christ came to finish by his death and resurrection. The covenantal knowledge of God is not an epistemological idealism but a practical realism rooted in God's own revelation (Deut 29:29). This knowledge in the natural order was first engraved in man at the time of creation, and still effective in the common grace realm of life: "For in him we live and move and have our being. As some of your own poets have said, 'We are his offspring.'" (Acts 17:28).

In his well-known work *Knowing God*, J. I. Packer said that the knowledge of God is never an abstract or boring concept but a practical and indispensable guide to journey through this hostile world.[7] He tells a parable of a native person in the Amazon pulled out of "his world" and left alone in the streets of London to survive on his own, and how cruel and dreadful that might be. He concludes that mankind in a fallen world, expelled from the paradise he once belonged to, is faced with a similar fate. Apart from knowing God, fallen mankind is simply not equipped to survive in this world on their own though they try to avoid and suppress the truth.[8] The knowledge of God engraved in man's heart is now darkened, and his thinking became futile; he is lost in this world without a God-given map and direction.[9] The probationary state

---

6. Vos, *Eschatology of Old Testament*, 75.
7. Packer, *Knowing God*, 19.
8. Packer, *Knowing God*, 19.
9. Packer, *Knowing God*, 19.

in paradise meant a probationary knowledge of God, which needed to be expanded and confirmed through obedience. God is the efficient cause of all things so the authentic and sufficient knowledge revealed by him is eternal life (Deut 29:29). The tree of knowledge and the tree of life in paradise were intended to indicate to man that there is to be a process of growth and expansion of that knowledge that will lead to the eternal life. The growth of the knowledge of himself as the creature made in God's image was part of the covenantal arrangement. Again, the mutual knowledge of the Father and the Son in eternity is the model after which this covenant knowledge is designed (John 17:25–26). As Calvin stated, man's knowledge of himself depends on the knowledge of God and the two are inextricably connected through the covenantal arrangement.[10] The covenantal arrangement is the foundation of the possibility, not to mention the integrity, of all of man's knowledge (Rom 1:18–23). As a creature made in God's image and possessing some of his communicable attributes, man is designed to respond to God either as a covenant keeper or a covenant breaker, but never on a neutral ground with respect to him.

Blessedness of God

The law of God manifests his attributes and is said to have been given to man for his own happiness as the image-bearer of God (Deut 10:13). The covenant includes intimate knowledge, affectionate love, faithful obedience, and mutual blessedness:

> And now, Israel, what does the LORD your God ask of you but to fear the LORD your God, to walk in obedience to him, to love him, to serve the LORD your God with all your heart and with all your soul, and to observe the LORD commands and decrees that I am giving you today for your own good?" (Deut 10:12–13)

The Hebrew *towb* (good) meant the goodness of the original state of the world created *ex nihilo* with a potential to reach the eternal state of blessedness. The goal of creation was to attain to God's goodness or blessedness. God is called a "blessed God"—*makarios* means blessed in Greek and is equivalent to *towb* (Gen 1:31; 1 Tim 1:11, 6:15; Matt 5:3). God's own blessed nature and man's happiness are closely interrelated from creation, and its consummation surprisingly came through redemption in Christ. In this sense, Geerhardus Vos said that there is a "redemptive plus" to the original version of blessedness.[11] The Covenant of Grace is an eschatology 2.0, as it were, in the sense that God's blessedness and man's happiness are sealed through the redemptive work of the Second Adam (1 Cor 15:22). The redemptive process is not merely sin's remedy but the realization of the eschatological goal of God's own blessedness in man. The everlasting life in the non-redemptive state of Eden, then,

---

10. Calvin, *Institutes*, 1:35.
11. Vos, *Eschatology of Old Testament*, 77.

already had envisioned the blessedness of God as man's chief end and the participation in the divine nature as the highest state of his existence. In paradise, epistemology (knowledge) and eschatology (blessedness) could no more be separated than the tree of knowledge and the tree of life (Gen 2:9; 3:22). Adam would have remained in God's blessedness within the epistemological boundaries drawn by the tree of knowledge (Gen 2:17). The serpent, however, had crossed those boundaries set by God and deceived Adam in a lie that his knowledge could be like that of God's: "For God knows that when you eat of it your eyes will be opened, and you will be like God, knowing good and evil" (Gen 3:5). But, the integrity of man's knowledge of good and evil would be protected only within the proper boundaries of covenantal obedience to God.

The interrelation between covenantal knowledge and blessedness is first found within the eternal fellowship of the Trinity as Jesus' prayer revealed:

> Righteous Father, though the world does not know you, I know you, and they know that you have sent me. I have made you known to them, and will continue to make you known in order that the love you have for me may be in them and that I myself may be in them. (John 17:25–26)

The goodness of God was generally revealed in the work of creation, but more particularly in the creation of man and woman: "The Lord God said, 'It is not good [*lo towb*] for the man to be alone. I will make a helper suitable for him" (Gen 2:18). It is interesting to note the negation of blessedness that it was "not blessed" for Adam to remain alone so God made Eve to complete the blessedness through their marriage union. The blessedness of the covenant union led to covenant knowledge that "Adam knew [*yada*] his wife, and she became pregnant and gave birth to Cain" (Gen 4:1). The Hebrew verb *yada* may mean either to know or to make love, both of which are significant for the covenant union. For a Hebrew reader, true knowledge is covenantal knowledge that involves two parties who will " become one flesh" in a blessedness union (Gen 1:24). The covenantal knowledge is a relational knowledge and man is said to be "not blessed" when he is alone. In the same way, man is blessed when he is with the blessed God in covenantal union and fellowship. The image of God in truth, righteousness, and holiness is given to man for this purpose, that he may walk with God in paradise (Gen 3:8; Eph 4:24). J. I. Packer made a useful distinction that "a little knowledge *of* God is worth more than much knowledge *about* God."[12] The covenantal knowledge brings God's blessedness to man so that he may "participate in the divine nature, having escaped the corruption in the world caused by evil desires" (2 Pet 1:4). The attribute of blessedness so shared with man is a sign of the transcendent God's immanence in the world.[13] God does not remain in the supernatural realm but involves himself in the natural world in order to make his eternal will come to fruition. Those who know God and are known by God

---

12. Packer, *Knowing God*, 26.
13. Van Til, *Introduction to Systematic Theology*, 233.

are blessed because in the covenant union and fellowship they are growing to know more of God.[14] The knowledge of God is neither wholly rational nor wholly irrational, but it is always covenantal and personal rooted in God's self-revelation. The natural knowledge of God in man and nature is revelatory of God and it still serves as a point of contact between the Creator and the creature. In the nature of the case, man knows God instinctively as the Creator, though not as the Redeemer.

The blessedness of God is brought to its fruition and clearest manifestation in the gospel (good/blessed news) of Christ. The High-Priestly Prayer of Christ allows us to peek into the blessed Trinity, who is the model of the blessedness of believers (John 17:5, 21–24). Jesus brings our attention to the particular "place" that he wishes his disciples to arrive at as a result of their knowledge of the Father and the Son: "Father, I want those you have given me to be with me where I am, and to see my glory, the glory you have given me because you loved me before the creation of the world" (John 17:24). He first prays for their unity, and then makes an extraordinary request that they might also be in the fellowship of the Father and the Son (and of course, the Spirit). The particular "location" Jesus prayed for believers to enter was actually not a place but a Person—the Persons of the Trinity. The intra-Trinitarian fellowship in mutual glory, love, and knowledge is where believers may enter and foretaste God's blessed attributes through covenantal union. The prayer for union and communion with God was also made earlier when Jesus promised to send the Holy Spirit to the disheartened disciples: "And I will ask the Father, and he will give you another Counselor to be with you forever . . . On that day you will realize that I am in my Father, and you are in me, and I am in you" (John 14:16, 20). Whoever is in Jesus is also in the Father because he is the perfect mediator between God and man, and possesses the two natures for that purpose. The two natures of Christ (divine and human) are used for substitutionary atonement but also for that blessed union with and participation in the divine nature. Those who are united to him can participate in the divine nature and share the blessedness of God through the perfect God and the perfect man (Ps 8:5). The covenant with God thus means that God's blessed nature and attributes also becomes their own blessedness and happiness: "For in Christ all the fullness of the Deity lives in bodily form, and in Christ you have been brought to fullness" (Col 2:9–10). The blessed news of the gospel lies first in the forgiveness of sin, but then in the blessed union with a holy, loving, and righteous God. The Covenant of Grace is gracious but also covenantal so that believers might not perish but dwell (*yada*) forever in the Father with the Son (John 17:12, 21).

Union with the Son through the Spirit means with union with the Father, and believers are expected, as Jesus prayed, to share in the blessedness of the Trinity.[15] In this sense alone, Christ is more than sufficient to be the mystery of God in whom the divine nature and the human nature are conjoined in order that he might bring

---

14. Packer, *Knowing God*, 33.
15. Murray, *Redemption Accomplished and Applied*, 171.

believers into the blessedness of God: "Blessed [*makarios*] are the pure in heart, for they will see God" (Matt 5:8). There is no better means to "the chief end of man to glorify God and to enjoy Him forever" than to be filled with God:

> I pray that you, being rooted and established in love, may have power, together with all the saints, to grasp how wide and long and high and deep is the love of Christ, and to know this love that surpasses knowledge—that you may be filled to the measure of all the fullness of God. (Eph 3:19)

On the one hand, Christ's human nature is used for atonement of sin, but, on the other hand, it is used to bring believers into union with God and fill them with the fullness and blessedness of God. In this sense, the gospel can truly and properly be the blessed news of Jesus Christ. The blessed God who walked with man in the temple of paradise is forever with us through Christ's work as the eternal High Priest in the heavenly tabernacle not made by hands (Gen 3:8; Heb 9:11–12). He entered the inner sanctuary in heaven in his humanity, in the order of Melchizedek, so that believers might approach God with freedom and without fear (Heb 6:19–20).

> For we do not have a high priest who is unable to empathize with our weaknesses, but we have one who has been tempted in every way, just as we are—yet he did not sin. Let us then approach the throne of grace with confidence, so that we may receive mercy and find grace to help us in our time of need. (Heb 4:15)

The full scope of the doctrine of God such as the Trinity may not have been revealed clearly in the earlier stages of the history of revelation. The volume of revelation then would have been relatively small and its content more typological in form until the personal incarnation of the Son of God. "The Word became flesh and made his dwelling among us" so that in the end man might dwell in God (John 1:14). The revelatory knowledge of the depth, width, breadth, and height of God's love in Christ was a gradual and progressive growth that culminated with Christ, through whom God spoke "in these last days" (Heb 1:1–2).

2.2 NATURE AND GRACE

Eschatology and Revelation

Eschatology and epistemology are interconnected in the organic growth and progress of the biblical revelation. As we have seen before, the knowledge is covenantal by nature, and the knowledge of God is the foundation of all knowledge. As the biblical covenants move forward and upward to their consummation in Christ, God's people thirst after a deeper knowledge of God (Hos 6:3). Jesus is the highest form of divine revelation and the incarnation of the Son of God meant a termination of the prophetic era: "In the past God spoke to our forefathers through prophets at many times in various ways, but in these last days he has spoken to us by his Son, whom he appointed heir of all things, and through whom he made the universe" (Heb 1:1–2). The intrusion of the perfect revelation in the Person of Christ is coextensive with the inauguration of the last days. Christ now personally reveals the Father and those who have seen him have seen the Father (John 14:9; 17:6). The knowledge of the Son is the most direct and intimate knowledge of the Father. The words given to him by the Father are the same words he now gives to believers: "For I gave them the words you gave me and they accepted them" (John 17:8). The "words" here refers to a covenant relationship, and in these words is the presence of the persons themselves. When such words are uttered to people, they are imbedded in their souls and have the power to alter them. Words unite or divide, kill or revive their hearers for they are the direct embodiment of the person: "The tongue has the power of life and death, and those who love it will eat its fruit" (Prov 18:21). "Words" means revelation in the Scriptures, and in the New Testament the Word (*Logos*) became flesh so that God may dwell (literally, to pitch a tabernacle) among its hearers and that they may know him (John 1:14). The knowledge of God is the bread to the soul: "Man does not live on bread alone, but on every word that comes from the mouth of God" (Matt 4:4; 1 Pet 2:2). Man was created in such a way that his soul thirsts after God like a deer searches for water: "As the deer pants for streams of water, so my soul pants for you, my God" (Ps 42:1).

In paradise, a part of the covenantal arrangement for Adam was the natural revelation of the knowledge of God as the Creator and as the would-be Consummator of the world (Rom 1:18–20).[16] The special revelation afterwards, however, was redemptive in that the fallen mankind might know God as the Redeemer through the Covenant of Grace (2 Tim 3:15–17).[17] The saving knowledge of God in the Scriptures transcends the natural revelation though it does not exclude it. In both kinds of revelation, the eschatological goal toward the higher order of consummation is evident even amid the soteric process in redemptive history. The natural (general) revelation is part of the natural order of creation that is unmistakably clear to man but suppressed due to the darkened mind (Ps 19:1; Rom 1:21). The special (redemptive) revelation is the Scriptures as the inspired Word of God given to prophets and apostles by the Holy Spirit (2 Pet 1:21; 2 Tim 3:15–17). By nature, the special revelation is soteric, given to the fallen humanity as its primary recipient, but it is not just a manual of personal salvation but a record of redemptive history toward the new order of creation in Jesus Christ. The progress of history from creation to consummation with an added redemptive gift thus necessitated the two kinds of revelation. The classification of revelation, then, is not merely to differentiate redemptive from non-redemptive knowledge but to understand the difference between the temporal and the eternal orders. In this sense, epistemology is a function of both soteriology and eschatology: the two important goals in history and the fallen world. Since the expulsion of man from paradise, the

---

16. Bavinck, *Our Reasonable Faith*, 32–43.
17. Bavinck, *Our Reasonable Faith*, 61–94.

world has been under the curse of the Covenant of Works and needed the provisions of the common grace and the natural revelation for its continuance until the Parousia. A need for the separate category of common grace arose subsequent to the entrance of sin for assistance of mankind through the history of redemption (Gen 3:16–24). The present order of the world makes use of both kinds of revelations until the distinction will no longer be necessary in the new paradise (Rev 21:1–2).

The progress of history in revelation has reached such heights in Christ that heaven and earth have been united in him, and the significance of this declaration can hardly be overstressed in biblical hermeneutics and theology (Eph 1:7–10). What this entails is that the two realms of earth and heaven are *spatially* unified through the risen Christ and their provisional unity becomes the new basis of faith and life. The nature/grace distinction that did not exist in paradise will not exist in the consummate state of the new paradise in heaven. In view of the consummation, therefore, the nature/grace separation is only provisional in the present order of things until the final reconciliation: "For God was pleased to have all his fullness dwell in him, and through him to reconcile to himself all things, whether things on earth or things in heaven, by making peace through his blood, shed on the cross" (Col 1:20). In Christ the substance of theology has been upgraded from the natural to the supernatural, and from the earthly image to the heavenly image (1 Cor 15:48–49). The progress of revelation has reached its climax in Christ so that it is organized into a unified system of knowledge (epistemology) sufficient to redeem and equip believers for "every good work" (Acts 16:4; 2 Tim 3:16–17). The inspired Word of God by the Holy Spirit is given to prophets and apostles in order that they may lay the foundation of the house of God with Christ as the Cornerstone (Eph 2:20–22). The foundation of knowledge is of such character that no more new revelation would be necessary besides Christ, consistent with the last days of revelation (Heb 1:1–2; Rev 22:18). Now, it has been transparently revealed that Christ is the *protos* and *eschatos* of all things, about which John and Paul both agreed (Col 1:15–20; Rev 22:13). Christ is the last of God's revelations in that he fulfilled and finished the eternal covenant ushering in these last days at the closing of the ages (Luke 24:44; John 19:30; Heb 1:2). In the soteric realm the natural revelation is non-saving but in the eschatological realm "the preeminence of the natural (the physical)" still holds true with the added blessing of redemption.[18] The significance of the natural revelation lies in the fact that Adam was "a covenant partner with God" and "a pattern of the one to come."[19]

Theophany is the most intense form of God's self-revelation, first appearing in Eden when God "was walking in the garden" with man (Gen 3:8; Isa 51:3; Rev 2:7). Theophany is the ground of and consistent with the chief end of man "to glorify God and enjoy Him forever." In what better way can man glorify and enjoy his Creator than through the most intimate and personal appearance of God? The paradise of God

---

18. Vos, *Eschatology of Old Testament*, 74.
19. Packer, *Knowing God*, 36.

reappears in Revelation as the consummate form of the temple of God, where man and God are reunited for everlasting fellowship (Rev 21:3): "Theophanies are personal representations of God in visible form. They go beyond the mere purpose of revelation; they express, in primitive form, God's approach to and communion with man. God does not merely speak in a theophany; he acts!"[20] The central aspect of eschatology is the nearness of God to man in speech and presence, characteristic of theophany fulfilled in *Immanuel*. Hence, the incarnation of the Son of God in flesh, who is the perfect image and revelation of God, is the fulfillment of all previous theophanies. The Word not only became flesh but did so to dwell with us on earth and in heaven (John 1:14). The Son of God in the Person of Jesus Christ is the preeminent theophany, for he built the temple of God and is the temple (John 2:21): "It is he who shall build the temple of the LORD and shall bear royal honor, and shall sit and rule on his throne. And there shall be a priest on his throne, and the counsel of peace shall be between them both" (Zech 6:13).

The Word of God is not merely a spoken and written revelation but a living Person in Jesus Christ, who walked and ate with his people: "For you have been born again, not of perishable seed, but of imperishable, through the living and enduring word of God" (1 Pet 1:23). The "living and enduring word of God" in its most personal form is Jesus Christ, in whom believers may now boldly approach and be approached by God. He walked in paradise with Adam, walked with the disciples in Palestine two thousand years ago, and will walk in the new paradise with the glorified children of God (Rev 21:3–4). But the most astounding truth is that Christ is seated next to the Father in the heavenly realms with those who are united with him. If theophany is the most intense form of God's self-revelation to man, there is no more clear theophany than this: God is now seated next to man with the risen Christ. In any case, eschatology, theophany, and epistemology (knowledge of God) are inseparable: "For 'All people are like grass, and all their glory is like the flowers of the field; the grass withers and the flowers fall, but the word of the Lord endures forever.' And this is the word that was preached to you" (1 Pet 1:24–25). Eden, Sinai, Canaan, and Gethsemane in one form or another all represent the garden of God, and were preparatory to the eternal garden where man will see God with "unveiled faces" (2 Cor 4:18). In the meantime, believers seated in the heavenly realms next to the Father already see God in preparation for the glorious encounter with him in the future:

> An approach toward permanent nearness is made by the building of altars, which are revisited as places that God might frequent. All this prepares for the permanent divine in-dwelling. Canaan prefigures the eschatological state of Israel. It is the land flowing with milk and honey; i.e., typical of Paradise. Note that Canaan was afterwards the scene of the highest permanent theophany of

---

20. Vos, *Eschatology of Old Testament*, 85.

the Old Testament (i.e., the temple) and therefore typical of the final consummative state of the theocracy.[21]

Integrity of Creation

The exact nature of the relationship between nature (creation) and grace (redemption) would be better viewed in the broader and higher context of eschatology. The discussion of nature and grace is often limited to the scope of soteriology and fails to take into account the eschatological nuance of creation and redemption. The continuity between nature and grace, for one, stems from the eschatology of nature in paradise, which envisions the eternal beyond the temporal. The new creation is truly new, yet not entirely distinct from the first creation for the two share the common goal of the everlasting life.[22] The redemptive eschatology, i.e., resurrection, is built on the integrity of the first creation and its sequel does not deviate from the original model except that it is new. The new creation transcends the first creation yet does not negate nor contradict it.[23] Its superiority lies in the transformation of the earthly image into the heaven image of man. The opposition of nature and grace in the soteric rectification of sin does not alter their common substance as God's creation. Grace and the flesh are antithetical, but grace consummates nature. The redemptive grace recreates the fallen nature and elevates it to the new order of creation in the heavenly realms (1 Cor 15:48; 2 Cor 5:17; Eph 2:5–6). Grace does not forsake the physical world precisely because God first said it was "very good" in the creation of it. The world is *creatio ex nihilo* (made out of nothing) and the integrity of the natural world was foundational to God's creation (Gen 1:1, 31). Unfortunately, the Augustinian view of *posse peccare* (ability to sin) in nature may have unwittingly contributed to a dualism later found in the semi-Pelagian theology of the Roman Church.

The world in its present form will eventually pass away and will be replaced by a new and eternal order (1 Cor 7:31; Rev 21:1): "I saw the Holy City, the new Jerusalem, coming down out of heaven from God, prepared as a bride beautifully dressed for her husband" (Rev 21:2). The bodily resurrection of Christ is a confirmation that redemptive grace will not abrogate nature but will perfect it with the heavenly image of man (1 Cor 15:48–49). The eschatology of nature in paradise merits attention in its own right in distinction from the soteric grace because of this fact. The everlasting life in the glorifying enjoyment of God is not a newly invented concept in redemption but preexisted prior to the fall in the natural world order (Rom 3:23). The immortality of man, symbolized by the tree of life, is promised to Adam in the probationary state as the reward of obedience to the Covenant of Works. It was not a mere test of obedience

---

21. Vos, *Eschatology of Old Testament*, 86.
22. Horton, *Covenant and Eschatology*, 6.
23. Horton, *Covenant and Eschatology*, 6.

but a covenantal arrangement for blessing and reward of God, whom he was to glorify and enjoy as the chief end of his being. The everlasting life in Jesus Christ is not exclusively a gift *of* salvation but a gift *through* it for the gift had been promised long ago to Adam in paradise. In this sense, "eschatology precedes soteriology."[24] Paradise and man were on their prescribed course toward eternal life with God when they were disrupted by sin, but God by grace redeemed and recreated them with a new Adam (Rom 5:12; 1 Cor 15:21–22). The fallen world is sustained by the common grace and providence until redemptive grace runs its due course and completes the salvation of the elect (Gen 3:16–24). In the consummate new world, grace will so completely recreate nature that heaven and earth will be united as originally had been planned in Jesus Christ.

The organic flow of redemptive history towards Christ indicates that heaven and earth will be united in the latter days foretold by the prophets. In this sense, the soteric division of the Spirit and the flesh will eventually give way to the eschatological unity of heaven and earth. In Paul, "the flesh" is contrasted with the Spirit but the earthly image is contrasted with the heavenly image (1 Cor 15:49). One is a soteric distinction whereas the other is an eschatological one. In the latter, the focus is the natural versus the supernatural, and both will be united eventually with no more need for such a division. Our interest here lies in the vertical perspective of the heavenly realms relative to the life in the horizontal dimension of the earthly realms (Heb 6:19–20; 8:5; 9:23). As seen earlier, redemptive history progresses in both dimensions, one toward the end in time and the other toward the supernatural in heaven. The earthly tabernacle is viewed as a copy and shadow of the heavenly tabernacle to be perfected by the new priestly order of Melchizedek. The order of Melchizedek is continuous with the order of Aaron in the horizontal direction, but superior to it in the vertical direction. This forms a triangle structure of redemptive history in which heaven comes down to earth in two stages, one by way of a copy and shadow and the other by way of the realities themselves (Heb 8:5; 10:1; 12:22). After Christ the High Priest entered the heavenly sanctuary, the "frustration" and "groaning" of the creation thus intensifies as history moves closer to the prophesied last days and the final judgment (Rom 8:20–22).

The anticipation of the "glory that will be revealed" grows as the first days of the coming age effectively began with Christ's resurrection (Rom 8:18–19; Eph 2:6; Col 3:1). In this movement toward the new order and time, the common grace is not negated by the special grace but works in tandem with it as Christ is exalted to be the Lord over all things. In the eschatological sense, therefore, the cosmic battle between Satan and Christ is a clash of unrighteousness and righteousness rather than nature and grace. Herman Bavinck once observed that a risk does exist in theology either to overestimate or underestimate the role of the common grace.[25] In his opinion, the natural world under the bondage of sin cannot avoid being a mixture of great

---

24. Vos, *Pauline Eschatology*, 45.
25. Bavinck, *Our Reasonable Faith*, 44.

optimism and pessimism, or a "laughter in tears."[26] The common grace upholds the intrinsic goodness of the natural order but cannot provide a lasting hope in it. The birth and resurrection of Christ in flesh, on the other hand, demonstrates that saving grace does not supersede or degrade the natural order but redeems and consummates it. In short, an ethical antithesis of unrighteousness and righteousness does not mean a metaphysical separation between nature and grace. The resurrection, in particular, proves that the integrity of nature is all the more upheld by saving grace rather than abrogated by it.

The history of revelation gradually offers a more clear view of the dynamic between the natural and the supernatural through the eyes of faith. Faith in Christ now embraces the visible and the invisible: "Now faith is confidence in what we hope for and assurance about what we do not see . . . By faith we understand that the universe was formed at God's command, so that what is seen was not made out of what was visible" (Heb 11:3). It even sees that the natural world was created *ex nihilo* in the goodness of God and sin was not due to any fault in nature itself (Gen 1:31).[27] The traditional definition of the two kinds of grace, the *common* and the *special*, in a sense already presupposes the provisional nature of the creation order.[28] The common and natural will inevitably turn into the special and supernatural and the God who decrees and creates will surely consummate. It was not always the case that *gratia communis* (common grace)[29] was understood relative to eschatology, nature largely confined to the scope of the doctrine of man and sin. In this sense, the natural is explained within the scope of the flesh (*sarx*) and creation only as a backdrop of redemption. In eschatology, however, the natural is viewed more as the object of the supernatural made into a newer and higher creation. The new creation in Christ, then, provides a theological framework in which to view creation in a more positive outlook relative to the upcoming world (1 Cor 7:31). In the beauty and splendor of the paradise in Eden, the physical element could not be equated with the *flesh* in the soteric situation of man (Ps 8:1; Rom 8:5–7). In the limited scope of the fall and redemption, therefore, it would be difficult to properly assess the value of the natural order and its original preeminence. The Scriptures declare that the glory and splendor of God's creation still shines through the cloud and darkness of sin. It is worth noting that heaven and earth are normally contrasted in the Scriptures rather than grace and nature, lest the latter be equated with grace and sin (Matt 28:18; 1 Cor 15:48–49; Eph 1:10; Col 1:20).

In medieval theology, grace is defined as *donum superadditum* (extra gift added) to nature that supplements the innate deficiency of the physical world. The Augustinian doctrine of *posse peccare* (able to sin) in creation might have initially contributed to this tendency, suggesting that the innate instability of the physical world succumbed to

26. Bavinck, *Our Reasonable Faith*, 45.
27. Bavinck, *Our Reasonable Faith*, 44.
28. Kuyper, *Lectures on Calvinism*, 53.
29. Kuyper, *Lectures on Calvinism*, 53.

Satan's temptation taking away the *donum superadditum*. As a result, the lower natural world with its innate penchant for sinful passions tailspins into further corruption resulting in the fall. Afterwards, it was understood that grace was infused back into the corrupt nature to rectify sin and restore the lost balance between nature and grace. The rite of baptism atones for the past sins, and the infused grace begins to cooperate with the sanctified person by means of penance and other forms of meritorious works for the forgiveness of future sins. In short, a doctrine of salvation is built on the notion of an original defect in nature rooted in a grace/nature dualism. The dualistic outlook on nature and grace essentially shapes the Scholastic theology of the Roman Church in the Aristotelian tradition.

The Reformation, on the other hand, made an effort to rectify this theological problem by rejecting the *donum superadditum* theory and affirmed the goodness and preeminence of nature in its own right prior to the fall. The probationary state ("able to sin") of paradise is due to the covenantal arrangement rather than any defect in the natural order itself. It was so designed to be a transition into the confirmed state of life everlasting as a reward and blessing of the covenant. In this sense, the subsequent redemptive grace provides the cure of sin but also fulfills the prior goal of reaching the supernatural order, the tonic of the everlasting life. The sharp division of grace and law in Lutheran theology may have been necessary against the semi-Pelagianism of the Roman Church but did not give due credit to the eschatological vision in paradise prior to the fall. In its view, redemption is practically a return to paradise in Genesis, which is deemed equivalent to eternal life. Based on these observations, a better definition of "nature" seems necessary to rectify the dualistic tendency in either the medieval or the Lutheran view. Neither the medieval synthesis nor the Lutheran division of nature and grace can fully account for the consummation of heaven and earth in Jesus Christ as a result of redemption.

Kingdom of God

It may be a diversion, but the above discussion begs the question of whether the present kingdom of God should be understood as *one* or *two* kingdoms.[30] The kingdom of God in the New Testament is semi-eschatological in nature in which the two ages coexist in Christ. In principle, heaven and earth are unified in Christ and believers live in this unique period and state called the "last days," seated in the heavenly realms. The authority given to Christ by the Father is that of heaven and earth (Matt 28:18) and the Lord's Prayer is given to believers living in the kingdom age: "Our Father in heaven, hallowed be your name, your kingdom come, your will be done on earth as it is in heaven" (Matt 6:9–10). The sovereign reign of Christ over all creation is clearly one unified kingdom but for the time being provisionally ruled by the risen Christ

---

30. VanDrunen, *Living in God's Two Kingdoms* and *Natural Law and Two Kingdoms*; Wolters, *Creation Regained*.

until delivered to the Father (1 Cor 15:24). The heavenly kingdom has intruded the earthly realms in advance in the closing of this age and the beginning of another age started by the Messiah (Mark 1:15; 4:26–29). The presence of the future in the form of the kingdom means a foretaste of the heavenly realms for believers still living on earth (Luke 17:21; John 6:47; 10:10; Col 3:2). In the mystical union with Christ, heaven and earth have been united so that grace begins to restore and recreate nature, although not all things have subjected to Christ yet. By the cross and resurrection, Christ's authority over heaven and earth is undivided as believers have already been moved out of the darkness into "the kingdom of the Son" (Col 1:13). The kingdom of Christ, however, is semi-eschatological and provisional until the kingdom of God; it is in the world but not of the world (John 18:36). The proper division, therefore, is not between "two kingdoms" but between two ages separated by the two comings of Christ. It is one unified kingdom of God to be consummated in two successive stages.

The typological kingdom of Israel in Canaan prefigured the coming of the kingdom of God in the last days ushered in by Christ (Exod 19:5–6; Mark 1:15; Heb 8:5). Israel in Canaan was a form of intrusion, a copy and shadow of heaven on earth, so that Israel might become a symbol of theocracy. The intrusive nature of the kingdom of God is more fully manifested in the clash of the two ages at the time of Christ by his semi-eschatological kingdom that is not *of* this world (John 18:36). The kingdom of Christ in the present age, whose keys are given to the church, is thus said to be at war with the gates of hell (Matt 16:18–19). The eschatological kingdom of God from the coming age has already intruded this age, but will be consummated in the new heaven and earth (Rev 21:1). Therefore, the kingdom of God is *one* but realized in *two* successive stages since not all things in this evil age have submitted to Christ's authority yet. The two ages that characterize this unique period of Christ and the Spirit, however, are not equal to the "two kingdoms" as often understood today, i.e., the two realms of grace versus law. Based on the eschatological and christological considerations mentioned above, the messianic kingdom is no doubt unified and universal. This was made clear by Jesus himself to the disciples:

> Then Jesus came to them and said, "All authority in heaven and on earth has been given to me. Therefore go and make disciples of all nations, baptizing them in the name of the Father and of the Son and of the Holy Spirit, and teaching them to obey everything I have commanded you. And surely I am with you always, to the very end of the age." (Matt 28:18)

In view of this, the description of "two kingdoms" as used today seems to be neither accurate nor desirable since it appears to suggest that God's kingdom and his reign are divided. In the crucifixion and exaltation of Christ, he is declared as both Lord and Christ (Acts 2:36; Col 1:15–18). The supremacy of Christ over all creation, as the apostle Paul declared in no uncertain terms, means the unity and finality in his reign over the universe, both in the natural and the supernatural realms. The notion of two kingdoms seems to suit better the limited scope of soteriology, and a temporal distinction between law and grace. The division still exists in the present world where the realms of law and grace remain divided to a certain extent. But in a real and eschatological fashion, the kingdom of God has arrived in its unity and the last days of this age have already begun. The horizontal and temporal distinction remains, but the vertical fulfilment of earth and heaven has been once and for all fulfilled with a radical change in worldview for the earthly journey of believers.

It may be possible, however, to take "two kingdoms" as an expression of the already-but-not-yet kingdom that maintains the division of grace versus law. We are living in an imperfect world and in the outer man we are still citizens on earth while in the inner man we are seated in the heavenly realms with Christ (Rom 13:1–4; Eph 2:6). Even Jesus recognized the present reality of the two realms: "Then give to Caesar what is Caesar's, and to God what is God's" (Luke 20:25). Abraham Kuyper and the neo-Calvinistic vision of transforming every sphere of the kingdom of God very much stresses the present reign of Christ over the whole universe. The two kingdoms view, on the other hand, highlights the division of grace versus law in this fallen world, divided into two distinct realms of the spiritual and the natural. In the neo-Calvinistic view, the spiritual is somewhat collapsed (de-eschatologized) into the natural realm, but in the two kingdoms view, the spiritual is kept separate (over-eschatologized) from the natural until the end, which comes as a crisis. In any case, it cannot be denied that the kingdom of God is *already* here, but also *not yet* here (Mark 4:26–29; Luke 17:21; John 18:36). The distinction between the "inner man" and the "outer man" means that believers live as citizens of both heaven and earth (2 Cor 4:16–18). They belong to the invisible and eternal world in the coming age, but belong also to the visible and temporal world in this age: "So we fix our eyes not on what is seen, but on what is unseen. For what is seen is temporary, but what is unseen is eternal" (v. 18). The two citizenships, as it were, are kept apart for the time being as the two ages (the upper and the lower strata) are kept separate until the kingdom is fully given over to the Father (1 Cor 15:24). As Bavinck noted, pessimism and optimism will paradoxically coexist in the present state of the kingdom with "laughter in tears." Christ has so conquered evil that heaven and earth are united in principle, but the unity is provisional until the final judgement, when grace will consummate law. Then there will be a complete and consummate reversal of weeping and laughter: "Blessed are you who weep now, for you will laugh" (Luke 6:21; Rev 21:4).

2.3. Pactum Salutis

Eternal Origin of Covenant

The origin of biblical covenants is traceable to the intra-Trinitarian covenant taken place before the creation of the world (Eph 1:4–14).[31] The Eternal Counsel called the *Pactum Salutis* within the Trinitarian God precedes all historical covenants between God and man (John 17:4–6). This covenant in eternity is fulfilled in history through two other major covenants called the Covenant of Works and Covenant of Grace. The covenant by the Persons of the Trinity, in turn, reveals God's communicable attributes with man, which became the foundation the image of God in man (Gen 1:26). A central feature of the Eternal Counsel is the "free" and "voluntary" obedience of the Son to the Father.[32] This voluntary obedience of the Son in joy and glory is the essence of the image of God and central to the covenantal arrangement in paradise. It is also the ultimate goal of the Covenant of Grace so that grace, having saved sinners, engenders in them a conformation to the image of Christ, who voluntarily and joyfully obeyed the Father (Rom 8:29; Heb 5:8).

The covenantal image of the Father, the Son, and the Spirit in eternity is manifested in mutual glory, love, and knowledge (John 17:21–26). Jesus prayed for his disciples "that they may be one as we are one," and that they "be with me where I am," and "see my glory" (vv. 22, 24). This revealing prayer manifests the nature of the intra-Trinitarian relationship, but also how it becomes the basis of God's covenantal arrangement with man (Deut 6:5): "Love the Lord your God with all your heart and with all your soul and with all your strength and with all your mind; and, Love your neighbors as yourself" (Luke 10:27). Here we can make an important distinction between the legal stipulation of a covenant, whether it is fulfilled by obedience or faith, and the substance of covenant itself requiring joyful obedience out of the image of God. The legal stipulation of the covenant may have changed from *works* to *grace* subsequent to the fall, yet its substance spelled out in Deuteronomy 6:5 remains unchanged. The covenantal arrangement is, and has always been, free and voluntary, reflecting the image of the Persons of the Trinity. "The free deeds performed in a covenantal way" by the Son was then a rightful means by which the plan and execution of redemption were carried out (John 17:4; Eph 1:1–14). "The perfect freedom required of the covenant can only be found in the Trinitarian God"[33] and believers can have a glimpse into the glory of that relationship in their own covenant with God. Jesus came to fulfill the covenant with the Father: "Now this is eternal life: that they may know you, the only true God, and Jesus Christ, whom you have sent. I have brought you glory on earth by finishing the work you gave me to do" (John 17:3–4). Nevertheless,

---

31. Vos, "Doctrine of Covenant," 247.
32. Vos, "Doctrine of Covenant," 244–45.
33. Vos, *Redemptive History*, 245–46.

lest man may boast in his obedience, Vos is careful to note that a perfectly bilateral, free, and voluntary covenant, ideally speaking, is possible only within the Trinitarian arrangement of the *Pactum Salutis*.

The "voluntary condescension"[34] of God to make covenant with man in order to reward him for obedience is consistent with the creation of man as God's image-bearer. It is not surprising that the covenantal arrangement in paradise was modelled after that of the Father and the Son. There is no doubt that the adoption to sonship in the *Ordo Salutis* has something to do with the conformation to the image of the Son, who freely and joyfully obeyed the Father (Rom 8:29). "The eschatology of nature is typical of the eschatology of redemption" in that it expresses "God's approach to and communion with man."[35] Again, theophany during the course of redemptive history is significant for eschatology because "it marks the first step toward the return of the primitive, normal intercourse."[36] The Son's free and voluntary obedience to the Father was a form of their covenantal communion and in return "he was heard because of his reverent submission" (Heb 5:7–9). In the same way, the purpose of redemption is the conformation to the Son's image and to "become mature, attaining to the whole measure of Christ" (Rom 8:29; Eph 4:13). Biblical history is a covenant history; it is a school of God in which his children learn lessons on covenant obedience even as they are justified by faith alone. Christ's perfect obedience is performed for man, but more properly performed toward the Father as part of their mutual covenant. It is not just legal and ethical, but religious in nature, modelled after the Trinitarian communion. Hence, believers receive the Person of Christ as well as the benefits his work; they have faith in Christ—literally, "faith of Christ" (Gal 2:16). The gracious element of the Covenant of Grace does not alter or supersede the eschatological substance of covenant. In eternity, the Son volunteered to be the Mediator between God and man, but his obedience would not merely be imputed to them but reproduced in their walk with God.[37] They receive the grace of justification but also receive the grace of sanctification that they may conform to the image of the Son, through whom they enter into communion with the Father. The Covenant of Grace not only saves sinners but recreates them with "all the fullness of God" (Col 2:9; Eph 2:15; 3:19).

Predestination and Holiness

In the apostle Paul's mind, the first cause of God's sovereignty and the secondary cause of human responsibility are harmonized by way of the Golden Chain of the *Ordo Salutis* (Rom 8:30). There is no conflict or contradiction between eternity and time, heaven and earth, predestination and covenant in the biblical worldview, much less in

---

34. Westminster Confession of Faith, 7.
35. Vos, *Eschatology of Old Testament*, 85.
36. Vos, *Eschatology of Old Testament*, 85.
37. Vos, *Eschatology of Old Testament*, 85. Also see Bavinck, *Reasonable Faith*, 267.

its eschatology. God's election does not weaken the need for man's free and voluntary obedience or vice versa in the Covenant of Grace.[38] The apostle makes it a plain truth that God predestined some in order that they may become "holy and blameless in his sight" (Eph 1:4). The covenant is the means by which God executes the election, producing faith and obedience in those who are called by him. They freely believe and obey because they have been chosen, called, and given to Christ (John 17:4–6; Gal 2:16). They are justified by faith in Christ, which is not their own work but a gift of God so that no one can boast about it (Eph 2:8). The means of justification is the non-meritorious gift of faith but its goal is to produce free and voluntary obedience such as that of Christ. The reason for God's election and the gift of faith is to fulfill the chief end of man: "For we are God's workmanship, created in Christ Jesus to do good works, which God prepared in advance for us to do" (Eph 2:10). Even in the Abrahamic covenant, he was justified by faith alone yet not without the covenantal obedience out of the free and voluntary will: "I am God Almighty; walk before me and be blameless" (Gen 17:1). The Eternal Counsel, as seen before, is executed through the gracious covenantal arrangement that produces faith and obedience. The "free deeds performed in a covenantal way" in the Covenant of Grace is most simply yet beautifully expressed as "faith working through love" (Gal 5:6). It is loving faith or faithful love, represented in the Old Testament by goodness (*hesed*) and in the New Testament by *agape* love (Exod 34:6; Gal 5:6).[39]

The purpose of predestination, or the *Pactum Salutis*, is explicitly stated to be that of making holy and blameless children chosen in Christ out of love for the glory of God (Eph 1:4–14; 4:24). This purpose thus equally applies to both the Covenant of Works and Covenant of Grace although their means of achieving the goal may be different. It is worth quoting Vos once again: "The eschatology of nature is typical of the eschatology of redemption."[40] Beside the legal stipulations of the covenant, either by law or grace, both in the end relate to the image of God in man, represented either by Adam or the Second Adam (Rom 5:14). The free, voluntary, and joyful obedience of the Son to the Father in the *Pactum Salutis* is carried over into history and became the basis of the two covenants. They find a common origin and purpose despite their antithesis in the legal terms of the covenant, one by law and the other by faith. Yet again, the theory that the eternal decree and covenant are irreconcilable doctrines is erroneous and unsupported by the Scriptures. It has been wrongly argued that Calvin and the Puritans represent two entirely distinct theological systems of predestination and covenant.[41] This problem is resolved by the organic unity between predestination and covenant within the *Pactum Salutis*. In our view, the perceived problem is due to a failure to recognize what is a methodological difference rather than a theological

---

38. Song, *Theology and Piety*, 34–35.
39. Frame, *Doctrine of God*, 415.
40. Vos, *Eschatology of Old Testament*, 85.
41. Song, *Theology and Piety*, 32.

conflict.[42] One's perspective is the transcendence (predestination) of God's hidden will and the other's perspective is the immanence (covenant) of God's revealed will. These are not theological conflicts, but only a logical distinction between two perspectives of the same entity. The Scriptures know nothing of such conflict between the two aspects in God's plan of redemption. The Covenant of Grace is sovereign and unilateral in the eternal decree of predestination, but mutual and bilateral in the historical manifestation of the Golden Chain of the *Ordo Salutis*.

An important theological principle maintained by the historical Reformed Confessions, i.e., the Westminster Confession of Faith, is the dynamic between the primary and the secondary causes in the work of God. The first cause of all things is God and the secondary cause is man's liberty and contingency.[43] The liberty and contingency of the secondary causes is manifested in history and the various covenants in biblical history belong to this category. Hence, the eternal will of God in predestination is executed through the historical revelations of the covenants that require the human response. The unsearchable will of God in eternity is carried out through man's response in faith and obedience: "I have brought you glory on earth by finishing the work you gave me to do . . . I have revealed you to those whom you gave me out of the world. They were yours; you gave them to me and they have obeyed your word" (John 17:4, 6). The incomprehensibility of God's hidden will does not weaken the revealed will that demands faith and obedience, but on the contrary further establishes it: "Oh, the depth of the riches of the wisdom and knowledge of God! How unsearchable his judgments, and his paths beyond tracing out!" (Rom 11:33). In the end, therefore, all to the glory of God: "For from him and through and to him are all things. To him be the glory forever! Amen" (v. 36).

The outpouring of the Spirit in Pentecost, then, is the last stage (days) of the historical culmination of the *Pactum Salutis*: "Exalted to the right hand of God, he has received from the Father the promised Holy Spirit and has poured out what you now see and hear" (Acts 2:33). This is to be received by means of faith and repentance, the other end of the covenantal arrangement: "Repent and be baptized, every one of you, in the name of Jesus Christ for the forgiveness of your sins. And you will receive the gift of the Holy Spirit" (v. 37–38). The secret will and the revealed will have never been in conflict except that revelations have organically grown from infancy to maturity through the various covenants revealed in biblical history (Deut 29:29). The doctrine of predestination itself, however, is not identical to the *Pactum Salutis*, which looks into the intra-Trinitarian arrangement of how the predestination was to be executed (Eph 1:4–14). It adds covenant personality to predestination, characterized by the mutual glory, love, and knowledge among the Persons of the Trinity. The bilateral mutuality essential to man's free and voluntary obedience to covenant is rooted in the Son's obedience to the Father—which is not possible in the Sabellian or modalistic

---

42. Song, *Theology and Piety*, 32.
43. Westminster Confession of Faith, 3.

view of the Trinity. The mystery of God, as the apostle Paul understood it, lies in Christ, who is the embodiment of God's hidden and revealed will (Col 1:26–27; 2:2). The incarnation, life, death, and resurrection of Christ did not just fulfill the series of all previous covenants in biblical history but completed the *Pactum Salutis* in the vertical direction (Ezek 37:26; Heb 13:20). In him, heaven and earth are united vertically, as well as Old Covenant and New Covenant horizontally. Both decree and history are fulfilled in Christ, who entered "the greater and more perfect tabernacle that is not man-made, that is to say, not a part of this creation" (Heb 9:11).

Eternal Counsel and Means of Grace

Since the intra-Trinitarian covenant precedes the work of creation itself, it follows that nothing can separate God's children from the love of God in Christ once the covenant is historically ratified by him (Rom 8:31–39). The Covenant of Grace is the proper means by which the Eternal Counsel of Peace is fulfilled and executed in history. According to the arrangement, the Holy Spirit becomes the pledge of the inheritance of the Covenant of Grace once it is fulfilled by Christ (Eph 1:14). The efficacy of the Covenant of Grace and the work of Christ is unmistakable for the elect: "And this is the will of him who sent me, that I shall lose none of all that he has given me, but raise them up at the last day" (John 6:39). It could not have been perfect unless it is the work of the Father, the Son, and the Spirit: "This happened so that the words he had spoken would be fulfilled: 'I have not lost one of those you gave me'" (John 18:9). Hence, the sacraments of the Covenant of Grace are the sign and seal of the eternal promise of God made effective through the benediction in the name of the Father, the Son, and the Holy Spirit (2 Cor 13:13). The efficacy of the earthly means is authenticated by the certainty of the heavenly counsel. The Golden Chain of the *Ordo Salutis* from predestination to glorification is guaranteed not by man, or even by the means of grace, but by the covenantal promise of God alone. Faith is the instrumental cause of the covenant but the Counsel of Peace is the efficient, material, and final cause (Eph 1:3–14). The sacrament of baptism is a means of grace rooted in the promise of the Eternal Counsel by the Father and the Son, offered to believing adults and their children (Acts 2:39). Here is an important principle of covenant theology: the sacraments are the outward means of ratifying the Counsel between the Father and the Son, and they apply equally to circumcision and baptism, for their efficacies do not lie in man or even in the means themselves but in God's unfailing promise. Infant baptism is administered to the children of believing parents because the sacrament is a sign and seal of the Eternal Counsel rather than man's faith (Gen 17:7–14). The recipients of the Abrahamic covenant are very clear: "This is my covenant with you and your descendants after you, the covenant you are to keep . . ." (v. 10). The sacrament of baptism does not seal the believer's faith but seals God's promises rooted in the Eternal Counsel to the believing parents and their descendants. It was never intended that the efficacy of the covenant depended on the recipient's faith but on the Eternal Counsel of the Father and the Son. In short, believers "do not believe in the means of grace but in grace."[44] The believing parents and their covenant children thus receive the sacrament of baptism solely based on the promise of God in the Covenant of Grace that flows out of the Counsel of Peace.

The Eternal Counsel is the archetype of all other covenants in the Scriptures and their respective sacraments are the proper means of its execution and application. The Eternal Counsel, in the vertical perspective, is the mother of all covenants, whether in creation or redemption. The horizontal progress in the Covenant of Grace throughout the Old Testament history is its growth from infancy to maturity while the vertical element holds them together in unity. In this progress, the vertical goal remains unchanged, that God's chosen people must grow as a holy nation and priestly kingdom among nations. The vision of the kingdom matures but never abandoned: beside the soteric goal of atonement and justification, the chief goal of the covenant matures with the progress of revelation. God's primary interest throughout biblical history is expressed in the words "I will be your God, and you will be my people." It is consistent with the eschatology of nature as well as the eschatology of redemption: "Highest life is characterized by the most intimate connection with God."[45] Holiness before God and intimacy with God—"highly religious"[46]—are the dominant motifs in biblical covenants beside the soteric atonement of sin. This is undoubtedly the content of the Counsel of Peace between the Father and the Son: "For he chose us in him before the creation of the world to be holy and blameless in his sight. In love he predestined us for adoption to sonship . . ." (Eph 1:4). The election of Christ as the Mediator in the Counsel was a comprehensive plan that includes the penal, ethical, and religious elements: atonement, holiness, and intimacy with God.[47] The eternal plan of the Counsel was first implemented in paradise and will be completed in the new paradise which we now eagerly anticipate (Rev 2:7). In the meantime, the "most intimate connection with God," and the "highest life," have already begun in the Son, with whom we are seated in the heavenly realms. The imitation of the Son is made possible because of proximity to the Son: "For those God foreknew he also predestined to be conformed to the image of his Son, that he might be the firstborn among many brothers and sisters" (Rom 8:29).

The Scriptures do not often provide us with detailed logical arguments for the secret will of God such as the Counsel of Peace except where such a reasoning is inevitable and beneficial (Matt 22:14; Rom 9:19–29; Eph 1:4). These instances are not meant to be philosophical speculations but confessions of the splendid glory and abundant grace contained in the unsearchable will of God (Deut 29:29; Rom 9:1–33;

---

44. Vos, "Doctrine of Covenant in Reformed Theology," 262.
45. Vos, *Eschatology of Old Testament*, 75.
46. Vos, *Eschatology of Old Testament*, 75.
47. Bavinck, *Our Reasonable Faith*, 267.

Eph 1:4–14). In any case, the perception that God's secret will weakens man's moral duty is unfounded and foreign to the mind of biblical authors in their view of God (Rom 9:20–21). The Eternal Counsel *ipso facto* is highly ethical, intimate, and personal in nature. The eternal plans of God's creation, redemption, and consummation are so designed to reflect such a nature and character of the intra-Trinitarian counsel. The two particular attributes of the Counsel of Peace between the Father and the Son that Jesus mentions in his prayer are *glory* and *love*. It is perhaps not a coincidence that they appear again in Paul's detailed description of the Eternal Counsel in Ephesians (Eph 1:4, 6). In the prayer of Jesus for the disciples, glory and love are the basis for the Eternal Counsel and the chief reason for their union with him and the Father (John 17:21–24). This is precisely how the apostle understands the Counsel: "In love he predestined us to be adopted as his sons through Jesus Christ, in accordance with his pleasure and will—to the praise of his glorious grace, which he has freely given us in the One he loves" (Eph 1:5–6). He says, again, all this is "in order that we, who were the first to hope in Christ, might be for the praise of his glory" (v. 12). The *Pactum Salutis* by nature is so personal, ethical, loving, and glorious that its historical outcome in the life of believers cannot also be otherwise.[48] In this sense, the Sabellian view of the Trinity, which denies the Persons of God, or the Arian view, which denies the unity of God, cannot explain the Eternal Counsel, or the Covenant of Grace for that matter (2 Cor 13:13; 1 Tim 2:5).[49] The historical significance of the Councils of Nicea and Chalcedon is invaluable in this regard as these not only established the doctrine of the Trinity itself, but provided the foundation for the Counsel of Peace between the Father and the Son, from which the Covenant of Grace flows.[50]

Blessedness in Eschatology

The blessedness of God is the foundation of the eschatology of nature and the eschatology of redemption, being the foundation of the good (blessed) news of the gospel. Eschatology begins and ends with God, who is the Alpha and Omega of all things: "For from him and through him and to him are all things. To him be the glory forever! Amen" (Rom 11:36). The goodness (*towb*) of nature loudly attests to the blessed attribute of its Creator, who is good in and of himself (Gen 1:31; 1 Tim 1:11). His goodness is the basis of the chief end of man to glorify and enjoy God forever—the eschatology of nature. The state of blessedness is a hallmark of covenant union as demonstrated by Adam and Eve: "The Lord God said, 'It is not good [*lo-towb*] for the man to be alone. I will make a helper suitable for him" (Gen 2:18). And so God created Eve and brought her to Adam for the union of marriage, through which "they became one flesh" (Gen 2:24). Adam would not have been blessed had he remained alone without a covenant

---

48. Vos, "Doctrine of Covenant," 246.
49. Frame, *Doctrine of God*, 706.
50. Chalcedonian Creed (451 AD).

partner in Eve. Hence, the state of blessedness requires a covenant partner and their union is the necessary condition of consummating that blessedness.

Such a blessed relationship has already been seen in the Counsel of the Trinity as revealed in the prayer of Jesus. God is blessed because the Persons of the Trinity existed from eternity in the mutual glory, love, and knowledge they shared in themselves. The blessedness of man and nature is but a reflection of this blessedness of God, which became the model of the covenantal arrangement in paradise (1 Tim 1:11; 6:15). In these verses, when the apostle Paul says "blessed God," he does not mean that God is worthy of praise (which he certainly is) but that God is blessed in and of himself by nature. If praise of God was meant, *eulogetos* would have been used, but in this case *makarios* was used to express the blessed nature of God (Rom 1:25; Eph 1:3). Of course, God is worthy to be praised precisely because he is infinitely blessed in attributes. Because God is blessed by nature, those who are blessed (*makarioi*) will possess certain qualities characteristic of the kingdom of God: "Blessed are the pure in heart, for they will see God" (Matt 5:8). If it is true that "the eschatology of nature is typical of the eschatology of redemption," blessedness may well be the common ground that unifies both (1 Tim 1:11). God is most worthy to be blessed because he is supremely blessed by nature, and the author of everything that is good: "Every good and perfect gift is from above, coming down from the Father of the heavenly lights, who does not change like shifting shadows" (Jas 1:17).

The gospel of the good news is the gospel of the blessed news, and Paul could not have unwittingly said, "the *gospel* of the glory of the *blessed* God" (1 Tim 1:11). The gospel, then, is the eschatological fulfillment of the blessedness of God promised in the Counsel of Peace. There is this essential connection between the good news of the gospel and the good nature of God. "Eschatology precedes soteriology" because the infinitely good nature of God precedes everything else. In the nature of the case, the gospel does more than cure sin or evade judgment; it leads us to the glory and beauty in the blessedness of God (Rom 3:23). In this, nature is typical of grace and the two share the common feature of God's blessedness. But to the natural goodness of paradise is added the redemptive goodness of the Son of God, who is infinitely more blessed than Adam. The blessedness of the covenant union in the wedding of Adam and Eve is typical of the blessedness in the spiritual wedding of Yahweh and Israel, which in turn will be fulfilled in the eschatological wedding of Christ and the church (Deut 10:13; Matt 22:1–14; Eph 5:22–25). The wedding is one of the most often used and best metaphors associated with the blessedness of covenant in the Scriptures. The blessedness in the wedding metaphor is that of the union and reflects the blessedness in the union of the Three-in-One. In the natural eschatology, the good nature of the Creator was the good news, which is typical of the redemptive eschatology, where it becomes the blessed news of the gospel. The infinite blessedness of God has reached its consummate state in the blessed Redeemer. God, who is the Alpha and the Omega of all things, is now the Alpha and the Omega of every good and perfect news.

Whether the goodness in creation (*towb*) or in redemption (*euangelion*), therefore, the covenantal substance of "every good and perfect gift" lies in the blessed nature of the triune God. Hence, it is properly called the gospel of God (Mark 1:14; Rom 1:1; 2 Cor 11:7). Blessedness so defined is found within the specific boundaries of the covenant love and faithfulness of God expressed through *hesed* and *agape*. The covenant love and faithfulness, or blessedness, intuitively pursues union rather than disunion as in the case of Adam and Eve, and Yahweh and Israel (Exod 19:5–6). In paradise it was "they will become one flesh," but in the Promised Land it was "I will take you as my own people, and I will be your God" (Gen 2:24; Exod 6:7). It would not be good for Israel to be "alone" apart from Yahweh even in the would-be paradise of Canaan. Israel was reminded time and again that it was for their own happiness (blessedness) that God made covenant with them and required them to obey all the commandments:

> And now, Israel, what does the LORD your God ask of you but to fear the LORD your God, to walk in obedience to him, to love him, to serve the LORD your God with all your heart and with all your soul, and to observe the LORD commands and decrees that I am giving you today for your own good [*towb*]. (Deut 10:12–13)

The source of blessedness did not lie in themselves or paradise but in the blessed God who made a covenant with them. In his own blessed nature, God pursued Israel's happiness by offering them the covenant union of the spiritual wedding despite their continued rebellion (Hos 1:9–10). God's commandments were given not to enslave Israel but to bless them as a holy nation and priestly kingdom set apart from all other nations. The blessed nature of God was the foundation of his patience and mercy toward the rebellious Israel, who was to inherit the kingdom as the "children of the living God" (Hos 1:10). A family motif is clearly evident in this covenant metaphor of blessedness: God's spiritual wedding with Israel, his forgiveness of her adultery, and the adoption of her descendants to sonship. The blessedness of God is consummated in Jesus and in the spiritual family of God, whose firstborn is Christ (Rom 8:29): "And a voice from heaven said, 'This is my Son, whom I love; with him I am well pleased'" (Matt 3:17). The Father and the Son are blessed from eternity in the Counsel of Peace and it is now fully revealed to the adopted sons in the Son. In him, believers are adopted to be coheirs of the kingdom of God, as promised to Hosea through his forgiveness and acceptance of Gomer. The wedding of Christ and the church is the fulfillment of the prophesy and the church awaits its consummation in heaven (Eph 5:22–25). Paul's prayer "that you may be filled to the measure of all the fullness of God" summarizes the inexpressible joy anticipated of that consummate union (Eph 3:19). Soteriology proper seeks rectitude, but eschatology seeks blessedness; the redemptive eschatology is blessedness with a plus of rectitude. The covenant promise "I will be your God, and you will be my people" was unable to be realized in the temple of the natural eschatology, but now realized in the temple of the redemptive eschatology. In the temple that Jesus Christ built (John 2:19), God will be forever united with his people that they will never again be separated from his love (Rom 8:39). The Beatitudes express the reversed blessedness of God's kingdom modelled after the blessed (*makarios*) nature of God contrasted to the commonly understood blessings of this world (Matt 5:3–12; 1 Cor 7:29–31; 2 Cor 12:9–10). The way of the cross is the reversed blessedness, and the reversal of the patterns of this age: "known, yet regarded as unknown; dying, and yet we live on; beaten, and yet not killed; sorrowful, yet always rejoicing; poor, yet making many rich; having nothing, and yet possessing everything" (2 Cor 6:9–10).

The execution of the Counsel of Peace is as revealing as the content of it. The Father, the Son, and the Spirit glorify and love each other as they appear together to implement the Eternal Counsel in history with the closing of the ages (1 Cor 10:11). They do so in the order in which it was conceived in the Counsel (Eph 1:4–14) and in a manner that is pleasing and delightful among themselves: "And as he was praying, heaven was opened and the Holy Spirit descended on him in bodily form like a dove. And a voice came from heaven: 'You are my Son, whom I love; with you I am well pleased'" (Luke 3:22). The reason for the Father's delight must have been the free and voluntary obedience of the Son in suffering, and the evidence of the delight is the Spirit descending on him like a dove (Matt 4:1; John 17:4; Heb 5:8). The approval of the Son is so affirmative that the Holy Spirit is called "the Spirit of Christ" and "the Spirit of Jesus," or even the Spirit of "the Last Adam" (1 Cor 15:44). Hence, the joyful manner in which the Persons interact with each other is as revealing as the mission itself (John 17:21–24). The blessedness of God lies in the means as well as in the end of the redemptive mission because God deemed his reverent submission as important as the submission itself: "Although he was a son, he learned obedience from what he suffered" (Heb 5:8). The enjoyment of the covenant is as important as, if not more than, the execution of it, something which all God's covenant children must be mindful of and should learn from the firstborn of God's family (Rom 8:29).

What Jesus, as the Last Man, did in his reverent submission to the Father was to fulfill and complete the chief end of man. It means the fulfillment of the natural eschatology with the added gift of the redemptive: "Love the LORD your God with all your heart and with all your soul and with all your strength. These commandments that I give you today are to be upon your hearts" (Deut 6:5–6). The law was never intended to be a mere test of obedience just as the covenant in paradise was not intended to be a test of obedience but a means of reward and blessedness:

> And now, O Israel, what does the LORD your God ask of you but to fear the LORD your God, to walk in obedience to him, to love him, to serve the LORD your God with all your heart and with all your soul, and to observe the LORD's

commands and decrees that I am giving you today for your own good [blessedness]? (Deut 10:12–13)

Any sense of progress in redemptive history would lose its significance apart from how and where the law is applied at different administrations of the Covenant of Grace (Jer 31:31–34). The substance of the Covenant of Grace is the same regardless of administrations, but the means of its revelation and execution were different as the law can be written in stone, or in the heart. If written in the stone, the law is obeyed with relatively less delight and freedom than written in the heart. The veil that covered the fading glory on Moses' face may have diminished the glory and freedom in the Old Covenant when the law was written in stone. But the veil had disappeared in the New Covenant, the order of Melchizedek, and the law is written in the heart for more delight and freedom in the Spirit (2 Cor 3:1–18). The glory of the Lord is revealed to the fullest measure with the unveiled faces who are "transformed into his likeness with ever-increasing glory, which comes from the Lord, who is the Spirit" (v. 18). There would be no substantial difference in the strictly soteric sense between the administrations in terms of the curative function of the law. But there is a qualitative difference in the eschatological sense since the law written in the heart will transform believers by the unveiled and glorious face of Christ, who obeyed the Father "for the joy set before him" (Heb 12:2). God delights in the free and voluntary obedience of his people for their own blessedness but it comes from the freedom in the Spirit and the law written in the heart rather than in stone (1 Sam 15:22). It is blessedness *par excellence* because it transforms God's children into the likeness of the Son, with whom the Father is most pleased. It may be said that doxology in the end is the eschatological form of the blessedness of God—"Praise God, from whom all blessings flow; Praise Him, all creatures here below; Praise Him above, ye heav'nly hosts; Praise Father, Son and Holy Ghost."

Union with God

It is a great insight into the covenantal nature of redemptive eschatology that Calvin understood the bodily resurrection of believers in the future as "union with God."[51] Though the present resurrection of believers with Christ into the heavenly realms was not as much stressed, he did see the future resurrection in terms of the covenantal nature of man and his chief destination. The resurrection of Christ as the firstfruit of the final harvest, then, is the firstfruit of the final union with God beyond victory over death (1 Cor 15:20). The union with God is the best expression of the redemptive eschatology typified by the natural eschatology in paradise. Jesus prayed for the unity of believers, just as the Father and the Son are one: "May they also be in us so that the world may believe that you have sent me" (John 17:21). His prayer reveals that the

---

51. Calvin, *Institutes*, 2:988–89.

purpose of the Counsel of Peace was to bring God's children into the union with the Father in order that they may share in the glory, love, and knowledge of the Trinity. Albeit substitutionary in nature, the covenant union of believers with the Mediator renders them able to peek into and take part in the inner sanctuary of the Eternal Counsel of the Father and the Son. They are brought near to God in presence as well as being near to God in likeness, and the union completes it in the temple of heaven, "the heavenly Jerusalem, the city of the living God" (Heb 12:22).

In the Golden Chain of the *Ordo Salutis*, rectitude from sin ends with glorification, or the final approach to God in order to enter the most intimate and highest life (Heb 4:16; 9:24). The eternal life in redemption is typified by the everlasting life in nature promised to Adam in paradise as the reward of obedience to the Covenant of Works (Gen 2:17, 3:21–24; John 6:47). Of course, the redemptive is better than the natural: "I have come that they may have life, and have it to the full" (John 10:10). Until the Last Man, no man including Adam has ever approached so near God with so much confidence that God is called "*Abba*, Father" (Rom 8:15; Heb 4:14–16). The redemptive nearness in this union is intimate, inseparable, and everlasting beyond the natural nearness to God in the probationary Eden. It is noteworthy that sin is defined as falling short of the glory of God rather than falling from the goodness of creation (Rom 3:23). Even though the latter is certainly true, the former is the highest standard against which the apostle measures sin. He could have defined sin in terms of the depth of the fall, but instead he defines it under the height of God's glory. The height from which mankind fell is the everlasting life in union with God, and in this sense the apostle also sees the meaning of resurrection beyond rectitude from sin: "Set your minds on things above, not on earthly things. For you died, and your life is now hidden with Christ in God" (Col 3:4). Calvin did not miss this point, that resurrection is more than rectitude of death, but the final approach to God and entrance into the glory from which mankind fell (Heb 9:24). The crucifixion was for the cure, and the exaltation was for the union; he now "serves in the sanctuary, the true tabernacle set up by the Lord, not by man" and we too are seated with him next to the Father (Heb 8:1–2).

The high priests of the Old Covenant in the order of Aaron were allowed to enter the inner sanctuary only once a year for their priesthood was imperfect and temporary (Heb 6:19–20). This meant that Israel's union with God in the earthly tabernacle was temporary and indirect for their priests could never become a perfect mediator. The priesthood of Melchizedek, however, is for the direct and permanent union with God in the heavenly sanctuary set up by God: "A mediator, however, does not represent just one party; but God is one" (Gal 3:20). In the new order of priesthood, there is a direct union with God through the Mediator, who is the Son of God, and those united with him can enter the inner part of the sanctuary in heaven to be seated next to the Father. Due to the spatial restrictions, Israel could not physically enter the sanctuary but had to be content with the substitutionary presence of the high priest, and even that only once a year. The new Israel, however, is not limited by the spatial restrictions, and can at once enter the inner sanctuary in heaven with the eternal High Priest (Heb 4:16). The most important work of a high priest is to enter the inner sanctuary in behalf the people of God, and in this sense, "If he [Christ] were on earth, he would not be a priest" (Heb 8:4). Through his resurrection and exaltation, Christ brings the people of God through the now-wide-open curtain into the inner sanctuary for the permanent union with the Father (Heb 6:19–20). His work of the eternal priesthood would have been incomplete until he spatially entered the heavenly sanctuary and pled with the Father, and this time, unlike the Aaronic order, the new Israel may approach before God with him (Heb 9:24–26). In the priesthood of Christ, therefore, the crucifixion and resurrection are inseparable and indispensable for the blessed union with God. The priestly work at the altar (cross) and in the sanctuary (resurrection) are both necessary to complete the work of the Mediator (Heb 9:1–12). The earthly tabernacle in the Aaronic order merely served as "a copy and shadow of what is in heaven" until the substance of heaven itself arrived for the blessed union (Heb 8:5, 9:24, 10:1, 11:39–40, 12:22–23).

In conclusion, perhaps no other biblical concept more properly captures the redemptive eschatology manifested in the priesthood of Christ than that of "God with us" (*Immanuel*). The apostle John fittingly portrays the new heaven and earth as the place of the consummate wedding union between God and his bride:

> Then I saw a new heaven and a new earth, for the first heaven and the first earth had passed away, and there was no longer any sea. I saw the Holy City, the new Jerusalem, coming down out of heaven from God, prepared as a bride beautifully dressed for her husband. (Rev 21:1–2)

It is noteworthy that the new paradise as described above is unlike the first paradise in one particular aspect: the cherubim that guarded its gates are no more to be seen. The absence of the cherubim in the new paradise means that there is free and unlimited access to the tree of life by believers with no further hindrance or possibility of death (Gen 3:24; Exod 25:22; John 17:21; Rev 22:2). The final union with God in the new paradise will never again be probationary for the eschatological purpose of God's creation will have been fulfilled with an added redemptive gift. In glory and freedom, believers will no longer see God "as through a mirror" but see him face to face, "filled to the measure of all the fullness of God" (1 Cor 13:12; Eph 3:19).

Chapter 3
Man and Eschatology

3.1 Image of God

The notion of the *imago* Dei is significant in all aspects of theology as it correlates the nature of man to the nature and attributes of God. The image of God is constitutive of the image of man at creation, who became the image-bearer of the Creator. Accordingly, it is a key feature in all aspects of theology including the creation, redemption, and consummation of man and the world. The purpose of the eternal election in Christ is the consummation of that image:

> For he chose us in him before the creation of the world to be holy and blameless in his sight. In love he predestined us to be adopted as his sons through Jesus Christ, in accordance with his pleasure and will—to the praise of his glorious grace, which he has freely given us in the One he loves. (Eph 1:4–6)

The adoption to sonship as the completion of the image of God in man is the key link that connects God and man, and man and the world, tying together all facets of redemptive history from Genesis to Revelation. The image of God *in* man is relevant to eschatology, in particular, since the scope of soteriology is often limited to the vicarious work of Christ finished *outside* of believers. The restoration and completion of the divine image bears more directly on the renewing work of Christ in believers through the Spirit, leading to the final glorification (Eph 4:24; Rom 8:30; Col 3:10).

The creation of man in the image and likeness of God is part of the eschatology of nature that precedes redemption but foreshadows the eschatology of redemption. The natural order and its eternal purpose for glorifying and enjoying God precedes the curative and salvific grace, but is also further augmented by the latter. It merits attention in its own right in the non-soteric order because the redemptive grace is introduced later to restore and consummate the original purpose of nature. The first Adam is typical of the Second Adam, and the image of God in nature is perfected in Christ, whom believers must conform to (Rom 5:14, 8:29). In this sense, Christ's work goes beyond the forensic justification of sinners to the recreation of the old man into the new man (Eph 2:15; 4:23–24). It goes beyond the unification of ethnicities, Jews and Gentiles, to the recreation of man into a new order of humanity whose head is Christ. The work of redemption—"put off the old self, and put on the new self"—is at the same time the work of the redemptive eschatology. In the new order of creation, the new birth of regeneration in believers is equivalent to the resurrection in the Spirit to the heavenly image of man (Eph 2:5–9; 1 Cor 15:46–49). The new birth of man in the baptism of the Spirit means a change in the order of man rather than a mere change in man. It is based on the original view of man as a covenant partner of God and the goal of redemption is to fulfill that purpose in a far better way than the first. The foundation of the image of God is the communicable attributes of God, especially revealed through the Counsel of Peace, shared with man for covenant partnership and fellowship. It was seen previously that the natural revelation of God in man and nature is the epistemological foundation of all natural human knowledge (Rom 1:18–23; 2:14–15). The use of the image of God to fulfill the eschatology of nature was expected of the first Adam, but it is now fulfilled in the eschatology of redemption by the Last Adam (Rom 5:14; 2 Cor 4:4).

As a result, common grace and redemptive grace nowhere more clearly overlap than in the image of God from the perspective of the chief end of man. The recreation of man in order to make him participate in the blessed nature of God is not a tertiary but a primary goal of redemption in Christ (Eph 4:24; Col 3:10; 1 Pet 1:4). The union with Christ, in this sense, means union with God and "the light of the gospel of the glory of Christ who is the image of God" (2 Cor 4:4). The gospel of the glory of Christ is the eschatology of redemption that saves and takes man from the earthly image to the heavenly image. It involves the imputation of Christ's righteousness for justification but equally results in sanctification through conformation to Christ (Rom 8:29). One is the cure of God; the other is the power of God: "So will it be with the resurrection of the dead . . . it is sown in dishonor, it is raised in glory; it is sown in weakness, it is raised in power . . ." (1 Cor 15:43). The image of God in resurrection, then, is the image of God in redemptive eschatology, which is "created to be like God in true righteousness and holiness" (Eph 4:24). The redemptive is better than the natural, but not unlike it, in the covenantal purpose of the chief end of man to share in the blessedness of the Father. The Last Adam consummated the chief end that the first Adam could not complete with an addition of redemption so that the new humanity in him might participate in the same goal: "Instead, speaking the truth in love, we will in all things grow up into him who is the Head, that is, Christ" (Eph 4:15). What was probationary in nature and lost in sin had been regained in the grace of redemption, and will be consummated by the same grace.

The image of God as a receptacle of the blessedness of God is unique to man, and no other creature had been given this special gift and privilege. Beside man, no other creature was promised eternal life as the reward and blessing of the Creator by way of a covenant. It was equipped with truth, righteousness, and holiness after the nature of God in order that the new man may share in the glory, love, and knowledge of the Father and the Son. At the time of creation, the image of God has had threefold significances in relation to God, man (self and others), and nature.[1] The vice-regent of the Creator was to exercise the image of God to love God, love fellow human beings, and to care for the world (Gen 1:26–28, 2:15). Hoekema could not have summarized any better the uniqueness of the image of God in man: no other creature, beside angels, is commanded to "serve" God; no other creature, not even angels, is commanded to "love" neighbor; no other creature, including angels, is given the authority to "subdue" the earth.[2] The image of God is the clearest indication that man was created superior to all creatures, even including angels in some sense, for the glory and enjoyment of God. Adam was properly the prophet, priest, and king in nature according to the pattern of truth, holiness, and righteousness in respective order. The prophetic, priestly, and kingly offices of Adam in the natural eschatology prefigured Christ in the redemptive eschatology (Col 3:10). In these three offices of Adam, nature was typical of grace (Rom 5:14; Col 1:15). The creation is recreated into the new creation through the "redemptive plus" of the work of Christ. In it, the image of God is elevated to the highest level in the adoption to sonship in order that believers may freely and voluntarily serve God, love neighbor, and rule over nature.[3] The covenantal duty in the chief end of man in nature can now be completed through the redemption and consummation in grace.

Earthly and Heavenly Man

The exact nature of life in paradise is not revealed in great detail but the tree of life and the tree of knowledge provide us with a few important details. The two trees signify a choice between eternal death and eternal life, placed before Adam by way of a covenant (Gen 2:17). In case he obeyed God and kept the covenant, he would proceed from the probationary state of the natural life to the confirmed state of the eternal life. Hypothetically, the eschatology of nature and the chief and of man would have been reached. The first parents of mankind enjoyed for a while temporary immortality until they violated the forbidden tree and transgressed the law of God in the covenant (Gen 2:17, 3:22; Rom 2:14–15). During this unique period in history, the natural order of life had not yet transformed into the eternal order and the fallible state had not yet reached an infallible state. The image of God had the potential to reach the highest state through the Covenant of Works but has not yet reached the glorified state beyond the possibility of death (Gen 1:26–28; Rom 3:23; 8:30).[4]

1. Hoekma, *Created in God's Image*, 75–82.
2. Hoekma, *Created in God's Image*, 75–82.
3. Hoekma, *Created in God's Image*, 73–75.
4. Vos, *Doctrine of the Covenant* (ebook), 174. "When we compare the representations of the

> Just as the blessedness of God exists in the free relationship of the three Persons of the adorable Being, so man shall also find his blessedness in the covenantal relationship with his God ... Therefore, he must not immediately and prematurely possess the highest enjoyment, but be led up to it along a rational way. The image of God within him must be brought out in the full clarity of his consciousness. In a certain sense, it must be extended, for in that he can still sin and die man is not God's image bearer. In his life it must be formed by keeping the divine law ... so that, by completing it, he might enter the full joy of his covenant God.[5]

God's creation was complete but man's work of cultivation has just started, which required the covenantal use of the image of God so that it may be fully consummated. As the Westminster Confession made clear, the covenant with Adam was not so much a test of obedience as the means of God's voluntary condescension to reward and bless him with life eternal. It was called a covenant rather than a test of obedience because "reasonable creatures do owe obedience" to God anyways as the "distance between God and the creature is so great."[6] The adoption to sonship in the redemptive grace is particularly significant in this regard as it signifies the permanent extension and formation of the image of God in man to receive the blessedness of God. God designed and created man so that he might be adopted to sonship through a covenantal arrangement akin to the relationship of the Son to the Father. In the fulfillment of this arrangement, the image of God would to be transformed from the earthly to the heavenly for "the highest enjoyment" of God's blessedness (1 Cor 15:48). A probationary state in paradise was given for that progress in the image of God to be formed in man through the Covenant of Works but with the possibility of sin and death (Hos 6:7). Insofar as man could sin and die, the image of God in him had not reached its highest state. The designation of the arrangement as the Covenant of Works toward a higher state of life thus sheds significant light on the eschatology of redemption in Reformed theology. The entrance into the highest possible realm of man's existence as God's image-bearer was not natural or automatic but required a period of schooling in obedience. The Covenant of Works reveals that since the beginning God has been more interested in the state of man's heart backed by obedience than his outward service or performance (1 Sam 15:22).

Even in the paradise of Eden, the natural (earth) was yet to unite with the supernatural (heaven) as man was required to complete the obedience to the covenant (Eph 1:10). This union required a free and voluntary obedience of Adam to God as

---

original state of man as they have been developed by the different theological traditions, there immediately arises a fundamental difference of great importance for the doctrine of the Covenant of Works. According to the Lutherans man had already reached his destination in that God had placed him in a state of uprightness. Eternal life was already in his possession."

5. Vos, *Doctrine of the Covenant* (ebook), 242–43.
6. Westminster Confession of Faith, 7.

that of the Son to the Father in the Counsel of Peace. It is the proper response of a reasonable creature from the point of view of creation, but all the more so because of the covenantal arrangement of God with the creature. The covenant is of an ethical and religious character in that Adam owes obedience God but also enjoys intimacy with him. It would be a relationship akin to that of the Father and the Son marked by mutual glory, love, and knowledge (John 17:21–26). If sustained, it would have elevated Adam to the state of glorification and the image of God in the fullest extent (Rom 3:23; 8:30). For mankind, the loss of glory (falling short of God's glory) in sin was the greater tragedy than the fall from the original righteousness. It is more about where man could have reached in glory than about where he fell from in sin. The immeasurable worth of man lies in his nature as the image-bearer of God and the glorification reserved for him in life eternal. The depth to which mankind fell is measured against the height which he could have reached had the covenant been sustained for a period of time. The glory envisaged is foreshadowed by the seventh day of creation, when God rested and the day and night pattern ceased (Gen 2:3). Bavinck's views on the Covenant of Works, the image of God, and the natural eschatology are as follows: "Although Adam was made in the image of God, it did not immediately reach its form in the fullest sense. Moreover, Adam was not the image itself. All the abundance of the image of God cannot be known until the present and future destiny of man is considered."[7]

It is rather clear that there is a direct correlation between the Covenant of Works, the image of God, the chief end of man, and the eschatology of nature. These foreshadow and are typical of what is ahead in the redemptive eschatology and the Covenant of Grace as far as the image of God is concerned. Participation in the divine nature by way of the recreated image of God has been envisaged in the work of creation and remains as the paramount vision in the work of redemption (2 Pet 1:4). The pursuit of the heavenly image of man had been premeditated in paradise rather than accidentally occasioned by the fall. The Eternal Counsel of the Trinity is the proper origin of it to be more accurate, and the incarnation, obedience, and resurrection of the Son sealed it (1 Cor 15:46–49).[8] The heavenly image of man, in contrast to the earthly image, is the image of the Son in the Counsel of Peace. In this, the Covenant of Works and Covenant of Grace share a common ground in "the three Persons of the adorable Being." Eschatology precedes soteriology, as Vos said, but redemptive eschatology is an essential part of soteriology. The eschatology as the end of history should be augmented by the eschatology in the *telos* of the image of God which Christ came to complete. The natural order of law precedes the redemptive order of grace but does not supersede the supernatural order accomplished by grace. The use of the law in grace is proper in the sense that the image of God is still the primary interest of God.

---

7. Griffith and Muether, *Creator, Redeemer, Consummator*, 169.
8. Vos, *Redemptive History*, 245.

The law is necessary in grace not just for the soteric use of repentance and atonement, but for the eschatological goal envisaged in the Covenant of Works.

Narrow and Wide Sense

The redemptive eschatology in Christ recreates rather than abrogates the creation in Adam, and this is nowhere more clearly seen than in the image of God. The distinction between the narrow and the broad senses of the image of God in the Reformed view of man illustrates this point.[9] Whether creation is regained or recreated in redemption, the distinction at least indicates that creation is not completely abrogated by redemption or by its eschatology. In the narrower sense, the image of God is lost by sin, which altogether suspended its ethical and religious functions: "For although they knew God, they neither glorified him as God nor gave thanks to him, but their thinking became futile and their foolish hearts were darkened" (Rom 1:21). The moral and religious function of the image of God enables man to worship and love God with all of the heart, soul, mind, and strength. It also renders him to love fellow man and take care of the natural world as vice-regent of God. Sadly, this central feature in man was lost in the fall with tragic and fearful consequences: "The wrath of God is being revealed from heaven against all the godlessness and wickedness of men who suppress the truth by their wickedness" (Rom 1:18). The doctrine of the total depravity of man in Reformed theology means the extent rather than the degree of the corruption by sin, which destroyed the moral function of the image of God. In this religious and moral feature of the image of God, man became totally incapable of sustaining ethical and spiritual functions in relation to God and man. The image of God, in its broader sense and capacity, however, is still able to execute the natural mandates with regard to duties in the realm of culture. The structure of the image of God, including intellect, volition, conscience, or general morality in mankind, is not completely destroyed. He is able to sustain by way of these faculties the natural and physical duties within the realm of common grace. In this broader structural sense, the image of God is still operational even when man is spiritually dead, unable and unwilling to worship, love, and obey God (Eph 2:1). With the religious and ethical function lost in sin, he is banned from God's presence in paradise, left only with the basic faculties to execute natural duties in human civilization (Gen 3:22–24).[10]

When nature was cursed and paradise was lost in sin, the temporary continuance of life under common grace became the primary goal of nature until redemption and consummation are completed by the Second Adam (Gen 3:15). A new and eternal order of the world would be inaugurated by him in substitution of the old and corrupted order. But, under common grace, the broader sense of the image of God preserves the structural integrity of man's rational faculties for the stated purpose.

---

9. Hoekema, *Created in God's Image*, 68.
10. Hoekema, *Created in God's Image*, 68.

The argument that redemptive grace does not abrogate but restores the created order (work, rest, family, culture) is thus founded upon the broad sense of the image of God. It serves to remind us that nature is not totally abrogated by redemption, at least not until the world as we know it is consummated into the new heaven and earth (2 Pet 3:9–13): "That day will bring about the destruction of the heavens by fire, and the elements will melt in the heat. But in keeping with his promise we are looking forward to a new heaven and a new earth, the home of righteousness" (v. 13). In the eschatology of redemption and grace, Christ does not abrogates but recreates the image of God in truth, righteousness, and holiness (Eph 4:24). The substance of the image of God is not altered but elevated and perfected in redemption and consummation. The covenantal function in the newly created image of God is no longer probationary, but gradually extended and perfected in Christ.[11] In the new heaven and the new earth, the two senses of the image of God would be a moot point in the same way that saving grace and common grace would be. Redemptive grace temporarily restores nature but eventually will transform all things into the eschatological order. God chose the redemptive eschatology of the new creation rather than let mankind remain in the state of immortality after the spiritual death (Gen 3:22). The ban from the tree of life was a better way as it closed the door to the fallen creation and opened the door to a new creation in the Second Adam. The chief end of man was never defined as immortality itself apart from the glory and enjoyment of God. The natural order is not totally destroyed but provided the constitutive elements to the new order exemplified by Christ's bodily resurrection. The moral direction has been damaged but the structure remains: "An eagle, for example, propels itself through the air by flying—this is one of its functions. The eagle would be unable to fly, however, unless it had wings—one of its structures."[12] The wings of the image of God have not been destroyed completely by sin in order that it may not only fly again, but fly into eternity.

The image of God is sometimes used as the basis of the redeeming of creation in the form of the Cultural Mandate. It is viewed as the primary goal of the creation in Genesis, and accordingly the main purpose of the Great Commission (Matt 28:18–20). At the risk of oversimplification, it may be said that the purpose of the Evangelical Mandate is the Cultural Mandate. In redemption, therefore, the image of God is redeemed and restored so that mankind might return to fulfilling the original mandate of creation as spelled out in Genesis 1:26–28. In *Creation Regained*, Wolters explains how God's image has lost its covenantal function but not its natural structure in the fall. The ethico-religious function of the image of God is lost but its constitutive elements are retained so that redemption may restore mankind to "regain" creation.[13] Despite the damage, the structure of the image of God is alive and operational, waiting to be redeemed and reused for the restoration of creation. After all, mankind is created

---

11. Hoekema, *Created in God's Image*, 69.
12. Hoekema, *Created in God's Image*, 69.
13. Wolters, *Creation Regained*, 72–73.

as God's vice-regent for this purpose and redemption does not abrogate it. It is a great irony of sin, however, that even the act of rebellion against God and suppression of the truth needs the structural capacity of the image of God. The so-called neutral faculties are used as a weapon to rebel against the Creator and blaspheme him (Rom 1:18–23). In any case, the argument goes that if the direction of the image is restored in the Evangelical Mandate, the redeemed may return to completing the Cultural Mandate. The primary goal of the gospel, then, is defined in terms of the restoration of creation rather than the recreation of it. The purpose of redemptive grace is defined largely in terms of completing the unfinished task of the Cultural Mandate given to mankind at creation.

Wolters echoes the general principle of Reformed theology that grace restores rather than abrogates nature. God's redemption is in harmony with his creation and providence, and its purpose is to redeem and regain the original creation.[14] What appears to be lacking, however, is the redemptive eschatology that grace does not just restore nature, but elevates it to the eternal and the supernatural—heaven and earth united in Christ (Eph 1:10). There seems to be lacking a crucial distinction of the eschatology of redemption from the eschatology of nature. The purpose of resurrection, for instance, is not to regain the earthly image of man (Adam) but to elevate it the heavenly image of man (the Last Adam). The eschatology of redemption is nowhere more clearly revealed than in the apostle Paul's understanding of resurrection as a movement from the earthly image to the heavenly image of man (1 Cor 15:44–49). While resurrection consummates the earthly into the heavenly, and the natural into the supernatural, it completely conquers death: "When the perishable has been clothed with the imperishable, and the mortal with immortality, then the saying that is written will come true: 'Death has been swallowed up in victory.'" The redemptive grace is doubly significant for man in the state of sin in that while it achieves the soteric deliverance from sin it also fulfills the eschatology of nature. The image of God redeemed by grace, then, cannot stop at regaining creation but should reach recreation in true righteousness and holiness (Eph 4:24). This requires a deeper look into the condition of the image of God in the fallen state than a simple distinction between the narrow and the broad senses. The notion that the image of God in its narrow sense is lost but in the broad sense preserved is true to a certain extent, but, if truly "corrupt and perverted" by sin as Wolters recognizes, it should be assessed more comprehensively in light of the redemptive eschatology.[15]

New Order

The definition of the *imago Dei* should take into account the new and eternal order of creation in Christ beyond the recovery of the natural order (2 Cor 5:17). The notion

14. Wolters, *Creation Regained*, 72–73.
15. Wolters, *Creation Regained*, 68.

that grace restores (regains) creation holds true in the provisional kingdom of Christ until "he hands over the kingdom to the Father after he has destroyed all dominion, authority and power" (1 Cor 15:24). When the new order of heaven and earth appears, it will replace the first creation, which has been corrupted and perverted to its core by sin (Rom 8:18–25; 2 Pet 3:12–13). "Cursed is the ground because of you," said God, and the earthly image of man has been profoundly altered by the curse: "for dust you are and to dust you will return" (Gen 3:17, 19). The curse of God on man and the ground together and the effect it brought on the world may have meant a constitutive change involving annihilation of the elements of the first creation despite its continuance under the common grace. On account of sin, something deeply troubling happened to man and the world as a whole such that the very constitution of it needed to be destroyed and made anew. The revelation of what will happen and how it will happen at the end of the world suggests a total deconstruction of the present pattern of the world (1 Cor 7:29–31; 2 Pet 3:12–13). A closer look into the present evil age as a result of the curse and its final destiny, therefore, should be taken into account for the proper view of the image of God at the present time.

These considerations taken together suggest that redemptive grace is recreative in the final analysis. The transformation from the earthly image to the heavenly image of man is the evidence that there is a fundamental restructuring of the earthly order by the resurrection of Christ (1 Cor 15:44–49). At first, the apostle begins with the soteric problem of sin and death, but he then moves on to the contrast of the earthly and the heavenly images of man (vv. 48–49). The focus on the hope of resurrection became an occasion to bring up the crucial distinction between the natural and the supernatural state of man. It begins with a restorative significance of resurrection as victory over death but then elevates it to the entirely different topic of the eschatology of resurrection. It has moved into a topic of the eschatology of nature and the eschatology of redemption occasioned by the initial contrast between death and resurrection. Thus, the apostle's interest seems to lie not just in creation regained, but more properly in creation supernaturalized. The conventional distinction of the narrow and the broad senses of the image of God does not necessarily address this vertical shift from the natural to the supernatural order of man. Hoekema rightly cautions the risk involved in an oversimplification of the image of God in either direction:

> Earlier theologians said that the image of God in man was to be found primarily in his structural capacities . . . whereas his functioning was thought of as a kind of appendix to his structure. More recent theologians, however, have affirmed that the functioning of man . . . constitute the essence of the image of God . . .[16]

The reason why emphasis is limited to the two senses of the image of God is because the scope of the discussion is limited to the horizontal domain of redemption

---

16. Hoekema, *Created in God's Image*, 69.

as regaining creation. The traditional approach to the doctrine does not seem to have given sufficient attention to the vertical domain of heaven in regard to the image of God. It underscores the use of the image of God for the fulfillment of the Cultural Mandate, or the recovery of the original state of creation lost by sin. But, unless the heavenly image of man is made the focus, the scope of the doctrine will be strictly limited to the two senses with the goal of redeeming culture. The principle that grace restores nature holds largely true in the earthly scope of redemption, but does not fully account for the heavenly scope, namely, the eschatology of redemption. As seen before, it does not sufficiently address the curse of sin, which fundamentally distorted the first creation as to require a new creation. The doctrine of redemptive grace ought to be consistent with the already-but-not-yet kingdom of Christ as a prelude to the final kingdom of the Father (1 Cor 15:24). Saving grace is both soteric and eschatological by nature, envisaging the progress of redemptive history moving forward and upward to the new creation. Grace redeems the fallen world from the bottom of the pit of sin but at the same time transforms it from the earthly to the heavenly realms. The progress of history from creation to consummation requires an analysis more comprehensive than the conventional scope of the image of God. Sin did not merely affect mankind in the ethical direction alone but altered the very essence of its constitution as "dust" (Gen 3:19). The decomposition of man to dust was so radical that it required a deeper and lasting remedy than a temporary restoration from the dust.

These considerations complicate the question as to the precise state of the image of God under the present curse and the decaying effects of sin. Thus, it must be admitted that a razor-sharp distinction between the aforementioned senses of the image of God is rather arbitrary. The extent of the distorted image of God is not easily identifiable, and it is difficult to estimate to what extent its function or structure had been damaged. The damage is so deep-seated and comprehensive that the condition of the fallen mankind does not fit neatly into the two categories: "The Lord saw how great man's wickedness on the earth had become, and that every inclination of the thoughts of his heart was only evil all the time" (Gen 6:5). The distinction between the function and the structure in the image of God serves a limited and useful purpose, but does not fully explain the state of the total depravity: "The heart is deceitful above all things and beyond cure. Who can understand it?" (Jer 17:9). Therefore, even the relative integrity of the structure of the image of God cannot be conclusive as the depth and degree of the depravity is immense. As Bavinck cautioned, the common grace of nature cannot be overestimated and the return of man to dust cannot be underestimated. A change in the direction of the image of God does not necessarily mean a full and complete restoration of the first creation. In view of these considerations, the mandate to regain creation ought to be qualified by the necessity of a new order of creation in Christ (2 Cor 5:17). The Scriptures make it clear that the first creation has expired in the eschatology of redemption, and a new creation in the form of the new heaven and earth awaits in the future (2 Pet 3:10). Grace does not abrogate the natural order for the time being in the horizontal perspective, but qualifies its life span by the consummation in the vertical perspective (Rom 8:20–21). The earthly image of man to be returned to dust is temporary and provisional, thus it ought to be lived in the eschatological vision that the "world in in its present form is passing away" (1 Cor 7:31). The revelation of the final days of this world is both fearful and hopeful:

> But the day of the Lord will come like a thief. The heavens will disappear with a roar; the elements will be destroyed by fire, and the earth and everything done in it will be laid bare . . . But in keeping with his promise we are looking forward to a new heaven and a new earth, the home of righteousness. (2 Pet 3:10)

The cosmic transformation at the last day involves the creation order as a whole and that all temporal distinctions, including that of the image of God, will be erased and be replaced by the new order of righteousness. Its suggests the doctrine of the total depravity of man ought to be applied uniformly to the natural world as a whole and in that day those distinctions would be a moot point.[17] In short, the idea that redemption regains creation may be necessary and useful in upholding the original goodness of nature against a Gnostic dualism, but it ought to be seen within the comprehensive scope of the redemptive eschatology. In redemption, grace temporarily regains nature, but in the consummation it will unify heaven and nature in Christ. The two are held in the already-but-not-yet tension for the time being until the Parousia for the sanctification and perseverance of believers.

Apologetic Significance

The two senses of the image of God can be useful for the preaching of the gospel making use of the proper relationship between grace and nature. Since the fall of mankind, common grace operates in tandem with the faculties of man as part of the image of God for the preservation of human civilization (Gen 3:16–21). This also provides the foundation of the gospel's communication with the fallen world since both believers and non-believers live in the world under common grace. Due to the broad sense of the image of God, an internal communication between God and man takes place even though the fallen man suppresses the truth. There are no true atheists in the sense that every man possesses the innate knowledge of God, thought there could be practical atheists who suppress that knowledge (Rom 1:19–21). Atheism is a product of agnosticism, which is the belief that God and the supernatural world are unknowable or unproved, but the Scriptures make it clear that man knows God and is therefore "without excuse" (Rom 1:20). This knowledge, a sense of Deity, is postulated on the Covenant of Works with the Creator even after the fall. Saving grace makes use of this innate knowledge of God in man for the preaching and the invitation of mankind to

---

17. Hoekema, *Created in God's Image*, 69.

the gospel. "The eschatology of nature is typical of the eschatology of redemption" and is now used for the latter in the preaching and apologetics of the gospel.

As the apostle Paul wrote, the world in its present form will cease and will be replaced by a new world in immortality. Man is created in God's image in order that man can forever be with God, and God with us, never again being separated from his love (Rom 8:39). Although this does not negate the duty to preserve and cherish life on earth, it does set proper boundaries for those who look forward to the coming world (1 Cor 7:29–31). The focus, however, is not the world or even what kind of world, but God and his glory as the chief end of man for his own blessedness. For this reason, mankind at all times cannot evade God or the knowledge of God for epistemology flows out of theology. Again, the possibility of all knowledge stems from the prior knowledge of God in man and, though fallen and distorted, the image of God is a clear testimony to the glory of the Creator. The innate knowledge of God is so built into its fabric that man instinctively strives to procreate, fill the earth, and fulfill the original mandate as God's vicegerent (Gen 1:26–29). Mankind in its basic constitution is so reliant on God that even its existence and preservation cannot be sustained apart from God (Acts 17:28). The ethical antithesis and the spiritual separation did not mean a metaphysical separation from God, which would have meant an autonomy and independence of man from the Creator (which is inconceivable). Fallen man is separated from God in the ethico-religious sense, but not in the ontological sense so that he can never hide from the Creator (Gen 3:8–9; Job 34:21–22). In this sense, the broad sense of the image of God has been useful for the preaching and defending of the gospel: "By means of their distinction between the image of God in the broader and narrower sense Reformed theologians have most clearly maintained the connection between substance and quality, nature and grace, creation and redemption."[18]

The image of God reveals and imitates the Eternal Counsel of the Father, the Son, and the Spirit, in whose image man is created, redeemed, and will be consummated (Gen 1:26; John 17:21). In particular, it sheds significant light on the adoption to sonship in Christ, who is the fulfillment of Adam (Rom 5:14). Through the Spirit of adoption, believers seated next to God call him "*Abba*, Father" in conformation to Christ, the Son, who is the firstborn in God's family (Rom 8:15, 29). Adam was the probationary son in the paradise of Eden until the everlasting adoption to sonship is sealed by the Second Adam. By the obedience of the Second Adam to the Father, the image of God is recreated in order that man can consummate the covenant union with God that began in the first paradise. The Prodigal Son represents fallen humanity, who lost the sonship in Eden until the eternal Son came and sealed the everlasting sonship for those united to him (Luke 15:11–32). The image of God, then, is the very image of "the three Persons of the adorable Being" that started in the Counsel of Peace and was given to man in paradise. Hence, the adopted sons of God as coheirs with the firstborn should properly share in the blessedness of the Trinity and his kingdom (Rom 8:17).

---

18. Bavinck, *Reformed Dogmatics*, 2:590–94.

They are recreated in truth, righteousness, and holiness after God so that the ethico-religious end of man in nature might be fulfilled in the redemptive-eschatological realm of grace. The two senses of the image of God is a useful distinction for unity and correlation of creation and redemption, and provides a common ground for evangelical purposes. The theological, apologetic, and missional significance of the image of God, however, would be far more illuminated by its covenantal nature, which envisages the final purpose in the adoption to sonship.

Constitution of Man

The goodness of creation that flows out of the blessed of God bears out the constitution of man as a holistic being in the perfect union of body and soul. The integrity of the union is inherent to the natural order and was meant to persist until it is confirmed in the form of the eternal life. The body and the soul were never meant to be separated, barring the expulsion from paradise due to sin and the return of the body to dust (Gen 3:19, 22–24). The natural union of the two components in man precedes their unforeseen division by sin and the curse imposed upon mankind with the tragic consequences that followed (Gen 2:17, 3:16–19). The question of dichotomy or trichotomy (two or three parts) in the constitution of man's being would have been a moot point had Adam obeyed and remained in paradise, where death had not yet entered. Just as in the constitution of the image of God, the composition of man's being in the pre-fall situation would not have had to have been raised. Adam as a psychosomatic being could have possibly kept the covenant and fulfilled the chief end reaching God's glory (Rom 3:23). He could have reached the eternal state of immortality without ever having to contemplate nor experience the temporary separation of his body and soul. The two parts or three parts equally seem to find an appeal in the Scriptures because there are many instances that appear to support either view (Gen 2:7; Ezek 37:5; Matt 10:28; Mark 14:38; John 19:30; 1 Thess 5:13). In any case, the distinction is more relevant in the fallen state of man in which mankind experiences the effects of the flesh (*sarx*) and must inevitably face the separation of the two in death. In some instances, there is even a mention of four parts in man such as "heart, soul, mind, and strength," making it even more perplexing (Mark 12:30).

The proof-texting of the Scriptures for support obviously will not resolve the question of man's constitution, which requires a more fundamental consideration. Adam was undoubtedly created as a psychosomatic being possessing both physical and non-physical parts, generally called "body" and "soul" (Gen 2:7; 1 Cor 15:45). The first Adam became a "living soul" with a body and this distinction would have been less relevant as long as Adam remained in paradise. The constitutive parts of his being would not have had to undergo a separation by physical death in view of the eschatology of nature, and that would be even more true in the eschatology of redemption and eternal life. With the different aspects of the image of God in perfect harmony, the question of man's constitution in immortality would not have been raised. In creation *ex nihilo* (out of nothing), man was made with integrity in all his parts, holistic to such a degree "God saw that it was very good" (Gen 1:31): "Then the LORD God formed a man from the dust of the ground and breathed into his nostrils the breath of life, and the man became a living being" (Gen 2:7). For all intents and purposes, it was sufficient for Adam and Eve to know their being was the composite union of "the dust of the ground" and "the breath of life" made in the blessed image of God. The unified existence of body and soul served the moral and religious purposes of man in paradise to fulfill the commands God gave him (Gen 1:26–28). In soul and body, Adam was fit to serve as the vice-regent of the Creator until sin entered him and the constitutive parts became a problem that affected soul and body through imputation of guilt or the corruption of the sinful nature. Since then, the fallen state of man required an explanation in terms of his constitutive parts: "For the sinful nature desires what is contrary to the Spirit, and the Spirit what is contrary to the sinful nature. They are in conflict with each other, so that you do not do what you want" (Gal 5:17).

The sinful nature, or the flesh, has now become a representative pronoun of sin in the fallen state, and the physical component of creation has now become a symbol of the depraved nature. This was all due to the curse of the ground and man, who was to return to dust from which he came (Gen 3:19). Such a description of the *flesh* would not have been appropriate in the pre-fall context, when God saw that all creation was good after the blessedness of God (Gen 1:31; 2:1–3; 3:22–24). The question of man's constitution possibly would not have been raised at all, much less the flesh used as a symbol of the sinful nature. The analysis of man's constitution would have been unnecessary with the prospect of the eternal life in a perfect psychosomatic unity. With no death in paradise, the intermediate state of man's soul after death would have been a premature or even a strange question. All the constitutive parts of man's being would have functioned harmoniously in the integrity of the natural order; it is important in this regard that the image of God would have been respective to the whole man, and not to any one particular part of man. Adam's obedience to the Covenant of Works would have led him to the state of immortality where the constitutive parts would not have been subject to separation, confusion, or decay (1 Cor 15:45). The bodily resurrection of believers, then, would be all the more so since it is more than a reversal of death, but the redemptive arrival at the immortal state through the Second Adam. It is the redemptive and final conclusion by the Last Adam to what failed and was left unfinished by the first Adam (1 Cor 15:46–48). The resurrection of believers is first a soteric victory over death, but equally important, if not more, is the transformation from *protos* to *eschatos* man. In short, the biblical doctrine of man does not *a priori* postulate a division in man's constitution, whether two, three, or more parts, beyond the bodily and non-bodily parts generally called "body" and "soul." It assumes a psychosomatic unity of the parts in man and God intends to deal with man as such regardless of what state he is in.

After the fall, the division of the constitutive parts in man started to appear largely to address the fallen condition of man affected by sin and to prescribe its cure. The so-called noetic effect of sin (sin's influence on man's knowledge) also shows the depth and extent of its infection in man's inner being, fit to be called "dead in your transgressions and sins" (Eph 2:1). It is true that in the curative mode of redemption the two constitutive parts of man are sometimes invoked separately to address a particular aspect of sin's corruption. Sometimes the body is called out and other times the soul is called out, depending on the situation, but it is never implied that God intends to deal with man in any other way than as a whole being:

> Watch and pray so that you will not fall into temptation. The spirit is willing, but the flesh is weak. (Mark 14:38)

> Do not be afraid of those who kill the body but cannot kill the soul. Rather, be afraid of the One who can destroy both soul and body in hell. (Matt 11:28)

> Jesus called out with a loud voice, "Father, into your hands I commit my spirit." When he had said this, he breathed his last. (Luke 23: 46)

These scriptural texts seem to address man in terms of the parts rather than the whole, but they were not actually intended to address the makeup of man's being itself, much less to put spirit and body into an existential conflict. The first is about the importance of resilience in prayer in the midst of disappointments and fatigue; the second is about the importance of faith in the sovereign authority of God in the face of physical danger or loss of life; the third text is about a temporary separation of spirit and body in Jesus during his death on the cross. The separate parts of man in these texts are called out to address a particular symptom or the corresponding cure of sin rather than to answer the question about the composition of man's being. One common feature in all these texts is the reference to some type of predicament (separation or conflict) in which spirit and body are placed as a result of sin's influence on man. The discord, disruption, or division of the constitutive parts of man is unnatural and was never intended in the eschatological version of man. In short, the question of the dichotomy or trichotomy is raised more by curative concerns in the redemption of man rather than by the eschatology of redemption with regard to man.

Inner and Outer Man

Another significant category with regard to the biblical view of man is what the apostle Paul calls the "inner man" and the "outer man" (2 Cor 4:16–18). The believers united to Christ are called a new creation—they are in the semi-eschatological state in the kingdom of God (2 Cor 5:17; 1 Cor 15:24). In Christ, the outer man is said to be "wasting away" whereas the inner man is "being renewed day by day." This unique description of man properly belongs to the eschatology of the new creation characteristic of the present state in the Spirit, who is "a deposit, guaranteeing what is to come" (2 Cor 5:5). In Christ, believers live simultaneously in the two shores of heaven and earth overlaid at top and bottom until the final consummation of the world. The inner man is rescued and renewed but the outer man is in bondage and decaying: "Grace and peace to you from God our Father and the Lord Jesus Christ, who gave himself for our sins to rescue us from the present evil age, according to the will of our God and Father . . ." (Gal 1:4). The one same man already belongs in the future age (the inner man) renewed daily by the Spirit, but has not yet overcome the present age (the outer man) subject to physical decay and death. This is not a soteric issue but an eschatological tension in the new order of man, where the two ages coexist. This does not mean that a man is redeemed in the inner man but remains unredeemed in the outer man; that would be a logical fallacy since a man is either redeemed or not. It addresses the tension in the present state of the man already united to the risen Lord, on the one hand, but still awaiting his return in glory on the other. In contrast, the "old self" and the "new self" would more properly fit the soteric difference between the regenerate and the unregenerate (Eph 4:22–24).

A few further observations can be made with regard to the distinction of the inner and the outer man. First, the inner and outer man cannot possibly mean there are two men in the believer, one saved and the other unsaved, which would be outright absurd and irrational. Second, they are not references to the two parts of man, spirit and body, which would amount to a Gnostic dualism. Third, it also cannot mean that one part of man is saved now but another part will be saved in the future, which is equivalent to saying that the man is not saved yet. A man is either saved in his whole person or not saved at all. Furthermore, the "wasting away" of the outer man does not merely refer to the physical aspect but to the whole person, soul and body, having been affected by the corruption of this present evil age. It is not just the body that ages, but the mind also ages, facing the inevitable decay and death as part of the present reality to which the outer man belongs. The troubles are said to be "light" and "momentary" compared to the "eternal glory that far outweighs them all," but even so they are troubles to the whole man (2 Cor 4:17). Again, to say that "the spirit is willing but the flesh is weak" is not equivalent to a theological distinction of the inner and the outer man. Even when Paul urged believers to "offer your bodies as a living sacrifice, holy and pleasing to God—this is your true and proper worship," the body does not refer to a part of man but is representative of the whole person (Rom 12:1). Despite the moment of death, when the two parts of man are temporarily separated, it was never intended as part of the eschatology of nature, and will never be part of the eschatology of redemption. The distinction conforms to the semi-eschatological state in Christ and its purpose in Paul's mind was optimism rather than pessimism. It was meant to underscore the eschatological hope of the coming age, whose glory will far outweigh the present suffering. The hope that cannot fail is thus guaranteed for the inner man, who for now sees it by faith but will see it by sight at the new creation, which has already started taking place in his inner man. The tension, then, does not lie in soteric uncertainty within the Golden Chain of the *Ordo Salutis*, nor within the parts of man's being, but lies between what is already (inner man) here and what is not yet (outer man) here (Rom 7:22–23). The apostle is not split between body and spirit, or before and after regeneration, but between the two different laws (orders) at work within him: "For in my inner being I delight in God's law; but I see another law at work in the members of my body, waging war against the law of my mind and making me a prisoner of the law of sin at work within my members."

The coexistence of this age and the coming age is built into the redemptive eschatology of the New Testament as God has rescued believers out of this world at once and into the kingdom of the Son (Col 1:13). It is the new order of creation and history that arrived with the kingdom of Christ in which the inner and the outer man can be properly explained and applied. The inner man is raised and seated with Christ in the heavenly realms, but the outer man is part of this evil world with troubles that are comparatively light and momentary, at least from the perspective of the inner man (2 Cor 4:16; Col 3:1–5). The inner man is at once elevated to the heavenly realms but the outer man is still under the earthly realms, having to put to death his "earthly nature" (Col 3:5). In short, the semi-eschatological kingdom coalesces with the semi-eschatological man. The secret of this lies in their mystical union with the risen Christ, the Last Adam, who now lives in them through the Spirit (1 Cor 15:45). Interestingly, the inner man and the outer man almost perfectly fit the earthly image and the heavenly image of man (v. 48). They are saved *from* the sinful state of the earthly image *into* the blessed state of the heavenly image of man, a unique view of believers as part of the scope of resurrection and the Spirit as its guarantee (2 Cor 4:16–5:5). The distinction is not so much derived from an anthropological interest in man himself but from the redemptive-eschatological interest in Christ's finished work. The Spirit and the flesh are in a mortal conflict in the horizontal purview of redemption but the inner and the outer man are in an optimistic tension in the vertical view of eschatology (Gal 5:17). A believer is redeemed as a whole person in Christ, neither divided nor confused about himself, with access to every spiritual blessing in the heavenly realms (Eph 1:3).

3.2 Adam and Last Adam

The two Adams represent creation and redemption or the eschatology of nature and the eschatology of redemption, respectively. They are the two fountainheads of the human race and the Scriptures define the history of mankind by way of the two covenants: the Covenant of Works and Covenant of Grace (Rom 5:12–18; 1 Cor 15:22). In a soteriological sense, Adam and Christ are at the opposite ends of history, separated by the great gulf between the lost paradise and the regained paradise. In eschatology, however, they share a common ground in terms of the chief end of man, particularly through the image of God and the image of man (1 Cor 15:48). Adam is a type of Christ, "a pattern of the one to come," and Christ is the fulfillment of him through redemption (Rom 5:14; 1 Cor 15:45). In order to properly understand Adam and the Covenant of Works, we must fast-track history forward to the Second Adam and the Covenant of Grace: "For as in Adam all die, so in Christ all will be made alive" (1 Cor 15:22). The antithesis of the two Adams in the soteric sense does not negate or exclude their similarity in the covenantal and eschatological sense. They are the representative federal heads of the two covenants except the latter is the greater with a "redemptive plus."[19] There is a common goal in both covenants with regard to the union and communion with God already envisaged from eternity in the union and fellowship of the three Persons in the Counsel of Peace.

In the soteric scope, the imputation of guilt or righteousness through the two Adams is foundational to the forensic justification by faith (Rom 5:12, 18–19). In the manner in which Adam's guilt is imputed to all mankind through the Covenant of Works, Christ's righteousness is imputed, "credited as righteousness," to all believers through the Covenant of Grace (Rom 4:5). The difference lies in the fact that Adam's posterity are born by the ordinary procreation whereas Christ's are born of the Spirit (John 3:5–8). Believers are not born through a hereditary relationship with Christ but through their mystical union with him in the Spirit:

> Therefore, just as sin entered the world through one man, and death through sin, and in this way death came to all people, because all sinned . . . For just as through the disobedience of the one man the many were made sinners, so also through the obedience of the one man the many will be made righteous. (Rom 5:12, 19)

Aside from the imputation and forensic justification, however, it is equally significant that both Adams possess the image of God. The significance of the covenant lies in the moral and religious nature of man, which reflects the blessed nature of God:

> The distance between God and the creature is so great, that although reasonable creatures do owe obedience unto Him as their Creator, yet they could never have any fruition of Him as their blessedness and reward, but by some voluntary condescension on God's part, which He hath been pleased to express by way of covenant.[20]

Besides the imputation of righteousness, the Covenant of Grace recreates the image of God in man so that God may become his blessedness and reward as originally intended in the Covenant of Works. The chief end to glorify and enjoy God is achieved with a greater result and greater means in the Second Adam. Adam was not so much tested as he was covenanted with God in paradise for which purpose he was

---

19. Vos, *Eschatology of Old Testament*, 77.
20. Westminster Confession of Faith, 7.

made in the image and likeness of God (Gen 1:26–28; 2:17). The chief end of man thus expressed through the covenant precedes the soteric rectitude of atonement and justification. The probation in paradise was not about a test of obedience that the creature owes God regardless, but God's condescension to reward and bless man (Gen 2:17).

Besides the exchange of guilt and righteousness, therefore, the contrast of *protos* and *eschatos* man is the primary focus of the redemptive eschatology. The paradise of Eden was a temple of God where Adam watched God walk in the garden—the theophany of nature (Gen 3:8; Rev 2:7). It typifies the theophany of redemption in Christ and the Spirit: "And we, who with unveiled faces all reflect the Lord's glory, are being transformed into his likeness with ever-increasing glory, which comes from the Lord, who is the Spirit" (2 Cor 3:18). The soteric scope of atonement does not necessarily touch or dwell on this subject because its focus is limited to the rectitude of sin. The eschatology and theophany of redemption expands the scope of the rectitude, taking it further into the temple of God, where man encounters his glory with unveiled face. These latter topics perhaps tended to be more incidental rather than intentional in the traditional approach to the doctrine of man. Beside the substitutionary aspect of Christ's work *for* many, there is also the recreative work *in* them (2 Cor 5:14, 17). The new man in Christ is said to be recreated in truth, righteousness, and holiness after God's image in the redemptive eschatology of Christ (Eph 4:24). The work of Christ is both substitutionary and recreative toward the consummation of the wedding in the temple of the new creation. Christ is the "perfect image of the invisible God," or conversely, Adam was a type of the Last Adam, in order that we might walk in the garden of God (Rom 5:14; Col 1:15; Rev 2:7).

The question of the origin of the human soul itself would not have been particularly relevant in the pre-fall situation, where man's body and soul would have remained in organic unity. The soteric interest in how the imputation or infusion of sin takes place in man would not have been necessary. It becomes particularly relevant to the fallen state of man, where the constitution of man in body and soul have direct bearings on these questions. In nature or the eschatology of nature, man was a whole being of body and soul that remained in unity and harmony. A holistic being created *ex nihilo* in God's image would have been a sufficient knowledge of man for creation's purpose. The preexistence of the human soul in Greek philosophy, on the other hand, was a dualistic view of soul and body that contradicted the biblical view of creation. For our purposes, the two contrasting views are of particular interest: (1) Traducianism (a soul is hereditary produced through the process of ordinary procreation); (2) Creationism (a soul is created by God individually at the time of a child's conception in the womb). A simple soteric implication of this is how the guilt and corruption of the Original Sin of Adam are transferred to all men (Rom 5:12). The question of imputation of guilt and infusion of corruption are central to soteriology since the justification and sanctification of a sinner correspond to the guilt and corruption of Adam's sin. The question is exactly how these are imparted to his posterity in terms of man's soul and body; the hereditary process through body is obvious but the question remains with regard to soul. The origin of the human soul might, in fact, may affect the nature of sin and how it might be transferred to all men. If a soul is inherited from parents down to their posterity through ordinary procreation, it begs the question whether sin must needs be imputed at all. It may all be inherited, rather than imputed, since soul and body are all hereditary; the unnecessity of imputation of sin means the unnecessity of imputation of righteousness for justification of a sinner. The hereditary view of the human soul seems to nullify the need for imputation of sin (guilt), and in turn nullifies the need for imputation of righteousness for forensic justification.

The covenant headship of Adam means that his sin is imputed to all and inherited by all so that all men became sinners. The same principle is applied to the obedience and righteousness of the Second Adam: "Consequently, just as the result of one trespass was condemnation for all men, so also the result of one act of righteousness was justification that brings life for all men" (Rom 5:18). After the first covenant failed by man God graciously offered him a second covenant: "Man, by his fall, having made himself incapable of life by that covenant, the Lord was pleased to make a second, commonly called the Covenant of Grace; wherein he freely offereth unto sinners life and salvation by Jesus Christ . . ."[21] God perhaps could have chosen a method other than the covenant union between Adam and all men but he did choose that particular arrangement as his way of dealing with humanity (2 Pet 2:4; Jude 6). If every person in the human race were tested individually in probation and be responsible for his own destiny, it is possible that none would attain eternal life.[22] Out of his infinite love and wisdom, God has chosen to make a covenant with Adam to bless and reward him along with his posterity (Hos 6:7). The central concept in the covenant arrangement is that of imputation as the means of transfer, whether righteousness or guilt, as the apostle Paul explained in Romans.[23] This is based on the understanding of sin primarily as the breaking of God's law and offending the holy and righteous God. The guilt of sin is understood to be imputed at the moment of conception when a soul is created, but the corruption of sinful nature is understood to be inherited through the natural process of procreation. The original sin thus inherited to Adam's posterity produces the actual sins of every person, which "are truly and properly sin" (Gen 6:3; Rom 8:5–7).[24] In short, both the original sin of Adam and the actual sin of all men are truly and properly sin because they are the transgression of God's law and offense to his justice and holiness. As David confessed, then, everyone is born with the imputed guilt and the inherited sinful nature of original sin: "Surely I was sinful at birth, sinful from the time my mother conceived me" (Ps 51:5). And every person on account of

---

21. Westminster Confession of Faith, 7.
22. Hodge, *Confession of Faith*, 111.
23. Hodge, *Confession of Faith*, 111.
24. Westminster Confession of Faith, 6.

their actual sin must give account before God because they have truly and properly sinned against him (Rom 5:12; 1 John 1:8–9).[25]

In view of the above considerations, the view that supports the origin of the soul by creation at birth would be more consistent with the covenantal definition of original sin and its relation to forensic justification. The view that supports the origin of soul by the natural procreation (traducianism) would pose a greater challenge in explaining the validity and necessity of imputation of guilt in distinction from hereditary corruption. If soul and body are both hereditary through natural generation, the imputation of sin's guilt may seem to be arbitrary and redundant. It may still be argued that guilt is imputed to each person regardless, but then it may be difficult to practically differentiate imputation from inheritance since both soul and body are hereditary. Adam's sin would solely be hereditary instead of having the two aspects to it; its guilt imputed and its corruption hereditary. The covenant arrangement between Adam and all men fits more naturally into the definition of sin as guilt and corruption of creation. The certainty of imputation of guilt entails the certainty of the imputation of Christ's righteousness as the sure foundation of the penal substitution and forensic justification. Furthermore, the hereditary view of soul might not be able to prevent the false concept that righteousness and holiness might be hereditary too, passed down to posterity. Though not without difficulty of its own, the view that every man's soul is created at conception appears to be more consistent with our soteric understanding (Job 31:15; Ps 51:5; Eccl 5:15). In short, the imputative and hereditary aspects of sin, and their counterparts in justification and sanctification, must be kept logically distinct. In the eschatology of redemption, however, the distinction is unnecessary for the *Ordo Salutis* will be unified in the Person of Christ (1 Cor 1:30). The covenantal nature of man's relationship with God in paradise seeks the unity of soul and body, and makes the question of the origin of soul redundant, but for the time being they are to remain logically distinct.

The holistic view of man created in the image of God requires a combined perspective of anthropology, soteriology, and eschatology. God deals with man through covenants and elected representative heads throughout history; all men were in Adam's covenant, the salvation of Jews and Gentiles were in Abraham's covenant, and all the elect were in Christ's *Pactum Salutis* before time. A covenant is personal but also communal in that it involves a family, a tribe, or a nation, and finally a kingdom (Rom 8:17, 29). There is the representative as well as the conforming character in a covenant; while Christ died for many, he also lives in them. The Covenant of Grace by nature fulfills the Covenant of Works in both the substitutionary and the recreative aspects. The origin of the human soul is an example of how mankind ought to be seen in light of its federal union of Adam, and how redemption is likewise to be seen in union with the Second Adam. Eschatology undergirds anthropology and soteriology so that the new creation will reunite soul and body in the Last Adam into the heavenly image of

---

25. Westminster Confession of Faith, 6.

man (1 Cor 15:45–48). The main focus will no longer be soul or body, imputative or hereditary, but the newly created man after God's image (Eph 2:15; 4:24; 2 Cor 4:16).

3.3 Covenant Being

Purpose of Covenant

"The tree of life, although a sacrament, does not give life magically."[26] The tree of knowledge and the tree of life themselves do no intrinsically possess magical powers (Gen 2:9, 17; 3:22; Rev 2:7; 22:2). They are the sacramental symbols of death and immortality for the Covenant of Works and the eschatology of nature. They are typical of the eschatology of redemption in that the natural life in Eden was to be transformed into the supernatural life. In the Genesis narrative of creation, Adam was not a mere backdrop to the ensuing history of salvation but was a covenant partner with God (Gen 2:17; 3:22; 1 Cor 15:48). In the probation of the covenant, the two trees functioned as a sign and seal of what could have been for Adam if his obedience had been confirmed. He was given the honorable role of the covenant partner with God in nature which envisaged the supernatural and the immortal. The validity and integrity of the Covenant of Works is substantiated by the fact that Christ came to fulfill it as the Second Adam (Rom 5:12–21; Hos 6:7). Apart from the redemptive aspect, there was the consummative aspect to Christ's work since he achieved the latter through the former. It was consummation with added redemptive power: Adam was the earthly image of man whereas the Last Adam was the heavenly image of man (1 Cor 15:48). The "preeminence of the natural (physical) element"[27] undergirds the greatness of redemption and eventually fulfilled by the latter. The Covenant of Works in paradise assumes the integrity and splendor of nature that it could have been rewarded with the supernatural life. The "voluntary condescension" of the Creator to bless and reward man with the supernatural life is a proof that it was a covenant rather than a test of obedience.[28] It reveals the excellence of creation and God's great pleasure in the outcome of his work so that the creature may enjoy the covenant partnership in nature.[29] The greatness of redemption lies in the mystery that through the accidental fall of man in paradise, and its rectitude in salvation, God produced an even better version of creation in Christ (2 Cor 5:17).

The Covenant of Works preceded the Covenant of Grace, but could not qualitatively exceed the latter. The natural and the earthly man became the supernatural and heavenly man in the Covenant of Grace through redemption from sin and death (Gen 2:7; Ezek 37:5; John 3:5; 1 Cor 15:46). In paradise, there was a difference between the

---

26. Vos, *Eschatology of Old Testament*, 75.
27. Vos, *Eschatology of Old Testament*, 74.
28. Vos, "Doctrine of Covenant," 242–45.
29. Wolters, *Creation Regained*, 48.

temporary immortality of Adam and the higher life of the supernatural order represented by the tree of life. At the time of creation Adam did not know death, yet that came later with the fall, so the probationary state should be distinguished from the eternal and supernatural life (Gen 3:22–24). The goal of the Covenant of Works was to reward Adam with the blessed state of life in order that he may forever glorify and enjoy God. The covenant was patterned after the Counsel of Peace so that Adam was gifted with the image of the blessed God to obey him freely and voluntarily. The substance of the Counsel of Peace is that of the Covenant of Grace but the obedience of the Son to the Father is reflected in the Covenant of Works: "The relationship between God and man is essentially and fundamentally covenantal, because it inherently exists in the Divine Being."[30] The obedience of Adam made in the image of God reflects the Son, who thus obeyed the Father in the Counsel of Peace. The Father-Son relationship is the archetype of all covenants, and the promise-reward takes after the pattern of the Father and the Son (John 17:4–6). The Covenant of Works must have been modelled after the "free deeds in a covenantal way" first found in Counsel of Peace in "the three Persons of the adorable Being."[31] As mentioned earlier, Paul defines sin as a fall *from* God's glory rather than a fall *to* death, because he envisaged the highest possible standard by which to measure sin (Rom 3:23). The greatest loss in sin is the fall from the glory of the three Persons of the blessed Being for which Adam was created (John 17:21). The loss of that knowledge is the most sad and tragic consequence of sin, and the eternal life is defined accordingly: "Now this is eternal life: that they may know you, the only true God, and Jesus Christ, whom you have sent" (John 17:3). The eternal life, defined in the redemptive way, is to know God, and to possess the covenantal knowledge of the Father, who sent the Son as the Redeemer. Adam was originally created for this end in nature but did not reach it, while believers reach it in redemption through the Son (John 17:21–24). The chief end of entering into God's glory remains the same whether in nature or redemption, except that it is achieved with the blessedness of the Son in the latter.

Mankind created as covenant being after the image of the triune God is of particular interest to us because it precedes the fallen image of man, who has forgotten the chief end of his existence. The redemptive-eschatological progress toward the heavenly image of man thus properly ends with the Last Man (Adam), who is also the Savior. The heavenly image of man is now achieved through the redemptive work of the Last Man instead of the natural work of the first man. The redemptive-historical progress is a soteric process with the higher goal of union with God, which Jeremiah called "the eternal covenant"—the Eternal Counsel of Peace (Jer 50:5; Zech 6:13). It points to the eschatological-salvific wedding in the new Jerusalem (Rev 21:2). When the horizontal progress of history reaches the fullness of time, the new and eternal covenant is sealed (Ezek 16:60; 37:26; Heb 13:20). The new and eternal covenant is

---

30. Gentry and Wellum, *Kingdom through Covenants*, 164.
31. Vos, *Redemptive History*, 245.

more than substitutionary atonement, which also existed in the types, the law, and the prophecies. It also includes the fulfillment of the Covenant of Works by which the eternal adoption to sonship is forever sealed between God and man.[32] The image of God in man is eternally sealed and confirmed by Christ, who is the perfect image of God, and his bodily resurrection meant a victory over death into the heavenly image of man (1 Cor 15:47–49). In conquering death, mankind is redeemed from death, but instead of returning to the natural state is moved to the supernatural state. In this vein, Calvin was right to define the resurrection state of believers as their final union with God. This union amounts to the fulfillment of the covenant in paradise except it is redemptive and better. Thus, the ontological significance of Adam as covenantal being is carried over into redemption, which envisages its consummation: believers are commanded to put off the "old self" rather than the "old man" (Eph 4:22–24). In redemption, the old self in sin must be put off, but the old man as created in God's image is recreated to forever glorify and enjoy God.

The work of Christ is not just to undo the work of Adam and return to paradise but to establish a new paradise, the "garden of God" (Rev 2:7). The undoing of sin was necessary and a redemptive gain in reaching the glory of God: "for all men have sinned and have fallen short of the glory of God" (Rom 3:23). In eschatology, the glory of God takes the central place and is the chief end of all things whether in nature or in redemption (Rom 11:36): "God does not exist because of man, but man because of God. This is what is written at the entrance of the temple of Reformed theology."[33] The return to the first paradise cannot be the final goal of redemption where the perseverance of believers will not be guaranteed and they may again be separated from God's love (Rom 8:39). The story of the fall reminds us that the first paradise was not the eternal paradise and that there will be another "garden of God" where there will be a free access to the tree of life (Rev 2:7). The first paradise would be better than the fallen world but would fall short of the new paradise, where even the possibility of death is no more. When the apostle Paul said, "The Son is the image of the invisible God, the firstborn over all creation" (Col 1:15), Adam must have crossed his mind.[34] The image of God was to be perfected by the image of Christ, who is the image of the invisible God. Again, the natural is typical of the supernatural, and the image of God provides a common ground between the natural and the redemptive: "I make known the end from the beginning, from ancient times, what is still to come. I say: My purpose will stand, and I will do all that I please" (Isa 46:10). In the soteric sense alone, it would suffice to contrast Adam and Christ, but not the first Adam and the Last Adam (2 Cor 5:17; Col 1:20). The emphasis of the fall in the traditional doctrine of salvation seems to have shifted the focus more to the cure of sin away from the glory and enjoyment of God. This is where a renewed interest in the eschatology of nature can make a valuable

---

32. Wolters, *Creation Regained*, 47–56.
33. Vos, *Doctrine of the Covenant* (ebook), 174.
34. Ridderbos, *Paul*, 71.

contribution to theology. The apostle Paul championed the doctrine of justification by faith alone but never lost the sight of the paramount principle in theology: "For from him and through him and to him are all things. To him be the glory forever! Amen" (Rom 11:36). What was terminated by sin was not the eternal life but only the probationary state, and redemption is not just a recovery of the old creation but a new creation far better than the old (Gen 2:7; 3:22).

Grace does not abrogate nature but providentially preserves it until the eschatological kingdom of the Father (1 Cor 15:24; 2 Pet 3:7–13). Life under common grace continues and remains an important part of the earthly life of the redeemed. The blessed God is gracious toward all men, good and evil, in the natural realm and commands his children to be the same (Matt 5:44–45). The blessed nature of God does not change even in the fallen world: "And if you greet only your brothers, what are you doing more than others? Do not even pagans do that? Be perfect, therefore, as your heavenly Father is perfect" (vv. 47–48). The command to love our neighbors, not just our brothers, is the second part of the summary of the law, rooted in the blessed nature of God and the original goodness of nature. Redemption does not make believers go *back* to paradise but go *up* to the new paradise because they are no longer "under the law but under grace" (Rom 6:14). We are no longer under the natural order but under the supernatural order attained by grace. The supernatural is of the "spiritual body," or the resurrected version of the natural body (1 Cor 15:44). It is not a restoration of the old body but a new body created by the Spirit of the Last Adam. The new man, or the heavenly image of man, is recreated as a superbly moral and religious being in the truth, righteousness, and holiness of God (Eph 4:24). The covenant-filial relationship, modelled after the *Pactum Salutis*, is sealed forever and they can now be near God in presence as well as in likeness. "God with us" is no longer a future hope but a present and eternal gift through the one called *Immanuel*. Again, biblical history is not only a horizontal progress in time, but a vertical movement toward the union of God and man, a perfected version of the blessing and reward promised in paradise. The Covenant of Grace fulfills the Covenant of Works in this regard because God himself is the greatest reward in both. The Covenant of Grace is atoning of sin as well as everlasting for the redeemed: "I will make a covenant of peace with them; it will be an everlasting covenant" (Ezek 37:26). The law of God as the substance of the image of God is first placed in man's conscience at creation, and later written in the stone tablets at Mount Sinai (Jer 31:34; Rom 1:19–20; 2:15). It is then finally written in the heart of those in whom the Spirit dwells as the fulfillment of new covenant. Christ came not to abrogate the law but to fulfill it because the image of God cannot be abrogated (Matt 5:17). The administration "under the law" is abrogated but the administration "under the gospel" fulfilled it: "For he himself is our peace, who has made the two one and has destroyed the barrier, the dividing wall of hostility, by abolishing in his flesh the law with its commands and regulations. His purpose was to create in himself one new man . . ." (Eph 2:14–15). The image of God is proof that the greatest reward is the blessed God himself regardless of which covenant (Works or Grace) mankind was under. Only in the Covenant of Grace it is achieved through the obedience of the Last Adam with an "added soteric force."[35] Redemptive history is a process through which God's people receive the cure from sin in order that they might enjoy the tonic of God's everlasting presence.

Being and Doing

The progress of man is a part of the progress in redemptive history as the latter is the outworking of the eschatology of nature, which was later augmented to the eschatology of redemption in Christ (Eph 1:10; Col 1:20; Heb 8:5). As a matter of fact, the purpose of redemptive history is that all things in heaven and earth may be united and reconciled to God through the Last Man. The redemptive eschatology makes the progress in redemptive history invigorating of life as much as rectifying of sin. It is a process in which God's chosen people are cured of sin, brought to a new life, and gain a clearer vision of the eschatological kingdom of the Father. A sweet foretaste of the heavenly kingdom is not merely a future blessing but a present reward for those united to Christ through the Covenant of Grace. The creation narrative is but a prelude to the redemptive narrative of the final kingdom of the Father to be delivered by the Son (1 Cor 15:24). A perfect drama does not waste its carefully designed introduction but keeps it behind the stage and blows it wide open at the climactic conclusion. The final stage of redemptive history is a glorious return to a garden, but only this time it will be an eternal garden of God, where night is no more and the light of sun is unnecessary (Rev 22:5). In contrast to the first garden, the children of God in the new paradise will have free and unlimited access to the Father and the tree of life without the cherubim blocking the path. The stipulations of the Covenant of Works and Covenant of Grace may be opposite, but they have the same goal: "The fact that man stood in a covenant relationship with God before the fall brings us to expect that the covenant will also rule in redemption."[36] Man's goal as a covenant being is unaffected by redeeming grace, but even strengthened that he might be "filled to the measure of all the fullness of God" (Eph 3:19). His chief end is ethical and religious, envisaging union with God so that "God may be all in all" (1 Cor 15:28).

The work and rest contrast is an important subject in both creation and redemption, demonstrated by the distinction between the six days of work and the seventh day of rest. The final rest in the new paradise is revealed as follows: "He will wipe every tear from their eyes. There will be no more death or mourning or crying or pain, for the old order of things has passed away" (Rev 21:4). The Sabbath of God on the seventh day of creation suggests there will a new order beyond the cyclical pattern of work in six days (Gen 2:3). The Sabbath of God is set apart from the six

---

35. Vos, *Eschatology of Old Testament*, 74.
36. Vos, *Redemptive History*, 245.

days as the supernatural state above and beyond the natural order. The eschatology of nature, symbolized by the seventh day, is typical of the eschatology of redemption that is beyond any earthly rest. Even the great Moses could not enter the Promised Land, but what is more, not even his great successor Joshua could enter the Sabbath of God (Num 20:12; Heb 4:8). It was postponed to "another day" when God's people will enter the rest through another "Joshua" called Jesus (Matt 11:28–30). Moses and Joshua were God's servants and great leaders but even their entrance to and enjoyment of God's Sabbath remained as a future hope. The Sabbath rest Jesus brings to God's people is thus the culmination of the progress of the redemptive history that fulfills the eschatology of nature signaled by the seventh day of creation. The perfect obedience of Christ is the fulfillment of the work required in nature with the added grace of redemption. As a result, he is seated next to God in the heavenly realms and believers are seated with him (Eph 2:6). Since they are seated and resting next to God, "it is not by works, so that no one can boast" (v. 9). Jesus prayed that those who are in him may also be in the Father, and they enter the Sabbath of God through this union (John 17:21). God's rest on the seventh day is fulfilled by and the outcome of the Counsel of Peace; the three Persons of the blessed Being are the final resting place of man's soul. The contrast of Adam and Christ is more than a contrast of their works—obedience or disobedience—for they are contrasted as the representative beings in the image of God. Beyond the exchange of their works of unrighteousness and righteousness, they are about the fulfillment of the eschatology of nature in the seventh day. The eschatology of redemption "in Christ" fulfilled the eschatology of nature "in Adam" through the new creation (2 Cor 5:14–17). Those who are in Christ enter God's rest by entering the blessed union of the three Persons, while receiving the soteric benefits of Christ's work (John 17:21, 23). For this reason Old Covenant believers could not enter and enjoy God's rest despite having received the benefits of atonement (Heb 4:8).

God's Sabbath on the seventh day then points to more than a suspension of labor but the union and fellowship with the "adorable Being." The seventh day is distinguished from the six days not in terms of quantity but in terms of the quality of time and the quality of relationship with God (Gen 2:1–3). It is typical of the "fullness of time" in this age, and the subsequent seventh-day rest (the kingdom of God) secured by the High Priest of Melchizedek, who sat next to God (Mark 1:15; Heb 6:20). The six days of work in creation are not in conflict with the seventh day of rest, but they are two different orders of the natural and the supernatural. The latter fulfilled the former in the redemptive eschatology of the kingdom of God. The Covenant of Works in paradise, therefore, was not bare legalism but preeminent naturalism that envisaged the perfection of the six days into the seventh day. The real antithesis of God's rest is not works itself but the broken covenant with God:

> Eschatology deals with the expectation of beliefs characteristic of some religions that: (a) the world or part of the world moves to a definite goal (*telos*); (b) there is a new final order of affairs beyond the present. It is the doctrine

of consummation of the world-process in a supreme crisis leading on into a permanent state. As such, it is composed of two characteristic elements: (1) the limited duration of the present order of things; (2) the eternal character of the subsequent state. The correlate of eschatology is creation.[37]

The work-and-rest pattern was an integral part of the natural order and the two were mutually complementary. The six days of work was said to be good but they are followed by the seventh day of God's rest set apart as holy and with no mention of night (Gen 2:3). They are two different orders of the natural and the supernatural but are not inherently in conflict. The natural could have been confirmed to the supernatural state through the success of the Covenant of Works. In the Parable of the Vine and the Branches, the Vine itself is central to the fruit-bearing of the branches: "Remain in me, as I also remain in you. No branch can bear fruit by itself; it must remain in the vine" (John 15:4). If the branches remain (rest) in the Vine, they will be fruitful, but if detached (unrest) from it, they will be thrown away and be burned. The fruit-bearing work of the branches depends on the Vine, which supplies all that are necessary elements for the branches to bear fruit. It is the union of the Vine and the branches that supplies life to the latter and enables them to work and be fruitful. Likewise, God's rest is not a cessation from works but firmly resting in God: "Jesus said to them, 'My father is always at his work to this very day, and I, too, am working'" (John 5:17). And finally, the seventh day in creation is turned into the first day in redemption through Christ's resurrection: "Come to me, all you who are weary and burdened, and I will give you rest" (Matt 11:28). In the new creation, the order is reversed: first comes God's rest and then follows the six days. The six days of work is actually done in God's rest just as the branches remain in the Vine while working. So Jesus said, "my yoke is easy and my burden is light," meaning that while they remain in him the yoke and the burden are not theirs but Jesus'. The command to deny self and take up the cross to follow the Master is made "easy" and "light" for the Master already took the cross upon himself and finished the work. By the redemptive-eschatological work, believers may finally enter God's rest with Christ in the inner sanctuary of heaven (Heb 4:5; 6:18–19; 12:22–23). They are resting above with their life hidden in God while working below (Col 3:1–4); the earthly yoke and burden are carried through the heavenly rest and freedom.

In the soteric view, Adam is the representative of sinful disobedience, and Christ is his counterpart in obedience in order to rectify the unrighteousness. The particular emphasis falls on their actions rather than their beings (images), which are more soteric-eschatological. The final destination of mankind as a result of their actions is heaven or hell, defined in terms of a location rather than in terms of a separation from or union with the Being of God. It is of special importance to note that the final destination of God's people is called "my Sabbath" rather than the Promised Land (Heb

---

37. Vos, *Eschatology of Old Testament*, 1.

4:5). The land could not give God's rest to Israelites, and likewise nothing else could give God's rest to believers today other than the peace of God. The substitutionary work of the two Adams is an exchange of their actions for attainment of righteousness before God. But the final resting place for God's people is the fellowship of the three Persons of God rather than a particular location (Gal 2:20). Eschatology as a "new final order of affairs"[38] is more about the enjoyment of the union and peace with the Father through the Son (John 17:21–26). It looks beyond the works for the rectitude of sin into the Eternal Counsel of Peace marked by the mutual glory, love, and truth. Jesus thus prayed "that all of them may be one, Father, just as you are in me and I am in you. May they also be in us so that the world may believe that you have sent me" (v. 21). This was typified by Eden that the final resting place of Adam would not have been the garden itself, but the presence of God in the garden as the reward of the Covenant. Sin is a departure from God more than a departure from a place: "All men have sinned fallen short of God's glory" (Rom 3:23). In this, the eschatology of nature is quite revealing in that, despite the legalistic connotation, the Covenant of Works envisages but the ethical and religious being made for communion with God. The main focus of the covenant is not the works itself but the blessed being and image of God:

> When this principle is applied to man and his relationship with God, it immediately divides into three parts: 1. All of man's work has to rest on an antecedent work of God; 2. In all of his works man has to show forth God's image and be a means of the revelation of God's virtues; 3. The latter should not occur unconsciously or passively, but the revelation of God's virtues must proceed by way of understanding and will and by way of the conscious life, and actively come to external expression.[39]

The works are not to promote self-righteousness of man but to express through his moral and religious nature the image and virtues of God in the most conscious way, involving knowledge, will, and external life. All in all, it strongly suggests the splendor and excellence of man fit to be a covenant partner with God: "You made him a little lower than the heavenly beings and crowned him with glory and honor" (Ps 8:5). It is only fitting that the final resting place of man's soul is God's rest on the seventh day of creation fulfilled by the first day of resurrection: "There remains, then, a Sabbath rest for the people of God; for anyone who enters God's rest also rests from their works, just as God did from his" (Heb 4: 9–10).

The free and voluntary obedience of man is appropriate for the kind of being he was and for manifestation of God's virtues. And out of his own blessedness and goodness (Ps 100:5) God condescended himself and offered nothing less than himself as the reward of the obedience. This arrangement itself, in fact, did not change in redemption but was rather fulfilled through the obedience of the Second Adam (Gen

---

38 Vos, *Pauline Eschatology*, 48.

39. Vos, *Doctrine of the Covenant* (ebook), 174.

2:17). The creature could not grasp the gravity of his offense against God until he fully comprehended the glory from which he fell and the end for which the whole of nature was created. It was so glorious and splendid that "even angels long to look into these things" for they were not offered such a position and privilege (1 Pet 1:12): "The first covenant with man is the Covenant of Works, and promises life to Adam and his posterity, subject to perfect and personal obedience."[40]

The ethical and religious aspects of man's being have not been given sufficient attention in traditional soteriology, which did not fully incorporate the eschatology of nature. Without the eschatology of nature, soteriology could not take into account the eschatology of redemption. The scope of redemption was narrowed down to: the law against the gospel, nature against grace, obedience against faith, earth against heaven. But the Covenant of Grace was progressive under the law in Old Covenant, and under the gospel in the New Covenant. The moral law continues to be effective through the entire period under the Covenant of Grace while the ceremonial law was abrogated under the gospel's administration. The covenantal nature of man meant a continued use of the law in the Christian life, whose chief end is to glorify and enjoy God. The substance of the Covenant of Grace does not change throughout redemptive history while the means of grace were administered differently under the two administrations.[41] In the earlier stages of redemptive history, revelation was rudimentary and opaque about the whole counsel of God that began in the Counsel of Peace. In the fallen state, the soteric urgency of mankind would have loomed larger in which the eschatological vision may have been lost (Gen 3:15). The revelation of God was given in the earthly types and figures, which may have obscured the substance of the eternal covenant started in heaven (Heb 8:5). An eschatology of redemption with a view of man in covenant with God, whose chief end is to glorify and enjoy him, would not have been fully revealed until the incarnation of the Son of God (John 1:1–14). The covenantal nature of man created in God's image is no longer hidden in shadow and type but fully revealed through the Son (2 Cor 4:4; Col 1:15; Jas 3:9). He is "the mystery that has been kept hidden for ages and generations, but is now disclosed to the saints" (Col 1:26). In him the mystery of the Counsel of Peace is now fully revealed: mankind is not only to be remedied, but also to participate in the "tonic for sweet fellowship with God."[42] The redemption in Christ revealed that man is not just a fallen creature to be saved but a covenant partner with God to love him with all his heart, soul, mind, and strength: "God and man, man and God made a relationship through covenants. The relationship was expressed in a covenant manner both before and after the Fall."[43]

---

40. Westminster Confession of Faith, 7.
41. Westminster Confession of Faith, 7, "Of God's Covenant."
42. Vos, *Redemptive History*, 245.
43. Dunahoo, *Making Kingdom Disciples*, 106.

Adoption to Sonship

The adoption to sonship in redemption is the consummate state of man in view of Adam in the state of probation. It was still possible for him to be separated from God's fatherly love, yet to be formally called a child of God able to call him "*Abba*, Father" (Rom 8:14–15, 39). VanGemeren in *Progress of Redemption* observed that God's creation was "good" but was yet to be made "holy" in the seventh day of God's rest (Gen 2:3). There was a gap between the probation and the consummation in nature. In redemption, believers were chosen in Christ before the creation of the world that they may be holy and blameless children of God (Eph 1:4). In other words, the gap has been filled, the natural becoming the supernatural, through the redemptive work of Christ. Adam was a probationary child of God in Eden and was yet to reach the full adoption to sonship prior to the Covenant of Works. The full adoption is thus achieved in redemption by "the Spirit of the adoption to sonship" with Christ as "the firstborn" of God's family (Rom 8:15–17, 29). The redemptive adoption to sonship is a new order in man's relationship to God higher than the order of nature in Eden. Adam was yet to enter God's rest symbolized by the seventh day and would eventually be further removed from that rest after the fall. There is now an added chasm of sin to the probation further separating him from the glory of God and the adoption to his sonship. The forensic justification is followed by the adoption to sonship in the Golden Chain of the *Ordo Salutis* to ensure that believers are not merely restored to the state of Adam but recreated in the Last Adam.

In the eschatology of grace, the adoption to sonship is the greatest prize believers receive from the Father through their union with the firstborn. The Holy Spirit is given the unique title of the Spirit of the Adoption to Sonship, and the soteric grace enables believers reach the state of full adoption that Adam lost. As coheirs in the family of God, they have been given the right to the inheritance of God's kingdom: "For those God foreknew he also predestined to be conformed to the likeness of his Son, that he might be the firstborn among many brothers" (Rom 8:28). The goal of the Counsel of Peace is the participation of God's adopted children in the divine nature: "For he chose us in him before the creation of the world to be holy and blameless in his sight" (Eph 1:4). In the early stages of the history of redemption and revelation, believers were on a learning curve of the knowledge of God. The relationship largely depended on types, sacrifices, prophecies, and the ceremonial law as a guardian in preparation for the arrival of the Son. They were still a distance away from the fulfillment of the Covenant of Grace in the Son and the outpouring of the Spirit of adoption. "So the law was our guardian until Christ came" during which time the adoption to sonship was still only figurative and tentative engendering fear and uncertainty (Gal 3:24). Even with their faith in God through the sacrifices of atonement, they could not with full confidence call God "*Abba*, Father" until the day when believers enter the inner sanctuary of heaven with the risen Son. The key difference, in this regard, between the

Old and the New Testament is not the soteric atonement itself but the full status of adoption to sonship.

The ceremonial law of Israel as the guardian expired after the Son's arrival and the Spirit now directly indwells in believers, who are coheirs with the Son through the adoption to sonship: "You show that you are a letter from Christ, the result of our ministry, written not with ink but with the Spirit of the living God, not on tablets of stone but on tablets of human hearts" (2 Cor 3:3). The age of the New Covenant is the age of the Spirit in contrast to the letter, "for the letter kills, but the Spirit gives life" (v. 6). The age of the letter is marked by the incomplete, indirect, and tentative character of the priestly order of Aaron. In the overall scheme of things, it is a ministry that condemns as opposed to a ministry that "brings righteousness" (v. 9). The age of the Spirit, on the other hand, is marked by glory and freedom in the Son:

> For what was glorious has no glory now in comparison with the surpassing glory. And if what was transitory came with glory, how much greater is the glory of that which lasts! Therefore, since we have such a hope, we are very bold. We are not like Moses, who would put a veil over his face to prevent the Israelites from seeing the end of what was passing away. But their minds were made dull, for to this day the same veil remains when Old Covenant is read. It has not been removed, because only in Christ is it taken away. Even to this day when Moses is read, a veil covers their hearts. But whenever anyone turns to the Lord, the veil is taken away. Now the Lord is the Spirit, and where the Spirit of the Lord is, there is freedom. And we, who with unveiled faces all reflect the Lord's glory, are being transformed into his likeness with ever-increasing glory, which comes from the Lord, who is the Spirit. (2 Cor 3:10–18)

The glory and freedom in the New Covenant is the fulfillment of the Counsel of Peace between the Father and the Son, and the adoption of believers to sonship. They are now fully adopted by God as coheirs of the kingdom with the firstborn, who fulfilled the covenant by his perfect obedience and sacrifice: "Yet to all who receive him, to those who believed in his name, he gave the right to become children of God" (John 1:12). They are in God's rest and peace without the fear of rejection because they are not only free from sin's dominion but also free from the probation of Adam. They are not under the Covenant of Works, but under the Covenant of Grace rooted in the *Pactum Salutis* of the Father and the Son (John 17:4–6). The biblical view of man has now made a full circle in that the purpose of adoption to sonship in Adam is fulfilled in the Last Adam. God's children can at last begin to execute "free deeds performed in a covenantal way"[44] without the fear of losing sonship in the same way the Son has obeyed the Father.

The eschatology of adoption thus logically precedes the soteriology of justification though it follows the latter in the *Ordo Salutis*. This has to do with the ethical and

---

44, Vos, *Redemptive History*, 245.

religious nature of man even before the soteric need of man. The change from a "spirit of slavery" to "spirit of sonship" in believers does not negate the need for filial obedience to the Father (Rom 8:15). It is a contrast of status rather than denial of obedience; slaves are judged by what they do whereas sons are judged by who they are. The doctrine of adoption looks beyond the legal justification to the redemptive-eschatological sonship that freely and joyfully obeys the Father. Christ is not only the Mediator for sinners but the Firstborn of God's family: "During the days of Jesus life on earth, he offered up prayers and petitions with loud cries and tears to the one who could save him from death, and he was heard because of his reverent submission. Although he was a son, he learned obedience from what he suffered" (Heb 5:7–8). The throne of grace is the final resting place for those in Christ, who may now freely approach the Father "with confidence, so that we may receive mercy and find grace to help us in our time of need" (Heb 4:16). The redemptive sonship is the fulfillment of the natural sonship in Eden with the added soteric gift in the Covenant of Grace.

The scope of redemption is thus broadened and heightened to incorporate the preeminence of nature. The distinction between faith and work is not as sharp as that in the strictly soteric definition: "Then they asked him, 'What must we do to do the works God requires?' Jesus answered, 'The work of God is this: to believe in the one he has sent'" (John 6:28–29). Jesus equated faith with work or subsumed the latter under the former, for the greatness of faith does not lie in what it can do but whom it trusts. The works can be attributed to the person, but the person cannot be reduced to the works. Faith in the gospel administration produces good works because it places the believer, who is free, under the law of Christ (1 Cor 9:21). It is fitting that justification is followed by being under Christ's law, as Paul said, for sanctification that leads to glorification. The significance of redemption is not only in its victory over death, but in the consummation of the natural life into the supernatural one that "God may be all in all" (1 Cor 15:28). The resurrection is not only the means of immortality after death but the perfection of nature to be "filled to the measure of all the fullness of God" (Eph 3:19). In this, the *Historia Salutis* always logically precedes the *Ordo Salutis*: "For from him and through him and for him are all things. To him be the glory forever! Amen" (Rom 11:36). The blessed God in three Persons is the fount of every blessing and he is the chief end for which all things are created, redeemed, and consummated (1 Tim 1:11; 6:15):

> Come, Thou Fount of every blessing, tune my heart to sing thy grace; streams of mercy, never ceasing, call for songs of loudest praise. Teach me some melodious sonnet, sung by flaming tongues above. Praise the mount, I'm fixed upon it, mount of thy redeeming love.[45]

The failed covenant of Adam thus represents more than a loss of immortality or expulsion from paradise, but the loss of the union and fellowship with the blessed

---

45. Robert Robinson, "Come Thou Fount of Every Blessing" (1758).

Trinity. In this sense, the eternal life is not only immortal life (prolongation of life) but union with the immortal God. The sacrament of the tree of life in nature is typical of the eternal life in redemption. The new life in the gospel is not a return to the natural immortality in Eden but a transformation into a new order of life eternal (2 Pet 1:4). The mystery of the gospel is that God used the fall of nature to consummate nature in redemption (Rom 8:18–25). The preeminence of nature is upheld by the very fact that God used the lost paradise to recreate a new and everlasting paradise in the form of "the heavenly Jerusalem, the city of the living God" (Heb 12:22; Rev 2:7). It is also proven by the eager anticipation of all creation "to be liberated from its bondage to decay, and brought to the glorious freedom of the children of God" (Rom 8:19–21). Eschatology, whether that of nature or redemption, is ultimately about God, who is the *protos* and *eschatos* of all things and deserves all the praise and glory (Rom 11:36; Rev 22:13). The means of redemption is rectitude of sin, but the goal is the enjoyment of the blessed God (John 17:24; 1 Tim 3:15). God did not stop at the reversal of the curse, though an amazing grace in and of itself, but gave us a higher life in redemption than originally conceived in nature.

3.4 Knowledge of Creator

Sense of Deity

Eschatology brings creation, fall, and redemption all under the rubric of the glory God as the chief end of man and the final consummation of the world. The glory of God is the source of man's happiness so that the knowledge of God is the foundation of all man's knowledge. An antithesis in soteriology (i.e., law versus grace) may actually be a unity in the eschatology of redemption. A natural *sensus Divinitas* in man is a covenant sign that he is accountable to his Creator, unable to escape God's sovereignty over all things. Man's knowledge is grounded in the instinctive knowledge of God because the two are inseparable and existential in man. He is a moral and religious creature whose existence depends on the Creator: "For in him we live and move and have our being" (Acts 17:28). Even the possibility of a unified human knowledge is grounded in the constitution of man as being "in him." He will sooner plunge into an epistemological chaos than escape and hide from God (Gen 3:8). This is a moral and religious (covenantal) problem rather than a philosophical one: "Philosophers seek to find a unified view of the human experience. Philosophers want to get a comprehensive picture of all things. But the universe is constituted by diverse things. The problem of man is to find a unity in the diversity of things."[46]

The universe at first glance seems to be dictated by chance rather than by a definite purpose. Since the only one capable of resolving the conflict between unity (one) and diversity (many) in the universe is its Creator, the knowledge of God is

---

46. Van Til, *Defense of Faith*, 41, 48–49.

indispensable to man's knowledge of anything. A creature with finite wisdom cannot rationally unify or harmonize the many contradictions in the world unless a unifying feature is built into his existence. The natural revelation of God built into man and nature provides to a certain degree this knowledge for life under common grace. A great dilemma in human knowledge after the fall is unity without diversity (uniformity) or diversity without unity (relativity). A philosophical reasoning cannot resolve this paradox because man is unable to integrate the universals and the particulars without self-contradictions. Fallen mankind knows the truth about God but willfully suppresses that knowledge in hostility toward God (Rom 1:18). The religious and moral capacities of man as a covenant being accountable to God are lost:

> Although they claimed to be wise, they became fools and exchanged the glory of the immortal God for images made to look like mortal man and birds and animals and reptiles. Therefore, God gave them over in the sinful desires of their hearts to sexual impurity for the degrading of their bodies with one another. (Rom 1:22–24)

The natural revelation of God leaves him without an excuse of ignorance. The symptom of such an epistemological dilemma is vacillation between rationalism and irrationalism. The natural reason, having lost its covenantal function, cannot overcome the two extremes of self-pride or self-abasement: "The non-Christian philosophy always turns out to be an unstable mixture of arrogance and pessimism."[47] The problem of epistemology began with the tree of knowledge in the garden, and eventually led to religious idolatry and moral depravity. For a unified human experience in the knowledge of unity and diversity, man must start with a God whose is "One and Many."[48] The "three Persons of the adorable Being" is the absolute ground of unified world and knowledge. This is no longer possible in nature but only in redemption because "their thinking became futile and their foolish hearts were darkened" (Rom 1:21). The outcome of their futile thinking is either false pride or false humility, neither of which is from true knowledge. Fallen man thinks he must know everything or else he knows nothing. The failure of the moral and religious functions means that he is near God in likeness, but away from God in presence: "The man has now become like one of us, knowing good and evil . . . So the Lord God banished him from the Garden of Eden . . ." (Gen 3:22–24).

The tree of knowledge in the garden was proof that man's knowledge is covenantal and the serpent tested Adam with a false knowledge of God (Gen 3:5). The noetic effect of sin is evidenced by the fact that man's *thinking* became futile as a result of his heart turning foolish and darkened against God (Rom 1:21). The soteric scope alone tends to limit its view to the moral failure of man but the eschatology of nature brings the totality of man back into the overall picture. The soteric is set over against

---

47. Bahnsen, *Van Til's Apologetic*, 316.
48. Bahnsen, *Van Til's Apologetic*, 240.

the natural but the redemptive-eschatological is affirmative of the natural. Man's instinct for God lies in the innate sense of Deity by which he responds to God either in obedience or disobedience. In the nature of the case, either absolute knowledge or absolute despair is not possible for man due to his reliance on the Creator. He is not so autonomous as to possess absolute knowledge, and he is not so alone as to fall into total despair. All of man's knowledge is derivative of and secondary to the knowledge of God so that even the possibility of man's reasoning lies in his creaturely dependence on God. The *sensus Divinitas*, so called by Calvin, is an internal mechanism that reminds the soul that God is the foundation of all existence and knowledge: "God did this so that they would seek him and perhaps reach out for him and find him, though he is not far from any one of us. For in him we live and move and have our being. As some of your own poets have said, 'We are his offspring'" (Acts 17:27–28). Mankind owes such instincts to God, and does not need to be persuaded of the existence of God and the supernatural world (Eccl 3:11). Mankind's deep-seated longing for God renders him discontent with mere temporal existence and earthly life, which are but a fleeting reflection of the eternal and the invisible world.[49]

The natural revelation is a part of the religious and ethical makeup of man, so etched into his being that he cannot deny it. In fact, this knowledge cannot be erased or plucked out of him without destroying him as a creature made in the image of God. If mankind could ever exist apart from God, he would be self-destructive and would cease to exist. God would cease to be omnipotent and omniscient if man could escape from God to a region where he is unreachable by God. This is precisely what the serpent had hoped for when he injected in Adam the evil desire to be "like God," possessing knowledge of good and evil on his own (Gen 3:5). But the natural revelation of God imbedded in man cannot be metaphysically removed from him, though it is morally powerless to bring him back to God. The image of God can no more be erased from man's being than the image of parents can be removed from a child's consciousness. An ineffable mark of God has been stamped in every man's soul that he may know God as the Creator even if he is separated in presence: "Yet he has not left himself without testimony: He has shown kindness by giving you rain from heaven and crops in their seasons; he provides you with plenty of food and fills your hearts with joy" (Acts 14:17). This knowledge is an essential part of nature and the eschatology of nature, which, although powerless in redemption, is significant in the eschatology of redemption. The noetic effects of sin incapacitated the natural knowledge but its moral and religious purposes remain effective so long as man is a covenant being. It is sort of like an electronic device with a built-in memory for basic information storage that is protected and retrievable even if the main power is out (Rom 1:20). Likewise, the natural revelation of God is permanently stored in the human soul with important

---

49. Bavinck, *Our Reasonable Faith*, 19.

information about God. It cannot save mankind from sin, which requires the efficient call of the Holy Spirit, but it nevertheless renders man accountable to God at all time:[50]

> This evidence is unavoidable for anyone who is a rational creature. This evidence is a testimony of the Triune God who confronts man at any time and any place. Even sinners abandoned in sin cannot escape the revelation of God . . . So, he is confronted by God. Man is hearing God's voice. He exists in the relationship of covenantal interactions. In other words, he is a covenantal being . . . There cannot exist a non-being who will escape to avoid the voice of God and his face. If it were not for this knowledge of God that cannot be eradicated, then sin would not be sin.[51]

Coram Deo

The sense of Deity and the natural revelation contained in it renders man face to face with God at all times without an excuse. It is an internal testimony so clear that there is no way to evade it, just as the apostle Paul employed it to preach the gospel to those in Athens. He spoke of mankind's perennial search for God as evidence of the natural revelation that is also consistent with man's innate desire for eternal and supernatural life (Gen 9:16; Ezek 37:26; Heb 13:20). He is neither neutral nor autonomous but simply instinctive and inevitable in this search. One of the most important topics in theological debates throughout history, especially during the Reformation, was that of the freedom of the human will. The penalty of death for sin was not immediately executed after the fall, and for continuation of the earthly life God provided the "garments of skin" to Adam and Eve (Gen 3:21). Fallen man could no longer be in the presence of and fellowship with God out of his own knowledge and free will. The freedom and knowledge of man were always subservient to the ethical and religious relationship with God. Mankind could not love God on his free will, so God first loved him that he might forever be united with God (Matt 1:23). *Coram Deo* and the *sensus Divinitas* are covenantal concepts that are inseparable and the two sides of the same coin.[52]

Luther was correct when he said the fallen man's will is not free until it is set free by God's grace. Mankind can truly enjoy the freedom of the will when he is free from the bondage of sin to be in the presence of God. The will must be redeemed to be free and voluntary to glorify and enjoy God forever. The "zeal of the Lord Almighty will accomplish this" rather than the freedom of man's will itself (Isa 37:32). Again, the will is not free in redemption but is set free in the eschatology of redemption to perform the covenant duty. The covenantal end of redemption is union with God, and the covenant duty is to love God with his heart, soul, mind, and strength (Jer 50:5).

---

50. Calvin, *Institutes*, 1:43.
51. Van Til, *Defense of Faith*, 152.
52. Calvin, *Institutes*, 2:988.

The sense of Deity lets the fallen man maintain an internal dialogue with God, though suppressed beneath his consciousness. The rational faculties of man are not neutral in and of themselves, but conditioned by his moral and religious state. But even so, they have the natural capacities to carry out the natural life in the realm of the common grace. In this sense, human culture and civilization are a covenantal response to God as part of the natural eschatology in creation: "He causes his sun to rise on the evil and the good, and sends rain on the righteous and the unrighteous" (Matt 5:45). Mankind was a covenant partner with God in nature but the chief end of the covenant is fulfilled only through the means of redemption.

Adam had never been in a neutral state even in his relatively short tenure in paradise due to the nature of his being as covenant partner with God.[53] The tree of knowledge and the tree of life were the covenantal sacraments in nature. The knowledge of good and evil and immortality were mutually dependent and both relied on the integrity of the covenant. The constitution of man rules out the possibility of neutrality in man's knowledge, for Adam was either a covenant keeper or a covenant breaker. Neutrality and autonomy are not to be confused with liberty; man has always been free as a moral being to do as he pleases. Man in the broad sense of the image of God is free but never morally neutral before God. The *sensus Divinitas* is a point of contact between God and fallen man as shown by Paul in Athens, who reasoned with the sophists by invoking the intuitive knowledge of God that they could not disagree with: "Brothers and sisters, listen now to my defense" (Acts 22:1).[54] He reasoned with them based on the natural point of contact but did not presume the neutrality of their reasoning. The universal offer of the gospel is founded on all man as covenantal beings perpetually confronted by the sense of God written in their souls. After all, the call of the gospel is the outworking of the unconditional election and irresistible grace of God: "those he predestined, he also called; those he called, he also justified; those he justified, he also glorified" (Rom 8:30). In this sense alone, those assuring words of Jesus make a perfect sense: "I have not lost one of those you gave me" (John 18:9). God has the power to efficiently call out and awaken those whom he has chosen in Christ before the creation of the world, and the innate sense of the Creator functions a significant role in nature (Eph 1:4; 2:1, 8–9). The unregenerate would be unable to receive the efficient call except through an innate capacity to respond to it awakened by the Spirit. The collision of sin and grace alone does not fully account for this aspect of man, which, as Vos stated, is part of another strand in revelation that is older. It is a strand of revelation out of the eschatology of nature that provides the foundation for redemption: "Our metaphysical dependence on God was not erased by sin."[55]

The "metaphysical dependence" is the proof of the excellence and blessedness of nature. It is a witness to the adorable paradise where God walked with man. It is

---

53. Westminster Confession of Faith, 9.
54. Van Til, *Christian Apologetics*, 54–58.
55. Van Til, *Christian Apologetics*, 58.

also the earthly temple typical of the redemptive-eschatological temple to be consummated in the heavenly Jerusalem (Gen 3:8; Heb 12:22; Rev 2:7). The soteric cure of man from sin becomes an added force that reinforces this fundamental relationship in nature. In the preaching of the gospel, this aspect of nature becomes the point of contact for the efficient call of redemption. God does not have to be proven rationally from without as the evidence of him is available from within man. If no information were available from within man, then the so-called neutral evidences from without would have to be necessary. An excuse of ignorance could be made in his defense if no such revelation was already available within man. Sin is irreligious, unethical, and inexcusable, but not completely irrational in this sense. It is not that he is unable to think, but he is unable to think God-centered. Because he *a priori* alienated God from his thinking, no amount of external evidence will be sufficient to rationally convince him of God. The so-called brute facts from outside of him will be subsumed under his darkened heart and futile thinking. The facts have already lost neutrality and will only be used to corroborate his *a priori* presuppositions. They render fallen man so blind to the truth that God is a foolishness in his mind (1 Cor 1:18–25; Eph 2:1). The religious and ethical nature of human reason is so radically altered that wisdom is foolishness and vice versa. In this frame of mind, any notion of objectivity with regard to the external evidences are thrown out the window out of hostility toward God. A reversal of the roles between the Creator and the creature takes place; the Alpha and the Omega of all things is made subject to verification by the creature (Rev 1:8; 21:6). This futile attempt, however, will only make the mind descend further into a vicious circular reasoning between rationalism and agnosticism.

As a covenantal creature with the image of God, God does not need to be proven to him: "For it is in them [*en autois*] that they know God, that God has revealed it to them" (Rom 1:19). The knowledge of God is built into the self-knowledge of man; it is as *auto*matic as the "heavens declare the glory of God; the skies proclaim the work of his hand" (Ps 8:1–9; 19:1; Job 38:1–41). Paul's preaching of the gospel was such that the solution to the flesh is not more rational proofs of God, but the removal of hostility toward God: "The mind governed by the flesh is hostile to God; it does not submit to God's law, nor can it do so" (Rom 8:7). The mind governed by the flesh is at liberty to think but not at liberty to follow God's law for it is enslaved to the flesh. Enmity against God is concealed in the darkened heart, which generates a war of the flesh against the Spirit. Sin is unethical—Cain's murder of his brother Abel—but also blasphemous—worshipping of false gods and idols (Gen 4:8–9). When asked by God about his brother, Cain replied in anger, "Am I my brother's keeper?" (v. 9). He turned the evil act of murder committed in the fit of rage into a rational problem—"I don't know." As a religious creature, however, mankind cannot long sustain suppression of the knowledge of the true God but begins to worship false gods. He must by his religious nature "glorify" and "enjoy" a god even when he refuses to do so toward the true God. The so-called rational arguments against God are merely a form of disguise to cover up corruption that lies deeper in his depraved heart (Rom 1:23–25). The irony is that man's soul still thirsts after God like the Prodigal Son, who longs for his father although spiritually and morally incapable of doing so (Luke 15:11–21). The thought of his father could not be erased from his consciousness, and loomed even larger the harder he tried to deny him. In this existential dilemma, what the son needed was not more rational proofs of his father, but repentance and reconciliation with him.

Once enmity is removed from the heart, the mind can then be illuminated by the Spirit to understand and the will renewed to obey: "I believe in order that I may understand." The external evidences will become truly objective when God becomes most objective in his own mind. As Van Til said appropriately, there are "no brute facts" in the universe, and the objectivity and possibility of knowledge will be restored when God is enthroned in the seat of man's heart as the Lord. There are no neutral (uninterpreted) facts in the universe for they are interpreted either in obedience or disobedience to God. All facts are preconditioned in the mind by the spiritual and moral state of man out of his covenant relationship to God. His worldview will be governed by the precondition and the evidence will be used to justify the firmly entrenched presuppositions. Reason is a servant of the soul and the unregenerate mind vacillates between autonomy and agnosticism, which are both untenable.[56] Reason receives orders from the heart: "Flesh gives birth to flesh, but the Spirit gives birth to spirit. You should not be surprised at my saying, 'You must be born again'" (John 3:6–7).

In conclusion, the biblical view of man begins in nature and the eschatology of nature. It corresponds to the purpose of the Covenant of Works that envisaged perfection of nature. The covenant was a voluntary condescension on God's part to reward and bless mankind rather than a test of creaturely obedience. The tree of knowledge and the tree of life were the sacraments of the eschatology of nature typical of the eternal life in redemption. The natural law in man's conscience and the sense of Deity were the means to fulfilling the covenant duty and the natural eschatology. It can no longer be achieved in nature, thus God provided the redemptive-eschatological means to rectify and consummate the earthly man. Natural revelation signifies that the covenantal knowledge of God is foundational to all knowledge of man in nature. The chief end of man to glorify and enjoy God flows out of the covenantal relationship with the Creator, and typifies the redemptive eschatology in the Last Adam. The latter with an added soteric gift to the eschatology of nature is the substance of the Counsel of Peace between the Father and the Son. It is an added gift rather than a mere detour because the Second Adam is greater than the first Adam. Mankind was created to be near God in likeness and also in presence, and both are accomplished through the Covenant of Grace through the Second Adam.[57] The nearness in presence is *spatial* as well as spiritual (as in the Spirit) through union with the risen Christ. The Prodigal Son was never at any point separated from the father in his consciousness, but he

---

56. Van Til, *Defense of Faith*, 109, 179.
57. Van Til, *Defense of Faith*, 153.

became spatially present near the father by returning home.[58] The blessed news of the gospel is grounded in the fact that man is reachable by the blessed God through the sense of Deity, and will be awakened by the Spirit when he hears the call of the Father (Gen 3:8–9; Ps 139:7–8).[59] The sense of Deity as part of the image of God is evidence of God's fatherly love toward the elect seeking to be united with them in the blessedness of his own Being (Eph 1:4–5).

---

58. Van Til, *Defense of Faith*, 153.

59. Van Til, *Defense of Faith*, 153.

Chapter 4
Christ and Eschatology

4.1 Gospel and Law

Under Law

John Murray summarized the relationship of the gospel and the law as follows: "We must guard the doctrine of grace from the distorted works of the law, while at the same time guard the doctrine of the law from the false doctrine of grace."[1] Most would concur that the law without the gospel will result in legalism, and the gospel without the law in antinomianism. When the gospel and the law are confused or separated, it will create serious consequences in doctrine and life. "Insofar as there is an error here, there is an error in the understanding of the Gospel."[2] Nonetheless, as in the case of nature and grace, the relation of the law and the gospel needs more than soteriological perspective but a covenantal and eschatological outlook to be properly understood. The covenantal progress can be better visualized by redemptive history with the vertical as well as the horizontal perspectives. Redemptive history moves forward horizontally in time from typology to fulfillment, but it also grows upward until it reaches union with God through Christ. In view of the multidimensional aspects, the gospel and the law ought to be understood within the scope of union with Christ and the spatial ascension to the heavenly realms.

In order to do this, we must look into the use of law in the prelapsarian state of Adam's probation as well as its use in the state of sin. In this broader context, ethics and religion as the two central motifs in eschatology will be relevant to the definition of the law in addition to its soteric usage. Otherwise, believers would be prone to an antinomian view of the law once Old Covenant types and figures are fulfilled in Christ. In the horizontal perspective of redemptive history, the doctrine of common grace postpones the *eschatos* of the final judgment and consummation of the world (Acts 13:48). Thus, the historical process is a delay in time until the shadow is replaced

---

1. Murray, *Principles of Conduct*, 182.
2. Murray, *Principles of Conduct*, 181.

by the substance (Heb 10:1). But in the vertical perspective redemptive history would progressively mature until the covenant knowledge of God reaches its peak through union with Christ (Isa 7:14; Matt 1:23). God's earthly provision was not merely to extend history but to build the redemptive narrative until man's covenant union with God (Gen 3:16–24; Jer 50:5; Matt 5:45). The horizontal delay is not a mere extension of time to save souls and but organic growth of revelation toward Christ (Heb 1:1–3). Redemptive history is more than a collection of personal stories of salvation, but a gradual revelatory progress toward the heavenly wedding banquet (Matt 22:1–14). It is the grand narrative of salvation and consummation of history moving toward the last days of the world. The Covenant of Grace is distinguished between periods of being "under the law" or "under the gospel" within the progress of redemptive history. But the two periods only differ in terms of the means of grace or administration of the Covenant of Grace, rather than in substance. The period of being under the law is not merely a type to be replaced by the substance but itself "a copy and shadow of what is in heaven" (Heb 8:5). The law of God as an expression of the covenant requirement continues even though sign and seal of the Covenant of Grace have changed. The progress of redemptive history reaches its pinnacle in Christ with heaven and earth united, and this eschatological outlook must be brought to bear on the relation of the law and the gospel. Therefore, believers under the gospel are not under the law (under the types and shadows of Old Covenant) but still "under Christ's law" (1 Cor 9:21).

The Lutheran view, in contrast, sees the period of being under the law as a "tutor" to lead believers to Christ so that under the gospel the law is abrogated. It is a theological model largely dominated by the doctrine of justification by faith. It is true that Paul appears to pit the law and the gospel against each other but he does so only to refute the Judaizers—not to pit the two periods of being under the law and under the gospel as essentially in conflict (Gal 3:23–25, 4:1–5). We must consider the several ways in which the apostle uses the term "under the law" to put the matter in the proper perspective. In Paul, "under the law" could mean: (1) under sin (Rom 6:14); (2) under the Old Covenant (1 Cor 9:20); or (3) "under Christ's law" (v. 21). The first sense he outright rejects, but the second and the third he retains: the second use for evangelistic purpose, and the third use for sanctification and ethics. In short, the apostle does not support an antinomian view of the law under the gospel for those who are in Christ. The period of being under the gospel does not mean the law is abrogated but rather brought under Christ. The vertical perspective is of importance because believers are seated in the heavenly realms with Christ, where they are "under Christ's law." Eschatology enables us to see beyond use of the law in soteric justification to the image of God in sanctification and adoption to sonship. Christ's crucifixion and resurrection bear on the eschatological perspective on the law, which provides hermeneutical grounds for continuity between the two periods of the Covenant of Grace. "God had planned something better for us so that only together with us would they be made perfect" (Heb 11:40). The relation of the gospel and the law, therefore, is more properly and clearly understood under the scope of eschatology rather than just under forensic justification. The antithesis of the gospel and the law in justification should not be confused with the eschatological union of the two provisionally fulfilled in Christ. The typological unity of heaven and earth in the Old Covenant is fulfilled through Christ and his kingdom (Eph 1:10; Heb 8:5; Col 1:13). In the soteric sense, "you are not under the law, but under grace" (Rom 6:14), but in the eschatological sense, the gospel fulfills the law and brings believers under Christ's law (Matt 5:17; Rom 13:10; 1 Cor 9:21).

Law and Kingdom

God's covenant people are "a kingdom of priests and a holy nation" and the law was given for this covenantal purpose subsequent to the salvific event of Exodus (Exod 19:1–6). The mark of the kingdom is divine holiness exemplified by the typological kingdom of Israel, who were to wage the holy war of *herem* in Canaan (Lev 27:28). The emphasis of God's kingdom throughout redemptive history is not necessarily its triumph over the world but its distinction from it (John 18:36). The means of grace under the law (i.e., circumcision) may have been abrogated under the gospel but the spirit of the law for the New Covenant church is even more intensified. The kingdom of Christ fulfilled the typological kingdom of Israel, and the church now represents the eschatological kingdom of priests in covenant with God (1 Pet 2:9). The church is called out of this world (age) into the new pattern of the life to engage in spiritual war with the flesh. It is called out so that it can "put to death" the earthly nature just as the holy war of Israel in Canaan (Col 3:5). In redemptive-eschatological perspective, therefore, the law is far from being abrogated but is the primary means by which the distinctiveness of the kingdom of heaven is manifested in this world: "So then, the law is holy, and the commandment is holy, righteous and good . . . We know that the law is spiritual . . ." (Rom 7:12–14).

Christ fulfilled the law not only for reconciliation with God but for conformation to the firstborn of God and inheritance of the kingdom (Rom 8:29, 32–34). Christ's work is vicarious and vital in that it reconciles believers with God but further vitalizes them through holiness. Thus, the gospel and the law do not clash in Christ but mutually corroborate within the adoption to sonship. "Dear friends, let us love one another, for love comes from God. Everyone who loves has been born of God and knows God. Whoever does not love does not know God, because God is love" (1 John 4:7–8). The unity of the gospel and the law is most vividly manifested in the Person of Christ, who is our "wisdom, righteousness, holiness, and redemption" (1 Cor 1:30; 1 Pet 1:15). The gospel and the law can no more be separated in believers than Christ can be divided into parts because "without holiness no one will see the Lord" (Heb 12:14). In the Covenant of Grace, the works of the law for righteousness are abolished, but the law of the covenant is upheld: "Love does no harm to a neighbor. Therefore, love is the fulfillment of the law" (Rom 13:10). Paul defines the law in such a way that sin is more than a fall to corruption but a fall from God's glory and blessedness (Rom 3:23). The law is first and foremost a reflection of the divine image and its substance flows out from God's holiness and blessedness (1 Tim 1:11; 6:15). God is the fountain of "every good and perfect gift," whether in creation or redemption and in their respective eschatology (Gen 1:31; Matt 5:3–12; Jas 1:17). The law flows out of the goodness of God and produces good works: "The first characteristic of good works is conformity to the law of God. As we define sin as the violation of the law of God, so the good works are the opposite."[3] The gospel is more than "medical" as it seeks divine glory through recreation of the image of God and fulfillment of covenant union (John 17:24; Rom 5:1–2; Gal 5:6). The vertical and spatial ascension achieves this goal by union with the risen Christ, where believers are under Christ's law (1 Cor 9:21).

The fallen world could never again reach the vertical goal by means of the first covenant in Eden (Gen 3:16–24). The natural law written in the conscience of man to execute the natural duties of life under common grace (especially from the fourth to the tenth commandments that form the moral foundation of human society) is what remains of it (Rom 2:14–15). It is non-saving but still effective as part of the creation order for continuation of civilization until the final judgment of the seed of the serpent (Gen 3:15). In any case, the vertical perspective of the believer's union with Christ to the heavenly realms means that the gospel does not merely restore him to the state of the Covenant of Works. In the gospel, the new humanity reaches the higher order, where they "will see the glory of God" in Christ (John 11:40; 17:24; Rom 3:23). The final cause precedes the instrumental cause (eschatology precedes soteriology), that justification is in order that they might "rejoice in the hope of the glory of God" (Rom 5:1–2). The penal use of the law is thus preceded by its positive use in the covenantal promise of life eternal as the reward for Adam's obedience (Rom 2:12–13; 3:19–20). In the same spirit, the Decalogue was given to Israel as the substance of the Mosaic covenant that they might be a priestly kingdom and holy nation (Exod 19:1–6; 20:3–17). The striking similarity in the typology of garden and Canaan in terms of the law and the divine kingdom reveals the eschatological significance of the law. Even under the Covenant of Grace, the law had not been abrogated but further reinforced as the substance of the covenant for the priestly kingdom of God. The penal use of the law is for repentance and regeneration by the Spirit: "The mind governed by the flesh is hostile to God; it does not submit to God's law, nor can it do so" (Rom 8:7–8). In the eschatological perspective of the Covenant of Grace, however, the newly created man is expected to live in accordance with the law through the Spirit as the priestly kingdom of heaven (Rom 8:9; 2 Cor 3:6–7; 1 Pet 2:9). The Covenant of Grace is the eternal covenant in the vertical ascension with Christ, where believers are under Christ's law for the priestly kingdom. The obedience to Christ's law is not meritorious but conditional in that they will not "inherit the kingdom of God" apart from it (1

---

3. Vos, *Reformed Dogmatics*, 4:213.

Cor 6:9–10). "As the body without the spirit is dead, so faith without deeds is dead," and true faith always works through love that fulfills the law (Rom 13:10; Gal 5:6; Jas 2:26). In this, again, the goal of nature is typical of the final goal of redemption: "And this is love: that we walk in obedience to his commands. As you have heard from the beginning, his command is that you walk in love" (2 John 1:6).

Christ removed the curse of the Covenant of Works but not its lawful demand to be holy and blameless. There is a difference between abolishment of the *quid pro quo* principle in the Covenant of Works and abolishment of the condition itself: "The principle 'Do this then you shall live' is abolished, but 'Do this' is still valid"[4] because it is rooted in the very nature of man as created in God's image. The Covenant of Grace abolished justification by works of the law but did not abolish the works without which faith is "dead." It does not throw out the baby with the bathwater, for the law reflects God's glory, holiness, and blessedness: "So then, the law is holy, and the commandment is holy, righteous and good" (Rom 7:12). The covenantal way of dealing with man is grounded in the fact that God is blessed in himself and also the fountain of man's blessedness (Gen 1:31). The Mosaic law was given for Israel's own happiness (*towb*) without becoming a legalistic contract of *quid pro quo* (Deut 10:13). The gospel as "good news" in substance stems from the blessed nature of God and the Covenant of Grace does not abrogate this. The vertical union of heaven and earth through Christ's crucifixion and resurrection provides the theological foundation of law-in-grace. The precise understanding of the law and the gospel, therefore, must take into account the vertical as well as the horizontal perspective. The Old Covenant (under the law) is a type of New Covenant (under the gospel), but vertically speaking, it is a copy and shadow of heaven. It represents an intrusion of heaven on earth that prefigures the eschatological kingdom of God (1 Cor 15:24; Heb 8:5). In fact, the type of heaven on earth progressed through redemptive history and the dynamic of heaven's intrusion on earth is gradually intensified toward the last days (Gen 3:15; Mark 1:15; Acts 2:17). The covenants of Noah, Abraham, Moses, and David serve as types for the New Covenant under the gospel and they all foreshadow the eschatological kingdom in a progressive way. The Covenant of Grace under the gospel administration thus cannot be antinomian any more than the kingdom of God is antinomian. The interaction between the horizontal and vertical axes in redemptive history is the theological and hermeneutical key to unlock the multilayered relationship of the law and grace. A brief survey of the covenants from Noah to David will reveal how the soteric and eschatological perspectives are integrated in the progress of redemption in regard to the gospel and the law.

---

4. Vos, *Redemptive History*, 244.

Noahic Covenant

The first covenant in the era of the Covenant of Grace that typifies union of heaven on earth was Noah's covenant (Gen 6:18; 9:11). Amid the curse of the flood upon the fallen world God's provision of the ark for Noah's family represents a graphic intrusion of his kingdom on earth. But even in the salvific typology of the ark, God does not abandon the world and promises its preservation until the renewal of heaven and earth (Gen 6:17–18; 9:1–17). The words of God are strikingly similar to those spoken to Adam at creation: "Then God blessed Noah and his sons, saying to them, 'Be fruitful and increase in number and fill the earth'" (Gen 9:1). The covenant of Noah is not a bare repetition of the Covenant of Works but a reaffirmation of the natural order of creation that will be included in God's eschatological vision:

> I now establish my covenant with you and with your descendants after you and with every living creature that was with you—the birds, the livestock and all the wild animals, all those that came out of the ark with you—every living creature on earth. I establish my covenant with you: Never again will all life be destroyed by the waters of a flood; never again will there be a flood to destroy the earth. And God said, "This is the sign of the covenant I am making between me and you and every living creature with you, a covenant for all generations to come: I have set my rainbow in the clouds, and it will be the sign of the covenant between me and the earth." (Gen 9:9–13)

In the overall scheme, Noah's covenant upholds and strengthens the Adamic covenant by the affirmation of the natural order with the promise of preservation subsequent to the flood (Gen 9:1–2).[5] In the reaffirmation of the covenant at creation, however, Noah is freshly presented a "new Adam."[6] The ark represents a gracious domain of salvation provided by God amid the catastrophic event of the flood, which foreshadows the final judgment. The affinity of Noah to Adam particularly stands out in the view of man as created in God's image (Gen 9:6): "Noah's covenant was to reaffirm the image of God."[7] The image of God is one of the most important themes in creation and redemption as the link between the eschatology of both. An eschatological vision that started in creation and runs through the biblical covenants is the view of man as the temple of God created in God's image: "Don't you know that you yourselves are God's temple and that God's Spirit lives in you?" (1 Cor 3:16). The recreation of man in "truth, righteousness, and holiness" after the image of God is fulfillment of that original vision started in Eden (Eph 4:24; Col 3:10). God reinstates the eschatology of nature with the promise of preservation even as Noah is being saved

---

5. Dumbrell, *Covenant and Creation*, 15–26.
6. Gentry and Wellum, *Kingdom through Covenants*, 163, 168.
7. Gentry and Wellum, *Kingdom through Covenants*, 174.

from the judgment. A central feature in Noah's covenant, the image of God is really the ground of a "third" and "proper" use of the law for the sanctification of believers.[8]

Noah's covenant is thus salvific and eschatological with a dual purpose of deliverance from the flood and the promise of preservation (Gen 3:16–24; 9:13). A juxtaposition of these two purposes reinforces the fact that grace does not abrogate nature in the Covenant of Grace: "God's benevolent goodness and love to preserve the world through Noah's covenant provided the historical background for the unfolding of the redemptive plan for the world."[9] The covenant of Noah is a soteric story typical of and with particular implications for the last days of the world (1 Pet 2:5; 3:20; Rev 21:1–2). The promise and hope of the preservation of the natural world in contrast to the annihilation of life on the face of earth was paradoxical but perhaps necessary. In any case, the continuation of the world was necessary for the gradual maturation of redemptive history until the last days and the New Adam, who is the consummate image of God.[10] The promise of the extension of common grace history in Noah's covenant enabled the horizontal and vertical developments of covenant toward Christ. The natural law written in man's conscience for life on earthly kingdoms runs parallel to the divine law written on the heart of believers in the heavenly kingdom. In the overall scheme of redemptive history, Noah's covenant represents a small but a significant step in the right direction as it laid the foundation of the subsequent works of God. The magnitude of the flood event notwithstanding, the covenant accounts for a small progress in the history of special revelation with the ark and rainbow as its primary means of grace. A horizontal perspective alone would not represent much of a progress unless accompanied by the vertical perspective, and Noah's covenant was still in redemptive history's rudimentary stage. Noah's covenant, however, represents more than a type of deliverance from judgment, for in it the first steps toward the union of heaven and earth had already begun to unfold in no uncertain terms.

Abrahamic Covenant

In the *proto-euangelion* of the promised "seed," the Covenant of Grace started with the single person of Adam after he broke the Covenant of Works (Gen 3:15; Hos 6:7). The tree of life for the time being was inaccessible but a way will be eventually provided for man to approach and be reconciled with God. At that time, the angel who guarded the path to the garden will be withdrawn once and for all, giving way to the eternal Mediator (Heb 4:16; 9:24). The Covenant of Grace expanded from a person to a family in Noah's covenant, whose sign and seal was the ark and the rainbow. Noah's ark was a sign and seal of the covenant kingdom of God: "In it only a few people, eight in all, were saved through water" (Luke 17:27; Heb 11:7; 1 Pet 2:5; 3:20). The scope

8. Calvin, *Institutes*, 1:360.
9. Gentry and Wellum, *Kingdom through Covenants*, 175.
10. Williamson, *Sealed with an Oath*, 67–68.

and clarity of the Covenant of Grace is further magnified from a family to a tribe in Abraham's covenant with its substance and details in more clear terms. The Abrahamic covenant was the first in the Covenant of Grace with explicit means of grace and mention of forensic justification by faith (Gen 15:6; Rom 4:1–25). He and "every male in his household" were to be circumcised as the sign and seal of the covenant that the Hebrew tribe was set apart from the pagan world (Gen 17:27). The prologue to the rite of covenant ceremony, "I am God Almighty, walk before me faithfully and be blameless," reveals the theocentric and ethical nature of the covenant itself (Gen 17:1). The theocentric nature of the covenant shows the scope of the Covenant of Grace is wider and deeper than forensic justification by faith. The rite of circumcision signifies a chosen tribe of God who are to walk holy and blameless before him. The ritual of cutting of a carcass with blood dripping down made it visually clear that the covenant carried with it promise of blessing or warning of curse. The substance of the covenant itself did not change; it was still a matter of life and death as far as God was concerned, like the first covenant in the garden (Gen 2:17; 15:17). The standard of righteousness in the Covenant of Grace was the same as the Covenant of Works but only the mediator and the means changed. The shedding of blood in what was to be a gracious covenant bears out the mortal clash of two worlds already foretold in the promise of the seed (Gen 2:17; 3:15). Heaven's intrusion on earth has always created an epic clash of two worlds in biblical history, and reaches its pinnacle in the last days inaugurated by Christ: "From the days of John the Baptist until now, the kingdom of heaven has been forcefully advancing, and forceful men lay hold of it" (Matt 11:12).

Abraham's covenant is an expression of the eternal covenant in which believers are chosen in Christ out of God's love before the creation of the world (Eph 1:3–5). As in all other covenants, it requires a horizontal as well as a vertical perspective in order to account for its redemptive-eschatological significance (Heb 8:5; 9:23). The vertical union of heaven and earth and the horizontal fulfillment of the old by the new is a consistent theme running through the history of covenants. The goal of an everlasting binding with God to be consummated in "God with us" is implicit in all forms of the Covenant of Grace "under the law" administration, including Abraham's covenant (Jer 50:5). The eternal election (formal cause) is of a higher order than the faith (instrumental cause) of the covenant and the means of grace conform to the former (Eph 1:4; 2:8). The instrumental cause of faith is a gracious gift of God for that eternal election to be ratified in time, thus it cannot be the formal cause of the sign and seal of the covenant. As Paul stated, it is by grace, in Christ and through faith, that the covenant is received (Eph 2:7–8). Faith, therefore, is not the formal cause of the execution of God's gracious promise that began in the eternal covenant of the *Pactum Salutis*. In the vertical perspective of the covenant, union with Christ as the eschatological fulfillment of the eternal election precedes the subjective response of man—which could result in either legalism or antinomianism. It is precisely for this reason that the primary goal of faith is to be viewed as the appropriation of union with

Christ. The union with Christ permanently seals the everlasting covenant between God and man from which all other salvific benefits flow out. Abraham's covenant is no different in regard to giving preeminence to God's glory and sovereignty despite the particular attention given to faith. The spotlight faith receives in the Pauline Epistles is due to the urgency at the time to repudiate the "works of the law" by the Judaizers (Gal 3:2; 4:1–7).[11] The theme of eternal hope would have been "more prominent had it not been for the necessity of stressing the idea of faith on account of its controversial importance."[12] For Paul, the eschatological hope lies in union with the risen Christ, which logically precedes any subsequent stage in the order of salvation. "The bond between the believer and Christ is so close that . . . the severance of his actual life from the celestial Christ-centered sphere is unthinkable."[13] The urgency, then, to settle the doctrine of forensic justification occasioned by the Judaizers thrusted faith into the forefront of the controversy. The eschatological hope of union with Christ in reality was at the forefront of the apostle's mind had it not been for the soteriological controversy at hand.

In Abraham's covenant faith was required for the crediting of righteousness but not as condition of the rite of circumcision (Rom 4:3). The means of grace in circumcision, however, was the sign and seal of the covenant rooted in the eternal election of God, who is the formal cause of it. Faith, in contrast to the works of the law, is required as condition of justification, but not as condition of the covenant. If faith indeed had been a condition of the sign and seal of the covenant, it would not make sense to administer circumcision to the infant males (Gen 9:13). Everyone in Abraham's household, adult or infant male, was circumcised not because of their faith, but formally on the basis of God's promise. The administration of the means of grace, however, was to the believing male adults and male children (Rom 4:11; Acts 2:39). The male infants in the Abrahamic covenant were administered the rite of circumcision apart from faith based on the sovereign promise of God to be the seed of the covenant community. Abraham's covenant made it clear that administering the means of grace, originating from God's sovereign promise, is not formally contingent upon faith, which is but a gift (Gen 17:10; Eph 2:8). The efficacy of the means of grace in the covenant is rooted the promise and execution of God's eternal decree in Christ. After all, it is God alone who decrees, accomplishes, and applies the covenantal benefits to believers, and covenant children are not excluded from this promise (Eph 1:3–14).

The rite of circumcision in Abraham's covenant is a means of grace under the law that typifies baptism under the gospel. The promise of the covenant is spelled out clearly by Peter in his sermon in Acts: "Repent and be baptized, every one of you, in the name of Jesus Christ for the forgiveness of your sins. And you will receive the gift of the Holy Spirit" (Acts 2:38). He then extends the covenant promise to their children

---

11. Vos, *Pauline Eschatology*, 29.
12. Vos, *Pauline Eschatology*, 29.
13. Vos, *Pauline Eschatology*, 37.

as heirs: "The promise is for you and your children and for all who are far off—for all whom the Lord our God will call" (v. 39). The case for infant baptism obviously cannot be sustained if the Old Covenant is merely a shadow of the New Covenant and if its function has ended under the gospel. A total and substantial discontinuation between the two administrations would entail the means of grace (circumcision and baptism) have nothing in common whatsoever. The scope of the Abrahamic covenant would then be strictly limited to the benefits of justification to believing adults in the old administration. Infant baptism can be sustained, however, if placed within the redemptive-historical progress of the Covenant of Grace. The means of grace would then have a substantial continuity despite discontinuity in the method of administration. The substantial unity is that they are the sign and seal of union with Christ as the fulfillment of the eternal covenant. Infants were thus included as heirs in the covenant and the promise was for them as well as their believing parents. The substantial continuity in the means of grace is most clearly seen in Paul's view of baptism as circumcision by Christ:

> In him you were also circumcised with a circumcision not performed by human hands. Your whole self ruled by the flesh was put off when you were circumcised by Christ, buried with him in baptism, in which you were also raised with him through your faith in the working of God, who raised him from the dead. (Col 2:11–12)

The substance of baptism is no different than that of circumcision as both signal the burial of the old self and the birth of the new self in union with the crucified and risen Christ. The union did not just create a new man but a new order of man: "Neither circumcision nor uncircumcision means anything; what counts is the new creation" (Gal 6:15). The scope of the covenant is expanded to the new order of creation, and the means of grace is placed in the broader context of progress in redemptive-eschatology. In any case, the Abrahamic covenant illustrates that faith is not an instrument for one particular stage in the order of salvation, i.e., justification, but an instrument of union with Christ, in whom all the spiritual blessings in the heavenly realms are given to believers (Eph 1:3).

Mosaic Covenant

Despite the two previous covenants, it was not until the Mosaic covenant at Mount Sinai that the covenantal purpose of the law was manifested in more comprehensive terms through Israel as a theocratic kingdom. Starting with Moses, God clearly intends to reveal a concrete form of a kingdom bigger in scale than a family or tribe: "Now if you obey me fully and keep my covenant, then out of all nations you will be my treasured possession . . . you will be for me a kingdom of priests and a holy nation" (Exod 19:5–6). This covenant carries with it stipulations of blessings and curses specifically contingent upon Israel's faithful obedience, which renders it similar to the Adamic covenant (Deut 28:1–68).[14] In form, it does appear to be similar to that of the Covenant of Works: "Keep my decrees and laws, for the person who obeys them will live by them. I am the LORD (Lev 18:5)." Despite the legalistic form, the Mosaic covenant does not abrogate Abraham's covenant ratified four hundred years ago and the soteric principle of justification by faith remains unaltered (Gal 3:17).[15] The Mosaic covenant is not a repetition of the Covenant of Works in substance despite the similarity, nor can it possibly be so since it is established as part of the redemptive-historical progress within the Covenant of Grace. In the horizontal progress, the Mosaic law foreshadows Christ's atonement, but in the vertical perspective it typifies the eschatological kingdom of God, which requires perfect righteousness and holiness (Exod 19:5–6). The Mosaic kingdom and the radical nature of its use of the law foreshadows the kingdom of heaven to be revealed in the last days with the Messiah. Moses was a servant and Christ is the Son: "Moses was faithful as a servant in all God's house, testifying to what would be said in the future" (Heb 3:5). The stipulation of the covenant was that they would either inherit the Promised Land or lose it (Deut 28:63–64). Thus, the Mosaic law in its national-typological aspect is summed up as "Get in by grace, stay in by obedience."[16] This national covenant prefiguring the redemptive-eschatological kingdom of heaven is sometimes called "covenantal nomism" due to its emphasis on obedience to the law. Obedience, however, is not a soteric condition of personal justification but a typological language that befits the kingdom of heaven, which evildoers cannot inherit (1 Cor 6:9).[17]

Heaven's intrusion on earth is intensified as the typology progresses from a tribe to a nation with the Mosaic law at the forefront of the theocratic reign of God in Canaan. It represents a rudimentary form of the already-but-not-yet kingdom of God on earth and the theocratic nation of Israel ruled by the law stood in sharp distinction from the surrounding nations (Exod 33:16). The theme of heaven on earth progresses through the various types in the Old Testament (Adam's Eden, Noah's ark, Abraham's tribe, David's kingdom), but never so cataclysmic as the violent intrusion of Israel into Canaan.[18] Israel's conquest of the Promised Land is said to be closer than any prior typology to the consummate kingdom of God, graphically illustrated by the holy war of total destruction (Lev 27:28–29).[19] Eschatology engenders high ethical standards through a type of the kingdom so radical as to require a total destruction of the

---

14. Horton, *Covenant and Salvation*, 15.

15. Horton, *Covenant and Salvation*, 15.

16. Horton, *Covenant and Salvation*, 14, 37–52. Also see Sanders, *Paul and Palestinian Judaism*, 93, 178, 371.

17. Sanders, *Paul and Palestinian Judaism*, 75, 543–56.

18. Jeon, *Covenant Theology*, 307–14.

19. Kline, *Kingdom Prologue*, 321–22.

ungodly for the inheritance of the Promised Land.[20] In an eschatological sense, "the wicked will not inherit the kingdom of God" for their acts of evil are not fitting for the kingdom of priests and holy nation (1 Cor 6:9–10; 1 Pet 2:9). Exodus was a covenantal work of God that the great salvific event renders Israel enter into a covenant with Yahweh in rejection of the "gods" of Canaan (Exod 23:30, 32). Hence, "Do this, then you shall live" in the Mosaic covenant was effective and relevant only to the typological realm: "The works principle of the Mosaic covenant was limited to the earthly type of the kingdom of God."[21] As it turns out, the theocratic kingdom would only be temporary as Israel repeatedly failed and was uprooted from the Promised Land. Moses and Joshua could not lead Israel to God's Sabbath due to the temporality and weakness of the covenant (Jer 31:31–34; Heb 4:8–9). It was not a soteric issue of personal justification but a redemptive-historical issue of looking forward to one greater than Moses. "There remains, then, a Sabbath-rest for the people of God" which Moses and Joshua were unable to give Israel (Heb 4:9). In the progress of revelation, it wonderfully and fearfully prefigures the eternal kingdom to be inherited by a superior mediator (Heb 5:8–9). Moses was a mere servant but Jesus is the Son, who will bring God's people into the seventh day of God's rest (Heb 4:1ff.).

Moses did not fail in his own salvation, which is by grace alone, but failed in the national covenant by failing to trust God: "But the LORD said to Moses and Aaron, 'Because you did not trust in me enough to honor me as holy in the sight of the Israelites, you will not bring this community into the land I give them'" (Num 20:12). Jesus, however, will bring his own people into "Mount Zion, to the heavenly Jerusalem, the city of the living God," where believers have arrived in union with him (Heb 12:22). The inferiority of the Mosaic covenant was ironically expressed when Canaan turned into a wasteland in need of its own Sabbath rest from Israel (Jer 25:11; 2 Chr 36:21). The exile meant the national covenant had failed and the earthly theocratic model had runout its course. The elect are saved by grace and live by faith in all ages, but the typological kingdom failed and must await another mediator who will fulfill the new and eternal covenant (Hab 2:4; Rom 4:13; Heb 10:1).

The Mosaic covenant is a more advanced form of typology with an application of the divine law beyond personal justification and sanctification.[22] The kingdom of heaven is not of this world and the intrusion of Israel into Canaan prefigures it with emphasis on voluntary obedience (John 18:36; 1 Sam 15:22). In the horizontal perspective, the law prefigures Christ's atonement through sacrifices, but in the vertical perspective, the law foreshadows the kingdom of Christ ruled under his law (1 Cor 9:21). The Mosaic law resembles the Covenant of Works but only because it typifies the priestly kingdom that demands obedience befitting God's holiness. The Covenant of Grace under the law is still a gracious covenant, yet it is a covenant of the kingdom

---

20. Kline, *Kingdom Prologue*, 323.
21. Kline, *Kingdom Prologue*, 321.
22. Horton, *Covenant and Salvation*, 25.

that demands obedience to God's law. The Mosaic law has been confused with legal justification by Judaizers and Paul takes the occasion to repudiate the wrong sense of the Mosaic law (Gal 4:1–7). They were "zealous for God, but their zeal is not based on knowledge" because "they did not know the righteousness that comes from God and sought to establish their own, they did not submit to God's righteousness" (Rom 10:2–3). Hence, Paul qualifies the discourse in Galatians by saying Moses does not contradict Abraham in regard to justification by faith alone. The conditional clause in the national covenant of Israel only meant that the kingdom of God could not retain anything ungodly of this world (Matt 5:17, 48; 1 Cor 6:9–10; 1 John 5:3).

The language of conditionality in the Mosaic covenant law is appropriate for typology and must not be confused with righteousness gained through justification by the works of the law. Yet, the undeniable sense of conditionality specified in detail would be difficult to explain away merely from a perspective of personal holiness or sanctification.[23] The problem of conditionality is attributed to "symbolico-typical language" appropriate for Israel as a type of the kingdom of God.[24] In personal sanctification, the Christian life consists of "mortification of sin" and "vivification of life" by "the perfect law that gives freedom" (Jas 1:25). Life in a theocratic kingdom, however, consists of use of the law that reflects the totality of Israel's ethical and religious devotion to God (penal, moral, and doxological). The God who was called *Elohim* is now known as Yahweh, who is the husband of Israel (Exod 6:3): "As a bridegroom rejoices over his bride, so will your God rejoice over you" (Isa 62:5); "For your Maker is your husband—the LORD Almighty is his name—the Holy One of Israel is your Redeemer; he is called the God of all the earth" (Isa 54:5). The Mosaic kingdom in its symbolico-typological realm is designed to be a pattern of the eschatological kingdom of God, where nothing ungodly will be allowed to enter (1 Cor 15:24; Heb 8:5; 9:24, 26). A *Historia Salutis* perspective is necessary in order to properly interpret the conditional clause in the Mosaic covenant in order to avoid legalism or eisegesis.

The Mosaic law can be classified into moral, ritual, and civil laws essential to Israel as a type of the theocratic kingdom surrounded by heathen gods in Canaan. The moral law contained in the Decalogue (Exod 20:3–17) represents permanent moral principles of the priestly kingdom while the ritual and civil laws are transitory and unique to the symbolico-typical era of Old Covenant. The ritual and civil laws conform to the means of grace under the law that are abrogated once the progress of redemptive history reaches the New Covenant under the Gospel. The moral law, however, is not abrogated but written in the hearts of believers, who are under Christ's law. Once Christ ascends to heaven and establishes the messianic kingdom represented by

---

23. John Murray appears to be taking this position with regard to the conditionality in the Mosaic covenant. His analysis, however, seems to be limited to the scope of the *Ordo Salutis* without a sufficient consideration of the *Historia Salutis* or the eschatology in redemptive history.

24. Murray here cites Vos's view on the conditionality in the Mosaic covenant but does not discuss in detail the *Historia Salutis* aspect of the covenant.

his "body" on earth, the typological function of Israel and the Mosaic law is fulfilled (Heb 9:12; 12:22–23). In him, the church is now the new Israel: "You have not come to a mountain that can be touched . . . But you have come to Mount Zion, to the city of the living God, the heavenly Jerusalem . . . to the church of the firstborn . . ." (vv. 18, 22). Again, Judaizers turned the Mosaic law into legalism, failing to comprehend its typological nature, and misconstrued it as justification by the works of the law: "Before this faith came, we were held prisoners by the law, locked up until faith should be revealed . . . Now that faith has come, we are no longer under the supervision of the law" (Gal 3:23–25). Here the apostle places the two administrations of the Covenant of Grace into law versus faith, not to pit them against each other but to show the weakness of being under the law. It is more clearly explained when the apostle says:

> To Jews I became like a Jew, to win Jews. To those under the law I became like one under the law (though I myself am not under the law), so as to win those under the law. To those not having the law I became like one not having the law (though I am not free from God's law but am under Christ's law), so as to win those not having the law. (1 Cor 9:20–21)

But then he adds, "To the weak I became weak, to win the weak," defining "under the law" as a weaker administration in the Covenant of Grace. Judaizers misconstrued the weakness of the Mosaic law as justification by the works of the law precisely because they did not understand the organic relation between the two administrations of the Covenant of Grace (Jer 31:31–34; Gal 3:20).

The final destruction of Satan's kingdom will coincide with the suspension of common grace altogether: "He will punish those who do not know God and do not obey the Gospel of our Lord Jesus. They will be punished with everlasting destruction and shut out from the presence of the Lord and from the majesty of his power" (2 Thess 1:8–9). The Mosaic law demonstrates in typology that everything that imperils the integrity of the theocratic kingdom will be completely destroyed (Lev 27:28–29; Josh 2:1–24). At times it required a suspension of common grace ethics, when Israel was ordered to destroy the "devoted things," which, if unheeded, would bring about its own destruction (Josh 6:18; 7:11). The holy war meant "intrusion ethics"[25] of the theocratic kingdom such as the false testimony of Rahab against her own nation. The common grace ethic is suspended temporarily during the intrusive war, prefiguring the complete withdrawal of the common grace order at the last judgment. The annihilation of the ungodly seems cruel but is consistent with the final judgement and destruction of the world. The common grace ethic of "love your neighbor" is suspended temporarily during the holy war because it fundamentally alters the definition of a neighbor.[26] The enmity between the seed of the serpent and the seed of the woman

---

25. Jeon, *Biblical Theology*, 236.
26. Jeon, *Biblical Theology*, 236.

is not only a soteric clash of law and the gospel,[27] but the redemptive-eschatological contrast of heaven and earth (Gen 3:15). The intrusion of heaven on earth is to be fulfilled when heaven and earth are united in Christ as the inauguration of the heavenly theocratic kingdom (Eph 1:10). Israel in Canaan was a visual illustration of the eschatological kingdom in advance, or an Old Covenant form of the already-but-not-yet kingdom in the New Covenant. Forensic justification by faith alone remains unaltered under the Covenant of Grace and unaffected by the process of redemptive history (Gen 15:6; Rom 4:16; Gal 3:17):

> He remembers his covenant forever, the promise he made, for a thousand generations, the covenant he made with Abraham, the oath he swore to Isaac. He confirmed it to Jacob as a decree, to Israel as an everlasting covenant: To you I will give the land of Canaan as the portion you will inherit. (Ps 105:8–11)

The failure of a national covenant only made it more clear that the eschatological kingdom would to be established by a mediator superior to Moses. Moses was not exempt from the weakness of the administration under the law, a period characterized by "the letter" and by corporate unbelief (Heb 4:2). Even Moses demonstrated such weakness: "But the LORD said to Moses and Aaron, 'Because you did not trust in me enough to honor me as holy in the sight of the Israelites, you will not bring this community into the land I give them'" (Num 20:12). The inferior typology only added a greater longing to the anticipation of the heavenly Canaan with God's rest, which the Mosaic covenant could not guarantee. Thus, they look forward to another day in the future: "For if Joshua had given them rest, God would not have spoken later about another day" (Heb 4:8). The holy war of radical obedience and complete destruction of the ungodly failed but rendered them more hopeful of the perfect war of the messianic kingdom. The Abrahamic and Mosaic covenants do not differ in substance but only in typology, particularly in the wake of deliverance from Egypt.[28]

The Old Covenant is a copy and shadow of the heavenly realities that provides the basis of a unified view of history under the Covenant of Grace (Heb 8:5; 9:24). The Mosaic covenant with its emphasis on the law brings the importance of sanctification and ethics into focus as a matter of the theocratic kingdom. The moral law cannot be abrogated because the "devoted things" is central to the covenant community whether it be Israel or the church. The fundamental premise is that man is created to live for God's glory in all that he does and to do so consciously with all of the heart, mind, and strength (Deut 6:5; Matt 22:37). The Mosaic covenant reinstates this spirit in the strongest of terms so that grace is not mistaken for licentiousness (1 Cor 9:21). The positive use of the law for the sanctification of believers conforms to the theocratic standard that "without holiness no one will see the Lord" (Heb 12:14). Pursuit of holiness is the proper work of the image of God, whether it be in Eden, in Mount Zion,

---

27. Horton, *Covenant and Salvation*, 20–21.
28. Horton, *Covenant and Salvation*, 19.

or in the heavenly Jerusalem (Heb 12:22). The perfection of the image of God is the proper use of the law in "the city of the living God" and the radical demand in the Mosaic law gives expression to this aspect of man, which has not been altered by sin.[29] It foreshadows New Covenant ethics similar to the commandments of the "devoted things" in the conquest of Canaan (Matt 5:19–20, 29–30). The Sermon on the Mount sums up the moral standards of the kingdom of heaven this way: "Be perfect, therefore, as your heavenly Father is perfect" (Matt 5:17–48). The observance of the law that even surpasses the Pharisees and the gory details of how to deal with sin are reminiscent of the "intrusion ethics" of the theocratic kingdom in Canaan (Matt 5:20, 29–30). The standard and spirit of New Covenant ethics all but replicate those of Leviticus: "Put to death, therefore, whatever belongs to your earthly nature: sexual immorality, impurity, lust, evil desires and greed, which is idolatry" (Col 3:5; Lev 27:28–29). The Mosaic covenant, in this sense, is consistent with the purpose of the *Pactum Salutis*, that the chosen will be made holy and blameless children of God (Eph 1:4). The vertical perspective of the theocratic kingdom has not been given sufficient attention by the traditional view of the Mosaic law. It explains away the conditionality of the law simply as an intense expression of sanctification without giving much attention to the larger, typological aspect of Israel as a theocratic kingdom. God's intent was clearly spelled out in the prologue of the covenant, where it says he has chosen Israel as a kingdom of priests so that "out of all nations you will be my treasured possession" (Exod 19:5).

Davidic Covenant

The Davidic covenant is the most advanced form of covenant in the old administration under the law with the unified kingdom prefiguring the messianic kingdom of Christ. The proto-gospel promised to Adam has gradually matured through the covenants of Noah, Abraham, and Moses, but with the Davidic covenant the typology approached closest to the reality of the messianic kingdom.[30] The centerpiece of the Davidic covenant is the promise, "I will set him over my house and my kingdom forever; his throne will be established forever" (1 Chr 17:14). The first appearances of the prophecies regarding "the anointed" in the pre-Christ era emerged during David's reign (Ps 2:2; 18:50; 20:6; 28:8; 132:10, 17). In particular, it is linked with David: "He gives his king great victories; he shows unfailing kindness to his anointed, to David and his descendants forever" (Ps 18:50). In doing so, the covenant draws a direct line from David to Christ, the risen King, whose throne and authority will be everlasting over heaven and earth (1 Chr 17:11–12; Matt 28:18). The most striking feature, however, is that the anointed Messiah will be not just David's descendant but God's own Son: "I will be his father, and he will be my son. I will never take my love away

---

29. Vos, *Redemptive History*, 245.
30. Robertson, *Christ of Covenants*, 229.

from him, as I took it away from your predecessor" (1 Chr 17:13). Therefore, the Davidic covenant is the last dot that connects the pre-eschatological era of the Covenant of Grace to the semi-eschatological kingdom of the incarnate Son.[31] It was the most advanced type of revelation designed to foretell the approaching messianic kingdom of the crucified and risen Jesus: "For David did not ascend to heaven, and yet he said, 'The Lord said to my Lord: Sit at my right hand until I make your enemies a footstool for your feet.' Therefore let all Israel be assured of this: God has made this Jesus, whom you crucified, both Lord and Christ" (Acts 2:34–36).

By the time the history of covenants reached King David, heaven and earth became ever so close to being unified by the revelation of the unified messianic kingdom (Eph 1:10). David was clearly the direct prefiguration of the Son of God in whom "God was pleased to have all his fullness dwell" (Col 1:19). The Son would not only be the Priest who reconciles but also the King who reigns over heaven and earth, that God was pleased "through him to reconcile to himself all things, whether things on earth or things in heaven, by making peace through his blood, shed on the cross" (v. 20). The Davidic covenant, in particular, had more detailed revelations about the resurrection of the messianic king (Acts 2:25–27). There is more than any previous covenants a spatial transition from the earthly to the heavenly order of things: "regarding his Son, who as to his human nature was a descendant of David, and who through the Spirit of holiness was declared with power to be the Son of God by his resurrection from the dead: Jesus Christ our Lord" (Rom 1:3–4).

Christ fulfilled the prophecies in the horizontal perspective of history, but also finished (*tetelestai*) the covenant with the Father in the vertical sense (Luke 24:44; John 19:30). The crucifixion and resurrection of Christ, in addition to reconciliation, gave believers the eternal inheritance of the kingdom of God (Rom 8:17). The believers in New Covenant knew that the Davidic covenant was fulfilled when Jesus was crucified, raised, and seated in the heavenly throne as Lord and Christ (Acts 2:33–36; Eph 2:6). The spatial transition from earth to heaven in resurrection is the most distinguishing character of the New Covenant and brings all previous covenants to their final destination (Heb 1:1–3). The Davidic covenant comes at a time when religion and politics converge in the city of Jerusalem as the permanent center of the theocratic kingdom. It was a copy and shadow of "Mount Zion, the heavenly Jerusalem, and the city of the living God" (Heb 12:22–23). The authority given to David over the unified kingdom is a perfect symbol of the authority given to Jesus over heaven and earth subsequent to his resurrection (1 Chr 17:13–14; Matt 28:18). The progress of the Davidic covenant from the Mosaic covenant is the level of the conquest and lordship unknown to Moses. The Mosaic covenant was more about the intrusion of heaven on earth and a mortal clash between the sacred and the secular. The Davidic covenant foreshadows the Messiah and the everlasting kingdom of his reign, even as

---

31. Robertson, *Christ of Covenants*, 229.

Peter's sermon concludes, "God has made this Jesus, whom you crucified, both Lord and Christ" (Acts 2:36).

God made the covenant with David in the context of conversations about temple-building. Contrary to his wish to build it, David was told that "the Lord will build a house for him" (1 Chr 17:12). The Mosaic formula of the covenant was "Do this, then you shall live!" (Lev 18:5), but the Davidic formula was "The Lord will do this!" It was a natural progress in revelation fit for the times, when the war with surrounding nations all but ceased and the perspective changed to the messianic kingdom. The tabernacle and temple of the Old Covenant was but a shadow of "a greater and more perfect tabernacle that is not made with human hands, that is to say, is not part of this creation" (Heb 9:11). The theme and context of the covenant moved from intrusion to enthronement: "But when this priest had offered for all time one sacrifice for sins, he sat down at the right hand of God, and since that time he waits for his enemies to be made his footstool" (Heb 10:12–13; Ps 110:1). In his preaching, Peter saw the series of events that just took place as proof of the fulfillment of the prophecy in the psalm: "The Lord said to my Lord: Sit at my right hand until I make your enemies a footstool for your feet" (Acts 2:34–35). The intrusion of heaven progressed to the unification of heaven and earth in the resurrection of Jesus, who became Lord over all things.

The Davidic covenant was a clear progress in revelation in its scale and height: "Therefore, God exalted him to the highest place and gave him the name that is above every name, that at the name of Jesus every knee should bow, in heaven and on earth and under the earth, and every tongue confess that Jesus Christ is Lord, to the glory of God the Father" (Phil 2:9–11). Even so, a most intense form of holy war awaits believers on earth as a violent spiritual clash is anticipated with the coming of the kingdom of heaven in the crucifixion and resurrection of Jesus (Matt 11:12; Col 1:13; Col 1:5). The intrusive principle of heaven *in* the world but not *of* the world continues in the provisional kingdom of Christ with the most radical form of holy war (Eph 6:10–17).[32] In summary, the progress of covenants was relative to the amount and clarity of revelation as well as the spiritual maturity of the covenant community at the particular phase.[33]

4.2 New Covenant

In order to understand the full scope of the New Covenant as the fruit and flower of all previous covenants, we must understand how Christology and eschatology are interrelated. An eschatological approach to doctrines means that every teaching of the Scriptures is christocentric and should to be interpreted "in Christ." Ridderbos rightly stated: "The interdependence of eschatology and Christology in Paul's preaching is an

---

32. Robertson, *Christ of Covenants*, 27–63.
33. Gentry and Wellum, *Kingdom through Covenants*, 595.

important principle in understanding both."[34] The two subjects form the foundation of redemptive history and provide the substructure to all other doctrines in the Scriptures.[35] It is significant that Adam "was a pattern of the one to come," a type of Christ in the prelapsarian state of nature (Rom 5:14). Nature is typical of redemption in eschatology and the natural envisaged the supernatural. Christ is "before all things, and in him all things hold together" revealing that his work is redemptive-eschatological (Col 1:17). Christ is not only Savior of the church but Lord of all creation, and he is the mystery of God hidden in the Counsel of Peace from eternity (Col 2:2). The New Covenant is not only a progress from the Old but the fulfillment of the Eternal Covenant: "In reading this, then, you will be able to understand my insight into the mystery of Christ" (Eph 3:4). "The Word became flesh," and the mystery of the incarnation fulfills all prior prefigures and prophecies once for all (John 1:14).

In the Person and work of Christ, the horizontal and the vertical perspectives of history converge to usher in the last days of salvation and judgment. Thus, the New Covenant is called the "everlasting covenant" that completes the progress toward the union of "God with us" (John 17:21; Eph 2:6; Heb 13:20; Col 3:1). His incarnation, death, and resurrection constitute the substance of the New Covenant as the last phase of the Covenant of Grace for the fulfillment of the *Pactum Salutis*. These events set off the last days of history in motion, through atonement of sin, and the earthly image was changed into the heavenly image of man. He is the *Historia Salutis* from which the subjective application of the *Ordo Salutis* in the elect is made possible. The new order of the world in the objective and historical realm is foundational to the new order of man in the subjective and experiential realm (2 Cor 5:17; Eph 4:24). The redemptive-eschatological work of Christ made possible the subjective-personal application of the Spirit. It may be a rhetorical question, but the psalmist raised an important point with regard to the eschatology of redemption: "When the foundations are being destroyed, what can the righteous do?" (Ps 11:3).

Mystery of God

The Person of Christ is the "mystery of God" hidden from eternity revealed at the end of this age through the incarnation of the Word (John 1:14; Col 1:26; Mark 1:15). His divinity and preexistence before creation and his supremacy over all creation in the redemptive-eschatological work is unmistakable (Col 1:15–20). The hypostatic union of the two natures of Christ is indispensable to substitutionary work for atonement, but its eschatological significance is no less clear in Paul's discourse. The work of soteric reconciliation is the "redemptive plus" to the eternal inheritance envisaged in the eschatology of nature. His resurrection to the heavenly realms meant an intrusion of the future age in advance into the present age. The convergence of the two ages by

34. Ridderbos, *Paul*, 49.
35. Ridderbos, *Paul*, 49.

the vertical union of heaven and earth ushered in the semi-eschatological state in the form of union with the risen Christ. The current state of believers in the Spirit means nothing less than having been risen and seated above with Christ (Eph 2:6). The human nature of Christ is used for the substitutionary purpose and the priestly function in the heavenly realms (Heb 4:16; 9:24). The hypostatic union of two natures thus becomes the basis of soteric rectitude and the eschatological kingdom of heaven (Luke 17:21). Christ is "the image of the invisible God" and "the exact representation of his being," who came as the Last Adam to bring the elect to the eternal garden of God (Col 1:15; Heb 1:3; Rev 2:7). The focus of the eternal life is the three Persons of the blessed Being: "Now this is the eternal life: that they may know you, the only true God, and Jesus Christ, whom you have sent" (John 17:3). This knowledge of the Person precedes the benefits because the believer's union with Christ means union with the Father (John 17:21, 24, 25). The knowledge of the Person of Christ is so overarching and comprehensive that the entire work of God can be summed up as follows: "The work of God is this: to believe in the one he has sent" (John 6:29). The union with Christ is redemptive-eschatological because in it "you may be filled to the measure of all the fullness of God" (Eph 3:19).

The union with him brought soteric deliverance to the fallen world but in so doing the new humanity is transformed out of the earthly state of probation into everlasting life. Even the chief goal of justification is God's glory rather than man's liberty: "This mystery, which is Christ in you, the hope of glory" (Col 1:27; Rom 5:1–2). The salvific need of man is preceded by the completion of the image of God in nature, and for this Christ became the "radiance of glory and the exact representation of his being" (Heb 1:3). According to the apostle, it is primarily the knowledge of the Person of Christ that surpasses all other gains and renders them comparatively worthless (Phil 3:8). The traditional approach to soteriology tended to reverse the biblical order (work over person) due to its primary interests in the rectitude of sin. But the order must be restored: The "I am" clauses of Jesus in the Gospels invoke the self-testimony of Yahweh, who said to Israel, "I AM WHO I AM" (Exod 3:14). It cannot be overstressed that Jesus is given the title of Christ and Lord in Peter's Pentecost sermon (Acts 2:36). The benefits of his work rectify sin, but he himself is one of the three Persons in the blessed God; "I and the Father are one" is the ground of his work (John 10:20). The work of Christ is eternally efficient and binding because of who he is: "The priestly sacrifice of Christ and its effect are directly linked to the constitution of the person."[36] Progress in redemptive history is a forward and upward movement toward union with that unique Person called *Immanuel*. In him, God is not just for us but with us. The Spirit is the guarantee of resurrection who unites us with the risen Lord and the Last Adam (1 Cor 15:45–49; 1 John 4:13).

---

36. Murray, *Redemption Accomplished and Applied*, 15.

Election of Mediator

The *Pactum Salutis* was the archetype of covenant that engenders ethics, piety, intimacy, and devotion in man's relation to God. The Eternal Counsel of Peace was marked by mutual glory, love, and knowledge between the Father and the Son. The tendency in some circles to view the election as a theological antinomy to covenant is due to a lack of understanding of the character of the intra-Trinitarian covenant. The covenant by nature does not separate ethics (duty) from the person, especially when it comes to Christ (1 Cor 1:30). The Covenant of Grace is the earthly expression of the Counsel of Peace in which the Son freely and voluntarily obeys the Father (John 17:4–6). This obedience is reflected in biblical covenants as an essential part of the union and communion between God and man. The theory that Calvin's theology is essentially decretal whereas Puritan theology is covenantal thus seems quite arbitrary and unfounded.[37] In their view, predestination and covenant are mutually exclusive theological concepts because the former nullifies the need for ethics and the duty of man. The bilateral aspects of ethics and duty, however, are rooted in man as covenant being created in God's image, whose archetype is the Son who obeys the Father (2 Cor 4:4). In his voluntary obedience to the Father he was elected as the Mediator of the Counsel of Peace. He is the one whom believers must conform to subsequent to their adoption to sonship by the Spirit (John 17:4; Rom 8:29). In view of the nature of man's relation to God, therefore, the theological choice is not predestination or covenant. In the Golden Chain of the *Ordo Salutis*, realized by the believer's union with the Mediator of the Eternal Counsel, both find their fulfillment (Eph 1:4).

The redemptive-eschatological work of Christ is the direct result of the Person constituted by the two natures of divinity and humanity. The incarnation of the Second Person of the Trinity means perfect unity and harmony in the two natures for the execution of the Counsel of Peace (John 1:1, 14). The mystery of the two natures in Christ makes possible the reconciliation of God and man, but furthermore the consummation of man in the heavenly image (1 Cor 15:44–49). The personhood is particularly significant for the redemptive eschatology because covenant union and communion is predicated on it. The goal of redemption is to participate in the blessedness of the three Persons of the Trinity. The kingdom of heaven is the kingdom of the Son, whom the Father loves: "For he has rescued us from the dominion of darkness and brought us into the kingdom of the Son he loves" (Col 1:13). The union of the two natures in the Person of Christ is essential to the kingdom of heaven in which believers are to enjoy communion with the Father (John 18:36; Luke 17:21). The three Persons of the blessed Being is the final destination of redemption and the resting place of believers in Christ (Eph 2:6). The whole concept of covenant is predicated on the personhood of the bilateral parties. Hence, the human nature of Christ is not only

---

37. Song, *Theology and Piety*, 2.

for vicarious atonement, but more properly for union of God and man through the Person of Christ.

The mystical union of Christ and believers is not a direct union of God and man but union through the God-man (Matt 16:13; John 14:6, 20; 17:21, 23; Gal 3:20). Man cannot directly be united with God without a personal mediator who is both God and man. In this union, the humanity of Christ is not merely used to substitute believers for atonement but to bring them near to God for intimacy. In the new birth of the Spirit they are transformed into the heavenly image by being seated with Christ. He retained his human nature even after his work on the cross so that in his body he might ascend to the heavenly realms to approach God for and with believers (Heb 9:24). The use of his humanity did not end with his vicarious death but continues before God for intercession and intimacy. The former is to receive the righteousness of God through justifying faith but the latter is to sit next to God and rejoice. The Council at Chalcedon affirmed the hypostatic union of the two natures of Christ, which cannot be "divided, separated, mixed, nor confused."[38] They were constituted in such a way that he is not only the Savior but also the Last Adam—the eschatology of redemption. The work of Christ involves the two natures in such a way there is no conflict or contradiction within the Person: "Christ, in the work mediation, acts according to both natures, by each nature doing that which is proper to itself: yet, by reason of the unity of the person, that which is proper to one nature is sometimes in Scripture attributed to the person denominated by the other nature."[39] Christ obeyed the Father and earned the right to resurrection and the position next to the Father as the High Priest in the Melchizedek order (Heb 5:8–10; 6:19–20; 1 Tim 3:16). In his obedience, the divine nature did not violate the integrity of his human nature "with all the essential properties and common infirmities thereof, yet without sin."[40] He could not have truly obeyed and suffered as man if he had done so with the aid of divinity at his convenience (Heb 5:8): "We do not have a high priest who is unable to empathize with our weaknesses, but we have one who has been tempted in every way, just as we are—yet he did not sin" (Heb 4:15). Christ is now enthroned in heaven as the prophesied Messiah in the Davidic covenant, who is both divine and human (Acts 2:36; Rom 1:3–4). He is "the mystery that has been kept hidden for ages and generations, but is now disclosed to the saints" in order to execute the divine plan from eternity (Col 1:26). The blessed news of the gospel is that God has revealed to Gentiles "the glorious riches of this mystery, which is Christ in you, the hope of glory" (v. 27). The Old Covenant was but a copy and shadow of him until the full reality of his Person arrived in the fullness of this age to open up the redemptive heaven through his eternal priesthood (Heb 8:5; 10:1)

---

38. Chalcedonian Creed (451 AD).
39. Westminster Confession of Faith, 8.7.
40. Westminster Confession of Faith, 8.2.

The earthly ministry of Christ did not exhaust the mystery of God as he must "appear for us in God's presence" in heaven (Rom 8:34; Heb 9:24). In order to truly gauge the significance of the priestly work of Christ on earth, its antitype in heaven ought be the reference point (Heb 8:5; 9:24). The priestly work of Christ has often been linked only to his death on the cross as the ransom for sin but the priesthood of Melchizedek reaches into the heavenly sanctuary (Rom 3:10, 23; Heb 9:22, 26). God is both just and justifier of sinners through the Priest who simultaneously satisfied God's justice and love (John 3:16; Rom 3:26). This priestly work, however, consists of two parts: the first, sacrifice and the second, entrance into the inner sanctuary for intercession: "If he were on earth, he would not be a priest, for there are already men who offer the gifts prescribed by law" (Heb 8:4). Christ died on the cross as the paschal Lamb but his priestly work of intercession began when he entered the heavenly sanctuary. This is typified by the high priest of the Old Covenant, who prepares sacrifices at the altar outside of the tabernacle but whose work of intercession occurs after he enters the inner sanctuary of the tabernacle where he prays for Israel (Lev 16:1–22; Heb 9:1–12). The earthly work Christ finished at the altar of the cross must be brought into the inner sanctuary of heaven for reconciliation to begin to take effect: "For Christ did not enter a man-made sanctuary that was only a copy of the true one; he entered heaven itself, now to appear for us in God's presence" (Heb 9:24). The sacrifice at the cross is prepared "at the end of the ages" and the work of intercession in heaven is final and everlasting (Heb 9:26). Christ died his vicarious death on earth in order that he might execute the work of intercession before God in heaven. The immediacy of the resurrection after crucifixion (three days) was in order that his appearance in heaven may be immediate. With him seated next to God believers may boldly approach the throne, where they are declared righteous and receive grace to help in times of need (Rom 8:34–39; Heb 4:15–16).

The benefits of the Covenant of Grace thus flow from his priestly intercession in heaven logically prior to being applied to believers by the Spirit: "Praise be to the God and Father of our Lord Jesus Christ, who has blessed us in the heavenly realms with every spiritual blessing in Christ" (Eph 1:3; Rom 8:29). Believers have every spiritual blessing flow from heaven to them because they are united to the risen Christ and approach the throne of grace through him (Rom 8:32). In addition to the substitutionary atonement of the crucifixion, or more precisely through the soteric gift, the adoption of the Last Adam is achieved in the resurrection as the firstborn among believers (Rom 1:3–4; 8:15–17, 29). In Christ, the "redemptive plus" is the planned path to the eschatology of inheritance in the Father's kingdom (Rom 8:17; 1 John 4:16). The earthly work of his suffering is thus properly appreciated in light of the heavenly work of intercession and inheritance. The work on earth and in heaven joined together make the Covenant of Grace the gospel of the kingdom of heaven (Luke 16:16). It is called the "gospel of the kingdom" because the good news of Jesus Christ is redemptive-eschatological (Gen 2:18, 24; Jer 50:5; John 15:4–6). The boasting of the cross is actually boasting of the Person of Christ crucified on the cross rather than the cross itself (1 Cor 1:30–31; 2:2). The way of the cross is superior to the signs of Jews and the wisdom of the Greeks because it is of the Person of Christ, "in whom are hidden all the treasures of wisdom and knowledge" (1 Cor 1:24; Col 2:2). The work he finished on earth Christ brought into the sanctuary of heaven, where the mystery had been hidden for eternity in the secret will of the Father and the Son, but is now revealed at the closing of the ages and the opening of the age to come.

4.3 Union with Christ

In Christ

The union with Christ is expressed in the phrase "in Christ" and its theological significance is far, deep, and wide in view of what has already been said. In the Golden Chain of redemption, believers are predestined, called, justified, adopted, sanctified, and glorified *in* him (Rom 8:30). In the Old Covenant believers were not yet united with him in person since he was anticipated through types and figures. The incarnation of the Word is the long-awaited fulfillment of "God with us" as believers in union with him would soon be seated in the heavenly realms. The anticipation in the Old Covenant was not without progress, however, as the spiritual vision of Israel ever so gradually moved toward the eschatological hope. As the horizontal history moved forward, the vertical hope toward the covenant union heightened in proportion to increased revelations. In this progress, the newer revelations about the last days (or the "latter days") of the Messiah were gradually added for more clarity and intensity. The redemptive-eschatological hope was that all things in heaven and on earth would be united, ushering in the last days of this age through the Son (Heb 1:1–2).[41] This will mark "the end of the ages" and the beginning of the coming ages; the two ages overlap since Christ (Heb 9:26). The subjective *Ordo Salutis* is not detached from this historical shift but interpreted as part of the new order. The kingdom of heaven has forcefully advanced into the world from above preceding the application of redemption to individual believers (Matt 11:12).

The rite of baptism is defined in terms of participation into the historical crucifixion and resurrection of Christ (Rom 6:3–4).[42] The sacraments of the Covenant of Grace are the sign and seal of participation in the death and resurrection of Christ. The correlation of Christ *for* us and Christ *in* us is the most distinguishing feature of the eschatology of redemption (2 Cor 5:14–17). Ridderbos writes, "The declaration after 2 Cor. 5:14 is important because there is a clear shift from 'Christ for us' to 'Christ in/with us.'"[43] Since Christ, the cure of atonement and the tonic of the new

---

41. Ridderbos, *Paul*, 59.
42. Ridderbos, *Paul*, 59.
43. Ridderbos, *Paul*, 60.

CHRIST AND ESCHATOLOGY

creation have been conjoined through union with him, making the work redemptive and eschatological. Luther understood "in Christ" as justification by faith in Christ, but Calvin understood it as mystical union with him through the Spirit. This union includes and guarantees regeneration, justification, sanctification, adoption, and even glorification in the heavenly image of man. Union with the risen Christ means a fundamental shift in the order of things as earth and heaven have now come under his reign (Eph 1:10; 21). The eschatological element of "in Christ" brings a wider perspective to the interpretation of redemptive history and redemption itself.

The union with Christ integrates the *Ordo Salutis* and *Historia Salutis*, the subjective and objective aspects of redemption, and produces the eschatology of redemption. Much of the controversy in the areas of law, justification, covenant, ethics, and kingdom arise from separation or confusion of the two aspects of redemption. The historical type/fulfillment distinction belongs to the latter whereas the justification/sanctification distinction belongs to the former. The recent debate on the New Perspective of Paul on the law and justification is a case in point, as well as the debate on the conditionality in the Mosaic law. These are examples of the failure to distinguish personal soterics and the eschatological outlook of redemptive history. In any case, the final synthesis of the two categories in redemption does not occur until they meet in Christ's death and resurrection. Old Covenant believers received in advance the righteousness of Christ by faith through types, shadows, and prophecies. Yet they could not have known in advance the full extent of the mystery of Christ, which can only be known in the actual union with him. Theirs was the copy and image of the heavenly reality but the actual union with that reality was yet to arrive (Heb 8:5). A soteric knowledge and justifying faith are common to both covenants, but the eschatological knowledge of union with Christ was largely hidden in the Old. The following verse explains the redemptive-eschatological difference: "These were all commanded for their faith, yet none of them received what had been promised. God had planned something better for us so that only together with us would they be made perfect" (Heb 11:39–40).

The discontinuity of the New from the Old mainly lies in the realm of the *Historia Salutis*, especially in the redemptive eschatology. The perspective should be not only horizontal, between the shadow and the reality, but vertical, between earth and heaven. The issue is not just salvific but historical in that all previous types have been fulfilled (horizontally and vertically) by union with the crucified and risen Christ. In redemption, the natural is transformed into the supernatural. The church of the heavenly kingdom ruled by Christ is superior to Israel of the earthly kingdom ruled by Moses. In Christ, therefore, arrived the provisional kingdom of heaven echoed by Christ himself, "the kingdom of God is within [among] you" (Luke 17:21). Christ himself *is* the kingdom and anyone in Christ has entered the kingdom through the new birth in the Spirit (John 3:5). Sometimes Christ is said to be "in them" while other times they are said to be "in Christ," but both are both true (Gal 2:20; 2 Cor 5:17).

In union with Christ, the historical and the personal aspects of salvation have been joined to a degree never before experienced in the old administration of the law (Eph 2:6). As the two perspectives are merged through union with Christ, the soteric aspect is shaped by the eschatological element in ways Old Covenant believers could not have foreknown. In Christ, the future has arrived in advance and heaven is no longer merely an anticipation in hope but a present reality with a foretaste of its glory. The gospel in Christ is taken to a level unknown to the Old Covenant: "the good news of the kingdom of God is being preached, and everyone is forcing his way into it" (Luke 16:16). In Christ, the soteric order of salvation is not even possible to define apart from the new and supernatural order of creation (2 Cor 5:17).

Calvin viewed union with Christ as one of the most important teachings in the Scriptures, and John Murray echoed the sentiment: "There is nothing more central and basic than the union and fellowship with Christ."[44] The union with Christ means personal participation into the culmination of the history of redemption through baptism into his suffering and resurrection.[45] It is the final step, the once-for-all perfection of the promise that Old Covenant believers looked forward to (Heb 11:39–40). "It is finished," as Jesus said on the cross, in both horizontal and vertical senses: "And by that will, we have been made holy through the sacrifice of the body of Jesus Christ once for all" (Heb 10:10); "The death he died, he died to sin once for all; but the life he lives, he lives to God" (Rom 6:10). In this finished work, heaven and earth are unified; the Old Covenant is fulfilled by the New; believers are united with the risen Lord (John 19:30; Eph 1:10; Col 1:20). In humiliation Christ atones, but in exaltation he reigns (Acts 2:36; Col 1:18–20). There is a profound mixture of rectitude and perfection in this union: "In the same way, count yourselves dead to sin but alive to God in Christ Jesus. Therefore, do not let sin reign in your mortal body so that you obey its evil desires" (Rom 6:11–12). The exaltation is a vertical perfection that did more than fulfill Old Covenant prophecies in the horizontal direction by bringing the future into the present. Thus, the proclamations "if anyone is in Christ" and "Christ lives in me" mean the spatial movement from the earthly to the heavenly realms beyond personal experience of conversion (2 Cor 5:17; Gal 2:20). The vertical progress toward the risen Christ is the goal of redemptive history, and if not for this union the prior history would have been no more than a mere extension of time on earth. The progress in redemptive history is justified if it would one day reach the last days in the vertical as well as the horizontal sense, and Old Covenant believers would then have been meaningful participants in this progress (Heb 11:39–40).

---

44. Murray, *Redemption Accomplished and Applied*, 161.
45. Murray, *Redemption Accomplished and Applied*, 161.

Baptism in Christ

In the Covenant of Grace, the sacraments of circumcision and baptism are the sign and seal of God's election and covenant faithfulness. These can be traced back to the Counsel of Peace between the Father and the Son. The sacraments themselves are not so much the means of justification as they are the means of grace flowing out of the Eternal Covenant. As the sign and seal, the means of grace represent the Father's election in the Son and its execution in history through the Covenant of Grace. They point to the covenant faithfulness of the three Persons of the blessed Being, now actualized through Christ's crucifixion and resurrection. The chosen in the Son are given the gift of faith through the rebirth of the Spirit and given to the Son as the reward of his obedience (John 17:4–6; Rom 6:3–5). The formal cause of this covenant transaction is God's election in the *Pactum Salutis,* and the instrumental cause is believers' faith. In other words, the focus of the sacraments is the faithfulness of God rather than the faith of recipients. It is true that the rite of baptism is tied to the profession of faith in adults but not infants, for it signifies the Giver rather than the given of the covenant blessing. Faith is the instrumental, not the efficient, cause in this covenant transaction:

> In him you were also circumcised with a circumcision not performed by human hands. Your whole self ruled by the flesh was put off when you were circumcised by Christ, having been buried with him in baptism, in which you were also raised with him through your faith in the working of God, who raised him from the dead. (Col 2:11–12)

The crux of the apostle's argument lies in the phrase "through your faith in the working of God" (v. 12). It is God who works and is the efficient cause of redemption, and in this sense faith cannot be a formal condition of the sacrament of baptism. The circumcision in the Abrahamic covenant is thus fulfilled by the baptism in New Covenant—"circumcision" by Christ (Heb 11:39–40). The old form of shedding blood in circumcision is typical of the new form in the shedding of blood on the cross. The putting off the flesh in circumcision is fulfilled in the putting off the old self in baptism: "put off your old self" and "to put on the new self, created to like God in true righteousness and holiness" (Eph 4:22–24). But both forms are the sign and seal of the same the Covenant of Grace, which is the historical outworking of the Covenant of Redemption. In view of these considerations, the doctrine of believer's baptism (credo-baptism) does not account for the covenant as the means of execution of the *Pactum Salutis* by the Trinity, and is at odds with the covenant-eschatological view of redemptive history.

The unity of the Covenant of Grace lies in the horizontal fulfillment of types and prophecies but more so in the vertical fruition of the Covenant of Redemption: "In love he predestined us to be adopted as his sons through Jesus Christ, in accordance with his pleasure and will—to the praise of his glorious grace, which he has freely given us in the One he loves" (Eph 1:5–6). In the Old Covenant the knowledge of Christ was *mediate* through types and shadows whereas in the New Covenant it is *immediate* in the Person and work of Christ. The former is the order of Aaron, but the latter is the order of Melchizedek. As with Adam in nature, the goal of the covenant knowledge of God in redemption is the same in substance but superior (Gen 4:1; Jer 31:31–34). Isaiah prophesied, "the earth will be filled with the knowledge of the Lord as the waters cover the sea" and this eschatological vision is fulfilled in Christ (Isa 11:9; John 17:3). To know God is to be near God: "And God raised us up with Christ and seated us with him in the heavenly realms in Christ Jesus" (Eph 2:6). The different expressions of the Covenant of Grace differ in intimacy and spatial proximity to God but the vertical unity remains unchanged. The New Covenant fulfilled all previous covenants, and accordingly the kingdom of heaven has arrived with the messianic King (Luke 17:21). The traditional emphasis in covenant theology has been somewhat limited to the unity of various covenants finally fulfilled in the New Covenant. The unity of Jews and Gentiles, in particular, brings focus to the one new man formed in Christ (Eph 2:15). But as long as the purview of the covenant history remains within the horizontal development alone, the soteric-eschatological significance of covenant will not receive its due attention. As a result, the historical distinction of the New Covenant from the Old adds little to the vertical side of redemption. The difference between the earlier days, when God spoke through prophets, and the last days, when God speaks in the Son, is spatial as well as chronological (Eph 1:21; Heb 1:2).

Christ in Us

In Christ, the objective work accomplished by him becomes efficient in the subjective appropriation of it by believers through the work of the Spirit. The objective work done outside of believers, "Christ for us," applies to all periods under the Covenant of Grace on account of the election in Christ (Eph 1:4). But Old Covenant believers were unable to actually unite with the incarnate Christ but received only the benefits of his work through shadow of the law, types, and prophecies (Heb 10:1). Christ was *for* them in the objective sense, but he was not *in* them in the subjective sense of the actual union. The Word was yet to become flesh among them, yet to be crucified and risen, which would mark a significant difference between the two periods (John 1:14; Heb 11:39–40). The union "in Christ" is the redemptive-eschatological link between the *Historia* and *Ordo Salutis*. "Christ for us" is combined into "Christ in us" by the Spirit, rendering justification and sanctification inseparable (Rom 8:39; 2 Cor 5:14–17). In order for this mystery to be actualized, the Son of God had to break into history in person and be "among us." The weakness of the Old Covenant did not lie in the substance of the covenant but in the administration under the law (Heb 8:5). They looked forward to Christ from a distance: "Your father Abraham rejoiced at the thought of seeing my day; he saw it and was glad" (John 8:56). They were also saved by the Covenant of Grace but the historical disadvantage significantly limited the Old Covenant in religious and ethical tonic (Jer 31:31–34; 2 Cor 3:3–11). The Old Covenant period has yet to witness the level of violent clash the kingdom would have to withstand in the all-out attack of this dark world: "From the days of John the Baptist until now, the kingdom of heaven has been subjected to violence . . ." (Matt 11:12–13). In the days of the law and prophets the clash was more national and figurative, but in the days of Christ it became universal and eschatological (Eph 6:10–18). Seated in the heavenly realms with Christ and under his reign, believers engage in the cosmic battle against the kingdom of darkness (Col 1:13; 3:1–5). The clash triggered by the intrusion of the kingdom from above is now more intensified than it has ever been in scope and degree. As a result of the spatial and cosmic change, believers are raised and seated next to God, not only converted but made otherworldly (Eph 2:6; John 8:36).

John the Baptist was a man of great stature and authority by Old Covenant standards but considered to be the least in the kingdom of heaven; it refers to the greatness of the kingdom rather than inferiority of the Baptist (Matt 11:11; 2 Cor 5:17). Personal greatness was acknowledged to some measure in the Old Covenant but in Christ authority is no longer attributed to man but to the King and his kingdom, which far outweigh the greatness of man. The worth of any man must be pitched on the foundation of the kingdom in heaven rather than his own greatness: "What can the righteous do when the foundations are being destroyed? The LORD is in his holy temple; the LORD is on his heavenly throne. He observes the sons of men; his eyes examine them" (Ps 11:3–4). In the subjective realm, greatness may be relative to individual faith or performance but in the objective realm, it is attributed to the eschatological kingdom irrespective of the seated position (Matt 20:21–28). The least in the kingdom is still greater because his worth is estimated by the King he is seated with and the kingdom he is the coheir of. He is the greatest who is in Christ and Christ in him because that union signifies something even greater: "At the highest level, the union with Christ is likened to the union within the Triune God."[46] In Christ, believers are united with the blessed Father and gaze into his glory with the Son, and Old Covenant members could have only hoped for this (John 17:21–24). As the fulfillment of the Counsel of Peace, they have entered the fellowship of the blessed Trinity: "But as for me, it is good to be near God. I have made the Sovereign LORD my refuge; I will tell of all your deeds" (Ps 73:28).

Structure of Redemptive History

On the cross Jesus accomplished two things: he completed the Eternal Covenant and fulfilled the Old Covenant (Luke 24:44; John 19:30).[47] The fulfillment would have been sufficient for the Old Covenant but not without the completion (*tetelestai*) of the

---

46. Murray, *Redemption Accomplished and Applied*, 168.
47. Vos, *Redemptive History*, 354.

Eternal Covenant with the Father. Furthermore, even the Old Covenant is more than a mere shadow of the New but a copy and image of the things in heaven (Heb 8:5). The substantial unity and continuity of the two administrations in the Covenant of Grace is in fact preserved by the vertical element. On the horizontal side, discrepancy is significant between the two periods of being under the law and under the gospel. The unity, then, really stems from the vertical union of heaven and earth, held together by the Eternal Counsel and realized by Christ's death and resurrection. What Christ ratified on the cross by "God's own blood" fulfilled the Old Covenant but also finished the Eternal Counsel (Acts 20:28; Heb 13:20). There is a spatial and supernatural element associated with the inaugurated last days beside the redemptive part in atonement (Gal 1:14; 4:4; 6:14–15): "But he has appeared once for all at the culmination of the ages to do away with sin by the sacrifice of himself" (Heb 9:26). What is crucified on the cross is the old order of the world, and resurrected is the new and eternal order (Gal 6:14–15).

In the progress of revelation, the infancy of the Old Covenant is an integral part of the growth toward the adulthood in the New. It is not a mere shadow or dirty bathwater to be discarded afterwards; the form (guardian) is outdated but its substance (son) remains the same. The childhood under the tutelage of the law could not fully contain the adulthood under the Son, who arrived with the closing of this age (Mark 1:15; Gal 4:4; Heb 1:1–2; 11:40). The redemptive-eschatological knowledge during the progress would have been proportional to the amount and clarity of revelation available at a particular phase in history. A mature form of knowledge cannot prematurely be forced into the infancy of revelation without violating the level of spiritual maturity during that period. The knowledge of the Trinity or the two natures of Christ, for instance, would have been in hidden forms and premature in the early stages of revelation. The messianic kingdom of Christ was not clearly revealed until the time of the Davidic covenant, when prophecies concerning the "anointed one" first began to appear (Ps 18:50). The "offspring" promised in the proto-gospel would not have been immediately recognized as a prophecy about the messianic king akin to the Davidic sense (Gen 3:15).

The notions of type and antitype refer to the prophecies of the Old Covenant and their fulfillment in the New Covenant. The type in "the law, the prophets and the psalms" would be fulfilled by the antitype in the Person and work of Christ (Luke 24:44). A redemptive-eschatological disparity exists between the shadow and the reality despite their unity and continuity in substance (Heb 8:5; 10:1). Due to the clarity and quality of revelation, the reality far outweighs the shadow. In these last days of the fulfillment, God speaks through the incarnate Son, superseding all previous revelations. The mystery of God hidden for ages is now revealed through the Son, so much so that it is no longer just a matter of the old and the new but of earth and heaven. It was impossible for the shadow (smaller) to contain the reality (bigger) though the reverse is possible. Vos likened the Old Covenant to that of a cicada cricket, known as "the prophet of summer," and the New Covenant to the reality of summer itself.[48] A cicada cricket is a part of the summer but cannot be made equal to, much less substitute for, the summer. The reality is infinitely superior to the shadow in that without it the latter loses its very existence. A cicada cricket, too, is an image of heaven in the vertical sense, but nevertheless far inferior to the summer in the horizontal sense. The realities of the new order Christ brings could not have been substituted by the Old Covenant but only prefigured and foretold from a distance. If the Old Covenant could have fully contained the realities of the New Covenant, the Word made flesh would have been redundant. The New can sufficiently contain the Old but not vice versa, seen from the perspective of growth and progress. The soteric part can be found in the Old Covenant by means of the animal sacrifices and other types, but the eschatological reality can only be found in the Person of Christ. The soteric is uniformly governed by the Covenant of Grace throughout history, but the redemptive-eschatological is achieved only by the actual coming of the Son in person.

The greatness of the mystery is not the cricket in the summer but the summer in the cricket. The summer foretold by the cricket has not only arrived but actually united with the cricket, and lives in it. The shadow of the Old is fulfilled by the reality of the New but with it heaven and earth are also united. The vertical-spatial union in addition to the horizontal-time fulfillment has been achieved: "These were all commanded for their faith, yet none of them received what had been promised. God had planned something better for us so that only together with us would they be made perfect" (Heb 11:39). The soteric substitution and the eschatological union are both achieved when the summer entered the cricket. Augustine of Hippo also espoused the principle that the New is hidden in the Old, and the Old is revealed by the New.[49] But even this explanation but does not completely capture the vertical-spatial element of the union. There is far more to this union in the redemptive-eschatological sense than revelation of what had been hidden in the Old Covenant. It is a shift from one age to another age, or the presence of the future, and union of heaven and earth (Eph 1:10): "There God exalted him to the highest place and gave him the name that is above every name, that at the name of Jesus every knee should bow, in heaven and on earth and under earth, and every tongue acknowledge that Jesus Christ is Lord, to the glory of God the Father" (Phil 2:9–11). In short, this means the fulfillment of the long-awaited covenant vision, "God with us." The mystery of God that was hidden from eternity is now revealed in the mystical union of God and man through the Messiah (Col 2:2). The redemption in Christ is taken to a new level with the splendor and glory of the summer entering a lowly cicada cricket (Matt 13:31–33; Gal 2:20). Mankind fell short of God's glory and sunk to the level of a "worm" but God nevertheless enters those in Christ who repent and believe (Ps 22:6; Job 25:4–6; Rom 3:23; Jer 50:5). Out of his lovingkindness, God sent his Son to sinners, who cry out, "I am a worm and not

---

48. Vos, *Redemptive History*, 354.
49. Augustine, *Anti-Pelagian Writings*, 27, xv.

a man," so that they may be seated with him in the heavenly glory as coheirs of his kingdom (Rom 8:17, 29; Eph 1:4; 2:6).

4.4 Structure of Eschatology

Judaism and New Testament

History is divided into BC and AD but Christ represents more than a time shift from one period to another but a spatial transition from earth to heaven, from this age to the coming age (Eph 1:21). The transition from a horizontal plane in time to a vertical-spatial plane is one of the most striking features of Pauline eschatology.[50] Oscar Cullman similarly divides the biblical timeline as follows: "The timeline in the Bible is divided into three parts. The time before the Creation, the time from the Creation to Parousia, and the time after Parousia."[51] He then raises the question as to where is the precise location of the "mid-point" of history in the second part of this timeline. The mid-point in the time line between creation and Parousia is an important question in biblical eschatology because it dissects history into the eschatological before and after. It marks the point when the last days of this age are set in motion and God will pour out his Spirit for the church in full measure (Acts 2:17; Joel 2:28). The vertical-spatial part is particularly tied to the resurrection of the Messiah and his everlasting kingdom in the line of King David.

In Judaism, Cullman notes, the decisive shift in history takes place with the arrival of the Messiah and the eternal kingdom on earth. The decisive mid-point in the second stage of the timeline is based on the assumption that the Messiah will appear once and establish the kingdom on earth.[52] It is a linear concept of time since the messianic kingdom he establishes will be on earth and in history. Such a hope spilled over into the Jews at the time of Jesus as a great anticipation for the messianic kingdom was boiling up in them in part due to the Roman occupation (John 4:25; Acts 1:6). The redemptive-eschatological concept of time in the New Testament does not coalesce with the Jewish view of history or with its timeline. This is so because the Messiah appears not once but twice to establish his kingdom. The crucified and risen Jesus has been declared as the Messiah and Lord as promised in the Davidic covenant and he will reappear at the Parousia to consummate the kingdom (Acts 2:36; 1 Cor 15:24). In this new timeline, the decisive mid-point of history is not the Parousia but when he is declared as the Messiah and Lord. The Messiah comes in two successive stages so his reign will also begin and complete in two stages.

The semi-eschatological shift in history has already taken place when Jesus was declared as Christ and Lord. And the union with the exalted Christ meant that

---

50. Vos, *Pauline Eschatology*, 38.
51. Cullman, *Christ and Time*, 81.
52. Cullman, *Christ and Time*, 81.

believers have already been moved from the earthly to the heavenly realms (Eph 2:6). The new order of the age has begun after "the fullness of time" of this age, and the kingdom of God has come near so that all men are told to repent and believe (Mark 1:15). Unlike Judaism, therefore, the coming of the Messiah in the New Testament unfolds in two successive stages, the first as suffering servant and the second as victorious king.[53] The first coming is the critical mid-point of history in the redemptive-eschatological point of view because all things are essentially unified in him (Rom 8:30; Eph 1:3–14; Col 1:16–20). The eschatology of nature and the eschatology of redemption are now all provisionally achieved in Christ until they are delivered to the Father (1 Cor 15:24). The Counsel of Peace has been accomplished and it is so perfectly finished that not even one will be lost (John 18:9). The bodily resurrection of Christ, in particular, marks the cosmic shift—so central to the structure of Pauline eschatology.[54] Christ's resurrection meant transition from death to life, but also from the earthly to the heavenly realms, inaugurating the semi-eschatological era. The decisive events of Christ ushered in the last days of this evil age and the first days of the coming age, visibly manifested by the outpouring of the Spirit (Acts 1:6–8; 2:17). The provisional union of heaven and earth in Christ renders the redemptive eschatology of the New Testament different from the Jewish version of the kingdom, which never really grasped the notions of a servant king or suffering Messiah (Isa 53:1–12).

Time, Space, Being

The coming of the kingdom of heaven was preceded by "the fullness of time" (Mark 1:15). The appearance of the Messiah in history meant a radical breach with the previous age and the introduction of his reign as the Lord (Acts 2:36). A qualitative change of time, rather than a linear succession, took place in the resurrection of the Messiah to heaven. The "redemptive heaven" that Christ and believers entered is called "the kingdom," "the things above," or "the age to come."[55] With the end (fullness) of the previous time, a new time zone of the redemptive heaven started in Christ. Anyone who is in Christ begins to live in the new time zone or the schema of new creation (2 Cor 5:17). With the departure of the Messiah into heaven, where he rules "in this age and the age to come," believers begin to live in the two ages contemporaneously (Gal 1:4; Eph 1:21). The overlaying of the two ages in the semi-eschatological period is sometimes referred to as the already-but-not-yet kingdom that will be handed over to the Father at the Parousia (1 Cor 15:24). The shift in time concept, then, signals a shift from the pattern of this world (*kosmos*) to another pattern of the age to come:

---

53. Cullman, *Christ and Time*, 81.
54. Vos, *Pauline Eschatology*, 38.
55. Vos, *Pauline Eschatology*, 40.

> The close association between aion and kosmos compels the same conclusion, for of the kosmos it is said, I Cor. vii. 31 that its *schema* passes away: it passes away to make room for another *schema*. "The ends of the aions" have come upon believers, I Cor. x. 11. As will be afterwards shown the "pleroma too chronoo," "the fullness of time" has nothing to do in the first place with the idea of "ripeness of time"; it designates the arrival of the present dispensation of time at its predetermined goal of fulfillment through the appearance of the Messiah, Gal. iv. 4; cp. Eph. i. 10. Thus understood it signifies the immediate transition from chronos to something else.[56]

That "something else" is the age to come, the kingdom of God, where believers are seated with Christ through the rebirth in the Spirit (John 3:5). They are "in heaven" in the redemptive sense, and begin to live according the new pattern of the kingdom of God in a new definition of time. The age to come has intruded this age and the kingdom of heaven is a now present force in the war against the kingdom of darkness (Matt 11:12; Luke 16:16; 17:21). Faith and repentance, in particular, are the mark of the kingdom versus the flesh (*sarx*) governing this evil age (Mark 1:15). The new birth in the Spirit is personal regeneration but also an entrance into the new time of the age to come (John 3:5; Eph 2:6). It is the redemptive time in which the believer is recreated and renewed inwardly by the new order of heaven. Thus, believers contemporaneously exists in two opposing worlds: "Therefore we do not lose heart. Though outwardly we are wasting away, yet inwardly we are being renewed day by day" (2 Cor 4:16). The sanctification of believers is not just personal but aeonic: "Save the time [*kairos*], the hour [*chronos*] is evil" (Eph 5:16). Sometimes the two time concepts of *kairos* and *chronos* are used comparatively as representatives of the two ages of heaven and earth. But they are also used interchangeably, and the context determines the usage (Mark 1:15; 1 Cor 10:11; 2 Cor 6:2). In any case, Wright described the non-linear nature of the time concept in New Testament eschatology as follows: "What we are looking for is a different kind of time, not a change in time but a change of time itself."[57]

By being raised with Christ believers "inwardly" experience the newness of the heavenly time though "outwardly" they are bound by the corruption of the earthly time of this age (2 Cor 4:16). Insofar as the inner man is concerned, they have "crossed over from death to life" and their life eternal is hidden in God (John 5:25; 17:21–24; Col 3:1–4). Yet, the outer man is still under the dominion of this age, hence believers are exhorted to "continue to work out your salvation with fear and trembling..." (Phil 2:12). In Christ, however, the believer truly begins to live in the presence of God in "real time" before the throne of grace (Heb 4:15–16). In the schema of *kairos*, as it were, "he is a new creation," even though he is on a temporal journey through the horizontal time of *chronos* (1 Cor 15:19). The persistence and perseverance of believers on earth do not depend on the strength of their faith or piety but on the supernatural life and

---

56. Vos, *Pauline Eschatology*, 26.
57. Wright, *Paul and Faithfulness of God*, 1473.

energy from the "things above." They must set their minds "not on earthly things" and "put to death the earthly nature" (Col 3:2, 5). In the redemptive eschatology, there is the foundational support from those things above that strengthens personal faith to withstand the onslaught of spiritual forces from this age (Eph 6:10–18).

During the interim period until the Parousia, the vertical time in Christ is more significant for the church than the flow of time in the horizontal direction. The wait of the church subsequent to the D-Day of Christ is not merely an earthly extension of the previous time but a redemptive time of *kairos* within the final victory in Christ. Old Covenant believers looked forward to the time in Christ but New Covenant believers live in it as they foretaste the victory of heaven in advance (Rom 8:34–37; Heb 11:39–40). The weakness of the Israelites was not merely due to their personal shortcomings but also due to the inferiority of their time (age), which has yet to reach its fullness (Gal 4:4). The "last days" in the New Testament thus denotes the fullness of time rather than the terminus of history, with corresponding fullness of the new life (John 10:10). The fullness of life is effective immediately by being united into the death and resurrection of Christ: "I am the resurrection and the life. The one who believes in me will live, even though they die; and whoever lives by believing in me will never die. Do you believe this?" (John 11:25–26). Despite the cross-bearing on earth, believers can foretaste the righteousness, peace, and joy of the kingdom because they live on the higher plane of the age to come (Rom 14:17). In Christ, they will no more be raised in the future than they have already been raised and seated next to the Father with him.

The shift in time actually means a shift into the redemptive space called heaven. The space of the heavenly realms is given expression in such actions as "raised," "set your mind on things above," and "seated" in Christ (Eph 2:6; Col 3:1). These are the outcome of the "fulfillment of the ages" by the appearance of the Messiah, when the space of redemptive heaven opened up for believers to enter with him. The inner man is seated with Christ in the heavenly realms and "renewed day by day," while the outer man remains in this age with the inevitable reality of "wasting away" in time (2 Cor 4:16). The union of believers into Christ's resurrection is not a figure of speech but a real ascension to the new schema of the heavenly regions (Rom 6:4; Col 3:1). The crucified Christ resurrected in body and entered heaven to appear before God and to intercede in behalf of believers seated with him (Heb 9:12, 24). The semi-eschatological state is created by the ascension of the Messiah into the heavenly regions to reign as the Lord (John 3:5; Rom 6:3–5).

Some define the kingdom of God solely as a "reign of God" without considering the vertical ascension at present. Despite Christ's resurrection and a change of the schema to the coming age, the spatial element is postponed to the Parousia. Such a view fails to fully capture the significance of resurrection at present and the union with the risen Lord. The heavenly regions is a clear and present reality for those united into his resurrection, officially marking the closure of this age and inauguration of the next age:

> You have not come to a mountain that can be touched ... But you have come to Mount Zion, to the city of the living God, the heavenly Jerusalem. You have come to thousands upon thousands of angels in joyful assembly, to the church of the firstborn, whose names are written in heaven. You have come to God ... (Heb 12:18–24)

The change of *schema* from the earthly to the heavenly, in the redemptive sense, corresponds to the change of time from this age to the coming age. But the new creation in Christ is expected to effectuate a radical transformation in the objective sphere as well as in the personal life. In Christ, believers are not just heavenly citizens in name but in presence as they have been transferred from one dominion to another (Phil 3:20; Col 1:13). They do not have to wait until the Parousia to begin to experience life eternal and the supernatural because they have entered its spatial territory by faith (2 Cor 5:7). The new creation through union with Christ is the primary work of the Spirit[58]; it brings about a new world order as the foundation of personal faith and ethics in the subjective experience of the believer. Christ has first entered the heavenly sanctuary and approached God so that believers may approach the throne of grace to find help in times of their personal need (Rom 8:34; Heb 9:24):

> There has been created a totally new environment, or, more accurately speaking, a totally new world, in which the person spoken of is an inhabitant and participator. It is not in the first place the interiority of the subject that has undergone the change, although that, of course, is not to be excluded. The whole surrounding world has assumed a new aspect and complexion.[59]

Biblical history is redemptive-eschatological by definition, progressing toward the great shift at the mid-point where time and space receive new meaning in Christ.[60] The spatial overlay of heaven and earth is part of the mystery of Christ, and the intrusion of heaven has transformed faith and life of believers in ways never seen before. Their hearts and minds have been profoundly altered by the new order of heaven and earth so that they are given the power and resources to put to death the earthly parts (Matt 5:29–30; Col 3:5). If believers had been saved but were still of this world, they would be left to personal resources to deal with the forces of darkness on earth without a foundation from above. But the psalmist asks, "When the foundations are being destroyed, what can the righteous do?" (Ps 11:3). The rebirth in the Spirit, therefore, is a redemptive-eschatological event that involves a spatial shift to the heavenly

---

58. Calvin, *Institutes*, book III.[q which vol? cited differently than elsewhere]
59. Vos, *Pauline Eschatology*, 47.
60. Vos, *Pauline Eschatology*, 37.

regions as well as a soteric deliverance from sin.⁶¹ It is a movement from one region to another region on a cosmic level: "For he has rescued us from the dominion of darkness and brought us into the kingdom of the Son he loves . . ." (Col 1:13). The upward lift to where Christ is seated widens their vision to capture the full scale of the cosmos renewed by Christ and his reign. The epic battle in the spiritual realms against Satan's stronghold needs the new authority in heaven and earth (Matt 28:18): "For our struggle is not against flesh and blood, but against the rulers, against the authorities, against the powers of this dark world and against the spiritual forces of evil in the heavenly realms" (Eph 6:12). The vision of "Jacob's ladder" in which heaven and earth are bridged is finally fulfilled so that believers may pray God's will be done on earth as in heaven (Gen 28:12; Matt 6:10). The kingdom of Christ in this semi-eschatological era is perhaps best characterized by its radical antithesis to the dominion of this age, called "these last days" (John 18:36; Gal 1:4; Heb 1:2).

The division of earth and heaven, temporal and eternal, natural and supernatural began in creation as a type of the redemptive-eschatology in Christ. Created in God's image, man desires to be near God and possesses innate attributes to do so in life eternal (Gen 3:8; Rev 2:7). The redemptive aspect deals with rectitude of sin but eschatology is about the nearness to God unfulfilled by Adam. In Pauline eschatology, believers come near to God immediately upon their regeneration, rendering the soteric and the supernatural aspects combined into one (Rom 8:30; 1 Cor 1:30; Heb 4:16; 9:24). The spatial ascension to the heavenly realms is not a soul/body dualism, however, but a provisional union of heaven and earth through Christ.⁶² It is not a psychosomatic division but the fulfilment of the Covenant of Redemption. The apostle Paul condemned the Gnostic heresy in the strongest words possible and rejected a soul/body dualism (1 Cor 15:12). For him, redemption is the fulfillment of nature rather than the denial of it. The Golden Chain of the *Ordo Salutis* does not divide soul from body though it may be viewed in the semi-eschatological already-but-not-yet form. Salvation is never given in piecemeal fashion, i.e., half on earth and half in heaven, for the whole salvation is given at once in union with Christ. The unity of salvation despite the logical distinction in order is held together by the spatial ascension to the heavenly realms upon their union with Christ. The spatial categories of "above" and "below" in Paul are not a dualism of soul and body, but a semi-eschatological language appropriate for the present significance of resurrection (Col 3:1–4).⁶³ This provisional union of "above" and "below" in Christ are not to be prematurely collapsed or pulled apart until the eschatological kingdom of the Father (1 Cor 15:24). In a true and otherworldly sense, believers are seated in the heavenly realms as the eternal foundation of their earthly existence, or the supernatural foundation of their temporal life. The Father has "blessed us in the heavenly realms with every spiritual blessing in Christ" (Eph 1:3).

61. Vos, *Pauline Eschatology*, 38.
62. Wright, *Paul*, 609.
63. Horton, *Covenant and Eschatology*, 29, 39.

Eschatology by nature does not divide spirit and body, but places them together in the kingdom of Christ in order that God's will may be done on earth as in heaven. In this sense, "Biblical eschatology is not embarrassed by chronos and the historical time."[64]

The third category of change in union with the risen Christ is the definition of life and death, and the correlate meaning of existence. In the *chronos* time zone on earth, death is the decisive event that ends man's physical existence according to the terms of the Covenant of Works (Gen 2:17). The realm of the dead is the unknown side of man's existence, and a total separation from life in the earthly realms. In the traditional view, eschatology deals with the end of the world as mankind knows it. For believers, death will be overcome by their bodily resurrection at the Parousia, when immortality also begins. This is how Martha responded to Jesus when she was told that her brother Lazarus will live: "Martha answered, 'I know he will rise again in the resurrection at the last day'" (John 11:24). In other words, she believed that death will dictate man until "the resurrection at the last day." In the new view of resurrection, however, death and life are defined by the new and eternal order of creation for "anyone who is in Christ." The matter is not postponed to the future but immediately made relevant at present and Jesus defines it in the present tense: "whoever lives and believes in me will never die" (vv. 25–26). In Christ, death no longer has mastery over believers, in present or future, because the "sting" of death is taken out by the triumph of his resurrection (1 Cor 15:55–57).

Life eternal, therefore, is not just an extension of physical life (*psyche*) on earth but an intrusion of the new and eternal life (*zoe*) from heaven (John 6:47). In the eschatology of paradise, death was never intended to be a natural part of the creation, hence body and spirit were a unified whole. They are separated temporarily by sin and death, but they will eventually be unified in the new paradise (1 Cor 15:48–49, 55). The semi-eschatological structure of the two ages in the New Testament means that believers now exist as the "inward" and the "outward" man (2 Cor 4:16). The decisive element in this new order of existence is not death but resurrection because the risen Christ became the "life-giving Spirit" in believers (1 Cor 15:45). In him, believers are immediately brought into the heavenly state of life regardless of their outward state of being, which wastes away in time (2 Cor 5:17; Gal 2:20). Conversely, those that are outside of Christ still belong to this evil age, and they are considered dead even if outwardly remain alive (Eph 2:1). The line between life and death as mankind knows them is erased in Christ, for it is decided no longer by the time category of earth but by the spatial category of heaven. Paul's view of life and death is now redefined by the eschatological perspective in Christ:

> I eagerly expect and hope that I will in no way be ashamed, but will have sufficient courage so that now as always Christ will be exalted in my body, whether by life or by death. For to me, to live is Christ and to die is gain. If I

---

64. Horton, *Covenant and Eschatology*, 41.

am to go on living in the body, this will mean fruitful labor for me. Yet what shall I choose? I do not know! I am torn between to the two: I desire to depart and be with Christ, which is better by far ... (Phil 1:20–23)

The Old Testament view of the intermediate state of death was not as optimistic as that of the New Testament, relatively speaking. It was premature to know in detail the eschatological implications of Christ for he had not yet come in person. During the pre-messianic times believers could not profess in the same way as Paul did about death and life. The lack of revelation rendered them at best uncertain about the realm of the dead and despairing at the prospect of death: "On the whole it must be said that the general outlook on death was a dismal one ... there was something of a high degree of gloom about it. While falling short of despair, it remained an even farther distance from positive joy than from despair."[65] The realm of the dead, the grave (*Sheol*), was a place to go down rather than go up: "But Jacob said, 'My son will not go down there with you; his brother is dead and he is the only one left. If harm comes to him on the journey you are taking, you will bring my gray head down to the grave in sorrow'" (Gen 42:38). In contrast, New Covenant believers have redefined life and death with greater optimism because God now speaks directly through his Son (Heb 1:1–3). There is a striking disparity in the high optimism with regard to death in Christ: "If we live, we live for the Lord; and if we die, we die for the Lord. So, whether we live or die, we belong to the Lord" (Rom 14:8). The new order of life and death in him transcends the boundaries of earthly existence, and because their life is so identified with the risen Christ even death is deemed profitable (Phil 1:21). Once the view of life and death is thus reversed or redefined, what remains as the most critical piece of the puzzle is the "second death" as the final blow to the eternal fate of man (Rev 20:14):

> Women received back their dead, raised to life again. There were others who were tortured, refusing to be released so that they might gain an even better resurrection. Some faced jeers and flogging, and even chains and imprisonment. They were put to death by stoning; they were sawed in two; they were killed by the sword. They went about in sheepskins and goatskins, destitute, persecuted and mistreated—the world was not worthy of them. (Heb 11:35–38)

Martha's view of resurrection hope was clearly in the future for she knew death will be overcome at the last day in bodily resurrection. But, to her surprise, Jesus' reply was in the future and in the present tense: "I am the resurrection and the life. He who believes in me will live, even though he dies; and whoever lives and believes in me will never die. Do you believe this?" (John 11:25–26). In the new meaning of life and death, resurrection is ever in the present tense, which Jesus demonstrated by making Lazarus walk out from the grave. The first half of the verse, "he will live even though he dies," denotes the future resurrection but the second half, "he will never die," denotes

---

65. Vos, *Eschatology of Old Testament*, 11.

the present resurrection. The bodily resurrection of Lazarus, and that of all believers in the future, is but the proof of their present resurrection with the risen Christ. Thus, anyone in Christ will never die the "second death" since he has been raised already and has eternal life. He is not bound by the death of the outward man for the inner is being renewed (2 Cor 4:14). The verb "has" (*echei*) is in the present indicative tense and means "he is having the eternal life" (John 6:47). Physical life (*psyche*) will end but the new and eternal life (*zoe*) will never end for the new creation is not subject to death and its sting (1 Cor 15:55; 2 Cor 5:17).

The horizontal passing of time on earth is not of the essence in the new order of life and death but the only thing to be considered is one's calling. Paul desired to depart and be with Christ but said to them, "but it is more necessary for you that I remain in the body" (Phil 1:24). With regard to the time on earth, there is both a warning and consolation: "Do not forget that with the Lord a day is like a thousand years, and a thousand years are like a day. The Lord is not slow in keeping his promise, as some understand slowness. He is patient with you, not wanting anyone to perish, but everyone to come to repentance" (2 Pet 3:8). The essence of the new perspective on life and death is the vertical-spatial dynamic in which believers find a new form of existence in Christ. The shift from the earthly to the heavenly regions and the corresponding view of life and death are produced by the unique structure of the ages (1Cor 15:49; Eph 1:21). The structure may be unfamiliar to modern worldview, but unless this be true there can be no absolute basis for true hope in the invisible heaven. The eschatological hope is rooted in the veracity of the believer's everlasting lot in heaven, which renders their present journey on earth worthwhile: "If only for this life we have hope in Christ, we are of all people most to be pitied" (1 Cor 15:19). The true hope is based on the certainty that the "firstfruit" and the "harvest" of resurrection are one entity separated only by time on earth (v. 23). If this be true, nothing on earth can make them ashamed or pitied regardless of the cost. The unashamed hope of believers can only be properly understood in terms of the certainty of their present entrance into the eternal and supernatural state (John 6:47; 17:3). The new form of existence is not so much a personal possession of the new life but participation in the new order of heaven and earth. The modern reader may be startled by a worldview so turned upside down that even death is considered a "gain," and what is more, everything is considered a loss "compared to the surpassing greatness of knowing Christ" (Phil 1:21; 3:8; Heb 11:38). They lived by faith rather than by sight—not a sign of Gnostic dualism but of the eschatological hope (2 Cor 5:7). They cherished all things in nature as a gracious gift of the Creator but also knew the world in its present form will pass away (Matt 5:45; 1 Cor 7:31; 2 Pet 3:10–13). The new order of life and death does not mean abandonment of the world but placement of all things in heaven and earth under the lordship of Christ (1 Pet 3:1–22; Phil 1:20).

4.5 Eternal High Priest

Sabbath Rest

The vertical ascension to the heavenly regions as the culmination of redemptive history brings into focus the Sabbath rest in Christ. The eschatology of nature in Genesis envisaged the Sabbath rest in the everlasting life—on the seventh day, when "God rested from all his work" (Gen 2:1–3). The Sabbath rest is an important goal in Israel's history that they could not achieve even in the promised land: "For if Joshua had given them rest, God would not have spoken later about another day" (Heb 4:8). It is finally achieved in Christ as the savory fruit of union and fellowship with him, who lovingly invites anyone to himself to receive the rest (Matt 11:28–30). This union with Christ brings believers into the union with the Father as the fulfillment of the Counsel of Peace (John 17:21). The reward of the covenant is the blessedness of the "adorable Being" himself, from whom "every good and perfect gift" flows (Gen 1:31; 1 Tim 1:11; James 1:17). The union of Adam and Eve in Eden was a prophetic metaphor for the blessed union of God and man in Christ. The chief end of nature is typical of the chief end of redemption. In the Genesis account of creation, the repetition of the morning and evening during the six days ceased on the seventh day (Gen 2:1). In a remarkable metaphor, it foreshadowed the new heaven and earth, where the repetition of day and night will cease and the need for the sun will be no more (Rev 22:5). God's rest on the seventh day is typical of the immortality in Christ, who fulfilled it through redemption. In this sense, there is the great "plus" of redemption to the eschatology of nature, as Vos penetratingly observed. The order in the work-rest pattern of nature is reversed in the new creation: "Remain in me, and I will remain in you. No branch can bear fruit by itself; it must remain in the vine. Neither can you bear fruit unless you remain in me" (John 15:4). The resurrection day of Christ has now become the first day of the week followed by the six days of work—all work is done in the rest. In the invitation of Jesus, the "yoke" and "burden" are not eliminated but made "easy" and "light" for those who remain in Christ (Matt 11:28). Though the rest is temporal in the horizontal time on earth, believers in the New Covenant have it far better than in the Old: "Now we who have believed enter that rest . . . For if Joshua had given them rest, God would not have spoken later about another day . . . for anyone who enters God's rest also rests from his own work, just as God did from his" (Heb 4:3–10).

The soteric gift of atonement itself does not guarantee God's rest, as proven by Israel, who could not enter it even by Joshua. It is guaranteed only by union with Christ that is soteric-eschatological. The foretaste of this rest on earth is all the more critical for believers because of the wasting away of the outer man and the pattern of this world quickly passing away (1 Cor 7:31). The promise of rest is true for those who are seated above with Christ, for the eschatological sun has risen over the darkness of this world. The Counsel of Peace has been completed by the Son, who gives peace unlike this world can give: "Peace I leave with you; my peace I give you. I do not give to you as the world gives. Do not let your hearts be troubled and do not be afraid" (John 14:27). The prophecy of Isaiah is fulfilled in those who are given this peace of Christ that they will not "grow weary or be faint" and "will soar on wings like eagles" (Isa 40:28–31). The unrest of the soul comes from the broken covenant with God and Christ brings it back to the peace of God: "Then they were glad because they were quiet, So He guided them to their desired harbor" (Ps 107:30). Into the decay and fatigue of the whole creation awaiting its liberation intruded the kingdom of heaven along with the Prince of Peace (Isa 9:6; Rom 8:21–22). In the Last Adam man will not return to the state of sin or probation, but move upward to the state of peace and rest. The heavenly rest given in advance by the eternal High Priest, who is seated next to God, is the ground of hope that they will never be separated from the Father's love (Rom 8:35–39). The adoption to sonship in Christ guarantees the assurance of God's fatherly love and brings everlasting peace to the child's heart (Rom 8:32; Eph 1:3).

Interestingly, the Sabbath rest and Christian ethics are interrelated in Paul's redemptive eschatology. The hope and assurance in God's rest gives rise to a unique perspective in Christian ethics (2 Cor 4:16): "Because the saints know that they are now between the resurrection of Christ and Parousia, and between the already fulfilled indicative where all the imperative has been removed and the consummation in the future, Christian ethics cannot be an additional command."[66] The believer does not have to feel that he must protect his righteousness before God by additional obedience to the law as if it were unsecure or his outcome postponed to the Parousia. He is raised and seated with Christ, where he is declared righteous and set free from the curse of the law once and for all (Rom 8:31–39). He is not only delivered from the state of condemnation but advanced to God's rest, where he remains. In that rest, he is not "under the law" but "under Christ's law," which is neither a threat to his righteousness nor an extra burden to his walk with God (1 Cor 9:21). There are no new laws once believers are raised and seated next to God but only the old command to love God and love others in the freedom of the Spirit.[67] The restfulness in Christ makes obedience to the law not an additional burden but a joyful and voluntary participation in the Divine nature (2 Pet 1:4).[68] That was the chief end in nature, and even more the chief end in redemption. The assurance of God's rest will produce religious devotion and ethics of the highest order without falling into legalism: "I tell you, now is the time [*kairos*] of God's favor, now is the day of salvation" (2 Cor 6:2). The vertical rest in the heavenly regions will ensure that personal piety and ethics will be a sweet fruit of the Spirit instead of burdensome self-righteousness (Gal 5:22–24). The High Priest in heaven once for all sat down (*ekathisen*) next to the Father and this ensures that believers in Christ are also seated (rested) next to him:

---

66. Cullman, *Christ and Time*, 225.
67. Cullman, *Christ and Time*, 225.
68. Cullman, *Christ and Time*, 225.

> Day after day every priest stands and performs his religious duties; again and again he offers the same sacrifices, which can never take away sins. But when this high priest had offered for all time one sacrifice for sins, he sat down at the right hand of God. (Heb 10:11–12)

The high priests in the order of Aaron must be in standing position while they perform duties in the earthly sanctuary, for neither they nor Israel have yet to enter God's rest. The seated posture in the order of Melchizedek, on the other hand, signals God's rest and guaranteed perseverance of the saints on earth. Even the sustainability of justification by faith is not guaranteed by faith alone but by being seated with Christ next to the Father. The peace and confidence of the soul flows from God's rest, which feeds and sustains it from above.

In Acts, a rare scene of the glorified Christ is briefly revealed to Stephen prior to his martyrdom. The risen Christ is seen to be standing rather than sitting, perhaps due to the gravity and urgency of the situation as if to cheer on his beloved saint who is about to be received into heaven: "But Stephen, full of the Holy Spirit, looked up to heaven and saw the glory of God, and Jesus standing at the right hand of God. 'Look,' he said, 'I see heaven open and the Son of Man standing at the right hand of God'" (Acts 7:55–56). In this magnificent vision, God allowed Stephen to peek into heaven that he might peacefully bear his final suffering for Christ's sake. In Pauline language, however, though he is not there yet, he is already there in Christ. His self-denial and cross-bearing for Christ's sake has been sustainable on earth by his prior union with the risen Christ, and now he is about to return to that heavenly region, where he has been with Christ all along.

We are reminded of the promise of Jesus that his yoke will be easy and his burden will be light precisely because they are taken up from above rather than from below (Col 3:2). The yoke and burden would be unbearable and disheartening apart from the heavenly foundation of peace and rest (Ps 11:3) In the new schema of two ages, the outer man is not yet resting but the inner man is already rested and renewed (2 Cor 4:16). In the semi-eschatological period of Christ's resurrection, the believer is resting in heaven even as he is toiling on earth: "For the kingdom of God is not a matter of eating and drinking, but of righteousness, peace and joy in the Holy Spirit" (Rom 14:17). In the kingdom, believers live by the rest and energy supplied by the Spirit from above as they "live by faith, not by sight" (2 Cor 5:7). This is not a Gnostic division of spirit and body, but a provisional distinction between the two ages inaugurated by the entrance of Christ into the heavenly regions. The inner man thus can start to experience new life (*zoe*) in the Spirit: "Whoever believes in me, as Scripture has said, rivers of living water will flow from within them" (John 7:38). As much as the approach to the throne of grace is immediate upon union with Christ to receive help, heaven is open and available to all God's children (Heb 4:16). If Christ's resurrection had been indefinitely delayed in time, the approach to the throne and the needed help also would have been delayed (Heb 9:24; Eph 1:3). The delay was for the Old Covenant but not for New Covenant in Christ, who is "the end of the law" (Rom 10:4). The well-rested and energized army of heaven can successfully wage spiritual war, for "our struggle is not against flesh and blood, but against the rulers, against the authorities, against the powers of this dark world and against the spiritual forces of evil in the heavenly realms" (Eph 6:12).

The unique structure of redemptive eschatology creates a tension between the two ages but it is neither a state of confusion nor restlessly pulled apart from above and below. The kingdom of Christ is unified yet exists in the overlaying of the two ages with the upper regions leading the lower regions. Rather than two kingdoms,[69] therefore, the two ages more properly represent the current semi-eschatological state (Gal 1:4; Eph 1:21). This age and the age to come are in a conflict but not in confusion, for the life in Christ is already hidden in God and they are able to set their minds on things above (Col 3:1–4). It seems the debate over two kingdoms and neo-Calvinism can only be settled by a redemptive-eschatological view of the kingdom of Christ. Both uphold the supremacy of Christ's reign over heaven and earth and a continued importance of nature, but they differ on how grace and nature are to be construed. The new schema of the ages, however, must be given priority over the question of how to define nature in redemption.

The entrance into the inner sanctuary behind the curtain is like "an anchor for the soul, firm and secure" (Heb 6:19). They are seated next to the risen Christ in the unified kingdom, otherworldly and unashamed although poor in spirit in this fleeting world (1 Cor 7:29–31). They are liberated from this world since his kingdom is not of this world, but they are willing to be slaves to all for the sake of the gospel under Christ's law (1 Cor 9:19–21). The blessedness of believers, "unknown yet known, sorrowful yet rejoicing, poor yet making many rich, having nothing yet possessing everything," flows from the freedom of God's rest in heaven (2 Cor 6:9–10). If detached from this heavenly foundation, one might slip into to a false sense of security (antinomianism) or a false means to earn it (legalism). Without the vertical rest in the heavenly regions, believers await the Sabbath of the indefinite future, leaving them without a firm foundation for their present journey. Even the soteric principle of *sola fide* needs the eschatological foundation to ensure the perseverance of saints on earth. The extent to which the rest in God is real and present to them is the extent to which they will persist and persevere in the fight against evil (Matt 11:28).

---

69. The present author is of the opinion that the debate between the "two kingdoms" camp and neo-Calvinism can only be settled by an eschatological approach to the kingdom of Christ. Both uphold the supremacy of Christ's reign over heaven and earth and the importance of the creation order, but they differ in terms of how the structure of grace and nature is viewed in the present order of things.

High Priesthood

The high-priestly work of intercession in the order of Melchizedek continues in heaven even after Christ's death on the cross (Heb 4:3–5; 9:12). Christ satisfied God's justice at the cross but makes the final approach to the Father in resurrection to do the work of the high priest: "For Christ did not enter a sanctuary made with human hands that was only a copy of the true one, he entered heaven itself, now to appear for us in God's presence" (Heb 9:24). In him believers can confidently approach the throne of the Father just as the Son prayed for them (John 17:21; Heb 4:16). At the throne of grace they are declared righteous and adopted to sonship as children of God, being coheirs with Christ (Rom 8:35–39). Christ's work is substitutionary and intercessory; it is redemptive-eschatological. Based on the intercessory work in heaven, believers can pray the Lord's Prayer, for the Father's will to "be done on earth as in heaven" (Matt 6:10). The request of "thy kingdom come, thy will be done earth as it is in heaven" is contingent upon Christ's entrance into heaven and intercession before the Father (Acts 2:33). It is also the reason for the promise to the church: "I will give you the keys of the kingdom of heaven; whatever you bind on earth will be bound in heaven, and whatever you loose on earth will be loosed in heaven" (Matt 16:19). The cry of "*Abba, Father*" is the outcome of adoption to sonship through the firstborn, who interceded to the Father for them in the garden of Gethsemane that "not my will, but your will be done" (Rom 8:15). The intercession in the order of Melchizedek is above, direct, and seated (Eph 2:6). The human nature of the eternal High Priest is used again in this work in heaven (he is able to sympathize) even after its use in the substitutionary work on earth (Heb 4:15). There in heaven, all accusations of Satan against believers are muted and their righteousness is declared forever (Heb 10:12). Although the disciples were dismayed about the imminent departure of Jesus, they would have been actually left as orphans on earth if Christ did not leave them to send another Counselor (John 14:18). Christ's entrance into the heavenly sanctuary with humanity ensured that believers are not left on earth as fatherless but on the contrary brought before the Father. Precisely because Christ appeared before the Father in humanity, they are not left to themselves but given the keys to overcome "the gates of Hades" (Matt 16:18). It was to their benefit that he left them to appear before the Father: "But very truly I tell you, it is for your good that I am going away. Unless I go away, the Advocate will not come to you; but if I go, I will send him to you" (John 16:7).

The ascension of Christ into heaven reveals that the progress of redemptive history is not merely forward-moving but upward-moving so that "God is with us." Redemptive history is redemptive-eschatological in that the high priesthood of Melchizedek is not only an improvement over that of Aaron but the end (*telos*) of it (Rom 10:4). In this order, Christ's human nature is put to its final use for man's everlasting union with God (Jer 50:5). The finality of his work is revealed in that he is *seated* next to God; he is the *last* of all priests; he is the *sacrifice*. The intercessory work of Christ in heaven actually completes his priesthood, which began in his incarnation. The soteric part has traditionally received the spotlight on account of the soteriological controversies. With the rise of redemptive-historical hermeneutics and the eschatological outlook, the heavenly ministry of Christ's has gained more attention. The vertical perspective places the present life of believers on a different plane as they eagerly anticipate Christ's return. None of the high priests prior to Christ ascended to heaven to continue their work, and none of the sacrifices they offered reached the heavenly sanctuary in the same degree as that of Christ's. In fulfilling the Levitical order of priesthood he also perfected the Melchizedek order (Lev 16:1–34). The neglect of the latter is a great detriment to the health and vitality of the church because they have an unlimited access to inner sanctuary of God through it. It is what makes them "more than conquerors" even amid the present sufferings (Rom 8:37–39). The early believers so relied on the strength of the invisible to overcome the weakness in the visible: "Though you have not seen him, you love him; and even though you do not see him now, you believe in him and are filled with an inexpressible and glorious joy . . ." (1 Pet 1:9).

The significance of the seated posture of Christ in heaven is difficult to overstate. It is one of the most outstanding features of Christ's high priesthood in the New Covenant vertically considered. In Eden, Adam had been in the provisional state of standing in relation to God faced with the prospect of life or death. Under the law administration of the Covenant of Grace, Israel was standing outside of the camp as the high priest stood before the ark of the covenant in behalf of the people. Ever since creation, therefore, there was never a time mankind was able to sit in the presence of God until Christ sat next to the Father after ascension. In standing, mankind was never able to fully rest and call out to God *Abba*, Father" with filial confidence (Rom 8:15). Eden was a "garden of God" where Adam could have been seated next to God in life eternal but was expelled from his presence (Gen 3:8, 22; Rev 2:7; 22:14). The eschatology of nature, then, would be postponed until Christ, when it was fulfilled in the form of the eschatology of redemption. Even in the Old Covenant, no high priest was ever permitted to sit in the sanctuary (Deut 17:12; 18:5; Heb 10:12). The standing posture conspicuously revealed that the priesthood and the entire ritual system were of a temporary nature (Heb 10:11).[70] The seated posture of Christ next to God bears testimony to the final and eternal character of the covenant Christ completed—the Counsel of Peace between the Father and the Son.[71] The seated high priest visually and spatially sealed what Christ had already publicly declared on cross: "It is finished." Christ was crucified for our sins and "raised to life for our justification" and the High Priest sealed it by sitting next to the Father (Rom 4:25). The covenant thus sealed by Christ will never be broken again and God's children will never be in probation again or severed from God's fatherly love (Rom 8:39). The Spirit of adoption is fittingly sent to the church subsequent to Christ's ascension to be seated next to the Father (Acts

---

70. Hughes, *Commentary on Hebrews*, 400–401.
71. Hughes, *Commentary on Hebrews*, 400–401.

2:33). The Spirit not only redeems us from sin but also completes the probation in Eden: "The Spirit you received does not make you slaves, so that you live in fear again; rather, the Spirit you received brought about your adoption to sonship. And by him we cry, 'Abba, Father'" (Rom 8:15). The Spirit of adoption puts to rest any lingering fear of losing righteousness or sonship that may lurk behind the restless soul. For this reason, Christ is superior to all previous heads of covenants whether under the Covenant of Works or Covenant of Grace (Heb 3:5–6).

On the Day of Atonement, the work of the high priest is not finished until he enters the inner sanctuary with the blood of sacrifice prepared outside at the altar (Lev 16:14; 23:27). This final stage of the high priest's work is critical because it seals the covenant union of Yahweh and Israel. Besides not being allowed to sit in the inner sanctuary, the priests in the order of Aaron can only do this one day a year, having to repeat it annually (Heb 9:7; 10:12). The purpose of the comparison in Hebrews is to highlight the eternal efficacy of Christ's priesthood in contrast to the fleeting efficacy of the imperfect high priesthood: "But when this priest had offered for all time one sacrifice for sins, he sat down at the right hand of God, and since that time, he waits for his enemies to be made his footstool. For by one sacrifice he has made perfect forever those who are being made holy" (Heb 10:12–14). The priesthood of Leviticus is imperfect and temporary but the priesthood of Christ and the single sacrifice is eternally effective upon his entrance to the heavenly sanctuary (Heb 9:12, 24). The Aaronic order was good for a year but the Melchizedek order is good for eternity, for the latter is ratified vertically from the altar of the cross to the inner sanctuary of heaven. Israel had to stand outside of the tabernacle during the ritual but the new Israel goes into the tabernacle with the Mediator: "When Christ came as high priest of the good things that are already here, he went through the greater and more perfect tabernacle that is not man-made, that is to say, not a part of this creation" (Heb 9:11). Christ's entrance into the inner sanctuary thus consummates the union of God and his people—"You will be my people, and I will be your God." The cross of Christ on earth is the sacrifice at the altar, but his resurrection and exaltation was the entrance into the inner sanctuary in heaven to appear before God. Vos thinks that Christ's entrance into the inner sanctuary of heaven on behalf of believers is "the final and proper" use of his humanity.

The soteric rectitude and the eschatological perfection are thus marvelously conjoined through his death and resurrection. The one day is typical of Christ's ministry on earth ending with the cross, and the one year of his ministry in heaven with everlasting efficacy. The disappearance of the cherubim, who used to guard the garden of Eden and the ark of the covenant in the inner sanctuary, is a sign that the path has been cleared for free access to God (Gen 3:24; Exod 25:18–22; Rev 2:7; 21:1). The tree of knowledge also disappeared in the new Eden for the probation is over and only the tree of life is seen by the "river of the water of life" (Rev 22:2). The status of God's children will never again be threatened by the presence of the cherubim or the tree of the knowledge of good and evil. They are seen no more for their mission is complete with the Son seated next to the Father interceding for believers, who are adopted as coheirs to the kingdom:

> Therefore, since we have a great high priest who has gone through the heavens, Jesus the Son of God, let us hold firmly to the faith we profess. For we do not have a high priest who is unable to sympathize with our weaknesses, but we have one who has been tempted in every way, just as we are—yet was without sin. Let us then approach the throne of grace with confidence, so that we may receive mercy and find grace to help us in our time of need. (Heb 4:14–16)

The cherubim were not removed from the earthly sanctuary during the entire period of the Old Covenant and the Levitical order of priesthood. As long as they were guarding the temple and the ark of the covenant, Israel could not directly enter behind the curtain without a mediator; the cherubim started to guard the garden of God after the fall (Heb 4:8; Gen 3:24). Their continued presence attests to the weakness of the temporary and imperfect order of Aaron, hinted by the rope and the bells tied to the priest when appearing behind the curtain (Heb 7:11). The disappearance of the cherubim coincides with Christ's death when the curtain was torn apart and Christ's resurrection into the heavenly regions for free and permanent access to the Father's presence (Luke 23:45; Heb 4:16). That was the moment, then, when the Covenant of Grace, which began in the Counsel of Peace from eternity, is forever sealed to give us the anchor of hope:

> We have this hope as an anchor for the soul, firm and secure. It enters the inner sanctuary behind the curtain, where Jesus, who went before us, has entered on our behalf. He has become a high priest forever, in the order of Melchizedek. (Heb 6:19–20)

> Therefore, brothers, since we have confidence to enter the Most Holy Place by the blood of Jesus, by a new and living way opened for us through the curtain, that is, his body, and since we have a great priest over the house of God, let us draw near to God with a sincere heart in full assurance of faith . . . (Heb 10:20)

Chapter 5

REDEMPTION AND ESCHATOLOGY

5.1 REDEMPTION ACCOMPLISHED AND APPLIED

THE CRUX OF THE GOSPEL is contained the death and resurrection of Christ: "For what I received I passed on to you as of first importance: that Christ died for our sins according to the Scriptures, that he was buried, that he was raised on the third day according to the Scriptures, and that he appeared to Cephas, and then to the Twelve" (1 Cor 15:3). The once-for-all historical accomplishment of redemption thus precedes the application of its benefits to believers through the Golden Chain of the *Ordo Salutis*. For the benefits of redemption, one must be united into the Person and work of Christ (Rom 6:4). The foundation and the application are inseparable yet distinguished to better understand the redemptive eschatology or eschatological redemption. In this work, the soterics is placed within the larger scope of the eschatology of nature in Adam and the eschatology of redemption in Christ. Any single stage in the logical order of salvation is always viewed in light of the perfect work of mediation by Christ, who is also the Last Adam.[1]

The Lutheran view, for instance, "presents too narrow a view of the sacraments," limiting them to a particular stage in the order of salvation without regard to the whole of redemption contained in the Covenant of Grace and the *Pactum Salutis*. In the Reformed view, they "cease being signs of a particular grace and become particular signs of all comprehensive grace ... They seal Christ to us ... we cannot limit that sealing power to any single stage of the way of salvation."[2] Ridderbos agrees that central to Paul's thought was not justification by faith, but the perfect obedience of Christ on which the entire order of salvation rests.[3] The gospel is not limited to any single stage in the *Ordo Salutis* but embraces the Person of Christ and his work in death and resurrection. Soteriology cannot be separated from eschatology or vice versa in

---

1. Ridderbos, *Paul*, 44.
2. Vos, *Redemptive History*, 262.
3. Ridderbos, *Paul*, 44.

Christ: "The whole content of Paul's preaching is the declaration and explanation of the last times inaugurated by Christ's incarnation, death, and resurrection."[4]

Luther and Calvin understood that justification by faith alone is central to soteriology for it frees the guilty conscience of man from the heavy burden of works righteousness. They did not deviate, however, from the Person and work of Christ as the foundation of redemptive grace applied to believers. The shift in focus from the Person of Christ to his benefits took place later in history with the rise of pietism, moralism, and mysticism, which defined redemption more in terms of subjective reception of Christ's benefits.[5] The interest of theology was fixated more on the soteric application rather than on the christological and eschatological foundation. We are reminded again by Paul that the Christ who died for us is also the Christ in us; the Christ who redeems is also the Christ who recreates (2 Cor 5:14–17). The benefits of Christ's work cannot be separated from the Person of Christ, who is the Mediator in the Counsel of Peace. Eternal life is nothing less than knowing the Father and the Son in the Eternal Covenant. The *Ordo Salutis* is the historical outcome of the work of the three Persons of the blessed God applied to the elect (John 17:3; Eph 1:4–14). In substance, redemptive grace is redemptive eschatology which fulfills the eschatology of nature through salvation: "I make known the end from the beginning, from ancient times, what is still to come. I say: My purpose will stand, and I will do all that I please" (Isa 46:10).

Eschatology is often misunderstood as an "independent, neutral, or supernatural" idea in the distant future irrelevant to the present.[6] At times its scope has been limited to the apocalyptic events of the Parousia. But at other times redemption is so de-eschatologized that it has become a timeless entity without interest any further than the present. A realized eschatology is relevant at present but not so historicized to the exclusion of anticipation of the future. It is a restructuring of the salvation of believers in light of the victory already sealed by Christ ahead of the final conclusion of history.[7] It takes redemption to a higher order with far-reaching implications for the church placed between D-Day and V-Day. In its narrow sense, eschatology is a study of the last things, but in its wider sense, a study of the supernatural. The former is a horizontal perspective of the last days whereas the latter is the vertical perspective foundational to the former. As for the last days of history, no one but the Father in heaven knows the specific time (Matt 24:36). But the last days in the vertical and present sense are inaugurated with Christ's crucifixion and resurrection followed by the outpouring of the Holy Spirit (Acts 2:17, 33). These redemptive yet eschatological events signaled the end of this age and the start of the coming age (Heb 1:1–2). The last days of this age are prompted by the final revelation of the Son, especially his

4. Ridderbos, *Paul*, 44.
5. Ridderbos, *Paul*, 44.
6. Berkouwer, *Return of Christ*, 18–19.
7. Berkouwer, *Return of Christ*, 18–19.

death and the vertical ascension to the heavenly regions. The vertical union of heaven and earth leads and dictates the horizontal anticipation of the Parousia. The first and the second comings of Christ, therefore, are not two independent events, but two successive stages of the same event separated by time. New Testament eschatology is an integral part of redemption rather than its chronological sequel.

The new birth in the Spirit and the entrance into the kingdom of God are the same event in the new order (John 3:5). Eternal life is not only new life but a new order of life in the supernatural (John 6:47). As we have seen previously, it is a rebirth into the new order of time and space by union with the risen Christ (Rom 6:1–14). What was pre-eschatological in the Old Covenant now became semi-eschatological in the New Covenant, for anyone in Christ is a new creation.[8] This is consistent with the progress of redemptive history toward the new creation within the Covenant of Grace. The end of redemption in the Last Adam is a new creation that fulfills the first creation in Adam. In Christ, the believer is redeemed in order to be transformed into the heavenly image (1 Cor 15:48–49). The soteric is not defined merely in terms of deliverance from the old self but deliverance into the new image of God (Eph 4:24). The sacraments of the covenant union with Christ signify the eternal (supernatural) life beyond forgiveness: "Whoever eats my flesh and drinks my blood has eternal life, and I will raise them up at the last day" (John 6:54). Eternal life is the covenantal knowledge of God that is ethical and religious in the highest order (John 17:3, 21–24). Adam was created in God's image to obey and commune with God and the Last Adam achieved the same goal to the nth degree (Gen 1:26–28; 2:15; 3:8). The goal of immortality in nature precedes the salvific rebirth in this sense, but it is achieved through the latter in the Last Adam. The reappearance of the tree of life confirms that what started in Eden has been consummated in the new Eden (Rev 22:2). The sacramental tree in nature typifies the "bread of life" that gives the eternal life (John 6:47–48). It is a visual symbol that he who eats of it will be redeemed to join the fellowship of the Father and the Son through the Spirit (John 17:21). Eternal life is so arranged in the Covenant of Redemption that its Mediator is now the Son of God, who became the Second Adam.

The eternal life was not yet as clearly revealed in the Old Testament, being "a copy and shadow of what is in heaven" (Heb 8:5). The eschatology of redemption was in progress and the available revelation was limited in quantity and clarity. Old Covenant believers were at a disadvantage in this regard though the soteric part of the Covenant of Grace was equally available to them (Heb 11:39–40). The disadvantage was not in regard to the knowledge of salvation itself but in regard to the knowledge of the Son and the kingdom of heaven. This disadvantage is partly attested by the fact that they could not eat of the sacrifices from the altar on the Day of Atonement (Heb 13:10–11). In contrast, New Covenant believers may eat from the Lord's Supper: "We have an altar from which those who minister at the tabernacle have no right to eat" (v. 10). The altar of the cross is final and eternal in that those united into Christ can now

---

8. Beale, "Eschatological Conception," 18–28.

freely eat from the table.⁹ The sacrament of the Lord's Supper is not only permitted but commanded in the New Covenant: "This is my body, which is for you; do this in remembrance of me" (1 Cor 11:24). What was prohibited in the Old Covenant due to its weakness is now freely available in the New Covenant in the Spirit (2 Cor 3:17). The cross of Jesus is the last and final altar, for his is the eternal covenant by which believers have free access to the throne of grace in heaven.¹⁰ It is not only the fulfillment of the horizontal progress from the Old to the New, but also the vertical movement from earth to heaven. The Lord's Supper, in this sense, is a sacrament that manifests the fulfillment of the Covenant of Grace and Covenant of Works.

New Covenant believers are called "a chosen people, a royal priesthood, a holy nation, a people belonging to God" in fulfillment of the kingdom of priests (1 Pet 2:9; Exod 19:6). As Adam was a prophet, priest, and king as the vice-regent of God, who could have eaten from the tree of life, believers are priests "being built into spiritual house to be a holy priesthood, offering spiritual sacrifices acceptable to God through Jesus Christ" (1 Pet 2:5). They have become priests because Christ is the eternal Priest who through his perfect obedience to the Father fulfilled the Counsel of Peace. The eternal priesthood of Christ is redemptive-eschatological for God "blessed us in the heavenly realms with every spiritual blessing in Christ" (Eph 1:3).¹¹ Calvin's view of the sacraments as the "spiritual presence" of Christ sheds light on the covenantal aspect of redemption that has more than substitutionary significance.¹² The sacraments cannot be limited to recovery of the Adamic state, but ought to be expanded to completion of the Adamic covenant. It is the perfection of the *imago Dei* or the chief end of man in nature, and as a reward he would have been allowed to eat from the tree of life. It is only fitting, therefore, that believers have the right to eat from the tree of life: "Whoever eats my flesh and drinks my blood remains in me, and I in them . . . This is the bread that came down from heaven. Your ancestors ate manna and died, but whoever feeds on this bread will live forever" (John 6:56–58). The life eternal is not postponed to the indefinite future as a hope but is a present blessing in which man may glorify and enjoy God. In Christ they begin to experience "righteousness, peace and joy in the Holy Spirit" despite earthly troubles that are light and momentary (Rom 14:17; 2 Cor 4:17). The eternal life is not just a place believers go after death, but begins with the union in the fellowship of the Father and the Son. The rebirth is equated to entrance into the kingdom of heaven, for it is not just deliverance from below but ascension to above (John 3:5; Col 3:2). The cure of atonement and the tonic of the eternal life remained detached before Christ but unified in him.¹³ Redemption does not stop at

---

9. Hughes, *Commentary on Hebrews*, 575.
10. Hughes, *Commentary on Hebrews*, 576.
11. Calvin, *Institutes*, 2:1284.
12. Calvin, *Institutes*, 2:1362.
13. Vos, *Eschatology of Old Testament*, 74.

justification or return to the state of Adam but enters into the new order of life in the kingdom of heaven.

The Covenant of Grace unifies the Old and New Covenants but also unified the earthly and the heavenly through Christ (Eph 1:10). In the vertical perspective, history has entered the semi-eschatological state in which salvation is more than restorative but consummative.[14] Moses understood the presence of Yahweh as the chief end of Israel when he prayed it would be meaningless to enter the Promised Land without God's presence (Exod 33:12–16). The greatest reward for Israel is not the land flowing with milk and honey but God himself as Israel's husband. The chief end of man, as always has been, is to glorify and enjoy God whether in nature or in redemption. The covenant knowledge of union in the garden of God is the substance of the eternal life expressed by the word *yada* (Gen 4:1). The covenant union is marked by mutual glory, love, and knowledge as revealed by the Father and the Son in the Counsel of Peace (John 17:21–26). Conversely, the eternal death is moral and religious separation from the "adorable Being"; Adam and Eve faced death not so much because they left Eden but because they left God (Gen 2:17). Hence, believers are seated with Christ in heaven "that they may have life, and have it to the full" despite their earthly pilgrimage (John 10:10). The horizontal time keeps flowing, but the vertical union is unchanging regardless of time: "Jesus Christ is the same yesterday and today and forever" (Heb 13:8). God's purpose for redemption is: "[I will give] drink to my people, my chosen, the people I formed for myself that they may proclaim my praise" (Isa 43:20–21).

5.2 Salvation and Last Things

Eschatology and soteriology have been united into a single entity—the eschatology of redemption—in Christ (Heb 1:1–2; 9:26). The soteric knowledge of Christ was necessary in the Covenant of Grace whether under the law or under the gospel. But the knowledge of Christ under the gospel is particularly associated with the coming of the kingdom of heaven and inauguration of the last days (Luke 16:16; Acts 2:17). The resurrection of Christ into the heavenly regions is particularly relevant in this regard as foretaste of resurrection, and that the harvest is quite near. The harvest is so near that those who are united with the risen Christ are risen and seated with him (Col 3:1–4). It became necessary to distinguish the redemption already accomplished from the redemption not yet consummated. Heaven as a consummate place is not yet here, but as union with him in the heavenly regions it is already here. The covenant union and fellowship with God at the throne of grace is now immediate, unceasing, and uninhibited (Heb 4:14–16). Old Covenant believers could not have experienced this though they received forgiveness of sin through atonement in the law administration.

---

14. Vos, *Pauline Eschatology*, 38.

In recent times, more interest in the kingdom and eschatology have raised new questions about the traditional doctrine justification by faith. In particular, the New Perspective school raised doubts about justification strictly as a way of receiving personal righteousness from God, offering a new theory of justification by faith—as a matter of *entrance* into the new covenant community for Jews and Gentiles. It is based on their conclusion of research into Second Temple Judaism that a concept of legal justification by works of the law did not exist. Hence, they argued that justification in Paul was not about imputation of Christ's righteousness for personal salvation but about a *membership* into the new covenant community of Jews and Gentiles. It is true that the traditional view of salvation may have lacked the corporate aspect of redemption, but an outright denial of justification by faith for personal righteousness is a serious misrepresentation of Paul. Ecclesiology is important, but not at the expense of soteriology. The "New Perspective" may be helpful in widening the scope of salvation to ecclesiology but denial of it all together is regrettable. The eschatology of redemption, as we view it, is for personal salvation from sin and for recreation of all things in the kingdom of God. Christ came to save sinners but also to reign over all creation, and all races in the age of mission will be part of the "one new man" under his lordship (2 Cor 5:17; Eph 2:15): "The new community of Jesus is already an eschatological community that belongs to the new era he started. Justification is an eschatological event. It brought to present in advance the verdict of the last judgement."[15]

Redemption in the schema of the age to come is such that Christ is "our righteousness, holiness and redemption" and all benefits derive from him directly (1 Cor 1:30). Union with Christ is more than alien righteousness from without; it includes the inner righteousness of Christ bearing the fruit of sanctification. In this sense, the New Perspective may have done a service to the church by bringing into light the corporal and communal aspect of Christ's work which perhaps had been overlooked. The integration of eschatology into the soteric work of Christ actually has been done before the New Perspective appeared on the scene.[16] It was done, however, without having to tear down one of the most significant doctrines to come out of Reformation theology. In any case, the meaning of forensic justification to obtain righteousness cannot be fully grasped apart from the whole scope of Christ's work. It provides the redemptive-eschatological scope in which to define the obtaining of personal salvation.[17] Eschatology adds the wider and higher perspective to soteriology: "Eschatology, in other words, even that of the most primitive kind, yields *ipso facto* a philosophy of history, be it of the most rudimentary sort. And every philosophy of history bears in itself the seed of a theology."[18] Christ transformed the fallen mankind and world into a new creation with a "redemptive plus," and the two are inseparable. In Christ, salvation

15. Stott, *Cross of Christ*, 189.
16. Vos, *Pauline Eschatology*, 42–61.
17. Vos, *Pauline Eschatology*, 61.
18. Vos, *Pauline Eschatology*, 61.

of the fallen man and the eschatological purpose of nature have been accomplished simultaneously without one being subsumed by the other.[19]

The eschatological aspect of salvation is particularly expressed in the active obedience of Christ and the imputation his righteousness on believers. The passive obedience and the vicarious death on the cross satisfied the curse of the law, but the active obedience fulfilled the requirement of the law. The law was required for the chief end of man to glorify and enjoy God and Christ fulfilled it as the Last Adam. Hence, although believers are free from the curse of the law but "under Christ's law" to walk before God in holiness as Christ did (1 Cor 9:21; Heb 12:14). The vicarious atonement itself does not deal with this aspect of redemption, which is the key difference between the two administrations of the Covenant of Grace. It would almost be superfluous to mention the progressiveness of redemptive history if justification to obtain righteousness were the only matter in redemption. Abraham and Paul are equally justified by faith alone based on the vicarious work of Christ. The redemptive-historical progress in Christ, however, means that believers are under Christ's law for the perfection of the image of God. The vertical union of God and man comes into focus as well as the horizontal fulfillment of prophecies (Heb 8:5). This requires the active obedience of Christ, and is not sufficiently explained by the passive obedience alone. The active obedience is that which fulfills the Covenant of Works as the Last Adam. The justification, therefore, is now explained in terms of Christ's resurrection as well as his suffering (Rom 4:25). Baptism into his death and resurrection, then, is the key that unlocks the mystery of God in union with Christ.[20] Calvin may not have fully foreseen the eschatological implications of union with Christ to the same degree, but he certainly laid the ground by placing the whole of redemption on this foundation.

The purpose of redemption is more than deliverance from the curse of the law, but the fulfillment of the eschatology of nature. Mankind was created in God's image to delight in the law of God and walk with him. The obedience of Adam in nature was typical of the active obedience by Christ in redemption (Rom 5:12; 1 Cor 15:22; Heb 1:3; Col 1:15). The perfect obedience is Christ's own justification as the Second Adam and the ground of his resurrection (Rom 4:25; 5:18; Heb 5:8–9; 1 Tim 3:16). The active and passive obedience of Christ cannot be separated yet should be distinguished for this reason: "In the same way, count yourselves dead to sin but alive to God in Christ" (Rom 6:11). In Christ, the new man is dead to sin and alive to God unlike the first man, who was not yet alive to God without probation.[21] Christ's active obedience is not only the basis of justification through imputation of righteousness but also the perseverance of saints. The two sides of Christ's obedience are really a single entity and can no more be separated than his death and resurrection can be severed.[22]

19. Vos, *Pauline Eschatology*, 45.
20. Calvin, *Institutes*, 1:537.
21. Hoekema, *Saved by Grace*, 182.
22. Hoekema, *Saved by Grace*, 182.

His obedience, passive or active, is all "active," being free and voluntary, but also all "passive," done in humiliation and suffering. The logical distinction, however, is necessary because of the distinction between curse and requirement of the law. Christ's active obedience is also the ground of acceptance into the adoption to sonship and the inheritance of the Father's kingdom (Rom 8:14–17, 29). In the adoption, believers are not sent back to the state of Adam but united to the Father, unable to be separated from his love again (Jer 50:5). The obedience, in any case, is summed as one sacrifice: "But when this priest had offered for all time one sacrifice for sins, he sat down at the right hand of God . . ." (Heb 10:12).

"All have sinned and fall short of the glory of God," so the goal of salvation is more than restoration to the state of Adam; it is God's glory (Rom 3:23). A covenant always requires man to walk before God as blameless and be perfect as he is (Gen 17:1; Matt 5:48). The chief end of man remains the same in redemption so that even justification is to "rejoice in the hope of the glory of God" (Rom 5:2). In Paul, redemption is "Christo-eschatological" in that not only Christ is *for* us, but also we are *in* Christ (Rom 6:11; 2 Cor 5:14–17).[23] The redemptive benefits are the outcome of the Christo-eschatological union. The believer is baptized into the Person of Christ and as a result he is baptized into his death and resurrection: "Or don't you know that all of us who were baptized into Christ Jesus were baptized into his death?" (Rom 6:3–4). The redemptive benefits of baptism into his works follow the Christo-eschatological baptism into his Person. Likewise, Paul's knowledge of the Person of Christ precedes the benefits of the power of his death and resurrection: "*I want to know Christ* and the power of his resurrection and the fellowship in his sufferings, becoming like him in his death, and so, somehow, to attain to the resurrection from the dead" (Phil 3:10–11).[24] This knowledge is that of covenant union between persons (Gen 4:1; John 17:3). In union with Christ, believers receive all the spiritual benefits in the heavenly realms (Eph 1:3). In fact, it is Christology that renders the eschatology of redemption superior to the eschatology of nature. The redemption of Christ is covenantal, not just substitutionary, which means the person and his works are inseparable.[25] As Ridderbos has beautifully put, soteriology essentially flows out of Christology and flows into eschatology. In view of this, the *Ordo Salutis* is a logical rather than chronological order, making redemption a covenantal gift in the Person of Christ (Rom 8:29–30).[26] All the benefits of redemption are given to believers through union with the Person who fulfilled the covenant with the Father and is given the reward (John 17:6).[27] In Christ, the benefits can be logically distinguished but cannot be divided in chronological succession.

---

23. Ridderbos, *Paul*, 57–64.
24. Italics added.
25. Murray, *Redemption Accomplished and Applied*, 15.
26. Hoekema, *Saved by Grace*, 202–9.
27. Hoekema, *Saved by Grace*, 202–9.

5.3 Faith and Covenant

The object of faith is the Covenant of Grace, in which believers are united to Christ through the Spirit. In particular, faith "accepts, receives, and rests on Christ," who fulfilled Counsel of Peace with the Father.[28] Faith is sometimes more narrowly defined in terms of a particular stage in the order of salvation such as justification. But more properly defined, the object of faith is Christ, who fulfilled the Covenant of Grace and the *Pactum Salutis* of the Father and the Son. Hence, all stages in the way of salvation are present at all times through faith in Christ. Faith is not just an instrument of justification but a gift of the covenant to receive Christ from the Father by grace. In justification, faith is primarily pittied against the works of the law for imputation of Christ's righteousness. In the broader and more proper sense, however, faith embraces the Person of Christ for the Golden Chain of redemption; the object of faith is the Mediator in whom the Father has "blessed us in the heavenly realms with every spiritual blessing" (Eph 1:3). According to Calvin, the primary work of the Holy Spirit is to produce faith in the elect for the union with Christ, from whom all blessings of the covenant flow.[29] In this he was merely echoing the words of the apostle Paul: "And God raised us up with Christ and seated us with him in the heavenly realms in Christ Jesus . . . For it is by grace you have been saved, through faith—and this is not from yourselves, it is the gift of God—not by works, so that no one can boast" (Eph 2:6, 8–9). The Trinitarian way of redemption laid out in the opening words of Ephesians proves that faith is the means of reception of the covenant between the three Persons (Eph 1:3–14). Calvin noted that not everyone responds in the same way to the general call of the gospel because the efficient call of the Holy Spirit is grounded in the eternal election.[30] In this regard, Ridderbos credits Calvin for "decisively improved balance" in Reformed theology compared to the Lutheran view of faith defined as the means of justification. Luther's main interest lied in the imputation of Christ's righteousness from outside of sinners, i.e., "alien" righteousness for justification by faith alone.[31] Calvin regarded union with Christ, rather than justification, as the central principle in Paul's thought, and justification was understood as one of the gifts of that union.[32]

The union is also the basis of the covenantal use of the law for holiness, which fits the broader definition of faith whose object is Christ. It would not fit well into the view of faith defined narrowly as the means of justification whose main focus is liberty from the curse of the law. The law condemns and leads sinners to repentance in preparation for justifying faith. The third use of the law, however, is covenantal by nature in that it sanctifies the believer as the image-bearer of God who must conform

---

28. Westminster Confession of Faith, 14.
29. Calvin, *Institutes*, 1:541.
30. Calvin, *Institutes*, 1:537.
31. Luther, "Two Kinds of Righteousness" (1518).
32. Ridderbos, *Paul*, 14.

to Christ's obedience to the Father (Rom 8:29). The Reformers agreed in justification by faith alone, but differed in regard to the scope of faith. The alien righteousness and vicarious atonement for justification were important to all Reformers,[33] but without union with the Person of Christ, they were also open to antinomianism. In Christ, the law is also written in believers by the Spirit for sanctification as the fulfillment of the New Covenant (2 Cor 3:3). Both of these fulfillments of the law, by design, are part of the Covenant of Grace: the vicarious work of Christ for us and the recreative work in us (2 Cor 5:14, 17). In the horizontal perspective, believers are not "under law," but in the vertical perspective they are "under Christ' law" (1 Cor 9:19–21). The covenantal view of the gospel broadens the scope of faith to include the law, through union with Christ, because man is a covenantal being bearing the image of God.

The roles of faith and the law also progress as redemptive history in the Covenant of Grace progresses toward Christ. Faith embraces the redemptive-eschatological nature of Christ's work, which justifies sinners but also unifies heaven and earth. The justifying faith includes the eschatology of nature: "By faith we understand that the universe was formed at God's command, so that what is seen was not made out of what was visible" (Heb 11:3). The Covenant of Grace under the law was largely curative of sin, but under the gospel is curative and energizing by the union with the risen Christ, in whom "are hidden all the treasures of wisdom and knowledge" (Col 2:2–3). There is the "definitive" as well as the "progressive" aspects of redemption powered by the new order from above.[34] In a similar vein, William Perkins defined covenant as "the means of execution of the decree" in which the Golden Chain of redemption from election to glorification is completed.[35] God's decree does not weaken duty because the two are joined by the unbreakable chain of covenant first established between the Father and the Son. God's decree precedes all things, but "nor is violence offered to the will of the creatures; nor is the liberty or contingency of the second causes taken away, but rather established."[36] God's decree and man's liberty are not inversely proportional but directly proportional in the Golden Chain of covenant: "For he chose us in him before the creation of the world to be holy and blameless in his sight" (Eph 1:3). The Chain cannot be broken because nothing or no one in the whole universe "will be able to separate us from the love of God that is in Christ Jesus our Lord" (Rom 8:39). It is not faith that guarantees justification but the Father's promise and love in the Eternal Counsel effectuated by the Son. The assurance and perseverance of salvation do not depend on man's faith but on the Covenant of Grace which faith embraces.[37] It is true that man is justified by faith alone but the justifying faith is not alone. Faith is not an instrument for a particular stage in the *Ordo Salutis*, but "accepts, receives, and rests

33. Luther, "Two Kinds of Righteousness" (1518).
34. Hoekema, *Saved by Grace*, 177.
35. Perkins, *Golden Chain*, 53–54.
36. Westminster Confession of Faith, 3.
37. Westminster Confession of Faith, 17.

on Christ alone." It is "first to last" because Christ is first to last: "For in the Gospel the righteousness of God is revealed—a righteousness that is by faith from *first to last*, just as it is written: 'The righteous will live by faith'" (Rom 1:17).[38]

The scope of faith is widened in the covenantal view of redemption and eschatology. The means of grace cannot be greater than grace, which is redemptive-eschatological: "We do not believe in the means of grace but in grace."[39] The means of grace are the sign and seal rather than the actual grace that flows out of the Covenant of Redemption by the Father and the Son. The promise and faithfulness of God revealed through the Son are the actual grace that faith must rest on. The church thus baptizes believers and their children as the rightful members and recipients of the covenant. Professing adults are baptized but the baptized are not only the professing adults but also their infants according to the promise of the covenant. It is duty of the church to include these children as coheirs of the promise and baptize them—"The promise is for you and your children" (Acts 2:39). The practice of infant baptism illustrates how the scope of redemption has expanded from justification to the Covenant of Grace. It is expanded to the eschatology of redemption as the chief end of the soteric rectitude in atonement and justification. Faith as the means of covenant fulfillment may have changed from that of works; the end nonetheless has not changed, but rather been established (Eph 2:8–10). *Soli Deo gloria* as the chief end equally applies to all facets of theology including redemption, but the liberty of the second causes is established by it rather than discarded: "And without faith it is impossible to please God, because anyone who comes to him must believe that he exists and that he rewards those who earnestly seek him" (Heb 11:6).

5.4 Not by Sight, But by Faith

The definition of faith as the instrument of justification was necessary against the semi-Pelagian legalism as was the case with the Judaizers of Paul's time. But, perseverance in faith is another matter that requires a better and stronger foundation in the heavenly regions: "What can the righteous do when the foundations are being destroyed?" (Ps 11:3). For this reason, believers are told to fix their eyes on "the author and perfecter" of faith rather than fixated on their faith (Heb 12:2). The justified sinners liberated from guilty conscience by the righteousness obtained by faith do not remain there but reach to the risen Christ seated in the heavenly realms. The vision of believers are often limited to the substitutionary work of Christ because they do not see the heavenly places by sight. This is due in part to the doctrine of the alien righteousness of Christ, who is seen to remain outside of and apart from them. The gospel is often defined solely in terms of the soteric need for rectitude without sufficient consideration of its foundation in the heavenly regions. It is the supernatural regions

---

38. Italics added.
39. Vos, *Redemptive History*, 262.

above where Christ and believers are seated together next to the Father to receive grace in times of need. Without this foundation above, perseverance on earth will have to rely on the "perseverance of the means of grace" rather than on grace itself.[40]

In our view, Calvin's definition of faith in terms of union with Christ laid a significant ground for redemptive eschatology beyond the soteric rectitude of sin. The mystical union by faith is the work of the Spirit that produces rebirth in which believers ascend to the heavenly realms with Christ (Eph 2:6). This union opens up a new horizon visible not by sight but by faith and adds the vertical plane to redemption (2 Cor 5:7). The eschatological outlook inherent in redemption is no longer limited to horizontal history but incorporates vertical ascension to heaven (Col 3:1–4). In this vertical plane, opened up by the resurrection of Christ, the Spirit is given "as a deposit guaranteeing what is to come" (2 Cor 5:5). The union takes the application of redemption to new heights as it brings an immediate presence of the eternal and supernatural life to believers. At this point all the spiritual blessings in the heavenly realm are given to believers from above as the true and everlasting gift of the Covenant of Grace.

This is a multidimensional view of redemption with the soterics and heaven combined in union with Christ. The simple past (aorist) tense of the action signifies that the movement has already taken place: "God raised us up with Christ and seated us with him in the heavenly realms" (Eph 2:6). The vertical vision seen by faith does not refer to the future event but to a present state of believers in Christ through the Spirit (Rom 6:5). It is worth noting that the Johannine expression "born again" could also be translated as "born from above" (John 3:7; Col 3:3). John's view of rebirth from above (heaven) is consistent with Paul's view of the place where Christ is seated with believers. Hence, the eternal life is a new order of life born from the otherworldly schema of the Spirit. Paul exhorts believers to set their minds "on things above" because they are truly and presently seated above and the rest of their earthly living is controlled by that which is in heaven (Col 3:1–2). Their life "hidden in God" is lived on earth but flows down from heaven as faith now sees the vertical plane from below to above. The Golden Chain of the *Ordo Salutis* is "a logical arrangement of the graces applied to believers" through the vertical transaction from heaven to earth.[41] The primary object of faith is Christ, for whose sake the Father will not withhold anything from believers as promised in the Counsel of Peace (Rom 8:32). It is only natural that the Eternal Counsel between the Father and the Son for the redemption of the elect is "to the praise of his glorious grace" (Eph 1:6). Justification by faith is not an end in itself but a means to the chief end to "rejoice in the hope of the glory of God" (Rom 5:2).

The liberty of man in justification by faith is a benefit of that union but not its chief end. For this end, the eschatology of redemption fulfills the eschatology of nature. The blessedness of the Gospel is rooted in the blessedness of the three Persons of God who is the foundation of the goodness in creation and redemption (Gen 1:31;

---

40. Vos, "Doctrine of Covenant," 262.
41. Berkhof, *Systematic Theology*, 415–16.

1 Tim 1:11; 6:15). "Every good and perfect gift is from above, coming down from the Father of the heavenly lights," and this is the everlasting foundation of the Covenant of Grace or the Gospel. In the Sermon on the Mount, Jesus spoke of the blessedness in the kingdom of God which is "not of this world" (John 18:36). In the kingdom, the blessed delight in the law of God and mediate on it day and night because God is blessed in nature (Ps 1:1–2).[42] The blessedness of God in nature has now been fulfilled in the blessedness of God in redemption by the gospel of Jesus Christ. The law is given because the blessed nature of God is reflected in it: "Keep my decrees and laws, for the man who obeys them will live by them. I am the Lord" (Lev 18:5). In the two administrations of the Covenant of Grace, the difference between "the letter" and "the Spirit" is not law against faith, but transitory and surpassing glory (2 Cor 3:3, 6–11). The Spirit is not against the law itself, but against the flesh seeking justification by the works of the law.[43] The law administration was temporary but the law itself as reflective of God's attributes was given to Israel for their own happiness (Deut 10:13).

Faith justifies believers and brings them near God through Christ for "it is good to be near God," who is blessed and wants to bless his children (Ps 73:28). The faith "under the gospel" administration fulfills this blessedness in them reaching God in worship and adoration. The worship in nature must have been blessed, but the worship in redemption with the added soteric power of Christ is even more blessed. As Calvin noted, God's children would not want to offend God by sinning even if hell did not exist—the latter is not the proper motivation for love and worship of God.[44] Vos suggests that the everlasting hope might have been more prominent in the apostle Paul's thought than justifying faith if not for the pressing need at the time of addressing the legalism of the Judaizers.

> That the Apostle's religious mentality was of a forward-looking character appears first of all from the role played in his Epistles by the conception of 'hope.' The role would undoubtedly have been more prominent still, had it not been for the necessity of stressing the idea of faith on account of its controversial importance.[45]

In his view, the apostle's understanding of redemption is fueled more by the eschatology of hope than the soteric faith: "It no longer forms one item in the sum-total of revealed teaching, but draws within its circle as correlated and eschatologically complexioned parts practically all of the fundamental tenets of Pauline Christianity."[46] This underscores, at the least, the inseparability of justifying faith and the eschatological hope in the apostle's thought. Justification is a benefit of the salvific work of Christ

---

42. Calvin, *Institutes*, 1:360.
43. Calvin, *Institutes*, 1:360.
44. Calvin, *Institutes*, 1:43.
45. Vos, *Pauline Eschatology*, 29.
46. Vos, *Pauline Eschatology*, 11.

but it will last only as an inseparable part of having been seated above with Christ, where hope will not fail. That is the foundation of true and everlasting hope on earth and the reason believers will never have to be pitied in this world (1 Cor 15:19): "If we have turned out to be no more than Christ-hopers and staked on that our whole present life, then we are of all men most pitiable . . . hope without corresponding reality . . . is the most futile and ill-fated frustration of life-purpose . . ."[47]

5.5 Justified and Sanctified

C. S. Lewis said that man's nearness to God in likeness is not the same as the nearness in approach; one does not automatically guarantee the other, especially after the fall.[48] Even the nearness to God in likeness is corrupt to such an extent that mankind knows God but suppresses the truth, worshipping idols instead (Rom 1:18–23). The greatest gift of being made in God's image is turned into a weapon against God, making the willful rebellion even more sinister. The story of the Prodigal Son is an illustration of the tragic irony of fallen man's longing of the Father but his inability to turn back (Luke 15:11–32). The story ends with the son returning and approaching the father, who embraces him and throws a great banquet to celebrate return of the lost son. The son was always near the father in likeness but not near in presence until the final reunion. It has always been the hope of Israel to be near God—"God with us"—but they were never able to enter God's rest even in the Promised Land (Ps 73:28; Heb 4:8). It is not until believers are baptized into Christ's death and resurrection that the union is realized and sealed for eternity (Rom 6:4; 8:39). Finally in this union, God's children are not only near God in likeness but also in everlasting presence. "It is not blessed for man to be alone," said God to Adam, and this is the same principle that God equally applied to the covenant with his people, who are chosen as "a priestly kingdom and holy nation" (Gen 2:24; 4:1; Exod 19:6). As important as justification is, the covenantal union and its chief end of priestly kingdom is the eschatological goal of redemption. Justification is not an end in itself, but the means to the ethical and religious goal of man in the temple of God (Rev 2:7). The death and resurrection of Christ ushered in the last days of this evil age because these events opened the way to the reunion with the Father at the temple of the heavenly Jerusalem (Heb 12:22). The traditional doctrine of justification with its curative emphasis could be complemented with this vertical element: "He was delivered over to death for our sins and was raised to life for our justification" (Rom 4:25).

As discussed earlier, the New Perspective school attempted to redefine the doctrine of justification by faith in Paul.[49] Gaffin argues, however, that central to Paul's idea of justification is the comparison of two persons, Adam and the Last Adam,

---

47. Vos, *Pauline Eschatology*, 31.
48. Lewis, *Four Loves*, 19.
49. Wright, *What Saint Paul Really Said*, 125.

particularly in regard to their obedience to the moral law.[50] Justification for the apostle, then, was about righteousness obtained by faith rather than by works of the law (Rom 1:17; 4:25). The moral law was not a racial "boundary marker" for Jews but the standard of righteousness that must be obeyed for reconciliation with God (Rom 5:12).[51] The difficulties and differences aside, their insights still may be help us to put soteriology in the larger context of eschatology and the *Historia Salutis*. Stott welcomed the renewed interest in the centrality of cross and resurrection as the foundation of theology. He succinctly summarized that the historical death of Jesus on the cross makes us righteous "through Christ," while our personal union with him makes us righteous "in Christ."[52] Moreover, the corporate nature of Christ's work can breathe fresh air into the church, the new covenant community of all races, and its ethics in cultural and social renewal. The eschatology of redemption can provide a comprehensive context and more cohesion for all doctrines, soteriology included.

The redemption in Christ is never soteric alone but soteric-eschatolgoical: "In the period of the Reformation the problem of the obtaining of righteousness before God filled hearts and minds. For the time this forced the eschatological hope into the background, although even then it would have been by no means paradoxical to say that the two strands of the justifying faith and the eschatological outlook remained closely intertwined."[53] The secondary priority of eschatology perhaps caused a gradual separation of application of redemption from its foundation. The seventeenth and eighteenth centuries witnessed the rise of rationalism, pietism, and moralism and the doctrine of salvation was largely fixated on the logical order rather than on the redemptive-eschatological significance of Christ's work. Justification and sanctification became a matter of cause and effect in the logical order rather than gifts of union with the risen Christ. The analysis of the logical and the chronological order of redemption in the experience of believers took attention away from Christ, who is himself "our righteousness, holiness and redemption" (1 Cor 1:30). The logical cause and effect in the subjective experience of believers began to make certain stages in the *Ordo Salutis* subordinate to others, which produced more questions than answers.

The redemptive eschatology of union with Christ, in contrast, takes the question out of the realm of cause and effect and brings it into the regions above, where no stage in salvation has to be subordinate to another in him. As Vos stated, Pauline eschatology provides the substructure to his teachings on justification and the soteric process.[54] In Christ, salvation is orderly yet "every spiritual blessing in the heavenly realms" is available to believers without certain stages being subordinate to others. God's declaration of justification and the sanctification in his inseparable love occur

50. Gaffin, *By Faith Not by Sight*, 47.
51. Piper, *Future of Justification*.
52. Stott, *Cross of Christ*, 188.
53. Vos, *Pauline Eschatology*, ii.
54. Vos, *Pauline Eschatology*, 38.

simultaneously where believers are seated with Christ (Rom 8:31–39). The cause and effect in the logical order is preceded and preserved by union with Christ, which puts believers right before the throne of God. The vertical ascension of the "inner man" supersedes the subjective experience of the "outer man" in the horizontal realm of time (2 Cor 4:14). Salvation cannot be divided into broken pieces any more than Christ himself can be divided into parts. The placement of eschatology at the end of all other doctrines, therefore, is a misreading of Paul's theology.[55] Justification seen from the vertical-spatial perspective is truly an eschatological event that brings the future verdict of righteousness to the present (Rom 8:33–34).[56] The birth of the church in the New Covenant is a redemptive-eschatological event, which few seem to disagree with.[57] The kingdom of God and the birth of the church meant that redemption is now greater than the sum of its logical parts.

It is true that in this already-but-not-yet kingdom the church cannot prematurely celebrate victory or be overly triumphant (Col 1:24).[58] Regardless, Christ begins to live in believers through the Spirit and all the graces of redemption in its wholeness begin to flow into them from above (Gal 2:20). The logical order of redemption does not mean salvation is partly achieved or only a part of man is saved at the present time. The eschatological nature of salvation cannot be anything less than a whole redemption of the whole man in Christ. It is personal yet cosmic; there is a historical shift from the "this evil age" to "the coming age" (Gal 1:3; Eph 1:20–21). The gap between the definitive and the progressive aspects in salvation is due to the bisection of the world into the two ages rather than underachieved salvation. In this new order of affairs, the salvific is conjoined with the new creation and the eschatological outlook. Justification and sanctification are not just a personal matter in the subjective experience of believers, but these originate from and reside in the heavenly regions, where they are declared to be definitive (Rom 8:39). Sanctification is not subordinate to justification in the definitive vertical sense because "without holiness no one will see the Lord" (Heb 12:14). There it is no longer a matter of logical cause and effect, but a covenant matter of the chief end of man, who must be like his heavenly Father, holy, blameless, and blessed (Matt 5:48; Rom 8:29; Eph 1:4–5). Sanctification is not a subsidiary stage in the *Ordo Salutis* but part of the chief end in preparation for the glorification. Saving faith is redemptive-eschatological for it achieves the covenantal vision in nature through the gracious gift of redemption. The logical order is almost a moot point where believers are seated with Christ and the covenant is eternally sealed.

The present state of salvation, in terms of the spatial category, is already of the heavenly regions because an earthly state of salvation cannot guarantee its perseverance to the end. Even if a believer had been justified by faith, he might be tempted to

---

55. Sanders, *Paul and Palestinian Judaism*, 434.
56. Stott, *Cross of Christ*, 189.
57. Vos, *Pauline Eschatology*, 189.
58. Vos, *Pauline Eschatology*, 235.

retreat back to works of the law if he is uncertain that he has been taken out of the darkness into the kingdom of the Son (Col 1:13). He will persevere, however, if he stands justified before the throne of God in the regions above and knows that he will never be separated from the Father's love in Christ (Heb 4:16). If faith is defined solely in terms of personal righteousness without the vertical consideration, sanctification and perseverance are left to the individual believer to work out on his own—a hope "without the corresponding reality"[59] is no true hope. Such a state easily may fall victim to antinomianism or retreat back to legalism due to the lack of the supernatural foundation. The reason believers can live by faith rather than by sight is because they see the invisible reality of the union with the risen Christ in the upper regions. Again, it is an encouraging sign in recent times that Christology and eschatology are brought back into the scope of soteriology as their objective and foundation. The redemption in Christ, in the nature of the case, cannot but be a product of Christology and eschatology. The insight that the doctrine of justification cannot be separated from the doctrine of the church as the eschatological body of Christ is helpful in this regard.[60] In the inaugurated kingdom of God, salvation is both personal yet communal, present yet future, earthly yet heavenly (Luke 16:16; 17:21). The Golden Chain of redemption is now defined as part of the kingdom of God, which bears the fruit of righteousness, joy, and peace in the Spirit for both Jews and Gentiles (Rom 14:17). The progressive sanctification on earth flows down from the definitive sanctification in heaven, where justification is declared before the throne of grace. The process of sanctification, however, can quickly degenerate into works of the law apart from the vertical state, where it may turn into a sweet fruit and fragrance of the work of the Spirit. Seated and rested with Christ in the heavenly realms, they do not have to be "weary and burdened" in the progress of sanctification (Matt 11:28).

5.6 Seated in the Heavenly Realms

In the redemptive-eschatological period of Christ, the soteric and the eternal (supernatural) are inseparable: "Since, then, you have been raised with Christ, set your hearts on things above where Christ is, seated at the right hand of God" (Col 3:1).[61] The eschatology of redemption is superior to the eschatology of nature in this regard: the new humanity in the Last Adam are seated above next to God with the soteric deliverance from below. There the highest goal of man is achieved, definitively, in the state of blessedness: "The chief end of man is to glorify God and to enjoy him forever." The chief end in nature was typical of the chief end in redemption: "Set your hearts on things above," but only this time it is finished and superior to the nth degree in Christ. New Testament ethics is built on its theology—redemptive eschatology—that

---

59 Vos, *Pauline Eschatology*, 31.
60. Wright, *Justification*, 36; Stott, *Cross of Christ*, 189.
61. Vos, *Pauline Eschatology*, 45, 60.

what *ought to be* is based on what already *is*. The imperative of duty flows out of the indicative of the present state that Christians ought to be holy because they are holy, seated in the holy regions.[62] Their ethics in personal and public arenas is but a natural application of the new order in the upper regions and their identity in Christ. Between the two comings of Christ, therefore, there exists a healthy tension between what is already realized and what is yet to be realized.[63] This is a semi-eschatological reality where Christians are seated above while passing through this evil world below with the top controlling the bottom. There is a close correlation between Christian ethics and sanctification, and the new order in the upper regions that breathes the supernatural life and energy into Christians.[64] Ethics is possible and doable with the support of the otherworldly foundation, which makes it far more than a personal struggle in the journey toward heaven.

In Lutheran theology, contrition of the heart and the gospel are divided so that the former is of the law and the latter is of faith.[65] In this sense, the law and the gospel are divided: "One is contrition, that is, terrors smiting the conscience through the knowledge of sin; the other is faith, which is born of the Gospel, or of absolution, and believes that for Christ's sake, sins are forgiven, comfort the conscience, and delivers it from terrors."[66] But Reformed theology sees the contrition of repentance as an evangelical grace that flows out of the gospel.[67] The gospel so defined includes both contrition and absolution, repentance and faith; the use of the law is not restricted to grievances of sin but extends to sanctification "to walk with Him in all the ways of His commandments."[68] Thus, repentance is an evangelical grace of the gospel rather than a prior stage in preparation for the gospel. The covenantal use of the law for holiness does not work against justification by faith but accompanies it, producing the fruit of righteousness in God's children. In this way, the gospel is truly rectifying and consummative of man created in God's image. The redemptive eschatology of the gospel does not negate the use of the law in repentance or in sanctification but places believers under the law of Christ (1 Cor 9:21). The difference between the works of the law and faith as the means of justification does not amount to the division of the law and the gospel. The former is a soteric issue whereas the latter is a consummative-eschatological one. Paul harmonizes the gospel and the law through union with Christ and the vertical ascension of believers to the heavenly realms, where they are under Christ's law. They receive the Spirit of adoption and conform to the image of Christ, taking the use of the law to new heights previously unseen, where believers exercise

---

62. Cullman, *Christ and Time*, 224.
63. Cullman, *Christ and Time*, 224.
64. Cullman, *Christ and Time*, 224.
65. Formula of Concord, xii.
66. Formula of Concord, xii.
67. Westminster Confession of Faith, 15.
68. Westminster Confession of Faith, 15.

the recreated image of God (Eph 4:24). The use of the law against the earthly nature is rooted in the upper regions: "Set your hearts on the things above . . . Put to death, therefore, whatever belongs to your earthly nature . . ." (Col 3:1, 5). The law is written in the heart, rather than on stones, in the new administration of the Covenant of Grace: "No longer will they teach their neighbor, or say to one another, 'Know the Lord,' because they will all know me" (Jer 31:31–34; Heb 8:11). In the inner sanctuary of heaven, the veil that covered Moses' face is no longer needed, and is lifted so that God's glory might shine forth in its fullness through Christ (2 Cor 3:3–18). Christ does not need the veil, and believers have freedom in the Spirit: "And we, who with unveiled faces all reflect the Lord's glory, are being transformed into his likeness with ever-increasing glory, which comes from the Lord, who is the Spirit" (v. 18).

The apostle Paul would not command believers to do what they do not have the ability to do. The reason that they can set their hearts on things above rather than things below is because they are there. It is not just who they are, but also where they are that enables them to put to death the earthly nature. Christ fulfilled the law for us while he was on earth, and now fulfills the law in us bonded together through the Spirit (Gal 2:20). Paul viewed the life of believers already hidden in God by the union and the imperative of sanctification is issued on the ground of the indicative (Col 3:3–5). They are able to put to death the remaining earthly nature because "death no longer has mastery over" them—the life hidden in God in the upper regions is safe and untouchable (Rom 6:9–11). Only those who are assured of their presence in the otherworldly regions can put to death that which belongs to this world for the sake of Christ, including the earthly life (Phil 1:21). They possess the sufficient spiritual weapons from above to wage war against the earthly nature with assurance of the final victory guaranteed by Christ. The earthly members, or the remains of the flesh, do not belong to the heavenly realms, where the man in Christ is seated: "Put to death, therefore, whatever belongs to earthly nature: sexual immorality, impurity, lust, evil desires, and greed, which is idolatry" (Col 3:5). Only parts are left of those seated in the heavenly places, and they are to be put to death through the work of sanctification in the Spirit.

In Romans, the discourse on justification is followed by the exhortation for sanctification: "Therefore, I urge you, brothers, in view of God's mercy, to offer your bodies as living sacrifices, holy and pleasing to God—this is your spiritual act of worship" (Rom 12:1). It shows more than a logical order between the two for the emphasis is the union with the risen Christ rather than cause and effect. In Paul's other epistles, this union is more explicit: "Since, then, you have been raised with Christ, set your hearts on things above, where Christ is seated at the right hand of God" (Col 3:1). This means the apostle understood justification as part of being raised with Christ and sanctification flows out of (down from) it. The indicative of forensic justification is part of the semi-eschatological ascension to the upper regions from which the imperatives are derived. In the logical sequence of the *Ordo Salutis*, sanctification follows justification, but in the vertical ascension both are the fruit of union with Christ. They are viewed within the scope of union with Christ, hence without any sense of logical conflict. The progressive sanctification takes place in the horizontal plane of time but the definitive sanctification is an outcome of the vertical union with the risen Lord. The vertical does not weaken the horizontal: "It has sometimes been asserted that this deflection from the straight prospective line of vision to the upward bent towards the heavenly world represents a toning down of the eschatological interest."[69] But the vertical part actually supports the horizontal process of sanctification: "In reality this whole representation of the Christian state as centrally and potentially anchored in heaven is not the abrogation, it is the most intense and the most practical assertion of the other-worldly tenor of the believer's life."[70]

In the scheme of things, sanctification flows down from the entrance into God's rest in the upper regions: "And God blessed the seventh day and made it holy, because on it he rested from all the work of creating that he had done" (Gen 2:3). The seventh day represents the eschatology of nature, which has been fulfilled by the eschatology of redemption in the resurrection of Christ. As a result, believers enter God's rest, and that provides the ground and the energy needed for the spiritual war on earth (Heb 4:4–5). The seventh day is "not the seventh day in our weekly cycle," said Murray, and there "is the strongest presumption in favor of the interpretation that this seventh day is not one that terminated at a certain point in history, but that whole period of time subsequent to the end of the sixth day is the sabbath of rest alluded . . ."[71] It is unclear precisely how history would have unfolded if Adam had kept the covenant and the world continued without corruption by sin. The end of the natural eschatology is not specified: "What the ultimate eschatology would have been in this latter event we do not know. But it would not have been an eschatology without developments and achievements of temporal duration and succession."[72] The eschatology of redemption has taken a detour, as it were, but its final goal toward God's rest remains effective and its outcome superior in Christ (1 Cor 15:44–49). God's rest in redemption produces in believers the supernatural energy to fulfill the chief end of man left unfulfilled by Adam. The rest in the upper regions will be far superior to the natural one with a "redemptive plus" in the Last Adam. The natural Sabbath was typical of the redemptive Sabbath: "For in him all things were created . . . all things have been created through him and for him. He is before all things, and in him all things hold together" (Col 1:16–17).

The adoption to sonship is the reason for the redemptive rest because the spiritual children can rest before the Father. The adoption is perhaps the most significant in the way of salvation because of the finality associate with it—and the peace it brings

69. Vos, *Pauline Eschatology*, 39.
70. Vos, *Pauline Eschatology*, 39.
71. Murray, *Principles of Conduct*, 30.
72. Murray, *Principles of Conduct*, 41.

to the children of God. The imperatives of duty and ethics flow out of the indicative of God's adoption in Christ. Justification is a forensic notion that does not in and of itself guarantee perseverance, but adoption to sonship does: "Now if we are children, then we are heirs-heirs of God and co-heirs with Christ, if indeed we share in his sufferings in order that we may also share in his glory" (Rom 8:17). The glorification is preceded by sanctification into holiness for without it no one will see God. But the growth in holiness is grounded in the peace and assurance that they will never be abandoned by the Father. The logical order in the way of salvation, the *Ordo Salutis*, is guaranteed by nothing else than the unceasing love of the Father in the Son through the Counsel of Peace. Seated next to the Father, the distinction between the law and the gospel will be theoretical for the children. The indicative and the imperative will be unified and harmonious: "faith working through love" and "speaking the truth in love" (Gal 5:6; Eph 4:15). The adoption in Christ completes the unity of the legal and the practical aspects of redemption because the membership and fellowship of family are sealed, inseparable, and practical. No father would ever say to a child, "You are my child in the legal sense, but not in the practical sense." It would be absurd and senseless for a child to be told that he is adopted but not guaranteed to stay that way. Adoption renders the logical order of justification and sanctification almost a moot point in the practical sphere. The adopted child is sanctified definitively, and also progressively into the fellowship of the family and will never be forsaken (Heb 13:5–6). The adoption has taken place in union with the firstborn, hence it cannot be postponed to future but immediately effective upon rebirth by the Spirit. God's rest in nature is now the Father's rest in redemption through the Son and he said, "I have not lost one of those you gave me" (John 18:9). The child will not be able to sustain faith if there is even a slightest doubt that his status will be threatened by the performance of his duty in the family. With assurance, however, the child's obedience to please the Father will be carried out freely and voluntarily. The law cannot condemn a child seated next to the Father but can help him to fulfill the covenantal duty as the image-bearer of God (Rom 13:10). Faith in love and truth in love are the marks of the redemption in Christ; they are the fruit of the redemptive eschatology of covenant love (*hesed*).[73]

Sanctification is a spiritual war seen from the perspective of the kingdom of heaven ushered in by the finished work of Christ: "For our struggle is not against flesh and blood, but against the rulers, against the authorities, against the powers of this dark world and against the spiritual forces of evil in the heavenly realms" (Eph 6:12). It is called sanctification in a believer, ethics in a body of believers, but a holy war in the kingdom of God. These are not separate entities of holiness but different perspectives of the present reality of believers placed between the two ages. Israel was a type of the priestly kingdom called to wage a holy war of total destruction (*hêrem*) in Canaan (Lev 27:28–29). In a typological sense, the theocratic kingdom was to put to death everything dedicated to Yahweh and could not retain them under any circumstances.

---

73. Gentry and Wellum, *Kingdom through Covenants*, 586–87.

The holy war of total destruction by Israel progresses to the holy war of the new Israel in an exactly same format: "Put to death, therefore, whatever belongs to your earthly nature . . ." (Col 3:5). In fact, nothing wicked will inherit or even enter the kingdom of God (1 Cor 6:9). Sanctification is a personal growth in holiness but in the kingdom of God it is a clash of the two ages no less fierce in the spiritual realms than the holy war of Israel in Canaan (Gal 1:3). Personal holiness in the two ages also depends on the kingdom of God drawing its life and energy from above. In the spiritual theocratic kingdom, believers are not expected to live privately but as members of the kingdom engaged in a war with the spiritual forces of evil and darkness (Col 1:13). Since the days of John the Baptist, it is inevitable that the kingdom of heaven is "subjected to violence" from the kingdom of darkness and believers are engaged in this battle (Matt 11:12).

A person is no match for the organized forces of evil unleashed in these last days unless aided by the greater supernatural forces of the kingdom of heaven (Matt 26:41; Eph 6:12). The kingdom is greater than a single believer and "whoever is least in the kingdom of heaven is greater than" even the greatest of man prior to the coming of the kingdom (Matt 11:11). Without the foundation and support from the upper regions, individual believers are thrown into the world ill prepared to fight against the onslaught of evil. The devil and his army are launching a violent and organized attack against God's people: "Then I saw a beast and the kings of the earth and their armies gathered together to make war against the rider on horse and his army" (Rev 19:19). The marked difference in the spiritual condition of the disciples after Pentecost owes to the outpouring of the Spirit and the kingdom of God that came with it. The outpouring does not just mean the filling of the Spirit in a personal way but the arrival of the kingdom from above in full force.[74] The Spirit turned ordinary fishermen into extraordinary witnesses of the risen King and his kingdom announcing the arrival of the last days of this age. The outpouring of the Spirit is a proof of God's redemptive work entering a new phase rather than a model of personal fullness of the Spirit.[75] It is rather a model of how the theocratic kingdom ruled by the Messiah can make a difference in personal holiness and in the spiritual war against darkness. The fullness of the Spirit is for the war of total destruction of sin in the theocracy of the risen Lord (Acts 2:36). The intrusion of the theocratic nation into Canaan was typical of the arrival of the kingdom of the Messiah into this world. The beast and his army in the eschatological war cannot be matched by personal holiness alone but must be dealt with by the full force of the messianic kingdom (Matt 11:12).

The exhortation of Paul to "offer your bodies as a living sacrifice holy and pleasing to God-this is your true and proper worship" and not to "conform any longer to the pattern of this world" is a spiritual war (Rom 12:1–2). First, *sacrifice* and *worship* invoke the thought of a temple, the religious and spiritual core central to the life and

74. Ferguson, *Holy Spirit,* 80.
75. Ferguson, *Holy Spirit,* 80.

the holy war of Israel in Canaan. The conquest meant an intrusion of the priestly kingdom of Israel into a pagan world to wage a holy war of Yahweh with the nations. The politico-religious Israel was typical of the messianic kingdom, and the temple was a place of sacrifice yet also played a central role in the holy war that God fought in Israel's behalf. The ark of the covenant would stand in the forefront of the army of Israel and lead them into the holy war of total destruction, called *herem* (Josh 3:11). In the united kingdom of David, religious and political centers converged to a location in Zion and Jerusalem, where the ark was to be stationed permanently. There God established the everlasting covenant with David and promised to extend his throne and kingdom through a messianic son in the Davidic line (2 Sam 7:1–29). The movement of the ark toward the temple of Jerusalem was symbolico-typical of the heavenly Jerusalem and Zion, where Christ entered (Heb 12:22–23). The living sacrifice Paul mentioned, if read in this context, evokes an image of the temple and the holy war of Israel in Canaan. Second, the offering of their bodies as living sacrifices was so that they may not "conform to the pattern of this world" (Rom 12:2). The war is not just of a person but of a kingdom; since the beginning covenant has always been corporate as well as personal as in the case of the *Pactum Salutis*.[76]

God called out Israel from Egypt to become a holy nation and equally calls out believers from this evil age that they may be a priestly kingdom (Gal 1:4; 1 Pet 2:9). The new humanity in the Second Adam are image-bearers of God created in truth, righteousness, and holiness (Eph 4:24). In the cosmic perspective of the holy war, since believers already belong to the coming age, they must not conform to the ways of this age, which they have the power from above to do so. The renewal of their minds in this holy war is done as the army of Christ's kingdom rather than as an individual believer on his own. Third, the phrase "living sacrifice" is a peculiar concept not found elsewhere, for a sacrifice is usually dead, not living. But the one who is dead to sin but alive to God is a living sacrifice since he is united to the death and resurrection of Christ (Rom 6:4, 11). Christ is the ultimate example of living sacrifice, for "the death he died, he died to sin once for all; but the life he lives, he lives to God" (v. 10). And those who are united with Christ then also become living sacrifices the moment they are dead and risen with him, seated in the heavenly regions. Christ is the eternal sacrifice, dead but alive, and those united to him can experience this most radical form of holiness and sanctification. Christ himself epitomizes a life that did not conform to the patterns of this world and believers are expected live in the same pattern of life. The ethics of "do not conform to this age," therefore, are grounded in the fact that they belong to a different world. The logic is consistent with the command to put to death the earthly nature since they have been raised to the heavenly nature (Col 3:5).

The traditional view of salvation was not sufficiently equipped to explain sanctification from the vertical-spatial category of the two ages. It was largely due to its focus on the logical order of salvation, which turned holiness into a purely a personal affair

---

76. Gentry and Wellum, *Kingdom through Covenants*, 586–87.

that often results in antinomian or legalistic tendencies. Hence, the apostle tells us not to imitate the schema of this world as just observed in Romans 12:2. The clash of the schema of the two ages peaked at the union with the exalted Christ and since that time sanctification is not only personal rectitude but a holy war of the kingdom. This brings a wider and higher perspective in the cosmic level to the soteric issues of individual believers as their supernatural foundation. The supernatural space is an important motif observed in the Covenant of Grace, which is not just a forward movement but also an upward movement to the upper schema. The Scriptures often use "spaces" to denote the quality of covenant between God and man: Eden, ark, Ur, Palestine, Egypt, Desert, Canaan, Zion, Babylon, Jerusalem, etc. These are all typical of the schema or pattern of this age or the coming age subsequent to the time of Christ, when the kingdom of God is at war with the kingdom of darkness. In the pre-eschatological period the space was expressed in symbolico-typical language, but in the semi-eschatological period expressed as the two ages or heaven and earth.

The earthly type of the temple in Israel was but a copy and image of the heavenly temple Christ entered after resurrection (Heb 8:5; 9:12, 24). In him, believers too have already arrived at the temple of "Mount Zion, the heavenly Jerusalem, and the City of the living God" (Heb 12:22). This spatial movement from one region to another is not just from the Old to the New, but from earth to heaven, from this age to the coming age. Hence, salvation is no longer viewed just in terms of a logical or chronological sequence but defined within the scope of the spatial transformation from below to above (Col 3:1). The redemption in Christ is not just a soteric rectitude but a shift in the schema of things: "And just as we have borne the likeness of the earthly man, so shall we bear the likeness of the man from heaven" (1 Cor 15:48). It is a part of the new and eternal order rather than just a rectitude from sin, although the former is achieved through the added gift of the latter. It has become an anthropological question of the shift from the natural to the supernatural man, in addition to the redeeming of the fallen man from death. Since believers have already moved from the schema of the below to the above, there is no more need to keep moving from one place to another on earth as in the case of Israel. There is no more sacred place—a temple—on earth for they have arrived at the heavenly temple behind the curtain with Christ (Heb 4:16). Canaan was typical of the city of God in heaven, where believers can finally rest next to the Father: "Instead, they were longing for a better country—a heavenly one. Therefore God is not ashamed to be called their God, for he has prepared a city for them" (Heb 11:16). The earthly temple was the sacred space for Israel in the typological era, but the heavenly temple is the space of the consummate union with God for the church. Christ's High-Priestly Prayer was that believers might enter the eschatological temple in the union and fellowship of the Father and the Son through the Spirit (John 17:21–26).

The redemptive-eschatological work of Christ did not end with his death but continues after his resurrection in the heavenly temple as the eternal High Priest.

All the spiritual gifts of the Covenant of Grace flow down from that sacred space in the heavenly regions, received by those united to Christ through the means of grace. Christ's heavenly ministry behind the curtain renders his earthly ministry forever efficient; the sacrifice prepared at the altar takes effect behind the curtain and becomes "the anchor for the soul, firm and secure" (Heb 6:19–20). The schema of the heavenly regions, therefore, precedes and enables the order of salvation in believers on earth. The work of the kingdom of God depends on "all authority in heaven and on earth" belonging to Christ, who rules and intercedes in heaven (Matt 28:18). The power does not lie in us but in the schema of the upper regions, where Christ took us with him. The vertical vision of the heavenlies does not smother interest in earthly matters but liberates believers to faithfully fulfill their temporal callings (1 Cor 7:29–31). The present state of believers in heaven reassures them of their mission on earth and empowers them to carry it out with great fervor, for their eternal destiny is secure in Christ: "To this end, I strenuously contend with all the energy Christ so powerfully works in me" (Col 1:29).

Chapter 6

Spirit and Eschatology

6.1 Spirit and Kingdom

THE DESCENDING OF THE SPIRIT at Pentecost is a redemptive-eschatological event ushering in the last days of this age subsequent to the death and resurrection of Christ (Acts 2:33). The outpouring of the Spirit after Christ's enthronement signaled the coming of the kingdom of God, met by a violent reaction of this evil age (Matt 11:12). The eschatological character of Pentecost had been foretold by Jesus:

> But I tell you the truth: It is for your good that I am going away. Unless I go away, the Counselor will not come to you; but if I go, I will send him to you. When he comes, he will convict the world of guilt in regard to sin and righteousness and judgment . . . and in regard to judgment, because the prince of this world now stands condemned. (John 16:7–8, 11)

The significance of Pentecost is that kingdom of God, foretold through the type of Israel, has arrived in substance and fulfillment.[1] It is a redemptive-eschatological event that cannot simply be translated into a private experience of baptism in the Spirit. The once-for-all historical event of Pentecost can no more be repeated than Christ's death and resurrection can be repeated. Pentecost is the revelation that the work Christ finished is complete and ready to be applied by the Spirit according to the Counsel of Peace (Acts 2:33; Eph 1:4–14). The Spirit is the "deposit" of the final redemption in resurrection, "guaranteeing what is to come" (2 Cor 5:5; Eph 1:14). The Counsel of the Father and the Son is fulfilled and the Spirit is poured out in the age of the church's mission to gather the chosen, giving them the gift of faith (Zech 6:13; Eph 2:8–9). The Counsel of Peace from eternity and the Covenant of Grace in history have reached their final phase in the Son and the Spirit. The indwelling of the Spirit in believers is not just for personal rebirth or preparation for the future resurrection but is itself a state of resurrection (Eph 2:5–6): "[T]he Spirit is not only the author of

---

1. Ferguson, *Holy Spirit*, 176.

the resurrection-act, but likewise the permanent substratum of the resurrection-life, to which He supplies the inner, basic element and the outer atmosphere."[2] Union with the Spirit means union with the risen Christ and spatial ascension into the heavenly regions immediately upon rebirth. In the Spirit, the knowledge of God through the high-priestly order of Melchizedek is direct, intimate, and efficient, being written in the heart rather than in the stone (Jer 31:31–34). The outpouring of the Spirit at Pentecost thus represents the climax in the progress of revelation and a marked discontinuity from the order of Aaron. With the disappearance of the veil on Moses' face by turning to Christ, the glory and freedom in the Spirit are not temporary but everlasting (2 Cor 3:16–18).

The eschatological nature of the Spirit is revealed in the phrase "the deposit of what is to come"; he is not only a means of rebirth but a guarantee of the coming age (2 Cor 1:22; 5:5; Eph 1:14, 21). He is the guarantee of the eternal world, not of this world, which will culminate in the bodily resurrection of believers (2 Cor 5:5). When the Spirit comes into a believer, the supernatural order of life intrudes into the temporal world as the foundation of true and everlasting hope. The state of being "filled with the Spirit" at Pentecost is a signal that the risen Christ is Lord over all things and the age of mission has begun for all people, including Jews and Gentiles. They are now one new humanity united in the exalted Christ, formed into one body: "For we were all baptized by one Spirit into one body—whether Jews or Greeks, slave or free—and we were all given the one Spirit to drink" (1 Cor 12:13). This filling of the Spirit of Christ means that the risen Lord is now present in the body and the work of consummating the body has started in global mission (Matt 28:18–20).[3] Wherever or whoever is filled with the Spirit is now the holy temple of God, and it no longer resides in Jerusalem but in Christ, who is the Temple (John 2:19–21). In him, believers also become the temple of the Spirit so that wherever they go will be the place of worship (John 4:24; 1 Cor 6:19). The age of mission is correlated with the new definition of temple and worship ushered in by the Spirit, that wherever believers go in the name of Christ is where people can directly worship God. Hence, the "fellowship of the Holy Spirit" in the body does not only refer to the fellowship of believers in the Spirit, but also a direct fellowship with the Spirit (2 Cor 13:13; Phil 2:1).[4] In the fellowship of the Spirit at the temple believers can enter the fellowship of the three Persons of the blessed Trinity (John 17:21). The Counsel of Peace is executed by the Son and lived in the Spirit, fulfilling the great wedding of "I will be your God and you will be my people" (Eph 5:23).

The eschatology of the Spirit is clearly revealed with the arrival of the new administration of the Covenant of Grace "under the gospel."[5] The great distinction of the New Covenant lies in the glory and freedom previously hidden by the veil on Moses'

---

2. Vos, *Pauline Eschatology*, 165.
3. Ferguson, *Holy Spirit*, 178.
4. Ferguson, *Holy Spirit*, 175.
5. Westminster Confession of Faith, 7.

face, but now the veil is taken away in Christ: "Now the Lord is the Spirit, and where the Spirit of the Lord is, there is freedom. And we, who with unveiled faces all reflect the Lord's glory, are being transformed into his likeness with ever-increasing glory, which comes from the Lord, who is the Spirit" (2 Cor 3:17–18). The letter and the Spirit, a distinction in the administration of the Covenant of Grace, are substantially the same yet different in the degree of glory and freedom (Heb 3:5). They do not refer to different ways of receiving salvation (law versus grace) but different degrees and extent in the worship and fellowship of God (John 4:21–24). The coming of the Spirit at Pentecost was a shift from the veiled glory to the unveiled glory: from the pre-eschatological shadow to the semi-eschatological reality. The unveiled glory will then be consummated in the full glory of the kingdom of the Father: "Now we see but a poor reflection as in a mirror; then we shall see face to face. Now I know in part; then I shall know fully, even as I am fully known" (1 Cor 13:12; 15:24). The unveiled glory in the Spirit is unmistakable, however, consistent with the supernatural regions where believers are seated with Christ. The primary work of the Spirit is to reveal this unmasked glory to believers that they may have the knowledge of the Father and the Son as never before. The glory of God in the vertical worship and the "zeal" of God in the horizontal mission are now fully revealed by the Spirit (2 Kgs 19:31).

The descending of the Spirit meant the intrusion of heaven on earth in the form of the kingdom of God as the church is united with the risen Lord (Acts 2:36; Luke 16:16; 17:21). Accordingly, believers may now pray the Lord's Prayer, "Thy kingdom come, and thy will be done on earth as it is in heaven." In Peter's sermon at Pentecost, the crowd was told that the messianic kingdom in the Davidic covenant has been fulfilled precisely as it was told David long ago (Acts 2:30–36). There are many symbolico-typical forms of theocratic kingdom appropriate for the period of interest throughout redemptive history (Heb 8:5; 9:23). The messianic kingdom has always been the object of eschatological thirst, and the outpouring of the Spirit at Pentecost was the fulfillment of the prophecy by Joel. The kingdom, however, was no longer just an intrusive model, arriving in full force, prompting a violent reaction from the kingdom of darkness (Matt 11:12). The epic clash of the kingdom of the Son and the spiritual forces of evil that was foretold from the outset is now being realized by the coming of the woman's "offspring" and the Spirit in these last days of the holy war (Gen 3:15; Gal 1:4; Col 1:13). The intrusive model of a theocratic kingdom in Canaan and the war of total destruction typified the spiritual holy war of the redemptive-eschatological era. It is now the war of the church and the kingdom, ruled by the risen Christ and carried out in the form of the global mission led by the Spirit of God.

In Canaan, the holy war was carried out with a temporary suspension of common grace ethics, as it "refers to the irrevocable giving over of things or persons to the LORD, often by totally destroying them . . ." (Lev 27:29; Josh 2:1–21; 7:1). The theocratic kingdom of the covenant, by nature, is defined by the law of "Do this, then you shall live" and nothing unholy will enter it (Exod 19:6; Lev 18:5; 1 Cor 6:9). The total destruction of things and persons seems to violate common grace ethics but it was a holy war of Yahweh against the pagan gods with eternal consequences. It was a war in the Mosaic covenant typical of the last day for the final judgment of all evil and the consummation of the righteous (1 Cor 15:24). In the redemptive-eschatological sense, the holy war climaxed at the cross of Christ, where the decisive battle was finished for the reward and curse of the covenant kingdom (Gen 3:15; John 16:11). The cross, where "it is finished," meant the eternal curse for some and the eternal reward for others; the Parousia will only be the reaping of the harvest of the age of mission (Mark 4:26–29). In these last days of the mission of the Spirit, Christ is the absolute condition of the holy war of the gospel by which God will judge humanity: "Whoever believes in him is not condemned, but whoever does not believe stands condemned already because he has not believed in the name of God's one and only Son" (John 3:18). The resurrection of Jesus was understood by Peter as the historical fulfillment of the Davidic covenant and the priestly kingdom, for Jesus is "both Lord and Christ" (Acts 2:36). His reign and the holy war is no longer typical as the Messiah is enthroned with all authority over heaven and earth (Matt 28:18). The semi-eschatological kingdom is an intrusion of a higher order than the theocratic Israel for it brought "all things in heaven and on earth together under one head, even Christ" (Mark 1:15; Eph 1:10).

The kingdom arriving in full force is expected to be met by an equally strong reaction from the armies of darkness in a degree unknown before Christ, but also with a foretaste of the final victory when Satan and his forces will be totally eradicated (Matt 11:12; Rev 19:2). The outpouring of the Spirit at Pentecost "like tongues of fire" represents a new form of the holy war of total destruction in the age of mission. Those seated in the heavenly regions with Christ are ordered to "put to death the earthly nature" with the fire of the Spirit: "When he comes, he will convict the world of guilt in regard to sin and righteousness and judgment . . ." (John 16:8). Hence, a discontinuity of a historical proportion is witnessed with regard to the work of the Spirit between the Old and the New Testaments.[6] This is not surprising for the knowledge of the Spirit has always been directly proportional to the knowledge of the Father and the Son; the three Persons work together according to the *Pactum Salutis*.[7] The development of this knowledge was more horizontal in the past but now became vertical through union with the risen Christ; it became redemptive-eschatological in the new creation by the Spirit.[8] The Spirit of adoption will never depart God's children for he is now the "life-giving Spirit" of the Last Adam who did not fail (Gen 3:22; 6:3; 1 Cor 15:45). The bond of union and fellowship with God is everlasting and the children need not fear anymore that the Spirit might leave them again (Ps 51:11).

The eschatology of the Spirit is seen in Ezekiel's prophecy of the valley of dry bones, where God said, "I will make breath [*ruach*] enter you" and later again said, "I

---

6. Stott, *Baptism and Fullness*, 26.
7. Ferguson, *Holy Spirit*, 30.
8. Beale, "Eschatological Conception," 12.

will put my Spirit in you . . ." (Ezek 37:5, 14). The breath (wind) of the Spirit, then, is not the same breath God breathed into Adam in order to make him "a living being" (Gen 2:7). The "likeness of the earthly man" in Adam was made in the natural breath, but "the likeness of the man from heaven" in the Last Adam was made in the *Pneuma* of the Spirit (1 Cor 15:49). The breath (wind) in Ezekiel's prophecy was typical of the breath of the Spirit in the redemptive-eschatological era of Christ. Its revelation may have been symbolico-typical but it is sufficient for us to recognize the eschatological significance of the Spirit. The Spirit at Pentecost was the fulfillment of prophecy of the valley of dry bones, just as it was of the prophecy of Joel in regard to the last days. The wind of the Spirit breathed into the new humanity of the last days is the seal of the Counsel of Peace: "I will make a covenant of peace with them; it will be an everlasting covenant . . . I will be their God, and they will be my people" (Ezek 37:26–27). But in keeping with the holy war of the kingdom in the last days, the Spirit demands a radical and immediate surrender to God: "Now if we are children, then we are heirs—heirs of God and coheirs with Christ, if indeed we share in his sufferings in order that we may also share in his glory" (Rom 8:17). Ferguson suggests that of all the titles given to the Spirit in the New Testament, "the Spirit of Adoption" is the most prominent and rich in nuance.[9] The chief end of man in nature was to glorify and enjoy God, and the chief end in redemption is no different except that it is achieved through the redemptive adoption to sonship by the Spirit and being coheirs of God's kingdom.[10] The justification by faith guarantees a legal status and liberty of conscience from guilt, but adoption to sonship guarantees a far more glorious prospect of the inheritance of God's kingdom. The specific call of believers to share in suffering as well as in glory is grounded in the adoption to sonship, in which they are "heirs of God and coheirs with Christ." The dry bones in the valley needed more than legal justification; they needed the wind of the Spirit to energize them with the supernatural life and vitality in order to carry out the gospel mission in these last days.

Pentecost will not be repeated in the same sense that Christ's death and resurrection will not be repeated, except that believers in every age may share in the redemptive-eschatological effects of these events (Rom 6:3–5). The Spirit will not again have to descend from heaven in the same way that Christ will not again have to incarnate to be crucified. The eschatology of the Spirit must be distinguished from the soteriology of the Spirit. In the soteric part, every believer in every age will receive the benefits of the finished work of Christ through the rebirth of the Spirit:

> And you also were included in Christ when you heard the word of truth, the gospel of your salvation. Having believed, you were marked in him with a seal, the promised Holy Spirit, who is a deposit guaranteeing our inheritance until

---

9. Ferguson, *Holy Spirit*, 182.
10. Ferguson, *Holy Spirit*, 182.

the redemption of those who are God's possession—to the praise of his glory. (Eph 1:13–14)

The redemptive-eschatological foundation of the church is laid only once, but the building will continue to be built to "become a dwelling in which God lives by his Spirit" (Eph 2:18–20). The singularity of the Spirit's descension is of the same nature with the cross and resurrection, that they laid the foundation of the holy temple where God lives.[11] The Third Person of the Trinity always works in concert with the Father and the Son in accordance with the Counsel of Peace and the Covenant of Grace (John 17:4–6; Acts 2:33; 1 Cor 15:45). The promise of Jesus that he will be with the disciples "always, to the very end of the age" would be fulfilled through the presence of the Spirit of Christ in them. There is nothing the Spirit does independently of Christ so that he is called "the Spirit of Christ" or "the Spirit of Jesus" (Rom 8:9; Acts 16:7). The application of redemption is the task of the Spirit but it depends on the foundational work of Christ that goes back to the Eternal Counsel within the three Persons of God. One of the common errors is to view the Spirit operating on his own in mysterious and spiritual ways in disregard of the intra-Trinitarian Counsel. It is worth noting that the Eternal Counsel of the three Persons is marked by mutual glory, love, and knowledge (John 17:21–14).

The economic Trinity means that the three Persons have distinct roles based on the Eternal Counsel manifested through the Covenant of Grace in history. The work of the Second Person is foundational as the Mediator: "For God was pleased to have all his fullness dwell in him, and through him to reconcile to himself all things, whether things on earth or things in heaven, by making peace through his blood, shed on the cross" (Col 1:19–20). Accordingly, the Spirit does not work independently but always in and through Christ so that the Counsel of Peace is successfully completed (Eph 1:4). The Spirit is personal but not mysterious, supernatural but not devoid of realism, whose primary focus is to bring believers into union with the risen Christ.[12] The subjective must always be preceded by the objective, or the schema of the age to come in which God "rescued us from the dominion of darkness and brought us into the kingdom of the Son he loves" (Col 1:13).[13] The Spirit is the deposit of resurrection that guarantees the coming age, revealing to them in advance what they could only see through the eyes of faith at the present time (2 Cor 5:5–7):

> Therefore we do not lose heart. Though outwardly we are wasting away, yet inwardly we are being renewed day by day. For our light and momentary troubles are achieving for us an eternal glory that far outweighs them all. So we fix our eyes not on what is seen, but on what is unseen. For what is seen is temporary, but what is unseen is eternal. (2 Cor 4:16–18)

---

11. Ferguson, *Holy Spirit*, 87–91.
12. Ferguson, *Holy Spirit*, 177.
13. Ferguson, *Holy Spirit*, 177.

The eschatology of redemption in the Spirit is that he does not send believers backward to Eden but upward to the new Eden. It is to create a new humanity in Christ who can reach the ethical and religious goal failed by the first humanity—but this time with a soteric addition (Eph 2:15). The presence of the Spirit is the unfailing hope that believers have moved, provisionally, from the natural state of *posse peccare* (able to sin) to the supernatural state of *non posse peccare* (not able to sin).[14]

6.2 Works of Spirit

In our analysis of the work of the Spirit, the Christo-eschatological perspective will be maintained in keeping with the overall approach taken in this book.[15] The several key concepts in regard to the work of the Spirit in the believer on a personal level are the rebirth, the fruit, the gifts, and the *adiaphora* of the Spirit. When working together, ideally, these will produce the fullness of the Spirit, making most of every opportunity (*kairos*) in these evil days (*chronos*) (Eph 5:16, 18). The Spirit is the Third Person of the Trinity and must be revered as much as the Father and the Son: "And do not grieve the Holy Spirit of God, with whom you were sealed for the day of redemption" (Eph 4:30). The sealing of the Spirit is redemptive and eschatological in that it involves the rebirth and the raising of believers with Christ to the heavenly regions. The Spirit, through the sacraments, "seal[s] Christ to us, the rich and full Christ, with all that we have in Him."[16] The Golden Chain of the *Ordo Salutis* is not a mere chain of logical causes and effects in the spiritual experience of believers but the redemptive-eschatological process that brings them into the new and eternal order away from the schema of this world.[17] The soteric is part of the new schema of the Spirit wherein the personal and the spatial elements of redemption are conjoined.[18] The overspiritualizing of the Third Person of the Trinity is not only theologically incorrect and morally hazardous, but practically unbeneficial. It is true that some works of the Spirit may be viewed as more universal (normative) and others as more particular (personal and situational) in nature. But no work of the Spirit is to be regarded as more spiritual or less spiritual in the redemptive-eschatological sense of man and the world.

Rebirth in Spirit

The rebirth of believers into the family of God is the foundational work of the Spirit that brings them into the kingdom of heaven to be the heirs of God: "Very truly I tell you, no one can enter the kingdom of God unless they are born of water and the

---

14. Berkhof, *History of Christian Doctrines*, 134.
15. Ferguson, *Holy Spirit*, 79.
16. Vos, *Redemptive History*, 262.
17. Ferguson, *Holy Spirit*, 99.
18. Ferguson, *Holy Spirit*, 99.

Spirit" (John 3:5). The adoption into the family of God as coheirs with Christ is the normative work of the Spirit that logically precedes all other subsequent works: "He saved us through the washing of rebirth and renewal by the Holy Spirit, whom he poured out on us generously through Jesus Christ our Savior, so that, having been justified by his grace, we might become heirs having the hope of eternal life" (Titus 3:5b–7). The rebirth is a universal gift to all believers for the Father's inheritance of the kingdom is equally distributed to all children. The rebirth is where the soteric of personal redemption is taken to the schema of the eternal in the coming age. The corporate and spatial aspect is evident in the baptism of believers into the body of Christ, who is seated in the heavenly regions next to the Father: "For we were all baptized by one Spirit into one body—whether Jews or Greeks, slave or free—and we were all given the one Spirit to drink" (1 Cor 12:13). The Greek preposition *en* suggests that the rebirth takes place through the baptism "in" the Spirit rather than "by" the Spirit. It is the baptism in the Spirit that produces the rebirth of believers by which they enter the schema of the new world so that they do not conform to the schema of this world (Rom 12:2).

The rebirth is of the highest priority in the work of the Spirit for no one can confess "Jesus is the Lord" without the ethical and religious transformation in the Spirit (1 Cor 12:3). Jesus is not only the Savior of them but the Lord, whom they must submit to in the theocratic kingdom of the new schema. The normative and universal of all redemptive graces is the rebirth into God's family and entrance into the kingdom necessary for the spiritual war in the age of mission. The rebirth in the Spirit is the outcome of Christ being seated in the heavenly realms "far above all rule and authority, power and dominion, and every title that can be given, not only in the present age but also in the one to come" (Eph 1:21). In this sense, "born from above" makes as much sense as, if not more than, "born again" of the Spirit (John 3:3). The rebirth from above is supernatural as it is new, though invisible to the naked eyes: "The wind blows wherever it pleases. You hear its sound, but you cannot tell where it comes from or where it is going. So it is with everyone born of the Spirit" (v. 8). With the normative work of the Spirit in the rebirth of the new humanity, the age of mission can properly be opened for Jews and Gentiles on whom the Spirit is poured out (Acts 10:45). As a sign of the new schema, Pentecost will not be historically repeated but will be reduplicated in all ages in the rebirth of every believer in all races by the baptism of the water and the Spirit:[19] "Can anyone keep these people from being baptized with water? They have received the Holy Spirit just as we have" (v. 47).

---

19. Ferguson, *Holy Spirit*, 88.

Fruit of Spirit

The second work of the Spirit to consider is the fruit of the Spirit, which is the eschatology of redemption in fulfillment of the eschatology of nature in man (Gal 5:22). These are the ethical and religious attributes envisaged in the chief end of man to glorify and enjoy God in nature, but could not come to fruition in Adam. It is normative in the sense of equally desired of all believers in redemption. This is also hinted by the fruit spoken as singular—the acts of the flesh are plural—revealing the unified, holistic, and purposeful nature of the fruit (v. 19). The fruit is the growth of God's children in the Spirit to conform to the firstborn of the family and inherit the blessedness of the Father: "Like newborn babies, crave pure spiritual milk, so that by it you may grow up in your salvation, now that you have tasted that the Lord is good" (1 Pet 2:2). The fruit of the Spirit reflects Christ, who freely and voluntarily obeyed the Father and whom all believers thus must normatively imitate. The Son's obedience to the Father in the Counsel of Peace is the model of spiritual fruit that the Spirit instills in believers "until we all reach unity in the faith and in the knowledge of the Son of God and become mature, attaining to the whole measure of the fullness of Christ" (Eph 4:13). Again, the Spirit does not pursue his own agenda in some mysterious way apart from the Counsel of Peace, but forms the image of the Son in them for nothing pleases the Father more than the Son (Luke 3:22). The fruit of the Spirit is covenantal, normative, and personal just as the three Persons of the "adorable Being," and precisely what was required of Adam in the Covenant of Works through use of the image of God. In the narrow soteric scope, there could be a tendency to render the work of the Spirit as a secondary blessing apart from and independent of the substitutionary work of Christ. The Spirit, however, executes the redemptive-eschatological plan of the *Pactum Salutis* with the Father and the Son, mainly testifying to Christ's teachings: "But the Counselor, the Holy Spirit, whom the Father will send in my name, will teach you all things and will remind you of everything I have said to you" (John 14:26).

The rate of spiritual growth in every believer is different, however, and the pace with which one bears the fruit will depend on the particular situation of each believer. The normative purpose of holiness in sanctification will be progressive in time though definitive in Christ having, been seated with him in the heavenly regions. The vertical union with the risen Lord works out progressively in the horizontal flow of time on earth through God's providence. A child of God does not have to struggle on his own to bear the fruit of the Spirit or doubt whether his efforts will be good enough to validate his justification or sufficient enough for perseverance. The fruit does not depend on his moral/spiritual performance but on the upper regions to which he is raised with Christ. The Spirit is a "deposit, guaranteeing what is to come," which means his work is more about the schema of the age to come as the soil from which the fruit of personal sanctification grows. For those raised and seated above, a lack of the fruit is neither a sign of moral inferiority nor a failure as a child of God. The rate and degree of growth are particular to each person just as the many branches of the same Vine (John 15:1–8). But it is of absolute importance that the branches remain in the Vine: "I am the vine; you are the branches. If a man remains in me and I in him, he will bear much fruit; apart from me you can do nothing" (v. 5). The Spirit does not so much change the branches themselves as make sure that they firmly remain in the Vine. Holiness in sanctification is not the cause, but a proof of the spatial change that took place in union with the risen Lord. This is not to deny the importance of the free and voluntary obedience essential and indispensable to a bilateral covenant that seeks mutual glory and love. In fact, the fruit of the Spirit (love, joy, peace, patience, kindness, goodness, faithfulness, gentleness, self-control) is predicated on the very idea of mutuality and responsibility. Even the Scriptures are given for the normative use of producing good fruit: "All Scripture is useful for teaching, rebuking, correcting and training in righteousness, so that the servant of God may be thoroughly equipped for every good work" (2 Tim 3:16–17).

The priority of love over all other gifts is rooted in the chief end of man to love God and our neighbors. It is the summary of the law and the norm of the Christian belief and life (Luke 10:27; Rom 13:10). In this, the eschatology of nature and the eschatology of redemption share a common end. The adoption to sonship as the consummate end of redemption is protected by love of the Father in Christ, from which nothing in heaven and earth can separate the children (Rom 8:39). The love of the Father is the formal cause of redemption: "In love, he predestined us to be adopted as his sons through Jesus Christ, in accordance with his pleasure and will—to the praise of his glorious grace, which he has freely given us in the One he loves" (Eph 1:5–6). The norm of love is so unmistakable that no other gift can compare to its preeminence: "If I have the gift of prophecy and can fathom all mysteries and all knowledge, and if I have a faith that can move mountains, but have not love, I am nothing" (1 Cor 13:2). Love is better than any spiritual gift, and even superior to faith seen from the redemptive-eschatological perspective (1 Cor 12:31; 13:12–13). Nothing pleases the Father more than the Son, who shared love and glory with the Father from eternity in the Counsel of Peace (John 17:21–24).

Gifts of Spirit

The third category in the work of the Spirit is the spiritual gifts, which are not normative but particular to individuals. The various spiritual gifts are given to believers by the Spirit in order to edify and build up the body of Christ: "There are different kinds of gifts, but the same Spirit. There are different kinds of service, but the same Lord. There are different kinds of working, but the same God works all of them in all men. Now to each one the manifestation of the Spirit is given for the common good" (1 Cor 12:4–7). The spiritual gifts are unlike the fruit of the Spirit in that they are given to all believers in different ways for different services to build up the body of Christ. In this sense, the gifts are not normative but particular and situational, functional and instrumental gifts "for the common good." The gifts of the Spirit are meant to help produce the fruit of the Spirit, which is the more normative work of the Spirit for the benefit of the whole body. A very important distinction between the two is that the gifts are distributed but the fruit is grown, suggesting that the gifts are the tools whereas the fruit is the chief end. The apostle takes the argument even further by making a contrast between the less gifted and the more gifted in appearance: the "weaker" parts of the body are more "indispensable"; the "less honorable" are treated with "greater honor"; and the "less presentable" are more protected (1 Cor 12:22–24).

The spiritual gifts themselves, though useful and necessary, do not increase or decrease the intrinsic value of a member in the body of Christ. As an instrument of service, the most important quality of a gift is not its size or appearance but its usefulness for a given service. Like those in the Corinthian church, believers are often tempted seek after the more flashy gifts because these seem more precious to them or more esteemed by others. But such a view of gifts tend to stir up dispute whereas love builds up: "Also a dispute arose among them as to which of them was considered to be greatest" (Luke 22:24). Those with "lesser" gifts must not be envious of others with "greater" gifts because the Spirit distributes them to each believer "in accordance with the measure of faith" God has given them (Rom 12:3–5). They are differently apportioned to each member so as to build up the whole body in the most effective and edifying way.

A particular and individual gift must always serve the normative and foundational work of the Spirit. In the baptism of the Spirit, he produces rebirth from above; in the fruit of the Spirit, he recreates the image of God to conform to Christ; in the gifts of the Spirit, he edifies and builds up the whole body of Christ. Through the redemptive-eschatological work of the Spirit, a child is born into God's family, grows into Christ's maturity, and becomes a useful member of the church community (1 Cor 12:5). The gifts of the Spirit especially must not stir up envy or dispute among the children of God, for the chief end of redemption is to bring the Counsel of Peace to the church. The normative grace precedes a "second grace," which is more particular and situational.[20] The gift of tongues, a "second baptism" of the Spirit, and the like, tend to take the primary focus away from the normative work of the Spirit and cause a division in the church.[21] The miraculous gifts in the New Testament would be best interpreted by the distinction between foundational (normative) grace and particular (situational) grace. The foundational work has been done through the prophets and apostles with Christ as the Cornerstone, and the practical application of building the church is being done through the spiritual gifts of believers in every age (Eph 2:18–20).

---

20. Hoekema, *Saved by Grace*, 19.
21. Hoekema, *Saved by Grace*, 19.

Adiaphora

The work of the Spirit considered as most private and situational is called "the matters of indifference" or *adiaphora* (Rom 14:1). The "reasonings" (*dialogismos*, from which "dialogue" is derived) depend largely on the liberty of conscience on disputable issues in particular situations. The observances of certain religious days or dietary laws became disputable in the church of the New Testament as it was transitioning from the Old Testament period. For these sensitive issues for Jews, the apostle proposes a rather simple principle to view them from the kingdom perspective: "For the kingdom of God is not a matter of eating and drinking, but of righteousness, peace and joy in the Holy Spirit" (Rom 14:17). The kingdom of God is not about disputes over dietary laws or religious days but more about the fruit of the Spirit such as righteousness, peace, and joy. The solution to a most private matter of one's faith and conscience in this case is the most normative principle of the kingdom of God. Those united to the risen Christ by the Spirit ought to shift their attention away from the disputable matters of conscience to the kingdom of God, where they are presently seated with Christ.

They are to change the line of sight from the horizontal to the vertical and set their minds on things "above" rather than things "on earth" (Col 3:1–2). The focus on the kingdom of God means a change in the schema of the two ages rather than a compromise in conscience. It requires a spatial change of view from this age to the coming age rather than a discord in the body that destroys the fruit of the Spirit and violates the norms of the kingdom of God. The disputable matters are private and situational, to be judged by one's faith and conscience, hence ought to be settled by the higher principle of the kingdom (Rom 14:14). Passing judgment (*diakriseis*) must give way to the higher norm of peace in the body: "Let us therefore, make every effort to do what leads to peace and to mutual edification" (v. 19). The kingdom of peace should take precedence over the ceremonial disputes that may be judged differently by believers according to their conscience. The greatest norm of the kingdom is submission to the lordship of Christ in all matters of dispute: "For none of us lives to himself alone and none of us dies to himself alone. If we live, we live to the Lord; and if we die, we die to the Lord. So, whether we live or die, we belong to the Lord" (vv. 7–8). This is not a situational ethic because Christ is the absolute and normative standard by which all matters of dispute are to be settled. The standard of judgment is not one's own conscience but the kingdom of Christ, where everyone's conscience is mutually respected for the sake of peace, joy, and righteousness.

The normative principle is to be "under Christ's law," though in particular situations the apostle was willing, for the sake of the gospel, to be "under the law" for Jews or "without the law" for Gentiles (1 Cor 9:20–21). The ceremonial law of the pre-Christ era is no longer relevant to those that are seated above, where Jews and Gentiles have become one new humanity in Christ. The liberty of the gospel in Christ is illustrated by Paul's response to Peter's double standards in regard to the dietary laws and exposed the hidden hypocrisy (Gal 2:11–14). The liberty of the gospel is most dramatically displayed in his different responses to the Jewish rite of circumcision. When liberty was at stake, Paul did not let Titus be circumcised for the sake of preaching to Gentiles but, conversely, he allowed it for Timothy for the sake of preaching to Jews (Gal 2:3; Acts 16:1–3). The liberty was not reactionary to the law in an antinomian way but submissive to the lordship of Christ such that he was at liberty to circumcise or not to circumcise depending on the situation. He was operating in the higher schema of the coming age, where he considered himself free to all men but under Christ's law.

The eschatology of redemption in Christ provides the overarching structure to the particular redemptive graces appropriated through the work of the Spirit. The particular graces of the Spirit, on the other hand, can be mistaken for the "secondary gifts" independent of and apart from the foundational graces. The church is not a random collection of believers gathered out of their own will but a body of the elect that is given to the Son as the reward for his obedience to the Father (John 17:4–6). The church is the earthly body of the risen Christ in heaven: "I will give you the keys of the kingdom of heaven; whatever you bind on earth will be bound in heaven, and whatever you loose on earth will be loosed in heaven (Matt 16:19). The particular graces and gifts are not random or mysterious acts of the Spirit to satisfy the spiritual needs of man but the outworking of the Eternal Counsel by the three Persons of the blessed God. In short, the Golden Chain of the *Ordo Salutis* is not to be viewed as a chronological progression from the ordinary graces to the extraordinary gifts, or from the elementary salvation to the secondary blessings.

Lastly, the command to be filled with the Spirit, rather than be drunk on wine, is not so much a particular work of the Spirit as the combined state, ideally considered, of all the work of the Spirit (Eph 5:18). It refers to the fullness in the schema of the heavenly realms in which God blessed us "with every spiritual blessing in Christ" (Eph 1:3). The filling of the Spirit at Pentecost was the sign and seal of the coming age that has arrived as a result of Christ's finished work (Acts 2:4, 17). In this sense, the fullness of the Spirit is not a reference to a particular stage in the order of salvation but the state of being filled with Christ as coheirs of the Father (Gal 2:20). The contrast of fullness in the Spirit to getting drunk on wine is a contrast of the two schemas of the kingdom of God and this world (Eph 5:16). In Christ, believers can be full of the coming age while passing through this age: "Be very careful, then, how you live—not as unwise but as wise, making the most of every opportunity [*kairos*], because the days [*chronos*] are evil" (vv. 15–16). In this fullness of the Spirit, we may "approach the throne of God's grace with confidence, so that we may receive mercy and find grace to help us in our time of need" (Heb 4:16). The emphasis is not so much on the believer's act of filling as him being filled with the Spirit for the combined effect of all the graces of the Spirit.

6.3 Spirit and Church

Temple of Spirit

The New Testament church is built on the Cornerstone of Christ and the foundation of the prophets and apostles (Eph 2:20–22). It is "the holy temple in the Lord," and "a dwelling in which God lives by his Spirit." The temple is the "garden of God," where the ethical and religious end of God's covenant with man is fulfilled. In this sense, the church is the redemptive-eschatological fulfillment of the garden of Eden in nature. The church is built on the foundation of Christ's finished work, hence expected to grow into the temple of the Spirit and complete the body in the age of the global mission. The church may share in the benefits of the foundation through the Spirit but is not expected to reduplicate the work time and again—nor can it do so.[22] The reason that "the gates of Hades will not overcome" the church is because the Lord is the rock on which she stands (Matt 16:18). The emphasis on the redemptive-eschatological foundation of the building rather than on the building itself does not weaken the latter but strengthens it. The miraculous gifts during apostolic times were the signs of extraordinary offices to lay the everlasting foundation. The modern attempts to reduplicate these miraculous gifts of the apostles will actually undermine the foundation, which in turn weakens the church. Just as a tree with shallow roots cannot long sustain itself, or a building with unstable pillars will collapse, the church without the eschatological foundation cannot stand against "the gates of Hades." The Cornerstone and the foundation will guarantee the victory of the church to complete its body through the Spirit that not even one will be lost (John 18:9).

In the new schema of the kingdom, believers do not have to repeat one prayer from the Old Testament, "Do not take the Holy Spirit from me" (Ps 51:11; Eph 1:14). The Spirit of Pentecost is the fulfillment of Ezekiel's prophecy with regard to the "wind" (*rūah*) of God breathed into the dry bones. The Spirit has come to dwell in the church, the temple in the Lord, and will never again depart from her as long as she is not separated from that union with Christ.[23] The vertical union will never be threatened because it is as strong and everlasting as the union of the Father and the Son (John 17:21). The perseverance of the saints does not depend on their faith or on the sacraments of grace but on the Counsel of Peace. The church is the new Israel, the city of God, Mount Zion in the vertical ascension to the heavenly realms: "But you are a chosen people, a royal priesthood, a holy nation, a people belonging to God, that you may declare the praises of him who called you out of darkness into his wonderful light" (1 Pet 2:9). In keeping with the eschatology of the Spirit, there are no more new revelations that are necessary "for salvation" and "for every good work" in this age of mission (2 Tim 3:15–17). These revelations are organized into a unified and orderly

---

22. Ferguson, *Holy Spirit*, 88.
23. Stott, *Baptism and Fullness*, 26.

system of doctrines with the closure of the canon consistent with the redemptive-eschatological revelation in the Son (Heb 1:1–2; Rev 22:18–29). The narrow soteric scope alone is not equipped to explain the closure of the canon and the sufficiency (coherency) of the biblical teachings for salvation and the work of the church. The eschatology with the soteric gift, however, can provide the convincing theological basis for them.

In Christ, the ethnic division of Jews and Gentiles was no longer an essential matter, for the church is now a new humanity in the redemptive-eschatological sense: "Neither circumcision nor uncircumcision means anything; what counts is the new creation" (Gal 6:15). Besides the racial division at the center of which lies Jewish law, other social barriers and discriminations were reinterpreted under the lordship of Christ, which transcends all other relationships in the horizontal schema of this age. The lordship of Christ is not established just by the horizontal shift from Israel to the church, but by the vertical union of heaven and earth (Eph 1:10). The true and lasting unity of Jews and Gentiles was sealed vertically in the age to come, where the invisible church is seated with Christ. The horizontal flow of time from the Old to the New cannot resolve the disparities and divisions within fallen humanity on numerous levels. A mere shift of time and generations will not be sufficient to unify these divisions without a spatial change from earth to heaven, from the natural to the supernatural regions. Hence, the kingdom of God has succeeded the closing of the ages, and the spiritual war is being fought "not against flesh and blood" but against the "powers of this dark world, and the spiritual forces evil in the heavenly realms" (Eph 6:12). The lordship of Christ vertically unifies Jews and Gentiles, man and woman, master and slave into one family of God thereby bringing a radical spiritual, moral, social transformation. Despite the earthly journey in the flow of *chronos* time, they nevertheless form one new human race into the body of Christ because they have been raised above and seated with him through the rebirth in the Spirit. The mission of the building completing itself on earth, as the temple of the Spirit, is made possible by the new schema of heaven.

Kingdom and Church

The eschatology of redemption is the kingdom of Christ that will be given over to the Father at the consummation (1 Cor 15:24). It is superior to the eschatology of nature envisaged in Eden for its Mediator is the incarnate Son of God. The vertical and the horizontal progress of redemptive history thus climax in him, who is seated next to the Father and rules heaven and earth. Central to the realized eschatology is the spatial concept of heaven or the age to come, where Christ is seated with believers. The church belongs to the upper regions through the resurrection of Christ although it is at war with the schema of this evil age. It is the new holy war of the theocratic kingdom of Christ waged by the Spirit against the flesh. The gospel in the two ages is thus fittingly called the gospel of the kingdom of heaven (Luke 16:16). The kingdom is officially inaugurated through the resurrection of Jesus, who is therefore declared to be the Messiah and Lord (Acts 2:36). The faith and life of the New Testament church cannot be defined apart from the new order of things and the eschatological hope it engendered. It was not an idealistic hope but a realism on how Christians in this semi-eschatological era ought to live in this world that is passing away (1 Cor 7:31). The kingdom of Christ has intruded this evil age from above and that new reality has affected every thought process and action of those who eagerly anticipated a speedy sequel to what already transpired in Christ (Gal 1:4; 2 Cor 5:1–7).

Some think the kingdom of Christ and the church are identical while others think they are related yet distinct.[24] What is clear is the otherworldly nature of the kingdom: "Jesus said, 'My kingdom is not of this world. If it were, my servants would fight to prevent my arrest by the Jews. But now my kingdom is from another place'" (John 18:36). In any case, the church and the kingdom are closely related and the former represents the latter on earth in a visible form; the church has been given the keys to the kingdom (Matt 16:19). Simultaneously, Kuyper's well-known thought that there is not an inch of the universe that Christ does not rule would be a useful index of the scope of the kingdom. In this view, the kingdom affects every sphere of the Christian life in its religious and non-religious aspects all together.[25] Furthermore, all spheres of life are under the lordship of Christ, hence every sphere is sovereign within its own boundary. The church, nonetheless, is singularly called out of this world by Christ, as the new Israel, to be "a kingdom of priests and a holy nation." This semi-eschatological kingdom is particularly characterized as "not of this world, and from another place" by Jesus until Christ hands it over to the Father. In the meantime, the kingdom will be known for its intrusive (otherworldly) character rather than its coextensiveness with the world. Its disposition is so antithetical to this evil age that its intrusion will be met with a violent reaction by the kingdom of darkness (Matt 11:12). The coming of the new theocratic kingdom of Christ into this world fulfills the intrusion of Israel into Canaan for the holy war of total destruction. The difference between the present and the final kingdom is that in the latter case it is no longer an intrusion but consummation in the kingdom of the Father. The semi-eschatological kingdom is established by the "removal of the Messiah into the higher world" in which the vertical side has been already realized but the horizontal progress in time yet remains unconsummated.[26] The growth of the kingdom is gradual at the present time but its harvest will be catastrophic in the future (Mark 4:26–29).

The new Israel is "a chosen people, a royal priesthood, and a holy nation," yet they are still "foreigners and strangers" in this world (Heb 11:13; 1 Pet 2:9). The church is more like the embassy of the kingdom of God in a foreign and hostile world: "We are

---

24. Dunahoo, *Making Kingdom Disciples*, 41.
25. Dunahoo, *Making Kingdom Disciples*, 46.
26. Vos, *Pauline Eschatology*, 37–38.

therefore Christ's ambassadors, as though God were making his appeal through us. We implore you on Christ's behalf; Be reconciled to God" (2 Cor 5:20). The metaphor is particularly fit to convey the intrusive nature of the kingdom, that reconciliation with God presupposes underlying hostility. The kingdom of Christ is pervasive in extent yet intrusive in substance until the final consummation. As the flesh is hostile to the Spirit, this age is hostile to the kingdom, and the priestly kingdom is called to be ambassadors of the gospel. As ambassadors, believers are the citizens of heaven, members of the higher world, and only their earthly nature remains in this age to be put to death (Phil 3:20; Col 3:5). In this sense, the "redemptive heaven" is far different from the "cosmical heaven" in Greek dualism.[27] The final victory of the church in the spiritual holy war does not lie in its own power but in the authority of the risen Messiah, who reigns from the higher world (Matt 28:18). They are "more than conquerors" not because of their own creative resources, but because Christ implores on their behalf next to the Father (Rom 8:37). In a foreign country, the safety of citizens from another country is protected by the powers of their own nation represented through the ambassador and the embassy. Their entrance into the embassy building is equivalent to being in their homeland, where they are protected by the laws of their own country. Just as the Lord to whom they belong, they live in the world but are not of the world: "The Christian has only his members upon earth, which are to be mortified; himself, and as a whole, he belongs to the high mountain-land above, Col. iii. 5."[28] In the redemptive-eschatological sense, they belong to heaven rather than earth, protected by the powers of the kingdom:

> The heaven in which the Christian by anticipation dwells is not the cosmical heaven, it is a thoroughly redemptive heaven, a heaven become what it is through the progressive upbuilding and enrichment pertaining to the age-long work of God in the sphere of redemption.[29]

The church in the semi-eschatological kingdom is given the task of reconciliation on the one hand, and the holy war of heaven on the other (Matt 28:18–20; 1 Cor 15:28). The eschatology of redemption is the reconciliation of all things with God—the things in heaven and the things on earth (Eph 1:10). But the intrusive nature of the kingdom of heaven entails the remaining suffering in the holy war against the earthly nature (Col 3:5). The church must be the "living sacrifice" in this war of the priestly kingdom; "a minister of Christ Jesus to the Gentiles with the priestly duty of proclaiming the gospel of God, so that the Gentiles might become an offering acceptable to God, sanctified by the Holy Spirit" (Rom 12:1–3; 15:16). The relationship of the church to the world is defined by these conflicting tasks, the priestly calling without conformation to the schema of this world. It can neither totally identify with the world

---

27. Vos, *Pauline Eschatology*, 40–41.
28. Vos, *Pauline Eschatology*, 41.
29. Vos, *Pauline Eschatology*, 40.

nor totally separate from it as the provisional kingdom of Christ exists between the two ages.

In the age of mission, the gospel of the kingdom of heaven is contemporaneously a reconciliation (of peace) and a declaration (of war)—the cross reconciles and condemns at the same time. There was a time when the Christendom was identified with the dominant culture of the time and her message was accepted by society unchallenged.[30] But the uniqueness and absoluteness of Christianity are now being challenged more than ever, and salvation is no longer seen as a monopoly of the Christian church.[31] These challenges are a good and necessary reminder to Christians that they are in the world but not of the world. Nonetheless, the church is given the keys to the kingdom of heaven and the gates of hell will not prevail in the redemptive-eschatological sense. Its violent intrusion, in the redemptive way, is the evidence that this fallen world needs the blessed news of the gospel (Matt 11:12).[32] In the provisional kingdom, it was necessary to distinguish Christ's headship over the church from his supremacy over all creation, which will be unnecessary at the final consummation: "Then the end will come, when he hands over the kingdom to God the Father after he has destroyed all dominion, authority and power" (1 Cor 15:24; Col 1:18).

6.4 Spirit and Christian Life

The present resurrection of believers in union with the risen Christ is the invisible ground of the visible Christian life in the world. It is the redemptive-eschatological foundation of Christian sanctification and ethics in this world, whose present schema is passing away. The exhortation "therefore, put to death the earthly nature" is made possible by the heavenly foundation of having been raised with Christ (Col 3:5). The Christian life is being lived within the two ages, rendering it progressive in time but definitive in Christ. It is like the holy war of *herem* in Canaan but also unlike it, for the present battle is the Spirit's war against the flesh, and the radical breach with sin is even more intensified. The Christian life, considered in its totality, is a life in the theocratic kingdom of Christ that demands total eradication of the ungodly (1 Cor 6:9). The ethical and religious nature of the covenant life, which was the chief end of man in the temple of God, has reached its climax in the war of the Spirit against the flesh. In the Sermon on the Mount, Jesus uses radical metaphors of total destruction of sin:

> If your right eye causes you to sin, gouge it out and throw it away. It is better for you to lose one part of your body than for your whole body to be thrown into hell. And if your right hand causes you to sin, cut it off and throw it away.

---

30. Clowney, *Church*, 14.
31. Hick, "Non-Absoluteness of Christianity," 23.
32. Clowney, *Church*, 15.

> It is better for you to lose one part of your body than for your whole body to go into hell. (Matt 5:29–30)

This echoes the command for the war of total destruction in Canaan: "No person devoted to destruction may be ransomed; he must be put to death" (Lev 27:29). It is possible that the apostle's command to "put to death the earthly nature" was borrowed from this Levitical language (Col 3:5). The Christian life as a "living sacrifice" is similarly an image borrowed from the Old Testament, now central to the new *schema* that does not conform to this world (Rom 12:1–2). The sanctification and Christian ethics of the new life in Christ are not merely a logical order following justification but they are under the rubric of a holy war of the kingdom: "But nothing that a man owns and devotes to the LORD—whether man or animal or family land—may be sold or redeemed; everything so devoted is most holy to the LORD" (Lev 27:28).

The holy war of the intrusive kingdom is a radical reversal of the patterns of this world, the flesh (*sarx*), which must be put to death by the Spirit: "For the sinful nature desires what is contrary to the Spirit, and the Spirit what is contrary to the sinful nature. They are in conflict with each other, so that you do not do what you want" (Gal 5:17). The upside-down nature of the kingdom of heaven and its ethical standards are consistent with the nature of blessedness in the kingdom (Matt 5:1–12). The reversed nature of blessedness in the kingdom is even more telling in Luke's version of the Beatitudes:

> Blessed are you who are poor, for yours is the kingdom of God. Blessed are you who hunger now, for you will be satisfied. Blessed are you who weep now, for you will laugh. Blessed are you when men hate you, when they exclude you and insult you and reject your name as evil, because of the Son of Man. (Luke 6:20–21)

The kingdom of heaven cannot be understood, much less practiced, unless one understands the reason why the cross is foolishness to this world (1 Cor 1:18–31). The blessedness of heaven, in the redemptive-eschatological sense, is the exact opposite of this world. The reversal takes place when believers are raised and seated with Christ in the higher regions, where they begin to wage war against the flesh, led by Christ and the Spirit. Christ himself was the ultimate living sacrifice by his crucifixion and resurrection, and Christians are commanded to do the same through self-denial and cross-bearing. A living sacrifice is "dead but alive" and this analogy fits perfectly the union of believers into Christ's death and resurrection—they are dead to sin but alive to God (Rom 6:11). Jesus told his disciples the seemingly impossible command that unless they surpass the scribes and the Pharisees in righteousness, they "will certainly not enter the kingdom of heaven" (Matt 5:20). But what Jesus did here was to change the view of righteousness from the horizontal perspective of legalistic comparison to the vertical perspective of union with the righteous one. They may never surpass the scribes and the Pharisees in the former, but they can surpass them in the latter; the scribes and the Pharisees will never surpass Christ's righteousness and his disciples can surpass them only by the vertical union with the risen Christ.

The correlation between Christian worship and the holy war of the kingdom is evident in the language of living sacrifice. The offering of their bodies as a living sacrifice for the theocratic kingdom of Christ is the true and proper worship in which Christians can "taste the heavenly gift and the powers of the coming age" (Heb 6:4–5; Rom 12:1). The worship of God in offering themselves as a living sacrifice is the ethical and religious foundation of the holy war against the pagan gods. The taste of the powers of the coming age through worship is the "essence of Christian pilgrimage"[33] and the mightiest weapon of the spiritual war against the flesh. The church has been given the keys to the kingdom, and placed in the redemptive-eschatological heaven, to engage in the holy war of living sacrifice. In the holy war of living sacrifice, however, they are given a foretaste of heaven on earth during the interim age of mission. It is a present endowment of the eternal inheritance, and a partial taste of the consummate banquet.[34] In the schema of the new creation, the change of worship to the day of resurrection, the Lord's day, means precisely that—a partial experience of the eternal rest in the holy war of the kingdom (Acts 20:7). The new creation does not abrogate the preeminence of nature but redemptively consummates it; the eschatology of nature is redemptively consummated by the eschatology of redemption. Hence, the praise of God is sung in worship on the first (resurrection) day of the week so that the church may proceed to the battlefield of the kingdom for the six days (Gen 1:31; Rom 1:17). The notion of a living sacrifice as the true and proper worship of Christians and renouncement of the pattern of this age by the new schema of the coming age were not fully known to Old Testament believers (Heb 11:39–40). Worship in the redemptive-eschatological sense, therefore, means the victory of the seed over the serpent (Gen 3:15): "Let us not give up meeting together, as some are in the habit of doing, but let us encourage one another—and all the more as you see the Day approaching" (Heb 10:25).

The religious and political affairs were inseparable in the theocratic kingdom of Israel as a type of the consummate kingdom in the coming age. The temple was the place of offering sacrifices and the place of making a covenant with God as a priestly kingdom to fight the holy war of total destruction. It was typical of the kingdom of Christ so that the church today is not only a place of worship but a place of entering the covenant with God for the spiritual war against the flesh. The Covenant of Grace is redemptive-eschatological by nature and is the covenant of the kingdom of Christ. Jesus thus entered the heavenly temple not only by himself but also lead the church into the presence of God, who are offered as living sacrifices (Heb 10:19–21):

---

33. Horton, *Better Way*, 125.
34. Horton, *Better Way*, 125.

> But you have come to Mount Zion, to the heavenly Jerusalem, the city of the living God. You have come to thousands upon thousands of angels in joyful assembly, to the church of the firstborn, whose names are written in heaven. You have come to God, the judge of all men, to the spirits of righteous men made perfect, to Jesus the mediator of a new covenant, and to the sprinkled blood that speaks a better word than the blood of Abel. (Heb 12:22–24)

The theocratic center of the present kingdom of Christ and the church is the "greater and more perfect tabernacle that is not made with human hands, that is to say, is not a part of this creation" (Heb 9:11). That the heavenly temple is not a part of this creation, in the redemptive sense, reveals the substance of the Christian life as a pilgrimage in this world. The redemptive kingdom of God is not of this world and the Christian life, comprehensively considered, should be so defined (1 Cor 7:29–31).[35]

Cross-Bearing

The eschatology of redemption when translated into personal and practical terms is best summarized by "faith expressing itself through love" (Gal 5:6).[36] The higher life of the heavenly regions through Christ's death and resurrection is most convincingly lived out in the earthly life of cross-bearing. It is a covenantal response of believers to the Covenant of Grace started in the Eternal Covenant of the Father and the Son. It is also the most proper response as members of the theocratic kingdom of Christ in heaven, who are called to the holy war of total destruction of sin. Spiritual growth in the cross-bearing of discipleship will flow out from the schema of the coming age in the redemptive kingdom. Paradoxically, the self-denial and cross-bearing on earth is made possible by the rest of God enjoyed in heaven. In regard to discipleship, Clowney noted a shift in God's view of the covenant partner from the Old to the New Covenant: "The people of God became disciples of Jesus."[37] The disciples of Jesus are now the new Israel, the priestly kingdom whose life is distinctly marked by self-denial and cross-bearing after their Master. They are born from above by the Spirit and became members of the kingdom, which intruded this world to be its salt and light. Yahweh, the LORD, was to Israel who Christ, the Lord, is to the disciples; they "imitate, serve, and testify to" the Yahweh in Christ.[38] The schema of the new order is the covenant union, the wedding of husband and wife, or the bilateral treaty between a vassal and suzerain (Jer 50:5). Since the disciples are so united with the risen Lord, they ought to be like him and follow in his footsteps just as Israel was to be holy as God is holy: "I will be your God, and you will by my people." A disciple is someone who completely

---

35. Gentry and Wellum, *Kingdom through Covenants*, 593–94.
36. Vos, *Pauline Eschatology*, 49.
37. Clowney, *Church*, 46.
38. Clowney, *Church*, 46–47.

identifies with the Master and takes the intimacy to a deeper and personal level as to influence all spheres in the ethical and religious life.[39] For the disciples, Jesus is not just a crucified Savior of the world, but a resurrected Messiah and the Lord of life (Acts 2:36).

It was important for the disciples to "remain in Christ," like the branches must remain in the Vine, to bear much fruit. The proximity to Christ breeds intimacy with God in the new schema of the heavenly places, where they are seated together (Col 3:1–4). The substitution of the twelve tribes of Israel by the twelve disciples of Jesus is not a coincidence but a fulfillment in both horizontal and vertical direction. The development of the Covenant of Grace from under the law to under the gospel is a progression from the people of God to the disciples of Christ, who are called to the life of cross-bearing (a living sacrifice) with superior means of grace than the former. Nearness and intimacy is the hallmark of Christ's ministry with his disciples and even his departure was in order that he might be in them permanently through the Spirit (Mark 3:14): "And I will ask the Father, and he will give you another advocate to help you and be with you forever—the Spirit of truth" (John 14:16). Justification leads to adoption to sonship so that believers join the firstborn and remain close to the Father. The disciple's nearness to the Lord, in the new schema of heaven, breeds intimacy with him, and intimacy leads to imitation of the Master (Eph 4:23–24). The glory in heaven shines most brilliantly through the cross-bearing on earth: "Now if we are children, then we are heirs—heirs of God and co-heirs with Christ, if indeed we share in his sufferings in order that we may also share in his glory" (Rom 8:17).

The life of self-denial and cross-bearing is the most conspicuous outcome of the redemptive eschatology: "Then Jesus said to his disciples, 'If anyone would come after me, he must deny himself and take up his cross and follow me'" (Matt 16:24). The self-denial, cross-bearing, and following the Master are the "living sacrifices holy and pleasing to God—this is your spiritual act of worship" (Rom 12:1b). It is a pattern of life foreign to this evil age: "Do not conform any longer to the pattern of this world, but be transformed by the renewing of your mind" (Rom 12:2b). The self-denial and the cross-bearing means a death of the self, which is exactly the reversal of what this world seeks. They are as far from each other as heaven is from earth, in the redemptive sense. It started with Christ, whose incarnation, life, and death epitomized self-denial and cross-bearing. He learned to obey the Father in suffering so that his prayer was heard—that he might be raised from death (Heb 5:7–9). The obedience of the Son to the Father, in fact, was the very foundation of redemption in the Counsel of Peace. The cross-bearing is not just personal piety but sharing in the glory of the Son through sharing in his suffering: "Let us, then, go to him outside the camp, bearing the disgrace he bore" (Heb 13:13).

The change of the "old self" into the "new self" is not just a conversion but a new creation in the image of the blessed God in three Persons (Eph 4:22–23). The

---

39. Clowney, *Church*, 47.

post-baptism life of Christians as living sacrifices in order not to conform to the schema of this world reaches beyond the scope of soteric gift. In this sense, the view of sanctification as an appendix to justification does not do full justice to the nature of the Christian life and ethics seen from the chief and eschatological end of man. The redemptive use of the law in Christ thus far exceeds what the natural use of the law in Adam might have achieved. It is a covenantal response to the holy war of redemption that demands a total destruction of the flesh and its evil desires (1 Cor 6:9–10). Such a radical response to sin is impossible unless the old self is put to death by the vertical union with the risen Lord (Gal 1:4; 5:16–17; Col 1:13). The vertical plane of the definitive death to sin leads the horizontal plane of progressive death to sinful desires. The death of the earthly nature is to be a total destruction, a *herem*, of the remaining "members" of the Christian, who as a whole belongs to "the redemptive heaven" (Col 3:5). Those who belong to the flesh will not and cannot die to sin without first changing the "venue" from below to above so that they could fix their thoughts on things above (v. 2).

The imitation is predicated on the spatial nearness to Christ: "Those who belong to Christ Jesus have crucified the flesh with its passions and desires" (Gal 5:24). Jesus lovingly reminded his disciples, when faced with imminent departure, that his presence in them through another Counselor would be far more beneficial and everlasting. His leaving was not so much his departure from them as their arrival in him seated above so that they would never again be separated. Having arrived, they could begin to put to death the remaining members in the earthly nature. Postmodern culture has reduced religion to the private life or to a separate sphere in life, but this is contrary to what Jesus demanded of disciples, who have entered the kingdom that reigns over all spheres in life.[40] A disciple is reborn by the Spirit, vertically lifted to the eternal life, where every sphere of life is lived out by the new schema of the kingdom.[41] Therefore, the promise of the Lord is still effective today that he will always be with his disciples: "And surely I am with you always, to the very end of the age" (Matt 28:20). Furthermore, his promise of intimacy with his disciples also stands today as ever before: "Here I am! I stand at the door and knock. If anyone hears my voice and opens the door, I will come in and eat with him, and he with me" (Rev 3:20).

The interaction between the suffering of Jesus outside of the city gate and the eternal city of the heavenly Jerusalem is theologically and practically significant. The author of Hebrews uses analogies very familiar to the readers at that time, such as "the city gate," "the camp," "the enduring city," and "the city that is to come," in order to convey his message (Heb 13:12–13). On the face, the text seems to make a simple contrast between the Old and the New Covenants to stress that the gospel is for all men, whether Jews or Gentiles. "They" could not eat from their altar back then but now in Christ "we" can eat from ours, the Lord's Supper (Lev 16:1–34; John 6:55–56).

---

40. Dunahoo, *Making Kingdom Disciples*, 4.
41. Dunahoo, *Making Kingdom Disciples*, 4.

"They" could not directly approach God in the tabernacle, but "we" can approach the throne of grace without fear through the High Priest in the order of Melchizedek. Israel crucified Jesus at outside of the city gate, where it was ceremonially unclean, but precisely for that reason the cross became the gospel that saves Jews and Gentiles.[42] The city gate (of Jerusalem) at the time religiously divided Jews and Gentiles, and it was significant for the author that Jesus died outside the city gate, bearing disgrace for us. But the contrast goes deeper or higher as it develops into one between the earthly city and "an enduring city, the city that is to come" (v. 14).

First, it moved in the horizontal direction from the Old to the New, but then moved in the vertical direction from the earthly to the heavenly city. In short, the cross of Jesus (at outside of the city gate) was the soteric means for Jews and Gentiles, but it was also an eschatological door, as it were, into "the heavenly Jerusalem and the city of God" (Heb 12:22). In this view, the cross became the crossroads of the earthly and the heavenly cities, the new and eternal gate through which believers of all races may enter "Mount Zion" (Heb 12:22).[43] The author then exhorts believers to go outside of the city gate toward the cross of Jesus, where they will find the way to the enduring city, "Let us, then, go to him outside the camp, bearing the disgrace he bore" (Heb 13:13). Cross-bearing is an active rather than a passive act of entering the eternal city, where they, in principle, already belong with Christ: "For our light and momentary troubles are achieving for us an eternal glory that far outweighs them all" (2 Cor 4:17). The disgrace of cross-bearing in the world, paradoxically, is the only way his disciples can taste the "heavenly gift" and "powers of the coming age" (Heb 6:4–5). Departure from the earthly glory of the camp is actually the entrance into the eternal glory that far outweighs them all—it is a separation from the world but also a separation to God.[44]

The author in subsequent verses describes worship and good deeds as "sacrifices" pleasing to God: "Through Jesus, therefore, let us continually offer to God a sacrifice of praise . . . And do not forget to do good and to share with others, for with such sacrifices God is pleased" (Heb 13:15–16). In the overall context of Hebrews, these sacrifices of worship and deeds ought to be viewed in light of the heavenly temple Jesus entered as the High Priest in the order of Melchizedek. The sacrifices of believers, of whatever kind, are first offered in the heavenly temple through the intercession of Christ before they are practiced in the church by way of worship or good deeds. Only then they are deemed pleasing to God, strikingly similar to the spiritual worship of "living sacrifices" that do not conform to the schema of this world (Rom 12:1–2). In both cases, worship and good deeds are understood as a form of sacrifice offered in the heavenly temple of Jerusalem through the High Priest in the order of Melchizedek. This way, the two tablets of the law—worship of God and love of neighbor—are

---

42. Hughes, *Hebrews*, 580.
43. Hughes, *Hebrews*, 581.
44. Hughes, *Hebrews*, 581

properly obeyed as the redemptive-eschatological sacrifices "under Christ's law" (1 Cor 9:21). These are the marks of true discipleship, neither legalistic nor antinomian, because they are from the city above, where they are with Christ: "We have this hope as an anchor for the soul, firm and secure. It enters the inner sanctuary behind the curtain, where our forerunner, Jesus, has entered on our behalf. He has become a high priest forever, in the order of Melchizedek" (Heb 6:19–20). A full circle is made, then, first from the inside to the outside of the city gate, then from the earthly to the heavenly city, and finally back down to the earthly city, where Christians offer the sacrifices of worship and good deeds. They are not merely the moral, pietistic, or social exercise of holiness but an expression of the covenant love of God. They are but the temporal and visible manifestation of what is taking currently place behind the curtain of the invisible temple in the heavenly realms.

Social Renewal

The preaching of the gospel and a social renewal through good deeds are inseparable as both are contained in the two tablets of the law.[45] The blessed nature of God is revealed in the goodness of the creation but especially in the blessed news of the gospel (Gen 1:31; 1 Tim 1:11). The blessedness in "the three Persons of the adorable Being" is the attribute of God that runs through the eschatology of nature and the eschatology of redemption. The love of God always accompanies the love of mankind and the love of nature; the blessed of God will always bless others with God's love. In the past, saving souls was given priority over social issues in the preaching of the gospel. With the rise of interest in the kingdom of God as the present reign of Christ over all things, the social responsibility of the church was no longer seen merely as a means of preaching the gospel to win more souls but more properly as the substance of the gospel itself.[46] It was gradually accepted that the Great Commission of saving souls and the Great Commandment of loving neighbors are inseparable in the Gospel of the kingdom (Luke 16:16). It was proposed that the global church should obey the two greatest commandments of the Lord on "vocational, local, national" levels and make them integral components of the preaching of the gospel.[47] The expansion of the scope of the gospel to include social reform has been thus aided by the latest biblical teachings in the ethics of the kingdom of God and their social implications.[48]

The kingdom of God is the redemptive-eschatological outcome of the gospel, which is wider in scope than the cure of sin through atonement. In the Beatitudes, Jesus makes the point clear that the blessed nature and love of the Father should be the reason for our love of neighbors and even of our enemies:

45. Stott, *Christian Mission*, 15–34.
46. Stott, *Christian Mission*, 23.
47. Stott, *Christian Mission*, 29.
48. Stott, *Christian Mission*, 20.

> You have heard that it was said, 'Love your neighbor and hate your enemy.' But I tell you, love your enemies and pray for those who persecute you, that you may be children of your Father in heaven. He causes his sun to rise on the evil and the good, and sends rain on the righteous and the unrighteous. If you love those who love you, what reward will you get? Are not even the tax collectors doing that? And if you greet only your own people, what are you doing more than others? Do not even pagans do that? Be perfect, therefore, as your heavenly Father is perfect. (Matt 5:43–48)

We have seen that the eternal city called heaven is where worship and good deeds pleasing to God flow out of. The good works for social renewal thus stem from the blessed attribute of the Father himself, and from the arrival of the kingdom of God as the new order of affairs in Christ. The balance between the two tablets of the law will be difficult to sustain, and the practice of them will be even more difficult unless the church understands the gospel in its entire and holistic sense. This requires an eschatological view of man, the world, and redemption in Christ. The eschatology of redemption does not discard the eschatology of nature in preference to saving souls (Matt 5:45). Nonetheless, social renewal, like anything else in this fallen world, ought to be placed within the overall perspective of this world in its present schema passing away (1 Cor 7:31). The temporal and fleeting nature of this fallen world is the basis of anticipation of the new schema of the age to come:

> What I mean, brothers and sisters, is that the time is short. From now on those who have wives should live as if they do not; those who mourn, as if they did not; those who are happy, as if they were not; those who buy something, as if it were not theirs to keep; those who use the things of the world, as if not engrossed in them. For this world in its present form is passing away. (1 Cor 7:29–31)

The semi-eschatological kingdom puts such social issues in context and the kingdom of God cannot be equated with any form of social program or political ideology. The kingdom of God touches every sphere of life and places them under the lordship of Christ but its most notable feature at the present time does not lie in its extent but in its intrusiveness.[49] The kingdom is known not necessarily by the scope of its presence but by its disposition—it is not of this world (John 18:36). It will bring about social renewal in every sphere of society such as found in Paul's epistles, but it does not see that as an end in itself, nor can it be in the schema of this world. Instead, the writers of the New Testament use the vertical schema of the kingdom to explain the present world in its horizontal movement toward the Parousia. They would sometimes apply the *already* of the kingdom to lift the downcast to heaven, but other times would apply the *not yet* to exhort the weak or warn the backsliders to put to death the earthly nature. The vertical order in Christ will keep the church clear of the two pitfalls of

---

49. Kline, *Structure of Biblical Authority*, 157; *Kingdom Prologue*, 158.

legalism and antinomianism in regard to good works (1 Cor 9:21). It will remind us to keep pursuing the kingdom gospel rather than a social gospel. The church is now in the age of mission, but the mission is not to build again a theocratic kingdom on earth, which Hebrews made clear that we do not have here an "enduring city."

Chapter 7
Kingdom and Eschatology

7.1 Servant King

REDEMPTIVE-ESCHATOLOGICAL HISTORY is the movement from the fallen creation of Adam toward the new creation of the Second Adam. It envisages the fulfillment of the eschatology of nature but does so with the soteric grace that will consummate the natural into the supernatural. The redemptive grace in Christ does not abrogate nature but makes it far superior to its original form. The Person and work of Christ is the execution of the Counsel of Peace between the Father and the Son, in which the eschatology of redemption was conceived. Redemption by nature is eschatological and achieved far more than nature could ever have achieved. The gradual progress of the Covenant of Grace in history does not necessarily explain the vertical fulfilment of eschatology. The soteric and the eschatological are inseparable yet logically distinguished and gradually unified. First, the soteric scope alone does not fully explain the gradual development and superiority of New Covenant (Heb 11:39–40). Second, it also does not fully explain the rationale for the present need (use) of Old Covenant revelation (Heb 8:5). These questions can only be answered by the eschatological force at work within the historical process. The vertical and the horizontal forces have to be considered together to fully account for the growth and development of revelation. The Scriptures thus considered the New Covenant superior to the Old because eschatology has been fully revealed by the New, and the Old Covenant still relevant because eschatology is hidden in it: "They serve at a sanctuary that is a copy and shadow of what is in heaven" (Heb 8:5a).

There are two ways that neglect of either the vertical fulfillment or the horizontal progress can influence theology as a whole. The first is an "under-realized" eschatology, or the complete postponement of the eschatological affairs to the future. In this view, the vertical fulfillment in Christ's resurrection and entrance into the heavenly realms is either unrecognized or unappreciated for its present significance. At the other end of the spectrum is "over-realized" eschatology, or the premature unity of heaven and earth in the form of God's kingdom on earth.[1] In this view, the anticipa-

---

1. Horton, *Better Way*, 130.

tion of the Parousia as a historical event is reduced and the eschatological hope is an idealistic unity of the eternal and the temporal. The first view favors the kingdom realized as a sudden crisis in an indefinite future with little present significance, while the second view favors the kingdom as being already arrived at present with less desire for the future version. Vos thinks the first is to "ultra-eschatologize" while the second is to "de-eschatologize" the kingdom of Christ. The first view generally supports the millennial kingdom in the future, while the second view supports the present kingdom for the restoration of creation.[2] Both of the two extreme views are inconsistent with the biblical eschatology of redemption in Christ, characterized by a semi-eschatological structure of the two ages.

Hence, neither of the two extreme views accurately explains the meaning of "The kingdom of God is near" (Mark 1:15). The kingdom of the Son is a provisional and semi-eschatological kingdom that will be handed over to the Father "after he has destroyed all dominion, authority and power" (1 Cor 15:24). The central question, in our view, is how the finished work of Christ (death, resurrection, and exaltation) is related to the unfinished return of the Parousia (John 19:30; Rev 22:20). The eschatology of redemption in between these two events will decide the nature of the kingdom of God and define the current state of redemption. In other words, the current state between Christ's resurrection and Parousia will define the kingdom of God and affect one's view of redemption, ethics, and worldview (1 Cor 7:29–31). In any case, the current state of believers in heaven united with the risen Christ cannot be dismissed—though often it is not noticed or is mischaracterized (Eph 2:6). The three possible views of eschatology and the kingdom considered above are based on how one understands the significance of Christ's death and resurrection. First, if the emphasis falls on the cross but not the resurrection, it results in the "under-realized" kingdom postponed indefinitely to the future. Second, if the emphasis falls on the resurrection but not on the cross, it will be an "over-realized" kingdom with weakened anticipation of the historical Parousia. Third, if the emphasis falls on both the cross and the resurrection, it will be the provisional kingdom of Christ in the form of "already but not yet."[3] The eschatological tension is echoed in our Lord's teaching that his kingdom is not *of* this world—though *in* the world (Luke 17:21; John 18:36). The kingdom of heaven, in the redemptive and the eschatological sense, is already near so that it demands faith and repentance, but not yet so near that we only have a foretaste of the banquet (Mark 1:15; Gal 1:4).

In light of these considerations, it is quite obvious that the kingdom of God and the eschatology of redemption is a direct correlate of Christ's resurrection. The effect of resurrection is not limited to rectitude from sin or restoration to the natural state of Adam. It involves the entire vertical movement from the grave to the sky, as it were, from the pit of death to the throne of grace in the heavenly sanctuary. It is not only

2. Horton, *Better Way*, 130.
3. Horton, *Better Way*, 130.

a recovery from death but a recovery from death for the consummation of nature. The transfer to the heavenly realms through union with Christ is a transfer from the schema of this age to that of the coming age. And the descending of the Spirit on the church at Pentecost signaled the historic transfer of the ages (1 Cor 15:45). The redemptive heaven that believers have arrived at with Christ is called "Mount Zion, the city of the living God, and the heavenly Jerusalem" (Heb 12:22). It is the redemptive "garden of God" in contrast to the garden in nature (Rev 2:7). Jeremiah looked forward to that day of a better and everlasting Zion: "They will ask the way to Zion and turn their faces toward it. They will come and bind themselves to the Lord in an everlasting covenant that will not be forgotten" (Jer 50:5). The traditional *Ordo Salutis* tends to stop short of the present movement to the heavenly places and postpone the transfer to the future. The bodily resurrection is no doubt in the future but the vertical transfer into the new order of existence, the ground of true and everlasting hope, has already taken place in the present tense (Eph 2:6). Because the hope is not a wish but anchored in its corresponding reality, believers will not be pitied for the sacrifices they make in this world. The messianic kingdom is linked with the New Testament view of reality, in which the two ages coexist because the Messiah's appearance takes place "in two successive stages."[4] The first appearance ushered in the provisional kingdom and the second appearance will consummate it as the eschatological kingdom of the Father. The provisional nature of the present kingdom stems from Jesus being Christ and Lord at the same time (Acts 2:36). But Christ is the Servant King in his first appearance rather than the Conqueror who will judge the world in his second appearance, making the period in between a semi-eschatological kingdom.[5]

Just as the suffering and resurrection of the Servant King defines the kingdom where victory and suffering coexist, the church lies in the paradox of the resurrection state and cross-bearing: "Now I rejoice in what was suffered for you, and I fill up in my flesh what is still lacking in regard to Christ's afflictions, for the sake of his body" (Col 1:24). The resurrection state will safeguard believers with the eschatological hope but the cross-bearing will urge them to continue to go "outside the city gate," where Christ bore the shame. In the resurrection state, the church is already in the heavenly city of God, but in the cross-bearing, it has not yet arrived in the "enduring city." The holy war of the provisional kingdom against the remaining earthly nature will not be over for the church until the complete defeat of the enemies:

> For David did not ascend to heaven, and yet he said, 'The Lord said to my Lord: "Sit at my right hand until I make your enemies a footstool for your feet."' Therefore, let all Israel be assured of this: God has made this Jesus, whom you crucified, both Lord and Messiah. (Acts 2:34–36)

---

4. Vos, *Pauline Eschatology*, 36.
5. Robertson, *Christ of Covenants*, 271.

This is exactly echoed by Paul when he says the kingdom of the Son will be handed over to the Father "after he [Christ] has destroyed all dominion, authority and power" (1 Cor 15:24). Hence, the kingdom of the Servant King, until he has completely destroyed the enemy, is intrusive by nature and at war with this evil age: "The antithesis is between a world (age) that *is* and a world (age) that *is to come*."[6] The overlay of the two ages, heaven and earth in the redemptive sense, is produced by two successive appearances of the King. Accordingly, those united to him also experience the two ascensions associated with the appearances: one at the point of rebirth into the kingdom and the other at the point of their bodily resurrection. The reign of the Servant King has begun yet "we do not see everything subject to him" (Heb 2:8). In any case, the redemptive-eschatological kingdom is greater in scope than soteric rectitude or the regaining of creation. In this kingdom, the Redeemer saves *and* reigns until the whole crop is ready to be harvested into the eschatological kingdom of the Father (Mark 4:26–29).

The kingdom of Christ supplies sufficient otherworldly energy from above for the church to engage in the spiritual war against the remaining rule of the flesh. The expectation of an early Parousia did not materialize but it was never about the timing of Christ's return in the first place. It was more about the reality of resurrection itself as the ground of their hope that would not make them pitied. It was the vertical reality of the resurrection state that provided the unceasing flow of life and energy from above so that believers in every age, regardless of time, may enjoy union and fellowship with the risen Lord, even amid suffering. Thus, true eschatology should not weaken but strengthen Christian ethics, contrary to what is often witnessed in those who use it as a pretext to escape the present reality. Eschatology does not diminish motivation to fight against the flesh but raises its intensity to a level of holy war in theocratic kingdom—total destruction of the ungodly. The holy war of Israel in Canaan was typical of the holy war of the present kingdom in all of its ethical and religious potency. It is now a full-blown war with the flesh led by the risen Lord and the Spirit: "Put to death, therefore, whatever belongs to your earthly nature . . ." (Col 3:5). In the redemptive sense, the church is seated in the heavenly realms, yet at the same time it should put to death its remaining earthly "members." In the new schema, the Christian wholly belongs to heaven, and only has to kill his earthly members in the all-out war against the flesh.

The "fullness of time" meant the last days of this age, and the new schema of the age to come was introduced into the world with the appearance of the Messiah on the scene. In the old perspective of Judaism, the arrival of the Messiah would mean that this age ends and the coming age begins in the horizontal scope of time.[7] In this old schema, the Messiah appears once and establishes his kingdom in history, as exemplified in the question raised by disciples: "Lord, are you at this time going to restore the

---

6. Vos, *Pauline Eschatology*, 36.

7. Gentry and Wellum, *Kingdom through Covenants*, 599.

kingdom to Israel?" (Acts 1:6). In the new order of things, however, the Messiah will arrive in two successive stages: the first as Servant King to suffer for the redemption of his people, and the second as Judge of the living and the dead. Unable to conceive of a suffering Messiah or Servant King, the Jews of the Old Testament could not receive Jesus as their Messiah according to the old model (Isa 53:1–12). They were expecting a sudden and catastrophic shift from this age to the coming age in the chronological line of history with the arrival of the Messiah. The New Testament eschatology, however, was such that the shift was to unfold in two stages and the messianic kingdom would arrive in a new schema of the two coexisting ages.[8] The last days of history, the fullness of time, had begun and the consequent arrival of the age to come energizes believers with the supernatural life of the coming age (Heb 1:1–2; 9:26). The old model of the two ages in succession was developed into a new definition in spatial categories:

> In this way it will be seen that the scheme of successiveness had not been entirely abrogated but simply been reapplied to the latter half of the original scheme: the age to come was perceived to bear in its womb another age to come, so that with reference to the mother and the as yet unborn child, as it were, the category of what is and what is to be not only could, but had to be retained.[9]

> Side by side, however, with the continuation of this older scheme the emergence of a new one, involving a coexistence of the two worlds or states, can be observed. From the nature of the case this principle did not allow of application to the age-concept, for the two sequences of time are mutually exclusive. So long as one age lasts no other can supervene. It is different with regard to the worlds or states, for here the existence of one does not exclude the contemporary existence of another, and there is nothing logically impossible either in the believer's belonging to both or at least preeminently to one rather than to the other.[10]

7.2 Covenant and Kingdom

The progress of redemptive history from Adam to Christ is the progress in the Covenant of Grace, which is not just a "testament" but envisages union with God as the redemptive-eschatological fulfillment of the Counsel of Peace. In the soteric scope, the covenant is a testament (the last will) in the sense that Christ's death was necessary to seal the inheritance of the eternal life. But the Covenant of Grace is grounded in the *Pactum Salutis* and this latter aspect is the eschatological fulfillment of man as the

---

8. Vos, *Pauline Eschatology*, 36.
9. Vos, *Pauline Eschatology*, 36.
10. Vos, *Pauline Eschatology*, 37.

image-bearer of God—through the soteric gift. The Covenant of Grace not only satisfies the justice of God by the substitutionary atonement (testament) but also fulfills the ethical and religious vision of man through union with the Mediator. In this sense, it was usually more fitting to translate *diatheke* as covenant rather than as testament: "Beside the law written in their hearts, they received a command not to eat of the tree of knowledge of good and evil; which while they kept, they were happy in their communion with God, and had dominion over the creatures."[11] In view of this, the unity of various covenants is not merely a horizontal fulfillment by a new covenant, but a vertical completion of that union and communion with God. The superiority of the New Covenant (discontinuity) is obvious, but the relevance of the Old Covenant as a "copy" and "shadow" of heaven (continuity) must also be preserved in our understanding of covenantal history (Heb 8:5; Jer 50:5). The diversity of covenants in the horizontal progression is held together by the unity in the vertical union of God and man through the Mediator. The eschatology of redemption this way fulfills the eschatology of nature: "I will be your God and you will be my people"—"God with us." The entrance of the High Priest in the order of Melchizedek into the heavenly sanctuary was the redemptive communion of God and man, far superior to that which Adam, as the priest of nature, would have achieved had he kept the covenant in nature.

The covenant, in the eschatology of redemption, is not only for personal rectitude of sin but for the theocratic kingdom of God as an ethical and religious body of people. It is true that the covenant is the "means of execution of the eternal decree" in the Golden Chain of the logical order of redemption.[12] The covenant as the means of executing the order of salvation come to its fruition is an important element in the soteric process: "And those he predestined, he also called; those he called, he also justified; those he justified, he also glorified" (Rom 8:30). The logical approach complemented the historical approach to covenant—historical development of the biblical covenants.[13] The logical arrangement of the Counsel of Peace leading to the faith of believers does not conflict with the historical arrangement of the Covenant of Grace from Adam to Christ. A perspectival distinction between the horizontal and the vertical aspects of redemption is not a theological conflict.[14] Decree and covenant, in fact, are positively related if the latter is indeed the means of executing the Counsel of Peace with the goal of making holy and blameless children of God (Eph 1:4). The unilateral and the bilateral division of theology is a false dichotomy not found in the

---

11. Westminster Confession of Faith, 4.

12. Song, *Theology and Piety*, 34–35

13. See Witsius, *Economy of Covenants* (1677). Those who favor the historical approach assert that decree and covenant are mutually exclusive and contradictory. It is asserted that decretal theology cannot be harmonized with covenant theology because the former is unilateral while the latter is bilateral in nature. They are seen as inversely proportional and unable to be integrated into a unified system. Hence, a theory was put forth that Calvin and the Puritans represent two distinct lines of theological tradition.

14. Song, *Theology and Piety*, 34–35.

Scriptures. Again, covenant is a unilateral testament in the soteric process (Heb 9:16) but a bilateral pact, a union, in the eschatological fulfillment (Jer 50:5). Hence, covenant progresses toward Christ in history but it also unites believers to him vertically above history. The historical progress is meaningful only if it also ascends vertically to the union of God and man. The shift from the natural to the supernatural schema is the redemptive-eschatological goal of covenant that ushered in the kingdom of God.

In *Christ and Time*, Cullman explains how Christ's death and resurrection changed the concept of time and history. In the new scheme of things, history has entered the new sphere of *kairos* time (2 Cor 6:2) while marching toward the end of *chronos*.[15] Before Christ, history was moving from the Old toward the New, but after Christ it is moving from D-Day to the V-Day of redemption. The covenant moves forward and upward so that the redemptive grace is both rectifying cure of sin and the life-giving tonic of the supernatural life. The Old Covenant may have been largely curative in nature with substitutionary grace, but the New Covenant is both curative and recreative with the consummative grace. The difference lies in the coming of the kingdom of God in the vertical schema of the age to come established by the resurrection of Christ. The soteric covenant in the pre-Christ era has gradually progressed toward the redemptive-eschatological kingdom in Christ.[16] The redemptive kingdom has arrived as the fulfillment of all previous covenants though present in already-but-not-yet form (Col 1:24–25). In the theocratic kingdom of Christ, believers belong to heaven yet bear their cross on earth; this paradox defines the Christian life and worldview. The parable of the growing seed captures the provisional nature of the kingdom in its process and crisis: "All by itself the soil produces grain—first the stalk, then the head, then the full kernel in the head. As soon as the grain is ripe, he puts the sickle to it, because the harvest has come" (Mark 4:28–29). The growth of the kingdom may be gradual and invisible but the harvest will be abrupt and swift. The kingdom exists in between the two ages, already having come but not yet consummated; and this not only in theory but in a real and practical sense:

> The structure of two strata placed one above the other, with the higher stratum made regulative for the lower one in its laws and ideals, is, of course, older than Paul. It underlies the parabolic teaching of our Lord in the Synoptics, and more abstractly and principially reveals itself both in the setting and in the discourses of the Fourth Gospel. And this scheme, far from being a purely speculative construction, is of eminently practical import. It is the basis of what in devotional language we call other-worldliness.[17]

Paul's view of the redemptive universe is that the risen Christ is now the Lord of "this age" and "the coming age" and his lordship is exercised through his kingdom

---

15. Cullman, *Christ and Time*, 141.
16. Ridderbos, *Coming of the Kingdom*, xxiii.
17. Vos, *Pauline Eschatology*, 297.

(Eph 1:21). This new schema of the redemptive heaven and earth is the foundation of the Christian life and ethics in the provisional kingdom.[18] The church is called out of this age into the kingdom of heaven, but sent back, as it were, to complete the remaining mission in the world (Matt 16:18; 28:18–20). The redemptive heaven is a missional kingdom, not a philosophical idealism; it is realism with injection of supernatural energy from the place of the risen Christ through the Spirit. It is not a confused state of neither heavenly nor earthly, but a heavenly state in Christ with the remaining earthly members to be put to death (Col 3:5); it is not a "yes and no" but an "already but not yet."[19] The kingdom of the heavenly realms sustains and leads the temporal world of history, moving horizontally toward the end of redemptive consummation. The kingdom of Christ as the fulfillment of the Covenant of Grace will be superior to the eschatology of nature.

The "practical import" of the kingdom as an initial endowment of the eternal inheritance will be deep and far-reaching as the church can tap into the foretaste of the wedding banquet. It will be indispensable for self-denial and cross-bearing in the horizontal pilgrimage of the world. The *Ordo Salutis*, whether the indicative or the imperative stages, needs the spatial support of the redemptive heaven for the sustenance, empowerment, and perseverance of believers. The kingdom of God is the new order and schema of heaven, an organized force from the age to come, to aid them in their faith working through love. In the nature of the case, the order of salvation itself does not guarantee the perseverance of believers unless supported by the vertical schema as the immutable indicative of redemption. Faith alone justifies the sinner, but it alone cannot guarantee its own assurance and perseverance. It is faith in grace, not faith in the means of grace, whose efficacy the Covenant of Grace rooted in the *Pactum Salutis* alone guarantees. A soteriology that places the sustenance of the *Ordo Salutis* on faith alone is at a great risk. The eternal security in the Covenant of Grace and the Counsel of Peace is what ensures redemption as a whole, so that even when faith wavers the promise of God will not in the severest of trials. It is the zeal of the Lord and the authority of his kingdom that will sustain the glorification of believers:

> Of the increase of his government and peace there will be no end. He will reign on David's throne and over his kingdom, establishing and upholding it with justice and righteousness from that time on and forever. The zeal of the Lord Almighty will accomplish this. (Isa 9:7)

The renewed interest in the kingdom of God from the age to come meant that eschatology is placed at the beginning rather than at the end in the locus of theology. It is not so much that the soteric gives birth to the kingdom as the kingdom gives birth to the soteric; the two are inseparable, in fact, in the eschatology of redemption. The kingdom has propelled the last things of redemption into the present ahead

---

18. Vos, *Pauline Eschatology*, 36.
19. Gaffin, *By Faith Not by Sight*, 57.

of the historical Parousia, making them the first priorities of theology. The kingdom switched the first and the last things around in order to underscore the chief end of man in the world from the eternal covenant point of view. The kingdom is synonymous with the new creation in this sense for the redemptive process, at the end, leads to a new order of creation.[20] In Christ, the soteric rectitude of sin is in order that nature might be consummated, and no doctrine better explains this than the new creation (2 Cor 5:17).[21] A chronological definition of the age to come, historically understood sometimes as imminent or other times as distant, is actually irrelevant since a concrete form of that age has arrived in the kingdom with the departure of Christ into its sphere. In any case, the kingdom corrected the mischaracterization of the age to come as purely belonging to a point in the future. The kingdom is provisional, but nevertheless present and real through the new schema of things introduced into history by the enthronement of the King to the heavenly realms. The coexistence of the last days of this age and the first days of the age to come has started in the kingdom; the coming age is nothing less than "God with us."[22] The everlasting life in the kingdom of God is a present reality in *coram Deo*: "I tell you the truth, he who believes has everlasting life" (John 6:47). Regardless of the time of the Parousia in history, the most critical matter is the union with the risen Lord:

> The bond between the believer and Christ is so close that, from Paul's point of view, a detachment of the Christian's interest not only, but even a severance of his actual life from the celestial Christ-centered sphere is unthinkable. The latter consideration counts for more than the mere fact that through the appearance or resurrection of Christ the eschatological process has been set in motion. As soon as the direction of the actual spiritual life-contact becomes involved, the horizontal movement of thought on the time-plane must give way immediately to a vertical projection of the eschatological interest into the supernal region, because there, even more than in the historical development below, the center of all religious values and forces has come to lie.[23]

7.3 Millennial Kingdom

The debate over the "millennial kingdom" is as much about the nature of the present view of the church—and the kingdom of God—as its future state after the Parousia. It begs the question of the degree of presence or absence of the kingdom in the present mode of redemption and the church. In other words, the nature of the kingdom subsequent to the Parousia is predicated on the present view of the kingdom as a

---

20. Beale, "Eschatological Conception," 12.
21. Beale, "Eschatological Conception," 12.
22. Beale, "Eschatological Conception," 12.
23. Vos, *Pauline Eschatology*, 37–38.

precursor of the former. If "these last days" indeed means a semi-eschatological state, its sequel will not be an entirely different order but a harvest and handing over to the Father (1 Cor 15:24). The question of the kingdom, before or after the Parousia, thus requires more than an independent interpretation of the relevant texts in Revelation. It requires a structure of eschatology as a whole and the theological frame in which to understand those millennial texts. In our view, the inaugurated kingdom does not need the future kingdom to be another intermediary state but will immediately transform into the new heaven and the new earth (1 Cor 7:29–31; 2 Pet 3:13). The future kingdom after the Parousia will be no better than the provisional kingdom of Christ though its consummate form may be better. Insofar as the age to come has already come, there will be no substantial difference between the two. The resurrection of Christ is his departure into the age to come, whose kingdom is already among us (Luke 17:21; Rom 1:4). If Christ is the King and has started his reign over the kingdom, it cannot be made any better than what it is now.

The coming of the kingdom and the reign of the King renders it "near" and "in" us, so much so that the gospel is called the kingdom of God (Matt 11:12; Mark 1:15; Luke 16:16; 17:21). The present form of the kingdom cannot be inferior any more than the present form of the gospel is to be considered inferior. In fact, the four Gospels do not explicitly define the kingdom of God in terms of either now or later.[24] The kingdom is said to have come, but is also said to be "coming.[25] That no such distinction was necessary means the kingdom is both now and later; it is already here but not yet completely here. The risen Christ is already with us but not yet completely with us: "I am torn between the two: I desire to depart and be with Christ, which is better by far; but it is more necessary for you that I remain in the body" (Phil 1:24). Paul is obviously not contradicting what he said about his being with Christ in the heavenly realms. His view of Christ precisely coincides with his view of the kingdom that he is already with Christ in the heavenly realms, but he also desires to be with him. The disciples of Jesus also did not fully grasp the nature of the kingdom prior to the descending of the Spirit at Pentecost, when they asked the resurrected Christ, "Lord, are you at this time going to restore the kingdom to Israel?" (Acts 1:6). After all that time with the Lord, they still thought and hoped the restoration of Israel might be the kingdom. The view of the millennial kingdom after the Parousia, then, is not entirely unlike the Jewish vision of the kingdom because the current rule of Christ is somehow thought to be inferior to his rule in the future. The absence of or disinterest in the vertical view of Christ as the Messiah and Lord is the root cause of such a misunderstanding (Acts 2:36).

The view of the "thousand years" in Revelation thus requires the redemptive-eschatological structure of the New Testament as its hermeneutical foundation. The high state of the redemption begs the question: What is the precise nature of its subsequent stage when Christ hands over his kingdom to the Father? (1 Cor 15:24). The

---

24. Ridderbos, *Coming of the Kingdom*, 105.
25. Ridderbos, *Coming of the Kingdom*, 105.

subsequent state of the kingdom, at least, could not be a repeat of the provisional kingdom but a fully consummated kingdom of the Father. For all intents and purposes, therefore, the "millennial kingdom" in Revelation is best explained as the semi-eschatological kingdom of Christ. Hence, another post-Parousia kingdom on earth seems rather repetitive and the redundancy of having two consecutive kingdoms of similar nature leads to one conclusion. That is, either no kingdom of God is here at the present time or, if it is here, the subsequent state of it has to be the consummate new heaven and new earth. It would be illogical, based on the eschatological structure of the New Testament, to expect two consecutive intermediate kingdoms before the final consummation (1 Cor 15:24). An even more important reason is that the theory of a post-Parousia millennial kingdom inevitably dilutes the sufficiency of the Messiah's work in the redemptive-eschatological sense (Luke 16:16; 17:21). The frequent mention of the last days of this age in the New Testament proves that the kingdom has arrived in a real and permanent way after the Messiah's resurrection: "Then he opened their minds so they could understand the Scriptures. He told them, 'This is what is written: The Christ will suffer and rise from the dead on the third day, and repentance for the forgiveness of sins will be preached in his name to all nations, beginning at Jerusalem'" (Luke 24:45–47). The cross and resurrection of Jesus not only marked the end of the Old Covenant but also the end of this age, ushering in the age to come, which is equivalent to the kingdom of God. The resurrection of the Messiah, in particular, was the fulfillment of the Davidic kingdom God had promised him (Acts 2:36). This is not just an exegetical issue of the millennial texts of Revelation, but a theological issue that concerns Christology and eschatology.

The eschatology of the New Testament is a direct outcome of its Christology. As such, it is not limited to interest in the last things of history but more so in the chief end of man and history. The insertion of another in-between millennial kingdom after the Parousia runs contrary to the eschatological nature of Christ's finished work, particularly its fulfillment of the *Pactum Salutis*. The kingdom of the Son as opposed to the "dominion of darkness" is the direct outcome of the fulfillment, and its presence is immediate and efficient in the life of believers (Col 1:13). The present kingdom is true and real because the finished work of Christ is so, and nothing less than a consummate kingdom of the Father, after all enemies have been defeated, is fit to succeed it: "Living, then, in a world of semi-futurities there is every reason to expect that the thought of the earliest Christians should have moved backwards from the anticipated attainment in its fullness to the present partial experiences and interpreted these in terms of the former."[26] The mind of the New Testament believers did not so much move from the present to the future as from the future to the present, which made their anticipation of the Parousia even more eager. They took the eschatology of heaven not so much as the "crown of soteriology" but as the prior foundation of it: "In other words, the

---

26. Vos, *Pauline Eschatology*, 43.

shaping of soteriology by eschatology is not so much in the terminology; it proceeds from the actual realities themselves and the language simply is adjusted to that."[27]

The arbitrary interpretation of the millennial clauses, then, postpones Christ's messianic reign to post-Parousia times, which does not find support either from Christology or eschatology. The difference between the present and the future kingdoms does not lie in their substance but in the consummation of the first by the second: "But each in turn: Christ, the firstfruits; then, when he comes, those who belong to him. Then the end will come, when he hands over the kingdom to God the Father after he has destroyed all dominion, authority and power" (1 Cor 15:23–24). In this context, the end (*telos*) refers to the full harvest of the firstfruit in the resurrection of Christ. It does not refer to the beginning of another period of a millennium, but to the consummation of what had already been started. The *telos* of man and history, in principle, has been reached at the cross when he declared "It is finished" and proved it by his resurrection. The decisive question, therefore, is how the Messiah's suffering and resurrection, which ushered in the new schema of the age, relate to the post-Parousia state of affairs. The theological foundation of Christology and eschatology should provide the necessary basis for the exegesis of the "thousand years" rather than the reverse. In view of these, the "thousand years" is a striking symbolism for the provisional kingdom of the Messiah (Rev 20:1–10; 1 Cor 15:24). The sense of finality and intensity of the symbolism is fitting for the semi-eschatological nature of the age to come that has begun with the Messiah's departure into the new schema with believers. In any case, the New Testament neither teaches nor sanctions personal salvation apart from the kingdom of God in the present tense (John 3:1–5).

Based on the eschatology of redemption, the biblical history subsequent to the fall consists of three major periods: the pre-eschatological of the Old Testament, the semi-eschatological of the New Testament, and the full-eschatological of the new heaven and the new earth. In contrast, the theory of a post-Parousia millennial kingdom divides history in such a way that the period between the two comings of Christ is not the kingdom of God in the sense we have stated. Some premillennialists do recognize "God's reign," but as an intrusion rather than arrival of the kingdom.[28] Ladd, for instance, recognizes the kingdom of God in this sense: "If, however, the Kingdom is the reign of God, not merely in the human heart but dynamically active in the person of Jesus and in human history, then it becomes possible to understand how the Kingdom of God can be present and future, inward and outward, spiritual and apocalyptic."[29] The realized kingdom of the present and the millennial kingdom of the future are harmonized this way by the concept of the "reign of God" until the Parousia. The kingdom, so defined as the reign of God, will be succeeded by the millennial kingdom after the Parousia, which then will again be succeeded by the consummate kingdom

---

27. Vos, *Pauline Eschatology*, 46.
28. Ladd, *Presence of the Future*, 42.
29. Ladd, *Presence of the Future*, 42.

into eternity. In short, a definition of the realized kingdom is suggested in order that another kingdom of a "thousand years" after the Parousia is rendered justifiable and desirable.

It is obvious that a kingdom so defined is less than semi-eschatological in nature. A kingdom of God without a vertical union of heaven and earth would only be a kingdom in name rather than a true reality (Eph 1:10). God's reign itself does not suggest the coming of the kingdom since God has reigned since the beginning of history. The kingdom of God is a kingdom of hope, but "hope without corresponding reality, or at least a principle of realization, is the most futile and ill-fated frustration of life-purpose..."[30] The kingdom of Christ, however, is a kingdom with the "corresponding reality" of the redemptive heaven, where believers are seated with Christ and where their hope is anchored (1 Cor 15:19). It would be a contradiction in terms to have a kingdom of God that is less than eschatological or at least semi-eschatological. And the resurrection of the Messiah is nothing short of eschatological in that believers are counted as "dead to sin but alive to God in Christ Jesus" (Rom 6:11). It is the beginning of the new and eternal order of affairs, which can only be followed by nothing less than its own consummation:

> It must be admitted, however, that the likelihood of finding Chiliasm in Paul is not favored by the trend of the Apostle's teaching as a whole. Not merely does his general concatenation of eschatological events, in which the Parousia and the resurrection of believers are conjoined with the judgment exclude every intermediate stage of protracted duration, it is of even more importance that Paul conceives of the present Christian state, ideally considered, as lived on so high a plane that nothing less nor lower than the absolute state of the eternal consummate Kingdom appears worthy to be its sequel.[31]

In this vein, the state of believers painted in the "thousand years" of Revelation and the state of believers seated with Christ in the Pauline Epistles are strikingly similar (Rev 20:1–10; Eph 2:6; Col 3:1–4). The two cases mutually corroborate the vertical elevation of those in Christ to the heavenly realms of redemptive order. The special features of the millennium in Revelation are: (1) they have experienced the first resurrection in Christ; (2) they reign with Christ as priests of God; (3) their names are written on the book of life; (4) the second death has no power over them (Rev 20:4–6). These descriptions of the souls of the dead in Christ remarkably fit those who are currently united with Christ: they too have experienced resurrection to the heavenly places; they also reign as the kingdom of priests; their life too is hidden in God through Jesus Christ (Matt 28:18; 1 Pet 2:9; Eph 2:6; Col 3:4). They are justified by God in Christ and counted as "more than conquerors" because they will never be separated from the love of God in Christ—equivalent to their names being written in

---

30. Vos, *Pauline Eschatology*, 31.
31. Vos, *Pauline Eschatology*, 235.

the Book of Life (Rom 8:31–39). In both of these celestial places, believers (whether dead or alive) are seated with Christ, where the second death has no power over them. Both indicate vertical ascension from the earthly to the heavenly realms, resting next to the Father, a guarantee of what is to come (2 Cor 5:5). Regardless of life or death, the state of being in Christ will not be substantially different because of the risen Christ himself—"For to me, to live is Christ and to die is gain" (Phil 1:21).

The state of being in the new order of heaven through this union cannot be different whether Paul was in the body or out of the body (vv. 22–23). It was a matter of preference rather than substantial difference as the apostle would "prefer to be away from the body and at home with the Lord" (2 Cor 5:8). At times he considered it "far better" to be with Christ away from the body in preference for the consummate joy of being with him (Phil 1:23). In truth, the chief end remains the same whether by life or by death: "If we live, we live to the Lord; and if we die, we die to the Lord. So, whether we live or die, we belong to the Lord" (Rom 14:8). The union with Christ made him transcend the scope of physical life in the horizontal flow of time and set his mind on "things above" (Col 1:2–3). In light of this, the hermeneutical key for the millennium ought to be the "first resurrection" believers experience in Christ in the new birth of the Holy Spirit. It radically alters one's view of life and death rearranged by the union with the living Christ (Phil 1:21–23). In all likelihood, "the keys of death and Hades" in Revelation are "the keys of the kingdom of heaven" Jesus Christ gave the church (Matt 16:19; Rev 1:18).[32] The "thousand years" precede the final battle prior to the return of the Lord, hence the keys are given to the church during that millennium, when Christ exercises his authority over life and death (Rev 19:11–21).[33]

In view of the risen Christ's reign over all things in heaven and earth, the state of believers is qualitatively the same whether by life or death vertically considered. There is a qualitative equivalence between the heavenly state of believers in Paul's epistles and state of the millennium described in Revelation. The "redemptive heaven"[34] that Christ entered through resurrection is where all believers begin to exist in the moment they are united to him through the Spirit. If so, this at least in part explains the absence of a millennial concept in Paul's epistles in "that the likelihood of finding Chiliasm in Paul is not favored by the trend of the Apostle's teaching as a whole."[35] At the moment of rebirth in the Spirit, believers are rescued from this evil age and elevated to the kingdom of the Son, where they are seated and reign with Christ. There is a plausible ground that the inaugurated kingdom of heaven in the four Gospels, the kingdom of the Son in the Pauline Epistles, and the "thousand years" in Revelation are one and the same kingdom prior to the Parousia. It will be succeeded by the eschatological kingdom of the Father subsequent to the Parousia. The growing

32. Beale and Campbell, *Revelation*, 430.
33. Beale and Campbell, *Revelation*, 430.
34. Vos, *Pauline Eschatology*, 40.
35. Vos, *Pauline Eschatology*, 235.

nature of the kingdom in the Gospels, in particular, makes it difficult to sustain either the premillennial or the postmillennial view (Mark 4:26–29). The age of the Spirit, eschatologically considered, is neither devoid of a kingdom nor equal to an earthly kingdom prior to the Parousia.[36]

The consensus in the New Testament is that Christ fulfilled the prophecies of the messianic kingdom and believers enter the kingdom by the new birth of the Spirit (John 3:5). Hence, the postponement of that kingdom to after the Parousia is a hermeneutic that denies the christocentric view of the redemptive history. It is true, the kingdom of Christ is provisional: "What I mean, brothers, is that the time is short. Those who have wives should live as if they had none . . . ; those who mourn, as if they did not; those who are happy, as if they were not . . . For this world in its present form is passing away" (1 Cor 7:29-31). The apostle no doubt anticipated a speedy arrival of the eschatological kingdom since (and because) Christ has already entered heaven, and believers in principle belong in the new schema of the age to come. The expectation of an early Parousia was his personal preference rather than a revelation from God but nonetheless a reasonable hope in light of corresponding reality. In fact, the exact time of the Parousia is inconsequential compared to what he knew with certainty of Christ's resurrection and the new schema believers belonged to with him. The soteric and the eschatological significances of Christ's death and resurrection were far greater to the New Testament authors than the numeric significance of the millennium. Rather than letting a symbol in the apocalyptic revelation dictate the entire hermeneutic of the kingdom, they were fixated on what the Messiah accomplished once and for all to bring about the age from the future. In conclusion, the coming of a provisional messianic kingdom is more likely before, rather than after, the Parousia.[37] Vos is of the opinion that a post-Parousia chiliastic kingdom is not supported by the epistles of Paul in that it is "positively irreconcilable" with the apostle's thought. But the likelihood of a present kingdom in the apostle's thought is undeniable:

> The argument in no wise precludes Paul's having regarded the present reign of Christ, with its semi-eschatological character in the light of a provisional kingdom to be succeeded by an absolute kingdom at the Parousia . . . This implies plainly a distinction between the kingdom of Christ as a *present* and the kingdom of God as a *future* reality. In this place then Paul has plainly incorporated into his eschatology the idea of a twofold kingdom, just as in the teaching of our Lord there appears the same distinction between the present kingdom and the eschatological kingdom.[38]

---

36. Four major views on the millennial kingdom are explained in Hoekema, *Bible and Future*, 173–93.
37. Vos, *Pauline Eschatology*, 258–59.
38. Vos, *Pauline Eschatology*, 258–59.

The hope for the eschatological kingdom of the Father (1 Cor 15:24) is not diminished but increased by the present kingdom of the Son, which is a foretaste of the wedding banquet in the new heaven and new earth: "He who testifies to these things says, 'Yes, I am coming soon.' Amen. Come, Lord Jesus. The grace of the Lord Jesus be with God's people. Amen" (Rev 22:20–21).

7.4 HEAVEN AND EARTH

The overall structure of redemptive history is that it moves forward from the Old Covenant to the New Covenant, but also moves upward from earth to heaven in the redemptive-eschatological sense (Eph 1:10). Heaven and earth are unified "so that God may be all in all" through the Last Adam, and this is the redemptive fulfillment of the eschatology of nature (1 Cor 15:28). In Christ's resurrection, not only death is overcome but the earthly image of man is changed into the heavenly image (1 Cor 15:47–49). The cross of Christ is for the substitutionary work of atonement whereas his resurrection is for the consummative work of the new creation. In this, Christ fulfilled the Counsel of Peace to bring the elect into the union and communion with the three Persons of the blessed God. It is an eschatology that elevated nature to nth degree through the mystery of redemption. Biblical revelation before Christ was progressive toward and typical of the fulfillment of the Messiah, though the soteric element was not devoid in types and shadows. The fullness of time is succeeded by the new schema of the coming age, and Jesus Christ has become the Savior and the Lord "so that in everything he might have the supremacy" (Col 1:18). The old schema of this age still continues but it is "passing away" for sure and believers are told not to live as if it will last forever (1 Cor 7:29–31). In the New Testament, then, the *Historia Salutis* (kingdom) provides the eschatological frame for the *Ordo Salutis* (salvation) in a way the Old Testament could not do.[39] The forward and the upward progress of redemptive-eschatological history reached its apex in the crucified and risen Messiah, and the subsequent history is the age of mission of the Spirit. The kingdom of the Messiah is no longer limited to a geopolitical nation but is global in nature (Matt 28:18–20). In this kingdom, a distinction between the sacred and the secular is no longer determined by the ceremonial laws of Israel but by the law of Christ, who reigns equally over all spheres of life (1 Cor 9:21). The upward progress in covenant reached its final destination in God's rest through Christ, who is *Immanuel* (Isa 7:14; 8:8; Matt 1:23). The horizontal development of covenant history alone does not fully explain the supernatural goal of the New Covenant or, conversely, justify the present necessity of the Old Covenant as part of the whole biblical revelation. Unless the vertical fulfillment of the age to come is considered, it is difficult to explain the messianic

---

39. Gaffin, *Centrality of Resurrection*, 13.

kingdom and the new schema of heaven, where believers are seated with Christ. It is not just a regaining of creation but a gain of the new order of creation.[40]

These considerations bear on the nature of the kingdom and the reign of Christ in this world, including redeeming culture. The Cultural Mandate was a part of the Covenant of Works in nature for mankind created in God's image (Gen 1:26–28; 2:15). In the eschatology of redemption, however, the renewal of culture is not the final goal but a process toward the redemptive consummation of all things in Christ. It must take into account the decay of nature, having been cursed and without hope apart from the redemptive recreation in Christ. The primary issue in the post-fall situation, then, is not that of saving souls or saving culture, but that between creation and recreation. In the eschatology of redemption, nature (and culture for that matter) is not abrogated but placed within the new schema moving toward the new heaven and new earth. The mission of the church in the new schema, whether saving souls or saving culture, is to be carried out in view of the provisional nature of this world, whose present form is passing away. The whole creation, in fact, awaits its redemption and liberation from "its bondage to decay," not just a restoration to its original form (Rom 8:18–22). The original form of the Cultural Mandate cannot be the final goal of redemption, let alone the final destination of its eschatology. In Christ, the order of nature has been upgraded (resurrected) to the order of redemption in the Last Adam; the Covenant of Works has been fulfilled by the Covenant of Grace with a "redemptive plus."

In redemption, the basic constitution of man was changed in that the redemptive life in him is not just a "living soul" but the "life-giving Spirit" (1 Cor 15:45). The entrance of sin cursed nature and radically altered the natural order to the extent that mankind must return to "dust" until recreated in the Last Adam. The difference is not just restorative but recreative, not just soteric but aeonic in nature, but in all Christ reigns as the Lord (Phil 2:10–11). In the limited scope of rectitude from sin, the antithesis of saving souls or saving culture would be unavoidable, but in the broader scope of the redemptive eschatology, it is a false dichotomy. A logical distinction between the soteric and the eschatological may be made, but in the broader sense redemption is eschatological. Nature can never return to the form in which it was first given to man, for the corruption is so deep and widespread that it too awaits to be "brought into the glorious freedom of the children of God" (Rom 8:21). The order of nature (marriage, labor, and rest) would have been preserved had Adam obeyed, and in the "confirmed state" of obedience the order would have continued.[41] The eschatology of nature, though, did not fulfill yet typified the eschatology of redemption. The gospel cannot be equated to the renewal of culture but will bring a new schema to the existing culture. The two orders coexist in the horizontal perspective of time, but are antithetical in the vertical perspective of schema (pattern), or the flesh versus the Spirit. The

---

40. Wolters, *Creation Regained*, 44–56.
41. Murray, *Principles of Conduct*, 41.

respective constitutions of each are so fundamentally irreconcilable that Jesus said, "my kingdom is not of this world" (John 18:36).

Cultural renewal as part of the gospel mission is part of the aeonic shift that took place in the coming of the Messiah. It is true that the new order does not negate nature itself, for it is not a Greek dualism but a redemptive eschatology.[42] Heaven is not a *cosmic* heaven but a *redemptive* heaven that will consummate earth in the age to come (Rev 21:1–5). It is against the flesh but not against the body, is spiritual but not Gnostic. Redemption upholds nature by elevating it to the highest order of splendor and glory without minimizing the gravity of the fall and its effect on creation. The Scriptures declare the preeminence of nature while lamenting the greatness of sin, which rendered nature to fall short of God's glory (Ps 8:1; Rom 1:19–20; 3:23). Redemption establishes nature rather than abrogates it, but culture in the natural sense can no longer be demanded of believers as a lasting principle. The tragic irony is that nature was cursed soon after God declared its goodness (Gen 1:31; 3:14–24): "That day will bring about the destruction of the heavens by fire, and the elements will melt in the heat. But in keeping with his promise we are looking forward to a new heaven and a new earth, where righteousness dwells" (2 Pet 3:12–13). The constitution of the world in its present schema will be destroyed and replaced by a redemptive heaven and earth.

A simple regain of culture in this fallen world seems to be a hope and sentiment foreign to the Scriptures. The rejection of a Greek dualism is understandable, but the view of redemption as a regaining of culture should also be qualified by the eschatology of the New Testament.[43] In this sense, renewal of culture cannot be too white-collared in the sense of a premature victory or blue-collared in the sense of indefinite postponement of victory. The former stresses a kingdom already come, whereas the latter stresses a kingdom not yet come. The first does not sufficiently recognize the hopeless reality of sin and decay, while the second does not fully appreciate the reign of Christ over all things. The tension of already-but-not-yet in the semi-eschatological kingdom is a reality that cannot be resolved by resorting to either extreme. The kingdom is not of this world, after all, and the Christian must be prepared to live in the eschatological tension (2 Cor 4:16–18). In this sense, eschatology is the "crown of soteriology" rather than a regaining of nature.[44] In the new schema of Christ, "the Messianic provisional kingdom and the present soteria are identical and coextensive, so that what the Christian now possesses and enjoys is the firstfruits and pledge of the life eternal."[45]

---

42. Wright, *Resurrection of the Son of God*, 348.
43. See Wolters, *Creation Regained*.
44. Wolters, *Creation Regained*, 43–44.
45. Vos, *Pauline Eschatology*, 259.

7.5 Kingdom and Culture

Cultural Mandate was a part of the Covenant of Works: "The LORD God took the man and put him in the Garden of Eden to work it and take care of it" (Gen 2:15). The focus here is not so much on work itself but on the goodness of creation and the blessedness of man as an image-bearer of God. The Covenant of Works is typical of the Covenant of Grace; redemption does not abrogate culture but transforms it by grace with a new schema. The choice was never between the renewal or denial of culture—the garden of God—but between the two schemas of culture. The choice is between conformation to "the pattern of this world" or transformation by "the renewing of your mind" (Rom 12:2). The latter requires a change of schema, from this evil age to the age to come, by offering oneself as "a living sacrifice." The redemptive grace does not abandon culture but establishes it from a redemptive perspective on such spheres as marriage, work, and rest. The beauty and splendor of the garden of God is elevated rather than degraded by redemption (Rev 2:7). The "resurrection-eschatology" raises the integrity of nature and affirms the blessedness of the physical rather than denigrates it.[46] The pattern of this world is what is passing away "after he has destroyed all dominion, authority and power," rather than the garden itself (1 Cor 15:24). The prospective transition renders everything in this age temporary and fleeting, including culture, explained in no uncertain terms in regard to marriage, work, and general outlook on life such as joy and sadness (1 Cor 7:29–31).

The schema of this world is "dominion, authority and power" invisibly at work within the fabric of this fallen world that affects every aspect of human life: "The LORD saw how great man's wickedness on the earth had become, and that every inclination of the thoughts of his heart was only evil all the time" (Gen 6:5). The garden of God, as the ethical and religious core of man's natural life, is no longer what it once used to be. Every sphere of society is affected by bondage to the flesh and what was meant to be an everlasting order in nature has been made temporary and passing away. As Murray had pointed out, had Adam entered a "confirmed state," the natural order such as marriage and work would have continued in the eschatology of nature. However, the Cultural Mandate in the eschatology of nature and in the eschatology of redemption cannot be the same. In this sense, grace restores nature (culture) with a qualification, and a renewal of culture must be redefined accordingly. The Covenant of Works and Covenant of Grace are two distinct orders that remain as separate principles in this fallen world until that distinction will become unnecessary in the new heaven and new earth; the first is natural, and the second is redemptive-eschatological. Hence, a distinction became necessary: gospel/law, church/world, ministry/vocational calling.

Broadly speaking, the neo-Calvinistic view favors transformation of culture as part of the gospel and the two-kingdoms view favors separation of the gospel and culture. In our view, the question at hand must take the redemptive-eschatological approach

---

46. Ridderbos, *Paul*, 55.

as explained above. Since the risen Christ has supremacy over all things, his reign and kingdom will never be divided, whether in this age or in the age to come (Eph 1:20–21; Col 1:15–20). The lordship of Christ is over all things so that the things in heaven and the things on earth are united in him (Eph 1:10). Such is the order and magnitude of the finished work through his incarnation, crucifixion, and resurrection. Although not everything is subject to him at present, Kuyper was right when he said that there is not an inch of the universe that Christ does not claim as "mine" (Rom 1:4; Heb 2:8). In this sense, the terminology of "two kingdoms" may be misleading, though it was never meant to imply a division within Christ's kingdom or reign. A renewal of the garden of God under the unified kingdom of Christ, therefore, is a proper and necessary mandate of the church and the gospel. This is the foundation of vocational calling and "sovereignty of spheres." The purpose of the renewal, however, is not to conform to "the pattern of this world" but to be transformed by "the renewing of your mind" (Rom 12:1–3). The purpose does not lie in the culture itself but in the new schema of culture that radically redefines it in terms of its substance and duration. As Wright has rightly described, the kingdom of Christ during the interim period is neither purely spiritual nor purely material—neither Gnosticism nor materialism.[47] The only way to do so, in our view, is to view the gospel in terms of the eschatology of redemption. The redemptive paradox of putting to death the earthly nature while being seated with Christ in heaven, being a living sacrifice, is the substance of Christian renewal in this fleeting world. This redemptive-eschatological vision was foreshadowed in Jacob's vision of the heavenly ladder, typical of the union of heaven and earth in Christ (Col 3:1–4). The prayer of Jesus for his disciples lets us peek into the chief end of man in redemption: truth, glory, love of the Father through the Son (John 17:17–26). The gospel seeks not culture but beauty, blessedness, and love of God as the chief end.

In the redemptive order of heaven and earth, the garden of God will be consummated but the exact details are scarce besides the few chapters in Revelation (1 Cor 7:29–31; 2 Pet 3:10–13; Rev 21:1–2). Even the nature of man in the new and eternal order is not explained in detail other than that the earthly image will be transformed into the heavenly image of man (1 Cor 15:48–49). On the one hand, the present form of culture will pass away with the present form of this world, but on the other, the blessedness of the garden of Eden gives us a reasonable hope that cultural advancements at present will have significance in the consummate world. It is true that culture will continue in the eternal order of creation in a new form and that renders every sphere of the natural life in this world meaningful, but this is not the same as saying that transformation of culture is the purpose of the gospel, or grace does not add supernatural elements to creation but only restores it.[48] In brief, redemption is largely defined as a regaining rather than a recreation of nature. Culture then only needs a change in direction (redeem) without a change in substance (supernatural). It would

---

47. Wright, *Resurrection of the Son of God*, 349.
48. Wolters, *Creation Regained*, 58–59.

then be a redemption without a consummation; a return to the eschatology of nature without the eschatology of redemption. In this picture of the gospel, a redemptive heaven, "the things above," and the kingdom of God, of entirely different schema is absent (Col 1:13; 3:2). In the eschatology of redemption, a distinction must be made between restoration and recreation by adding eschatology to creation. In the recreation, the work of six days will have entered the rest of the seventh day and "there will be no more night" and the "need for the light of a lamp or the light of the sun, for the Lord God will give them light" (Gen 2:1–3; Rev 22:5).[49]

The regaining of creation should then be put in perspective, and seen as a process toward the new garden of God in the Last Adam. The transformation of culture by the gospel is a part of the horizontal process toward the consummation: "For the creation was subjected to frustration, not by its own choice, but by the will of the one who subjected it, in hope that the creation itself will be liberated from the bondage to decay and brought into the freedom and glory of the children of God" (Rom 8:20–21). These words indicate that the renewal of culture in its present form of "pervasive depravity" is at best provisional and anticipatory of the eschatological hope of glory.[50] Sin and its corruption so altered constitution of the natural world that only its recreation into a new garden of God and a new image of man would be able to fix the problem (1 Cor 15:40–46). The two opposing schemas that dictate the present reality of man's existence, including every sphere of the present world, are described as follows: "Therefore, we do not lose heart. Though outwardly wasting away, yet inwardly we are being renewed day by day. For our light and momentary troubles are achieving for us an eternal glory that far outweighs them all" (2 Cor 4:16–17). The imperative of the gospel in the outward life, including renewal of the garden of God, is based on the indicative of the gospel in the inner life of resurrection. The imperatives of "set your hearts on things above" and "put to death the earthly nature" are supported by the indicative of "you have been raised with Christ" (Col 3:1–4). In any case, the kingdom of God in the New Testament is not cultural, political, or national entity, which are to be distinguished from the redemptive-eschatological lordship of Christ over all spheres of life.[51] A particular form of culture or politics in the schema of this world, in its most idealistic form, still does not and cannot represent the kingdom of Christ. The best forms of human culture and civilization are but part of the provisional kingdom in progress, like the growing grain awaiting the sickle of the farmer and the final harvest (Mark 4:26–29). The garden of God and its culture today exists in the eschatological tension of the two worlds, one fallen and the other redemptive (Eph 6:12; Heb 2:8). In the redemptive garden of Christ, nothing that God has consecrated is impure to drink or eat (Acts 10:15), but the garden itself was never the chief end: "For the kingdom of God is not a matter of eating and drinking, but of righteousness, peace and joy in the Holy Spirit" (Rom 14:17).

49. Hughes, *Hebrews*, 159.
50. Hoekema, *Created in God's Image*, 150.
51. Gentry and Wellum, *Kingdom through Covenants*, 593.

Chapter 8
Worldview and Eschatology

8.1 Kingdom and Worldview

THE REDEMPTIVE HISTORY IN THE SCRIPTURES with its forward and upward movement created a provisional kingdom of heaven between the first and the second comings of Christ. The worldview of the semi-eschatological kingdom rejects a dualism of spirit and body, sacred and secular, faith and knowledge, gospel and culture. But due to the antithesis between the flesh and the Spirit the pairs exist within the provisional unity of heaven and earth. The gospel and the worldview it envisions is more than a regaining of creation; it is a kingdom in anticipation of the new heaven and earth.

The fundamental premise of creation is that the natural and the supernatural coexist but are not antithetical. The earthly body and the heavenly body are of different order but they are not ethically opposed (1 Cor 15:44–49). The corruption of the natural order is not due to creation but due to the decay started by original sin. The creation of the physical world *ex nihilo* does not inherently discriminate against body; it only distinguishes between the natural (*psychikon*) and the supernatural (*pneumatikon*). The issue is not about constitution but the order of man and creation respectively, represented by Adam and the Last Adam. One is of a "living being" by natural birth but the other is of the "life-giving Spirit" by spiritual birth. The former body is of the earthly origin, but the latter body is of the heavenly origin. Hence, a biblical worldview is a matter of difference in the order of man rather than in the constitutive parts of man. The difference in the order is substantial as well as directional because the redemptive eschatology means the vertical shift from *psychikon* to *pneumatikon*. It is about the progress from creation to redemption and again to new creation, rather than about division within man. The body was never meant to be set over against spirit under any circumstance, an important consideration in regard to the holistic worldview. Christ's resurrection goes beyond the soteric remedy from death to life, to consummation from the natural to the supernatural. The resultant worldview is not a Gnostic dualism of soul and body but an eschatological distinction of the eternal and the temporal. The integrity of the physical element in creation can hardly be overemphasized, not only for the integrity of the gospel itself, but for the biblical worldview.[1] The progress of bodily resurrection from the natural to the supernatural region in union with Christ is the beginning of a new and perfect world order.[2]

The semi-eschatological kingdom offers a very unique biblical worldview based on the resurrection of Christ that does not split the physical world itself into the sacred and the secular. The vertical-spatial elevation in resurrection allows believers to maintain a wide-angle view from which to see the world in its totality. The apostle Paul exhorted believers to set their minds on things in heaven and not on things on earth in order that the latter might be wholly and properly interpreted (Col 3:1–4). The early Christians perceived that the world in its present form would soon pass away and this became the basis of their ethics and spiritual war (1 Cor 7:29–31; Col 3:5). Since they believed that they were already seated above with Christ, even to die was gain because it was a return to the home where they are already with the Lord. From the upper strata of heaven powerful energy is poured down to the pilgrimage on earth, which rendered New Testament believers filled with the hope and anticipation of Christ's return (1 Cor 15:50–58; 2 Cor 4:16–5:7). They hoped the interim would to be short that they might even be able to see Christ's return while "clothed" in the body.

The interim worldview of the New Testament is dictated by the provisional kingdom of Christ, which will soon be handed over the Father (1 Cor 15:24). Such an intense hope is expressed in the words "we who are still alive," in contrast to "those who sleep in death" at the time of his victorious return (1 Thess 4:15, 17). In the strict sense, therefore, theirs was not so much a worldview but an interim worldview. It would be strange not to think in these terms from their vantage point in history that there is no reason the first and second resurrection should be far apart in time. Resurrection was not primarily a horizontal issue of delay but a vertical issue of their present union with the risen Christ. Their worldview thus naturally flowed out of their faith and hope in the true reality of their present state vertically. However much time and living left in this world, they were always held in check by the greater hope of departing to be with Christ (Phil 1:23). Their union with Christ and the eternal perspective there provided a panoramic view of the horizontal plane below. They did not expect an indefinite extension of history or such a delay of Christ's return on account of their current state with him. Their worldview was born out of the resurrection state in the Spirit and the historical consciousness that "the time is short" (1 Cor 7:29).

The interim character of their worldview was naturally disposed to the eternal rather than the temporal but with strong ethical imperatives for the latter (Col 3:1–5). The focus would be more on the interim nature of the spheres below than the nature of spheres themselves. The ethnic, political, social, economic, and cultural spheres below are reinterpreted in view of the soteric and eschatological significance of Christ's

---

1. Wolters, *Creation Regained*, 51.
2. Gaffin, *Centrality of the Resurrection*, 89.

finished work. The vertical perspective did not degrade the horizontal spheres themselves, but altered how they were to be reinterpreted in Christ. The new order of heaven and earth penetrated every sphere in life that all things sacred and secular must be done as unto the Lord. "For none of us lives for ourselves alone, and none of us dies for ourselves alone. If we live, we live for the Lord; and if we die, we die for the Lord. So, whether we live or die, we belong to the Lord" (Rom 14:7–8). The import of the new order is that the hope of believers is not of this world as they have been spatially removed from this world and their life is already hidden in God. The foundation of true hope is the otherworldly state of believers, who are no longer subjugated to the vain glories of this world. "If only for this life we have hope in Christ, we are of all people most to be pitied," which conversely means that believers will never be pitied because their state (hope) is not of this world (1 Cor 15:19). One's hope is predicated on the indicative rather than the imperative of their being, assured by their spatial ascension to the realm of eternity. Conversely, one is to be most pitied if his current existence is only of this world yet must suffer great loss in it. The true hope is the outcome of an absolute reality rather than a psychological state of being hopeful (1 Cor 15:20).

A soteric assurance solely based on substitutionary atonement does not necessarily lead to the eschatological worldview with a certainty of hope based on the objective reality of resurrection. The perseverance of justification cannot be assured by substitutionary atonement but by resurrection (Rom 4:25). The indicative of justification so guaranteed in the vertical ascension will provide to believers liberty, joy, and rest to urge the imperative of the Christian life. The biblical worldview is the outcome of the otherworldly state of believers in resurrection with Christ. They are not merely being hopeful of the future but their absolute hope is brought to the forefront and rendered a controlling motif in every facet of life. The provisional kingdom naturally and rightly produces a provisional worldview: "The end of all things is near. Therefore be alert and of sober mind so that you may pray" (1 Pet 4:7). The end (*telos*) of this age is near, spatially rather than chronologically, in the same way the kingdom has come near, so the gospel urges people to repent and believe the good news (Mark 1:15; 1 Cor 10:11). In Christ, the end (purpose) of all things has drawn near in the vertical sense regardless of the time in the horizontal plane. "With the Lord a day is like a thousand years, and a thousand years are like a day," meaning that the quantity of time in the horizontal plane is irrelevant (2 Pet 3:8). The apostle was not so much interested in the worldview per se as he was in the Person of Christ, who revealed "all the treasures of wisdom and knowledge" of God (Col 2:3). The biblical worldview, in general, and the otherworldly view of the kingdom of heaven, in particular, find their ultimate meanings in Christ, the "mystery of God." Hence, the biblical worldview and biblical eschatology would have been synonymous in the minds of the believers in the New Testament. The bird's-eye view of the world below is possible only at the top of heaven and earth, and no substantial difference exists between believers then and believers now as far as this spatial position. In this position alone, the splendor of the "one, universal, holy, and apostolic" church and the supremacy of Christ over all things form a coherent unity (Col 1:18).

In the present author's mind, the apparent delay of the Parousia appears to have added fuel to the debate over the biblical worldview throughout the course of church history. In anticipation of an imminent return of Christ, the early Christians did not so much wrestle with the question of worldview based on a postponement of the Parousia. They were captivated by the kingdom of heaven and how that affected the world rather than indulging in a worldview itself. The transformation of culture is a modern concept that was foreign to the consciousness of the early believers in the New Testament. It would be anachronistic, therefore, to read it into the mindset of New Testament believers, who did not anticipate indefinite extension of culture. In their view of the realized kingdom, they were living in the fullness of time (the last days of the *kosmos*) and Christ's second coming was thought to be imminent. The modern interest in the renewal of culture would have been a moot point to those who believed this age would soon come to an end based on Christ's death and resurrection. As the initial hope faded with time, Christianity began to shift its attention to worldview and the renewal of culture in anticipation of a longer history. With an indefinite postponement of the Parousia, a certain de-eschatologizing tendency in the Christian faith began to surface to deal with the rising tides of secular culture. The fading hope in Christ's return and the judgment of the world was already voiced during New Testament times by those who questioned the truthfulness of God's promise:

> They will say, "Where is this 'coming' he promised? Ever since our fathers died, everything goes on as it has since the beginning of creation." . . But do not forget this one thing, dear friend: With the Lord a day is like a thousand years, and a thousand years are like a day. The Lord is not slow in keeping his promise, as some understand slowness. Instead, he is patient with you, not wanting anyone to perish, but everyone to come to repentance. (2 Pet 3:4, 8–9)

In any case, an interest in the renewal of culture should not be a byproduct of an elongated history in the horizontal perspective. A biblical worldview is to be determined by the vertical ascension of Christ rather than by an arbitrary expectation of indefinite history. In Christ, heaven and earth are unified and a biblical worldview must naturally flow out of the new order of world in Christ (Eph 1:10; Col 1:20). The Sermon on the Mount represents the new order of the world, where the meaning of blessedness (*makarios*) is completely reversed (Matt 5:1–12). The radical nature of the new order is rooted in the kingdom of heaven, which is essentially the present world turned upside down: "sorrowful yet always rejoicing; poor, yet making many rich; having nothing, yet possessing everything" (2 Cor 6:8–10). In reality, however, the present world order is turned upside down by sin when contrasted to the created order in the beginning (Gen 1:26–28). In the prelapsarian world, mankind was to rule over (*katakurieuo*) things but in this fallen world mankind rules over each other instead of things (Gen 1:28; Matt 20:25). The created order was turned upside down by sin, resulting in men lording over other men. But Jesus again turns it upside down by using the same word, *katakurieuo*, telling them the kingdom of God is where they serve, not rule over, each other:

> Not so with you. Instead, whoever wants to become great among you must be your servant, and whoever wants to be first must be your slave—just as the Son of Man did not come to be served, but to serve, and to give his life as a ransom for many. (Matt 20:26–28)

The new world order of the kingdom of heaven is the reversal of the fallen world order as most eloquently demonstrated by the way of the cross, which put to shame wisdom of this world: "but we preach Christ crucified: a stumbling block to Jews and foolishness to Gentiles" (1 Cor 1:22–23).

8.2 Sacred and Secular

The vertical ascension with Christ in the Spirit provides believers with a panoramic view of the world from the top. It is a view from the coming age, the kingdom not *of* this world, and the distinction between the sacred and the secular is determined from this position. Therefore, believers are told to set their "minds on the things that are above" (Col 3:2) that they might not conform to this world (Rom 12:1–3). The definition of the sacred and the secular is based on a distinction of the two worlds (ages) rather than a division in and of this world. The apostle Paul, in particular, addressed racial, national, social, and sexual divisions, which cannot be standards of the sacred and the secular. In the typological times of the Old Testament such divisions may have been allowed but in Christ they are fulfilled and no longer effective: "For he himself is our peace, who has made the two one and has destroyed the barrier, the dividing wall of hostility" (Eph 2:14). The spatial-vertical intrusion of the kingdom into history destroyed such divisions, with the only exception being the division between the Spirit and the flesh: "The mind of sinful man is death, but the mind controlled by the Spirit is life and peace; the sinful mind is hostile to God; it does not submit to God's law, nor can it do so" (Rom 8:7).

The division of sacred and secular arbitrarily created is neither biblically sanctioned nor physically possible to maintain.[3] The Gnostic dualism that denies the goodness of the physical world was condemned by the early church as heresy and a serious threat to the gospel. The biblical view of creation *ex nihilo* is that the physical world reflects the blessedness of God's attributes (Gen 1:31; 1 Tim 1:11). David sang in awe that nature was beautifully and wonderfully made, revealing God's attributes: "The heavens declare the glory of God; the skies proclaim the work of his hands" (Ps 19:1, 24:1). In the modern day, Abraham Kuyper echoed the same sentiment that

---

3. Bavinck, *Dogmatics*, 1:360.

Christ rules over every "square inch" of the universe, which he created and redeemed.[4] The doctrine of creation says that all of nature in its beauty and splendor is sacred and divine. The biblical worldview is thus borne out of the view of the creation and consummation of the physical world. Traditional theology treated the creation account largely in terms of sin and as a transition to redemption. The lack of interest in creation, providence, and consummation resulted in a dualism of the spiritual against the natural. The underrated view of the natural results in a "split-vision" that divides the world into the two spheres of the sacred and the secular.[5] The dualistic worldview of fundamentalism is sometimes seen as the greatest obstacle to the "transforming vision" of the world.[6] The clash of the Spirit and the flesh, central to the gospel, is not to be confused with Gnostic prejudice against the physical. The Spirit is against the flesh but not against the natural just as God is against sin but not against the world (John 3:16). The Greek word *kosmos* sometimes refers to the fallen world but other times refers to the world as God's creation. In the latter sense, there is not division between the religious and the non-religious, or the sacred and the secular.[7]

The terms "sacred" and "secular" are often used to drive a wedge between the holy and the unholy within the created order of things. These terms are rather pejorative in nuance, causing a segregation of the different spheres of the world into fragments. In view of the abrogation of Israel as a national model of the kingdom of God, and the eschatological nature of Christ's finished work, such an worldview is no longer valid. In the typological world of the Old Testament it may have been valid to a certain extent but Christ has now risen and reigns over the universe as the Lord. With heaven and earth unified in Christ, such a typological distinction is already fulfilled and no longer valid in the new order of the world. The holy and the unholy are no longer distinguished within the horizontal scope of the world but by the vertical relationship with God in Christ. The eschatological vision of the New Testament toward the consummation of the world does not negate the world but rather affirms it. The criticism against separatism was raised earlier by the Reformers, who disavowed a religion closed in "closet, cache, and church."[8] The isolation of soteriology (*Ordo Salutis*) from eschatology and the kingdom of God (*Historia Salutis*) might have somewhat contributed to this kind of division in the traditional approach to theology. The clash of the Spirit and the flesh properly defined must not be reduced to a matter of personal holiness. The sanctimonious division between the religious and the non-religious is the outcome of such reductionism in the doctrine of the Holy Spirit.

The transforming vision of the world, however, needs far more than rejection of such dualism in the horizontal perspective. It needs the vertical vision of Christ's

---

4. Kuyper, *Abraham Kuyper*, 488.
5. Walsh and Middleton, *Transforming Vision*, 95.
6. Walsh and Middleton, *Transforming Vision*, 95.
7. Bavinck, *Dogmatics*, 1:360.
8. Kuyper, *Lectures*, 53.

sovereign reign over the world, in which believers already participate through union with him. It provides the panoramic view of the earthly from the heavenly realms that transcends all previous sacred and secular divisions (Col 3:1–4). Such unifying vision of the world from above was yet to be realized in the typological era of Israel, when the sacred and the secular were distinguished ethnically, nationally, and religiously. The religious observations of the Jewish ceremonies in the New Testament, therefore, were contrary to the new order established by Christ. In Christ the sacred is no longer to be sanctioned by Jewish laws as believers have already ascended and been seated above with him: "You have not come to a mountain that can be touched . . . But you have come to Mount Zion, to the city of the living God, the heavenly Jerusalem" (Heb 12:18, 22). The kind of "worldview" proposed by Hebrews in these last days is the heavenly perspective from above, where all previous earthly typologies have been realized. The sacred and the secular are no longer defined by the visible and touchable but by being in Christ. In Israel, as the national model of the kingdom of God, outside the camp was considered ceremonially unclean whereas inside the camp was considered clean (Heb 13:11). In Christ, however, such a physical distinction was erased and the physical Jerusalem is no longer the reference point of holiness; "here we do not have an enduring city, but we are looking for the city that is to come" (v. 14). In the new order and perspective of heaven, the vision of the church is not to go "Back to Jerusalem"[9] but always to go back to Christ.

The divine providence and the common grace are grounded in the goodness of God in creation despite its fall into sin and downward spiral into corruption. The integrity of the natural order in creation is the foundation of biblical worldview in redemption and sanctification. The positive biblical worldview based on the natural goodness of creation, however, ought to be qualified by the guilt and decay of sin. The fallen world needs a total makeover in the redemption, restoration, and consummation of all things. The debate over transformation of culture and worldview requires a broader perspective of redemptive history that covers the whole spectrum from creation to consummation. The world in its present form will pass away and the natural order (marriage, work, and culture) should be redefined within the provisional structure of history. The eschatological order is not set over against the creation order but only reaffirms it with better things to come. Eschatology does not negate redemption and restoration, but strengthens them by bringing them under the rubric of new creation (2 Cor 5:17). The transforming worldview of the renewal of creation then should be placed within the eschatological structure of the two ages. The Golden Chain of the *Ordo Salutis*, which contains the way of salvation from predestination to glorification of the elect in Christ, is the basis of a sound biblical worldview. The Old Covenant standard of the city gate of Jerusalem is now replaced by New Covenant

---

9. "Back to Jerusalem" is the slogan of a popular mission movement in Asia in recent times, stressing that the final stage of the Great Commission is to return to and evangelize national Israel, which signals the imminent return of Christ.

standard of union with the Holy One. The metaphor progresses from a religious location to the Person of Christ, and according to Hebrews, to go out of the city gate is to go in Christ. In this union, believers are no longer bound by the earthly city but are vertically transported to the heavenly Jerusalem. Seated with Christ in the city of God, believers can love God and neighbors through the "sacrifices of praise and doing good to others" (Heb 13:15–16). The sacred is now determined by being one with Christ rather than by being within the boundaries of the city gate. The biblical worldview, therefore, is not about the extent of its sphere per se but the nature of its otherworldliness. The sphere of Christ's sovereign reign over all creation addresses the problem of the dualism of soul and body, but does not sufficiently address the problem of the two ages caused by sin.

The new order in Christ is the new worldview by which New Testament believers interpreted all spheres of life, including race, nation, family, and work. It provided a unified picture of life that everything must be done as unto the Lord rather than unto men: "Whatever you do, work at it with all your heart, as working for the Lord, not for men, since you know that you will receive an inheritance from the Lord as a reward. It is the Lord Christ you are serving" (Col 3:23–24). The concept of a "living sacrifice" is essential to the new order as believers, dead to this world yet alive to God, are commanded to live in keeping with the eschatological worldview. In Christ, they are alive to the patterns of the coming world, but dead to the patterns of this evil world. It is also explained in terms of the natural man in the flesh and the regenerate man in the Spirit: "The person without the Spirit does not accept the things that come from the Spirit of God but considers them foolishness, and cannot understand them because they are discerned only through the Spirit" (1 Cor 2:14). Sometimes, Paul's contrast between the natural (*psychikon*) to the spiritual (*pneumatikos*) implies more than a soteric opposition of sin and righteousness. It alludes to the redemptive-eschatological conclusion to God's purpose in creation, a shift from the natural to the supernatural (1 Cor 15:44). In the chapter devoted solely to the discussion on resurrection, Paul in particular makes a decisive and sweeping comparison between Adam and the Last Adam, the natural and the spiritual, the earthly and the heavenly image of man (1 Cor 15:44–49). The apostle sees the resurrection of Christ as the greatest manifestation of this comparison between the two orders in addition to the soteric truth that resurrection overcomes death. The new worldview from high above transcends the old distinction between the sacred and the secular. The national and earthly kingdom in Israel is fulfilled by the heavenly kingdom as the new sphere of the sacred. The transforming vision of the new order of the world then no longer affords spiritual significance to a particular race or nation. The righteousness of the fishermen can indeed surpass that of the Pharisees because the latter's moral superiority is at best earthly apart from being in Christ (Matt 5:20). The scribes were religious but not necessarily righteous by the standards of the kingdom of heaven; their righteousness was comparative but not superlative. Their religious and moral hypocrisy invited harsh words and warnings from Jesus despite their outward performances superior to those of the fishermen. The only way an ordinary believer could surpass the righteousness of the Pharisees is for her righteousness to be out of the heavenly realms. In the vertical order of the kingdom, "I no longer live but Christ lives in me," and the righteousness boasted is not mine but Christ's (Gal 2:20; 1 Cor 1:3–31). Therefore, the apostle exhorts believers to set their minds on the things above rather than below, where their morals and religiosity will surpass those of the Pharisees (Col 3:1–2). It is from there that they can truly be wise, righteous, and holy, putting to death the earthly nature (v. 5). The vertical order of heaven is thus foundational to the New Testament worldview for personal sanctification, social ethics, and even the renewal of culture.

A unified worldview requires a unified and orderly world and such unity is found in Christ, whose redemptive work recreated Jews and Gentiles, and all races for that matter, into one new humanity (Eph 2:15). The unified worldview of Adam at creation was lost at once when he broke the covenant and was banned from the presence of God. The cosmic clash between the serpent and the woman since the broken covenant is the reason behind the broken worldview (Gen 3:15–24). In Christ, however, believers are made into one new humanity with a new worldview based on the new order of creation. A new redemptive order (rather than a restoration of the old) was necessary for the consummation of the world. This new order to be established by the incarnate Son does not negate the glory and splendor of the first creation but also recognizes its transitory and temporary character. The new worldview in Christ takes into account the vertical arrival of the last days of this age as history continues until the end in the horizontal plane. This worldview, then, anticipates the final judgement of this world, and moreover, "the Holy City, the new Jerusalem, coming down out of heaven from God, prepared as a bride beautifully dressed for her husband" (Rev 21:1). In this new order of the world, Christ has abolished racial, social, and sexual discriminations but more importantly, united earth and heaven themselves: "He is before all things, and in him all things hold together. And he is the head of the body, the church; he is the beginning and the firstborn from among the dead, so that in everything he might have the supremacy" (Col 1:17–18). The sacred and the secular together became one new camp in Christ and for that reason he was crucified at the cross to open for us the way to an "enduring city" (Heb 13:12–13). All earthly divisions in the horizontal plane are now transcended by the new order of the eternal city above: "neither circumcision nor uncircumcision means anything; what counts is the new creation" (Gal 6:15). In Peter's encounter with Cornelius and his vision of unclean animals coming down from heaven, God reveals the new order of the world in a dramatic way (Acts 10:9–13). As "heaven opened," the animals were "let down to earth," Peter was asked to eat them but refused to do so out of prejudice against Gentiles. Finally, the sheet was withdrawn to heaven, and God said to Peter, "Do not call anything impure that God has made clean" (Acts 10:15). With the arrival of the new order of heaven, the racial and national divisions used for typological purposes are abrogated. The "Yes" in

Christ did not just fulfill the Old in the New, but unified the temporal and the eternal all "to the glory of God" (2 Cor 1:20).

8.3 Faith and Knowledge

Like the sacred and the secular, faith and knowledge need the vertical perspective in order to avoid the pitfalls of a false dichotomy. The theory that knowledge concerns the natural and faith concerns the supernatural world is not sanctioned by the unified view of heaven and earth in Christ. The faith in Christ embraces the visible and the invisible, the temporal and the eternal, and the natural and the supernatural: "By faith we understand that the universe was formed at God's command, so that what is seen was not made out of what was visible" (Heb 11:2). The purpose of scientific knowledge is not the same as that of theological knowledge but all knowledge is unified in Christ "in whom are hidden all the treasures of wisdom and knowledge" (Col 2:3). The faith and knowledge in Christ are not subjugated to the modern philosophy of knowledge, which divides the natural and the supernatural. Hence, it would be wrong to simply presume that biblical faith is irrational and scientific knowledge is rational. The worldview of a unified heaven and earth unifies all knowledge except that in this interim age until the Parousia, the "upper room" where Christ is seated with believers is seen by faith, not by sight. This is the reason that a soteriological definition of faith alone cannot explain the full dynamic of faith and knowledge. The scope of faith only as the means of justification does not touch on the eschatological foundation of knowledge with the unity of heaven and earth. The great antithesis in the era of the two ages is the Spirit and the flesh rather than faith and knowledge. Reason, like other faculties in man, can serve as an "instrument of righteousness" or "instrument of wickedness" depending on whom it serves as the master (Rom 6:13). The common dualism of faith or knowledge stems from a closed worldview that suppresses the innate knowledge of God and the invisible, supernatural world (Rom 1:19). In Christ, the split vision of heaven and earth that bifurcates rationalism or anti-intellectualism is neither possible nor practical. Our forefathers of faith have avoided the two extremes of reasonability and absurdity: they believed in something neither because it is believable nor because it is absurd.[10] Neither reason nor absurdity can be the true foundation of faith, and in the unified world of heaven and earth in Christ, "We believe in order that we may know."[11]

The objectivity of knowledge based on the unity of heaven and earth is lost by the fall, which created an ethical antithesis between God and man, and between the natural and the supernatural. Man's knowledge has always been covenantal (ethical and religious) since the beginning, symbolized by the tree of knowledge and the tree of life. The covenant knowledge of man as the image-bearer of God is always defined

---

10. Reymond, *Faith's Reasons for Believing*, 27–32.
11. Reymond, *Faith's Reasons for Believing*, 27–32.

in relation to God as the source of all knowledge.[12] The ethical and religious nature of covenant knowledge meant that the latter could never be *neutral* in and of itself apart from God. The covenantal cannot be neutral and the neutral is not covenantal; fallen man is ethically hostile to God.[13] In view of total depravity, the noetic effect of sin (knowledge affected by sin) has rendered the unregenerate man's thinking biased toward God.[14] The antithesis has made it impossible for knowledge to be neutral so that there can be no such things as "brute facts," as it were. Fallen man thus requires redeemed covenantal knowledge through the redemptive atonement of sin and reconciliation with God. The apostle spoke in no uncertain terms that "their thinking became futile and their foolish hearts were darkened" (Rom 1:21). Covenant knowledge is *yada* in Hebrew (to know, to make love) as in Adam and Eve, who through the marriage covenant "knew" each other and became "one flesh" (Gen 2:24; 4:1). Covenant knowledge originates from the triune God, who from eternity existed in mutual glory, love, and knowledge. The eternal life by nature is covenantal because it involves the knowledge of the Father and the Son (John 17:3). This mutual knowledge is so engraved into man's heart that the knowledge of God and the self are inseparably interwoven in creation.[15] The Covenant of Grace is such that faith alone justifies but justifying faith is never alone, accompanying the image of God in truth, righteousness, and holiness (Eph 4:23–24). Calvin, too, understood saving faith in terms of union with Christ rather than merely as an instrument of forensic justification. The Covenant of Grace then harmonizes the indicative and the imperative in the *Ordo Salutis* into a holistic union. Saving faith is the means by which believers become conscious of the Golden Chain of salvation, which extends from election to glorification in Christ (Rom 8:30). Hence, ontology (theory of being), epistemology (theory of knowledge), and ethics (theory of behavior) are unified through faith in Christ.[16] The chief end of the Covenant of Grace is to render believers created to be like God in the Last Adam. The renewal of the mind, in particular, is an essential part of the new order of being: "Do not conform to the patterns of this world, but be transformed by the renewing of your mind [*noos*]. Then you will be able to test and approve what God's will is—his good, pleasing and perfect will" (Rom 12:2). The dynamic of faith and knowledge is a covenantal problem rather than a philosophical or epistemological one. Saving faith rejects rationalism but seeks the renewal of mind; it rejects irrationalism but rejoices in the supernatural realm. The renewed and recreated mind can be of great service to God and the kingdom of heaven, but the natural mind of the flesh will not accept the things of God.[17]

12. Bahnsen, *Van Til's Apologetics*, 146.
13. Van Til, *Survey of Christian Epistemology*, 18–22.
14. Van Til, *Survey of Christian Epistemology*, 187.
15. Calvin, *Institutes*, 1:35.
16. Van Til, *Defense of Faith*, 23–66.
17. Bahnsen, *Van Til's Apologetics*, 154.

In premessianic times God spoke through prophets but in these last days God speaks through his Son, making knowledge clear and sufficient (Heb 1:1–2). In him, redemption and revelation both reached their completion and culmination. So much so that all the treasures of wisdom and knowledge are said to be found in him while the Greeks seek wisdom and Jews want signs (1 Cor 1:18–25; Col 2:2–3). The answer to "Who do you say I am?," in fact, is the answer to all other difficult questions in life and in death (Matt 16:13). He is the exalted Prophet, Priest, and King next to God, and believers can interpret the world as "a royal priesthood, a holy nation, a people belonging to God" seated above with him (1 Pet 2:9). The vertical-spatial ascension of believers is now made possible and the exercise of the prophetic (interpretative) ministry is part of the new order. Since Israel's knowledge of God was typological with the law written on the tablets of stone, their knowledge was incomplete and obscure (Jer 31:31–34). The division of faith and knowledge may have been excusable then but it is no longer justifiable in Christ. They relied on types, sacrifices, prophecies, and the law for knowledge, but now believers rely on the direct union with the Son and the Spirit. In the former they believed despite their knowledge, but in Christ we believe because of the new order of knowledge. Even as history progressed horizontally toward Christ, faith and knowledge of God's people progressed ever more upward to the heavenly city. The heavenly Jerusalem is seen through the eyes of faith, which is foolishness to this world (1 Cor 1:18–25; Cor 5:5). But faith in Christ is the wisdom and power of God, a cumulative revelation that grew out of the copies and shadows of heaven throughout the prior history: "These were all commended for their faith, yet none of them received what had been promised, since God had planned something better for us so that only together with us would they be made perfect" (Heb 11:39–40). In Christ, believers are positioned so high above in heaven that "faith is being sure of what we hope for and certain of what we do not see. This is what the ancients were commended for. By faith we understand that the universe was formed at God's command, so that what is seen was not made out of what was visible" (vs. 1–3).

Seated in the heavenly realms, their minds are renewed, and though their knowledge may not be comprehensive it is sufficient and unifying.[18] The unity of faith and understanding cannot be achieved in the horizontal plane of earth but is finally achieved in the vertical plane of heaven: "I will put my laws in their hearts, and I will write them on their minds" (Jer 31:31–34; Heb 10:16). Hence, all knowledge in the new order of things must be tested as to whether or not it is approvable by the "pleasing and perfect will" of God (Rom 12:2). Believing knowledge does not conform to the patterns of "this" world but is transformed through the renewing of the mind. The renewal of hearts and minds according to the patterns of the "other" world precedes the act of knowing itself. This leads to the objectivity of knowledge, whether or not any knowing can be truly objective in this changing world: God alone can be truly objective in the world he created. Adam's knowledge in paradise was unified with

---

18. Van Til, *Defense of Faith*, 100.

regard to God, himself, and the world as there was no need for a "special" revelation. The proofs of God's existence were not necessary unlike the fallen state in which man suppresses the truth, does not glorify God, and worships idols (Rom 1:18–24). Natural reason retained its ability to think but lost its covenantal function to discern good and evil for it pretends to be autonomous. The mind needs renewal to discern God's pleasing and perfect will by recreation of the image of God:

> You were taught, with regard to your former way of life, to put off your old self, which is being corrupted by its deceitful desires; to be made new in the attitude of your minds; and to put on the new self, created to be like God in true righteousness and holiness. (Eph 4:22–24)

It is clear that knowledge is inseparable from being, especially a being created in the image of the Creator. The worldview is not limited to the soteric scope of atonement and justification, for it is now rooted in the *Historia Salutis* with regard to the last days. In addition to redemption, comprehensive knowledge of how man interprets himself and the world must take into account both ends of creation and consummation (Rom 1:18–23). The pretended ignorance of God and the suppressed truth in the fallen state does not sufficiently gauge the true state of man's knowledge. No amount of facts or evidence will be sufficient to persuade fallen man to accept God or the things of God adding difficulty to preaching the good news (Rom 8:7; Eph 2:1). The predisposition of fallen man against God requires more than factual evidence to overturn his willful suppression of the truth about God. The factual evidence is auxiliary rather than primary in the war between the Spirit and the flesh; the war is first and foremost a matter of the heart, not of the mind. The apostle could not have stated this more clearly or bluntly: "The mind governed by the flesh is hostile to God; it does not submit to God's law, nor can it do so" (Rom 8:7). This was true since the time of the fall, when revelation was scarce, but even more true in these last days of the Son of God, when revelation is given in its fullness. Faith preceded reason at all times in the history of redemption as the means of the Covenant of Grace but faith was never against reason. The tree of knowledge and the tree of life will eventually be unified into one so that the former does not reappear in the new creation of heaven and earth (Rev 22:1–5). The tree of knowledge will be subsumed under the tree of life in Christ, in whom are hidden "all the treasures of wisdom and truth" (Col 2:3).

The progress of faith and knowledge is similar to the progress of the sacred and the secular until they are unified in Christ. The panoramic view from the heavenly realms is a unified view of faith and knowledge where the two become coextensive and mutually inclusive. The division is no longer significant within the new order, where the only division that hinders true knowledge is the Spirit and the flesh. Faith does not compete with knowledge nor knowledge with faith because they are unified and harmonious in the Person and work of Christ. The number of the sparrows in the sky and the hairs on your head are accounted for in this new order of the world

(Matt 10:29–30). The new order also has significance for the nature of the knowledge entrusted to the church: "I will give you the keys of the kingdom of heaven; whatever you bind on earth will be bound in heaven, and whatever you loose on earth will be loosed in heaven" (Matt 16:19). The Lord has given church the true, eternal, and spiritual knowledge sufficient for believers to enter the kingdom of heaven. Hence, the phrase "we live by faith, not by sight" is neither mysticism nor blind faith, but an eschatological confidence in the present state of believers as to where they belong. The expression is not a dichotomous view of faith and reason, but an eschatological insight into the already-but-not-yet character of the kingdom of Christ.

The world below is known by sight, but the world above is known by faith; the two aspects of the same unified reality but temporarily separated by time. In the end, all will be seen by sight in the glorious resurrected body! The current state of believers belonging to two different ages expressed as heaven and earth will be completely unified in the end. The knowledgeable faith is not just an instrument of justification, but the eschatological vision to see the invisible world (Heb 11:1–2). The soteric scope alone does not necessarily explain this faith in terms of the eschatological knowledge and hope. The standard of knowledge in the new order is to know Christ and nothing else; the bar has been so set that everything else is considered "rubbish" in comparison to the "surpassing greatness of knowing Christ" (Phil 3:8). The "way of the cross" is not only a soteric means, but a powerful defense that destroys arguments of the philosophers of this age. Christ crucified on the cross is the wisdom and power of God against the "signs" of Jews and the "wisdom" of Gentiles (1 Cor 1:18–25). The cross is the crossroads that divides this age and the age to come: "Where is the wise man? Where is the scholar? Where is the philosopher of this age? Has not God made foolish the wisdom of the world?" (v. 20)

8.4 Eschatological Worldview

The biblical worldview originates from the sovereign God who decreed, created, governs, redeems, and will consummate the world. The chief end of man—the chief end of redemption—is to participate in the eternal glory, love, and knowledge of the Father and the Son (John 17:21–26). Christ saves his people from sin in order that they might be brought into the eternal union and fellowship with the Father and the Spirit. Hence, the biblical worldview is nothing less than the great confession of the Westminster Catechism: "the chief end of man is to glorify God and to enjoy him forever." In his prayer to the Father, Jesus mentioned three particular attributes that characterize the intra-Trinitarian fellowship: glory, love and knowledge. Man as the image-bearer of God also seeks glory, love, and knowledge of the Trinity as his chief end. How else are we to understand the prayer of Jesus that believers may be one with them as they are one with each other? The God in three Persons is the theological foundation of unity and diversity, or the universals and particulars of the universe.[19] The universe in creation was unified yet diverse without conflict in accordance with the purpose of God.[20] The world was coherent with the natural order and Adam in his duty as the vice-regent of God and caretaker of the garden fulfilled the mandate of creation (Gen 1:26–28, 2:17). He was at peace with God, with himself, and with the world, which was declared as very good in God's eyes. A productive relationship was maintained in paradise and this same blessed image is recreated in believers for good works (Eph 2:10, 4:24; 1 Tim 1:11).[21] Believers can be in the same productive relationship for the restoration of culture in the new creation until the consummation of all things. In the vertical direction, they may share in the glory, love, and knowledge of God, but in the horizontal direction, they may fulfill their mission on earth.

The biblical view of culture should be seen from both perspectives of creation (Adam) and new creation (Last Adam). Otherwise, redeeming culture will become the purpose of the gospel rather than its result. The so-called Cultural Mandate of Adam obviously cannot be the same mandate of the Last Adam, who is now seated in the heavenly realms. However culture is understood during the interim age between the present kingdom and the eschatological kingdom of God (1 Cor 15:24), it cannot be the final purpose of the gospel.[22] Culture in the original sense now exists between the two ages within the already-but-not-yet frame of the provisional kingdom of Christ. Seated in the invisible realms of heaven, believers have a wide-open view of the culture below in which earthly life continues. In this new order of history, culture is under the reign of Christ but also transitional in nature, giving way to the new heaven and earth (1 Cor 7:31). A biblical and theological analysis of culture, therefore, could not bypass the vertical aspect that transcends what Paul calls "this world in its present form." On the one hand, the public nature of the biblical worldview cannot be neglected since Christ's work is a "public statement" of his lordship over the whole universe,[23] but on the other, the world in its present form is "passing away." The biblical view of the world is an application of the *Historia Salutis* and *Ordo Salutis* to every area of life, both private and public; in his exaltation Christ is declared to be Lord over all races and all creation (Acts 2:36). Christ is the Master whose authority transcends all horizontal relationships in society precisely because he is exalted high above the *present* form of the world (Eph 6:5–9). While social duties are to be honored as part of the Cultural Mandate, therefore, they must be subordinate to the calling of the age to come. In short, the vertical victory of Christ renders the horizontal culture and all its present glory transitory: "Whatever you do, work at it with all your heart, as working for the Lord, not for men since you know that you will receive an inheritance from the

19. Van Til, *Introduction to Systematic Theology*, 22–23.
20. Van Til, *Introduction to Systematic Theology*, 25.
21. Van Til, *Introduction to Systematic Theology*, 23.
22. Wolters, *Creation Regained*, 44–56.
23. Wright, *New Testament*, 135.

Lord as a reward. It is the Lord Christ you are serving" (Col 3:23–24). Social duties must give way to the lordship of Christ that they must offer themselves as a "living sacrifice" to God as those seated in the heavenly place with Christ. This order of new creation, in service of the Master, must precede the present order in the private life and public service of believers. This eschatological outlook on culture, ideally considered, will strengthen the renewal of culture rather than weaken it. The eternal state of believers in the vertical sense enables them to be worthy of suffering for Christ's sake, and even to be able to treat cultural (social or economic) disadvantage in the world as a small price to pay in comparison to the surpassing glory of the world to come.

The notion of human culture first originated from God's command to rule over creation, to multiply and be fruitful (Gen 1:26–28). God then gave Adam a more specific command to work and cultivate paradise: "The LORD God took the man and put him in the Garden of Eden to work it and take care of it" (Gen 2:15). The Covenant of Works in its broad sense includes this work, whereas in the narrow sense it prohibits eating from the tree of knowledge (Gen 2:17). The work in the garden was an essential part of man's duty as the image-bearer of God; God's creation was to be followed by Adam's diligent and fruitful cultivation of it (Gen 1:26). The temporary probation until the confirmed state of the eternal life required a covenantal arrangement for Adam to make creative uses of the image of God. It was modelled after the intra-Trinitarian model of mutual glory and love rather than a mere test of obedience (John 17:21–24; Eph 4:24). In this sense, culture is a distinct concept borne out of the prelapsarian state of man as the image-bearer of the Creator. The significance of culture in redemptive periods, however, becomes temporary until the consummation of man and creation through the work of the Last Adam. He fulfilled the Covenant of Works through his active and passive obedience, also perfecting the image of God in behalf of man (Rom 5:12; Heb 5:8). The temporary significance and value of culture is now redefined in Christ, who has successfully obeyed and finished the Covenant of Works. The conformation to Christ, in his obedience of love of God and neighbors, is now the goal of believers (Rom 8:29; 2 Cor 4:4; Col 1:16; Heb 1:3). The primary work of the Spirit is redeeming of believers "until Christ is formed in" them rather than redeeming culture (Gal 4:19).

The transformation of culture is the outcome, rather than the goal, of redemption; the kingdom of heaven has now arrived and culture must be reinterpreted under the new order and light. The new creation in Christ is more than restoration of culture but a provisional start of the eschatological state of all things. How far the present culture will carry over into the future state is not specified other than that this world in its present form will pass away (John 18:36; 1 Cor 7:31; 2 Pet 3:10–13; Rev 21:1). As the interim period between this age and the coming age, the present culture also appears to be provisional and temporary. As Herman Bavinck noted, the view of culture in the fallen state of the world is at best "pessimistic optimism" or "laughter in tears." A high view of culture notwithstanding, even a higher view of the new creation and new culture in Christ are anticipated as its sequel in the eschatological kingdom. A pessimistic view of culture leads to a gospel of saving souls but downgrades the wonder and splendor of God's first creation. The mandate to preserve and care for nature for the benefit of humanity still stands as part of God's common grace in the interim age (Matt 5:45). This is still the age of the common grace and culture; though Christ reigns over all things, not all things have completely submitted to him (Heb 2:8). The original culture created in paradise is now so deformed, however, it can only return to "dust," cursed as it was along with the fallen humanity (Gen 3:16–19). Still, the natural law is written in man's heart, and his conscience bears witness to do things that are morally upright.[24] Without it, there is no possibility of relative order and peace in this world in which positive cultural activities of mankind may be carried out. The Covenant of Works binds the human conscience until the end and mankind is able to perform cultural duties for the betterment of their natural life. In this way, the new order in Christ does not abrogate man's cultural duties in the earthly life so that all things may be done unto the Lord. Christ's sovereign reign over every sphere of life ought to be part of the Christian faith and worldview but only so under the eschatological vision of the new order. There is tendency to view culture either as wholly evil or wholly good but neither view fits the biblical worldview of the New Testament.

The biblical worldview is rooted in the doctrine of God that "there is but one God, the Father, from whom all things came and for whom we live; and there is but one Lord, Jesus Christ, through whom all things came and through whom we live" (1 Cor 8:6). The positive estimation of culture is consistent with the view of God, for whose glory all things are created and sustained. Nevertheless, the present world and the positive aspects of culture must not be prematurely de-eschatologized in the name of the inaugurated kingdom of God. The high view of culture based on the sovereign reign of Christ over all things should not minimize the return of Christ and the final judgment of all things. Niebuhr put forth the view that "Christ is the Transformer of Culture," and that he is neither against it nor above it.[25] He too rejected the tendency to downgrade culture in traditional theology and proposed a transformational view as the proper biblical response to culture.[26] The social theories of the gospel such as this, however, often tend to bypass the eschatological vision of the early church, which puts the present culture in a provisional perspective. They help us to recognize the value of culture as part of God's creation order but they also lose sight of the transitional nature of human society, especially in these last days. In fact, Niebuhr himself recognized that we do not live "between the times" but live in the end times, called the "Divine Now."[27] In any case, culture is sometimes seen as a timeless entity, which

---

24. Westminster Confession of Faith, 4.
25. Niebuhr, *Christ and Culture*, 190–206.
26. Niebuhr, *Christ and Culture*, 193–94.
27. Niebuhr, *Christ and Culture*, 195.

throughout history believers are fixated on transforming rather than interpreting it in light of the coming kingdom of God.

The worldview is neither too spiritualized nor too materialized in the eschatology of the New Testament. It does not envision a spiritualized version of the world but a world in which all things, visible and invisible, exist for God's glory. In the biblical worldview, there is no conflict between taking medicine and praying for healing at the same time. In the consummated kingdom, all things will be renewed and there will be no more disease, sickness, or death to torment us: "He will wipe every tear from their eyes. There will be no more death or mourning or crying or pain, for the old order of things has passed away" (Rev 21:4). It is interesting that Calvin's argument for a Christian politician was not based on building a Christianized culture, but on the simple hope that all will be believers and a believer might as well be the politician. Politics might never be wholly Christianized, but neither are believers opposed to it (Rom 13:1). God is sovereign over all things but for the time being during the interim age, "Give to Caesar what is Caesar's and to God what is God's" (Mark 12:17).

The transformation of culture relies on the doctrines of creation, common grace, and providence in cooperation with saving grace. It is based on the assumption that grace restores nature, that human culture in general reflects God's universal benevolence toward the created world (Gen 3:16–24; Matt 5:45):

> And he is not served by human hands, as if he needed anything, because he himself gives all men life and breath and everything else. From one man he made every nation of men, that they should inhabit the whole earth; and he determined the times set for them and the exact places where they should live. God did this so that men would seek him and perhaps reach out for him and find him, though he is not far from each one of us. "For in him we live and move and have our being." (Acts 17:25–28a)

The principle that grace restores nature, however, does not sufficiently address the modern problem of culture in this semi-eschatological age. The provisional nature of common grace until the Parousia should be part of how culture is defined and related to the gospel mission.[28] Traditional theology looked upon culture as essentially secular and outside of the scope of redemption, only for the preservation of the world until the Day of Judgement.[29] This view is equivalent to Niebuhr's "Christ against Culture," in which the purpose of the gospel mission is to save souls and is largely indifferent to cultural transformation. But culture is neither wholly secular nor wholly sacred in the provisional kingdom of Christ, where heaven and earth are already united but not yet consummated. In recent studies in biblical theology, a better perspective on culture and history subsequent to Christ has been proposed from the viewpoint of eschatology. It provides us with the vertical dimension of the new order in Christ, which

---

28. Van Drunen, *Living in God's Two Kingdoms*, 15.
29. Van Drunen, *Living in God's Two Kingdoms*, 15.

neither negates culture nor equates it with the gospel. A radical abandonment, rather than transformation, of the present evil age is the essence of the cross and resurrection of Christ. A renewal of culture not based on a radical separation from this world and movement to the higher realms will amount to conformation to "the pattern of this world" (Rom 12:2). The intrusion of God's kingdom and the violent reaction against it by the evil one is characteristic of this age and of the present culture for what's its worth (Matt 11:11–12).[30] The intrusion of the kingdom of heaven means a clash of the two ages of opposing schemas as Jesus himself stated (John 18:36). The restoration of the created order and the renewal of culture by redemptive grace, then, ought to be qualified by the fleeting nature of the world in its present form.

The semi-eschatological kingdom already come rendered that early believers stay outside the camp where Christ was crucified for an enduring city. As Christ's return was apparently delayed in subsequent history, culture also became more relevant as believers prepared for the long-haul wait. Nonetheless, the early Christians did not shy away from the goodness of culture itself as they redefined various social relationships by Christ's lordship over all things. It is clear in the New Testament that believers were more interested in what had been accomplished by Christ and what that entailed for culture, rather than transformation of culture itself. Two thousand years have passed since then but the eschatological vision of the New Testament remains unchanged regardless of the length of history. The modern interest in the restoration of culture as a dominant theme in theology, on the other hand, may be the outcome of elongated history and the long delay of the Parousia. As for the former Christians, they set their hearts on things above rather than things below without losing love for God and neighbor (Rom 13:10; Col 3:2). Quite the contrary, the heavenly state of their being reinforced their passion for God and compassion for others without placing their hope in the things of this world. Their love was pure and authentic because they did not consider themselves to have any stake or vested interest in this world.

In subsequent periods, believers gradually increased their involvement and interest in the horizontal direction of life on earth away from the vertical perspective. The rather compulsory interest in transforming culture due to these practical reasons, however, cannot be a proper theological alternative. Engagement in culture ought to be seen as part of the creation mandate, and as part of Christ's sovereign lordship over all things. The vision of the exalted Christ seated above and the presence of the future that wholly captivated New Testament believers should be the proper motivation. The earthly and the temporal are not necessarily secular, but they are not eternal either. In this sense, the two ages may have some similarities to the two kingdoms (eternal and temporal) model of the Reformation.[31] As part of the temporal world, fallen as it may be, culture is an important aspect of human life preserved by God's providence and common grace. It is the natural outcome of God's grace and benevolence toward

---

30. Kline, *Structure of Biblical Authority*, 157; *Kingdom Prologue*, 158.
31. Van Drunen, *Living in God's Two Kingdoms*, 13.

mankind but cannot be made the chief end of the gospel. The catastrophic event of harvest in the Parable of the Growing Seed suggests an abrupt shift into the final kingdom of God rather than a gradual transformation from earth to heaven (Mark 4:26–29).[32] Some believe that the positive cultural achievements of mankind will carry over into the eschatological kingdom, hinted at by such biblical texts as "the kings of the earth will bring their splendor into it" (Rev 21:24–26).[33] This positive expectation is based on the creation of man as the image-bearer of God and a continuation of the goodness of the first creation into the new creation.[34] They believe God's command to cultivate the garden still stands effective and touches on the cultural as well as the religious aspects of all man's activities.[35] Much of this remains as a conjecture, however, because the Scriptures do not specify in detail precisely how much of present cultural advancements, if any, will be brought into the eschatological kingdom. Again, all things are under the dominion of Christ, but the new order is yet to be consummated and it remains to be seen how much of present culture will continue in the kingdom of God.

Jesus gave the keys of the kingdom to the church not that it might transform the world into heaven but to open the doors for the world to enter the kingdom. The present world exists between the provisional kingdom of Christ and the eschatological kingdom of the Father (1 Cor 15:24). Human culture is of a provisional nature and is passing away along with the world in its present form. The eschatological vision may not be harmonious with building Christian culture in this present world but that appears to be the extent of redeeming culture in an semi-eschatological era. A great theologian and politician in the Calvinistic tradition, Abraham Kuyper, warned the church of his day not to privatize the Christian faith lest culture be monopolized by secular society. He tried to take Christianity out of the closet into the public sphere that cultural transformation could take place when the mind begins to be transformed.[36] He refused to accept the religious/non-religious dichotomy, on the one hand, but also refused to let the secular world claim ownership of culture. His emphasis on transformation of mind and culture provided impetus to the birth of a Christian worldview movement later called neo-Calvinism. It is grounded in the belief that God is sovereign over all of life and Christ claims every inch of the universe under his dominion. This belief gave rise to the well-known Christian philosophy of "sphere of sovereignty," which rejects all forms of authoritarianism and allows for independence of every sphere in life under Christ's reign. Despite its positive contributions to a Christian worldview, however, the Kuyperian model did not rigorously take into account the eschatology of the New Testament. Culture is rightly placed

---

32. Van Drunen, *Living in God's Two Kingdoms*, 13.
33. Hoekema, *Created in God's Image*, 99.
34. Hoekema, *Created in God's Image*, 88.
35. Robertson, *Christ of Covenants*, 68–81.
36. Kuyper, *Lectures on Calvinism*, 50.

under the universal reign of God but the Scriptures also state that not everything in the world has submitted to Christ yet. The present kingdom of Christ is "God's salvific reign"[37] but not necessarily God's consummate reign (Luke 16:16). The proponents of the Christian worldview and transformation of culture do recognize that there is a discontinuity between the present and the future forms of the world.[38] Even so, there seems to be insufficient recognition by them of the eschatological vsion in the New Testament teachings on the kingdom of God. Salvation is defined in the New Testament as both restoration and recreation, and that transforming vision of the world cannot simply be predicated on restoration alone.[39] The transforming vision of the restoration of creation must be qualified by the otherworldly nature of God's kingdom with its supernatural inclinations. New Testament believers did not make proactive attempts to transform the surrounding culture itself for their vision was fixated on things above. If any transformation of society and culture took place, it was the earthly manifestation of their union with Christ that trickled down from the heavenly realms in "faith working through love" (Gal 5:6).

The biblical narrative from creation to consummation is the eschatology of redemption beyond regaining creation or redeeming culture. It is superior to the eschatology of nature to the extent that Christ is superior to Adam. It is the fulfillment of the Counsel of Peace in the vertical direction as well as the consummation of history in the horizontal flow of time. The end (*eschatos*) of it is the unification of heaven and earth in Christ, so the renewal of culture is part of the narrative but only until all things in heaven and earth will be made anew. The central theme that runs through biblical history is still the cosmic clash between the two seeds under which the present order of the world marches toward the end (Gen 3:15–24). However, the Scriptures make it clear that "the prince of this world now stands condemned" on account of Christ's finished work (John 16:11). The curse of the law so profoundly penetrated the natural order that only a new creation, rather than restoration, is expected to be its sequel. In keeping with the curse spelled out in Genesis, the fallen world and its conditions would not be favorable toward God's people at any time in the course of history. The antithesis runs so deep in the fallen world that the flesh (*sarx*) does not and will not submit to the Spirit of God (Rom 8:7). The kingdom of heaven has never been *of* this world as the two worlds run parallel to the Parousia; nevertheless, the gospel of the kingdom of heaven is to be preached since it has intruded this world (Luke 16:16). The mission of the church, therefore, is not to redeem culture but to preach the gospel of the kingdom that is already but not yet. In this new order of the kingdom, the biblical response to this evil age is spelled out clearly by the apostle in the introduction of the second half of Romans. He does not tell believers to transform culture but to be

---

37. Gentry and Wellum, *Kingdom through Covenants*, 595.
38. Wolters, *Creation Regained*, 58.
39. Bavinck, *Dogmatics*, 1:360–61.

transformed themselves, and does not tell them to renew culture but to be renewed themselves. The focus of renewal and transformation is not the world but themselves:

> Therefore, I urge you, brothers, in view of God's mercy, to offer your bodies as living sacrifices, holy and pleasing to God—this is your spiritual act of worship. Do not conform any longer to the pattern of this world, but be transformed by the renewing of your mind. Then you will be able to test and approve what God's will is—his good, pleasing and perfect will. (Rom 12:1–2)

In our view, the so-called transforming vision of culture appears to gain more currency and influence in parts of the world where the church and the state maintain a positive relationship. This general tendency is usually found in the West, where there is relatively more freedom of religion and speech. Despite separation of the church and the state, there is more room for the church to participate and make positive impact on the surrounding culture. But such a vision is usually less of an alternative in places where the church is under persecution and goes underground. In these parts of the world, it would be difficult to imagine, much less attempt, a transformation of culture run by an anti-Christian government. In the former case, the gospel may appear to be more pro-culture but in the latter case, the gospel may appear to be almost anti-culture, not by choice but by default. The war between the Spirit and the flesh, by nature, is not of this world: "For our struggle is not against flesh and blood, but against the authorities, against the powers of this dark world and against the spiritual forces of evil in the heavenly realms" (Eph 6:12). Jesus and Paul did not consider the authorities who persecuted them as the *real* enemy or treat the world as inherently evil. In the New Testament, believers were imprisoned but their consciences were free. They did not fight back or asked to be freed but used the opportunity to honor Christ and preach the gospel of the kingdom whenever possible. They did so because they knew their fight was not against flesh and blood, and their battle was not of this world. They did not use political means to avoid persecution or seek freedom but, on the contrary, proactively used the judicial system of that day to stand trial for the opportunity to preach the gospel and fulfill their God-given mission (Acts 25:10–12).

Modern readers of the Scriptures, especially the New Testament, feel almost a sense of nonchalance on the part of the early believers toward their surrounding culture. They neither directly condoned nor condemned culture but did everything as unto the Lord, and even their response to oppression was deceptively passive because they were motivated by the higher call: "But how then would the Scriptures be fulfilled that says it must happen this way?" (Matt 26:54). The prayer of Jesus, "Father, forgive them, for they do not know what they are doing," for those who crucified him on the cross is an active and radical form of resistance to evil (Luke 23:34). Others like Paul followed in the footsteps of their Master because they saw themselves seated in the heavenly realms and set their minds "on things above, not on earthly things" (Col 3:1–4). It would be reasonable to conclude that they did not prefer one kind of culture over another as their vertical state was the dominant factor in the social and cultural expressions of their faith. In a sense, the driving force behind their worldview was more super-temporal than anti-cultural (1 Cor 7:29–31). Here, the apostle's exhortation to believers to restrain extreme sadness or extreme joy in this world is not a reflection of pessimism, but a sign of true and eternal hope in the world to come.

Bibliography

Bahnsen, Greg L. *Van Til's Apologetic: Readings & Analysis.* Phillipsburg, NJ: Presbyterian & Reformed, 1998.
Barker, William S., and W. Robert Godfrey, eds. *Theonomy: A Reformed Critique.* Grand Rapids: Academie, 1990.
Barth, Karl. *Church Dogmatics.* Edited by G. W. Bromiley and T. F. Torrance. Translated by G. W. Bromiley. 5 vols. Peabody, MA: Hendrickson, 2010.
———. "Gospel and Law." *Scottish Journal of Theology Occasional Papers* 8 (1959) 1–28.
Bavinck, Herman. "Calvin and Common Grace." In *Calvin and the Reformation: Four Studies,* edited by William Park Armstrong, 99–130. Eugene, OR: Wipf & Stock, 2004.
———. *Our Reasonable Faith: A Survey of Christian Doctrine.* Translated by Henry Zylstra. Grand Rapids: Eerdmans, 1956.
———. *Reformed Dogmatics.* Vol. 1. Grand Rapids: Baker, 2003.
Beale, Greg K. *The Book of Revelation.* New International Greek Testament Commentary. Grand Rapids: Eerdmans, 1999.
———. "The Eschatological Conception of New Testament Theology." In *Eschatology in Bible & Theology,* edited by Kent E. Brower and Mark W. Elliot. Downers Grove, IL: InterVarsity, 1997.
———. *A New Testament Biblical Theology: The Unfolding of the Old Testament in the New.* Grand Rapids: Baker Academic, 2011.
Beale, Greg K., and David H. Campbell. *Revelation: A Shorter Commentary.* Grand Rapids: Eerdmans, 2015.
Berkhof, Lewis. *Systematic Theology.* Grand Rapids: Eerdmans, 1941.
Bratt, James D., ed. *Abraham Kuyper: A Centennial Reader.* Grand Rapids: Eerdmans, 1998.
———. *The History of Christian Doctrines.* Grand Rapids: Baker, 1978.
Bruce, F. F. *Paul: Apostle of the Heart Set Free.* Grand Rapids: Eerdmans, 1984.
Calvin, John. *Calvin's Commentaries.* 22 vols. 1863. Reprint, Grand Rapids: Baker, 1996.
———. *Institutes of the Christian Religion in Two Volumes.* Edited by John T. McNeill. Translated by Ford Lewis Battles. Library of Christian Classics 20, 21. Philadelphia: Westminster, 1975.
———. *Sermons on the Epistle to the Ephesians.* Great Britain: Banner of Truth Trust, 1998.
Chafer, Lewis Sperry. "Dispensationalism." *Bibliotheca Sacra* 93 (1936) 390–449.
———. *Dispensationalism.* Dallas: Dallas Seminary Press, 1951.
———. *Systematic Theology.* 8 vols. Dallas: Dallas Seminary Press, 1948.
Campbell, Constantine R. *Paul and Union with Christ.* Grand Rapids: Zondervan, 2012.
Clowney, Edmund P. *The Church.* Contours of Christian Theology. Downers Grove, IL: InterVarsity, 1995.

Cullman, Oscar. *Christ and Time*. Philadelphia: Westminster, 1964.

Dumbrell, William J. *Covenant and Creation: A Theology of Old Testament Covenants*. Nashville: Thomas Nelson, 1984.

Dunahoo, Charles H. *Making Kingdom Disciples: A New Framework*. Phillipsburg, NJ: Presbyterian & Reformed, 2005.

Dunn, James D. G. *The New Perspective on Paul*. Grand Rapids: Eerdmans, 2008.

———. *New Testament Theology: An Introduction*. Nashville: Abingdon, 2009.

———. "Works of the Law and the Curse of the Law (Galatians 3:10–14)." *New Testament Studies* 31 (1985) 523–42.

Edgar, William. *Created and Creating: A Biblical Theology of Culture*. Downers Grove, IL: IVP Academic, 2016.

Edwards, Jonathan. *A History of the Work of Redemption: Containing the Outlines of a Body of Divinity*. Lexington: Hard, 2011.

Ferguson, Sinclair B. *The Holy Spirit*. Contours of Christian Theology. Downers Grove, IL: InterVarsity, 1996.

———. *The Whole Christ: Legalism, Antinomianism, and Gospel Assurance: Why the Marrow Controversy Still Matters*. Wheaton, IL: Crossway, 2016.

Fesko, J. V. "Calvin and Witsius on the Mosaic Covenant." In *The Law Is Not of Faith*, edited by Bryan D. Estelle et al., 25–43. Phillipsburg, NJ: Presbyterian & Reformed, 2009.

———. "The Republication of the Covenant of Works." *The Confessional Presbyterian* 8 (2012) 197–212.

———. *The Theology of the Westminster Standards: Historical Context and Theological Insights*. Wheaton, IL: Crossway, 2014.

Frame, John M. *The Doctrine of God*. Phillipsburg, NJ: Presbyterian & Reformed, 2002.

———. *A History of Western Philosophy and Theology*. Phillipsburg, NJ: Presbyterian & Reformed, 2015.

———. *Systematic Theology: An Introduction to Christian Belief*. Phillipsburg, NJ: Presbyterian & Reformed, 2013.

Gaffin, Richard B., Jr. "Biblical Theology and the Westminster Standards." In *The Practical Calvinists: An Introduction to the Presbyterian and Reformed Heritage: In Honor of D. Clair Davis' Thirty Years at Westminster Theological Seminary*, edited by Peter A. Lillback, 425–42. Great Britain: Christian Focus, 2002.

———. "Biblical Theology and the Westminster Standards." *Westminster Theological Journal* 65 (2003) 165–79.

———. *Centrality of the Resurrection: A Study in Paul's Soteriology*. Grand Rapids: Baker, 1978.

———. *By Faith, Not by Sight*. Carlisle, UK: Paternoster, 2006.

———. "The Holy Spirit." *Westminster Theological Journal* 43 (1980) 58–78.

———. *Perspectives on Pentecost: Studies in New Testament Teaching on the Gifts of the Holy Spirit*. Grand Rapids: Baker, 1979.

———. *Resurrection and Redemption: A Study in Paul's Soteriology*. Phillipsburg, NJ: Presbyterian & Reformed, 1987.

———. "Systematic Theology and Biblical Theology." In *The New Testament Student and Theology*, edited by John H. Skilton, 3:32–50. Philadelphia: Presbyterian & Reformed, 1976.

———. "The Vitality of Reformed Dogmatics." In *The Vitality of Reformed Theology: Proceedings of the International Theological Congress, June 20–24th 1994, Noordwijkerhout, The Netherlands*, edited by J.M. Batteau et al., 16–50. Kampen: Kok, 1994.

Gentry, Peter J., and Stephen J. Wellum. *Kingdom Through Covenant: A Biblical Theological Understanding of the Covenants*. Wheaton, IL: Crossway, 2012.

Godfrey, W. Robert. *John Calvin: Pilgrim and Pastor*. Wheaton, IL: Crossway, 2009.

———. "Kingdom and Kingdoms." *Evangelium* 7 (2009) 6–9.

Golding, Peter. *Covenant Theology: The Key of Theology in Reformed Thought and Tradition*. Geanies House, Scotland: Christian Focus, 2004.

Griffith, Howard, and John R. Muether, eds. *Creator, Redeemer, Consummator: A Festschrift for Meredith G. Kline*. Jackson, MS: Reformed Theological Seminary, 2000.

Grudem, Wayne. *The Gift of Prophecy*. Wheaton, IL: Crossway, 2000.

———. *Systematic Theology: An Introduction to Biblical Doctrine*. Grand Rapids: Zondervan, 2000.

Gundry, Robert H. *A Survey of the New Testament*. 5th ed. Grand Rapids: Zondervan, 2012.

Hall, David W. "Calvin on Human Government and the State." In *Theological Guide to Calvin's Institutes: Essays and Analysis*, edited by David W. Hall and Peter A. Lillback, 411–40. Phillipsburg, NJ: Presbyterian & Reformed, 2008.

———. *The Legacy of John Calvin: His Influence on the Modern World*. Phillipsburg, NJ: Presbyterian & Reformed, 2008.

Hick, John. "The Non-Absoluteness of Christianity." In *The Myth of Christian Uniqueness: Toward a Pluralistic Theology of Religions*, edited by John Hick and Paul F. Knitter. Maryknoll, NY: Orbis, 1987.

Hodge, A. A. *The Confession of Faith*. London: Banner of Truth Trust, 1992.

Hodge, Charles. *Systematic Theology*. 3 vols. 1871–1873. Reprint, Grand Rapids: Eerdmans, 1995.

Hoekema, Anthony A. *The Bible and the Future*. Grand Rapids: Eerdmans, 1979.

———. *Created in God's Image*. Reprint ed. Grand Rapids: Eerdmans, 1994.

———. *Saved by Grace*. Grand Rapids: Eerdmans, 1989.

Horton, Michael S. *A Better Way: Rediscovering the Drama of Christ-Centered Worship*. Grand Rapids: Baker, 2002.

———. *The Christian Faith: A Systematic Theology for Pilgrims on the Way*. Grand Rapids: Zondervan, 2011.

———. *Covenant and Eschatology*. Louisville: Westminster John Knox, 2002.

———. *Covenant and Salvation*. Louisville: Westminster John Knox, 2007.

Hughes, Philip E. *A Commentary on the Epistles to the Hebrews*. Grand Rapids: Eerdmans, 1977.

———. *A The True Image: The Origin and Destiny of Man in Christ*. Grand Rapids: Eerdmans, 1989.

Jeon, Jeong Koo. "The Abrahamic Covenant and the Kingdom of God." *The Confessional Presbyterian* 7 (2011) 123–38, 249–50.

———. *Biblical Eschatology: Covenant Eschatology for the Global Mission Age*. Eugene, OR: Wipf & Stock, 2021.

———. *Biblical Theology: Covenants and the Kingdom of God in Redemptive History*. Eugene, OR: Wipf & Stock, 2017.

———. *Calvin and the Federal Vision: Calvin's Covenant Theology in Light of Contemporary Discussion*. Eugene, OR: Wipf & Stock, 2009.

———. "Calvin and the Two Kingdoms: Calvin's Political Philosophy in Light of Contemporary Discussion." *Westminster Theological Journal* 72 (2010) 299–320.

———. "The Covenant of Creation and the Kingdom of God." *The Confessional Presbyterian* 9 (2013) 123–42.

———. *Covenant Theology and Justification by Faith: The Shepherd Controversy and Its Impacts*. Eugene, OR: Wipf & Stock, 2006.

———. "Covenant Theology and Old Testament Ethics: Meredith G. Kline's Intrusion Ethics." *Kerux* 16 (2002) 3—33.

———. *Covenant Theology: John Murray's and Meredith G. Kline's Responses to the Historical Development of Federal Theology in Reformed Thought*. Lanham, MD: University Press of America, 2004.

Jones, G. H. "The Concept of Holy War." In *The World of the Old Testament*, edited by R. E. Clements, 299–322. Cambridge: Cambridge University Press, 1989.

———. "'Holy War' or 'Yahweh War'?" *Vetus Testamentum* 25 (1975) 642–58.

Karlberg, Mark W. *Covenant Theology in Reformed Perspective*. Eugene, OR: Wipf & Stock, 2000.

———. "Reformed Theology as the Theology of the Covenants: The Contributions of Meredith G. Kline to Reformed Systematics." In *Creator, Redeemer, Consummator: A Festschrift For Meredith G. Kline*, edited by Howard Griffith and John H. Muether, 235–52. Greenville, SC: Reformed Academic, 2000.

Kim, Seyoon. *Justification and God's Kingdom*. Tübingen: Mohr Siebeck, 2018.

———. *Justification and Sanctification: What Is Justification and Sanctification?* Seoul: Duranno, 2015.

———. *The Origin of Paul's Gospel*. 2nd ed. Tübingen: Mohr and Siebeck, 1984.

———. *Paul and the New Perspective: Second Thoughts on the Origen of Paul's Gospel*. Grand Rapids: Eerdmans, 2002.

Kline, Meredith G. *Essential Writings of Meredith G. Kline*. Peabody, MA: Hendrickson, 2017.

———. *God, Heaven, and Har Magedon: A Covenantal Tale of Cosmos and Telos*. Eugene, OR: Wipf & Stock, 2006.

———. *Images of the Spirit*. Eugene, OR: Wipf & Stock, 1998.

———. "The Intrusion and the Decalogue." *Westminster Theological Journal* 16 (1953) 1–22.

———. *Kingdom Prologue: Genesis Foundations for a Covenantal Worldview*. Eugene, OR: Wipf & Stock, 2006.

———. *The Structure of Biblical Authority*. 2nd ed. Eugene, OR: Wipf & Stock, 1977.

———. *Treaty of the Great King: The Covenant Structure of Deuteronomy: Studies and Commentary*. Eugene, OR: Wipf & Stock, 2012.

Kuyper, Abraham. *Abraham Kuyper: A Centennial Reader*. Edited by James D. Bratt. Grand Rapids: Eerdmans, 1998.

———. *Lectures on Calvinism*. Grand Rapids: Eerdmans, 1994.

Ladd, George Eldon. *The Blessed Hope: A Biblical Study of the Second Advent and the Rapture*. Grand Rapids: Eerdmans, 1956.

———. *Crucial Questions About the Kingdom of God*. Grand Rapids: Eerdmans, 1972.

———. *The Gospel of the Kingdom: Scriptural Studies in the Kingdom of God*. Grand Rapids: Eerdmans, 1959.

———. "Historic Premillennialism." In *The Meaning of the Millennium: Four Views*, edited by Robert G. Clouse, 17–40. Downers Grove, IL: InterVarsity, 1977.

———. *The Presence of the Future*. Grand Rapids: Eerdmans, 1974.

Bibliography

Lewis, C. S. *The Four Loves*. New York: Harcourt, Brace, 1960.

Lillback, Peter A. *The Binding of God: Calvin's Role in the Development of Covenant Theology*. Grand Rapids: Baker, 2001.

Luther, Martin. *Martin Luther's Works*. Edited by Walther I. Brandt. Philadelphia: Fortress, 1962.

Marshal, I. Howard. *New Testament Theology*. Downers Grove, IL: InterVarsity, 2004.

Mathison, Keith A. *Postmillennialism: An Eschatology of Hope*. Phillipsburg, NJ: Presbyterian & Reformed, 1999.

Middleton, J. Richard. *A New Heaven and a New Earth: Reclaiming Biblical Eschatology*. Grand Rapids: Baker Academic, 2014.

Murray, John. *Collected Writings of John Murray*. 4 vols. Grand Rapids: Banner of Truth Trust, 1976–83.

———. *The Covenant of Grace: A Biblico-Theological Study*. Phillipsburg, NJ: Presbyterian & Reformed, 1988.

———. *The Imputation of Adam's Sin*. Phillipsburg, NJ: Presbyterian & Reformed, 1959.

———. *Principles of Conduct: Aspects of Biblical Ethics*. Grand Rapids: Eerdmans, 1957.

———. *Redemption Accomplished and Applied*. Grand Rapids: Eerdmans, 1988.

Niebuhr, Richard H. *Christ and Culture*. New York: Harper and Row, 2001.

Olinger, Danny E., ed. *A Geerhardus Vos Anthology: Biblical and Theological Insights Alphabetically Arranged*. Phillipsburg, NJ: Presbyterian & Reformed, 2005.

Owen, John. *Biblical Theology: The History of Theology from Adam to Christ*. Translated by Stephen P. Westcott. Pittsburg, PA: Soli Deo Gloria, 2007.

Packer, J. I. *Knowing God*. Downers Grove, IL: InterVarsity, 1973.

Park, Hyung Ryong. *Dr. Hyung Ryong Park Systematic Theology*, vol. 6, *Eschatology*. Seoul: Reformed, 2017.

Perkins, William. *Golden Chain*. Puritan Reprints, 2010.

Pink, Arthur W. *The Divine Covenants*. Grand Rapids: Baker, 1975.

Piper, John. *The Future of Justification: A Response to N.T. Wright*. Wheaton, IL: Crossway, 2007.

Poythress, Vern S. *God-Centered Biblical Interpretation*. Phillipsburg, NJ: Presbyterian & Reformed, 1999.

———. *The Returning King: A Guide to the Book of Revelation*. Phillipsburg, NJ: Presbyterian & Reformed, 2000.

———. *Theophany: A Biblical Theology of God's Appearing*. Wheaton, IL: Crossway, 2018.

———. *Understanding Dispensationalists*. Phillipsburg, NJ: Presbyterian & Reformed, 1993.

Rad, Gehard von. *Holy War in Ancient Israel*. Translated and edited by Marva J. Dawn. Grand Rapids: Eerdmans, 1991.

———. *Old Testament Theology*. 2 vols. Translated by D. M. G. Stalker. New York: Harper and Row, 1962.

Ramsey, D. Patrick. "In Defense of Moses: A Confessional Critique of Kline and Karlberg." *Westminster Theological Journal* 66 (2004) 373–400.

Reymond, Robert L. *Faith's Reasons for Believing*. Great Britain: Mentor, 2008.

———. *A New Systematic Theology of the Christian Faith*. Nashville: Thomas Nelson, 1998.

Ridderbos, Herman N. *The Coming of the Kingdom*. Translated by H. De Jongste. Edited by Raymond O. Zorn. Phillipsburg, NJ: Presbyterian & Reformed, 1962.

———. *Paul: An Outline of His Theology*. Translated by John Richard De Witt. Grand Rapids: Eerdmans, 1990.

———. *Paul and Jesus*. Translated by David H. Freeman. Phillipsburg, NJ: Presbyterian & Reformed, 2002.

———. *When the Time Had Fully Come: Studies in New Testament Theology*. Grand Rapids: Eerdmans, 1982.

Riddlebarger, Kim. *A Case for Amillennialism: Understanding the End Times*. Grand Rapids: Baker, 2003.

Robertson, O. Palmer. *The Christ of the Covenants*. Phillipsburg, NJ: Presbyterian & Reformed, 1980.

———. *The Christ of the Prophets: Abridged Edition*. Phillipsburg, NJ: Presbyterian & Reformed, 1980.

———. *The Israel of God: Yesterday, Today, and Tomorrow*. Phillipsburg, NJ: Presbyterian & Reformed, 2000.

Rushdoony, Rousas John. *The Institutes of Biblical Law*. 3 vols. Nutley, NJ: Craig, 1973.

Russell, James Stuart. *The Parousia: The New Testament Doctrine of Christ's Second Coming*. Bradford, PA: International Preterist Association, 2003.

Ryrie, Charles C. *Basic Theology: A Popular Systematic Guide to Understanding Biblical Truth*. Chicago: Moody, 1999.

———. *The Basis of the Premillennial Faith*. New York: Loizeaux, 1953.

———. *Dispensationalism*. Chicago: Moody, 2007.

———. *The Ryrie Study Bible: ESV*. Chicago, IL: Moody, 2011.

Sanders, E. P. "The Covenant as a Soteriological Category and the Nature of Salvation in Palestinian and Hellenistic Judaism." In *Jews, Greeks, and Christians: Religious Cultures in Late Antiquity*, edited by Robert Hamerton-Kelly and Robin Scroggs, 11–44. Leiden, 1976.

———. *Jesus and Judaism*. Philadelphia: Fortress, 1985.

———. *Jewish Law from Jesus to the Mishnah: Five Studies*. Philadelphia: Trinity, 1990.

———. *Paul*. Oxford: Oxford University Press, 1992.

———. *Paul and Palestinian Judaism*. Philadelphia: Fortress, 1977.

———. *Paul, the Law and the Jewish People*. Philadelphia: Fortress, 1983.

Schilder, Klass. *Christ and Culture*. Translated by G. van Rongen and W. Helder. Winnipeg: Premier, 1977.

Schreiner, Susan E. "Calvin's Use of Natural Law." In *A Preserving Grace: Protestants, Catholics, and Natural Law*, edited by Michael Cormartie, 51–76. Grand Rapids: Eerdmans, 1977.

———. *The Theater of His Glory: Nature and the Natural Order in the Thought of John Calvin*. Durham: Labyrinth, 1992.

Schreiner, Thomas R. *Covenant and God's Purpose for the World*. Wheaton, IL: Crossway, 2017.

———. *Faith Alone: The Doctrine of Justification*. Grand Rapids: Zondervan, 2015.

———. "Justification Apart From and By Good Works: At the Final Judgment Works Will Confirm Justification." In *Four Views on the Role of Works at the Final Judgment*, edited by Alan Stanley, 71–118. Grand Rapids: Zondervan, 2013.

Schweitzer, Albert. *The Mystery of the Kingdom of God: The Secret of Jesus' Messiahship and Passion*. Translated by Walter Lowrie. New York: Dodd, Mead, 1914.

Scofield, Cyrus I., ed. *The New Scofield Reference Bible: The Holy Bible Containing the Old and New Testaments*. Authorized King James Version. Edited by E. Schuyler English. New York: Oxford, 1967.

Sohn, Seock-Tae. *The Divine Election of Israel*. Grand Rapids: Eerdmans, 1991.

———. *YHWH, the Husband of Israel: The Metaphor of Marriage between YHWH and Israel.* Eugene, OR: Wipf & Stock, 2002.

Song, Young Jae. *Theology and Piety in the Reformed Federal Thought of William Perkins and John Preston.* Lewiston, NY: Mellen, 1998.

Stott, John R. W. *Baptism & Fullness: The Work of the Holy Spirit Today.* Downers Grove, IL: InterVarsity, 1977.

———. *Christian Mission in the Modern World.* Downers Grove, IL: InterVarsity Press, 1975.

———. *The Cross of Christ.* Downers Grove, IL: InterVarsity, 1986, 2006.

Strimple, Robert B. "Amillennialism." In *Three Views on the Millennium and Beyond*, edited by Darrell L. Bock, 81–129. Grand Rapids: Zondervan, 1999.

Turretin, Francis. *Institutes of Elenctic Theology.* Translated by George Musgrave Giger. Edited by James T. Dennison Jr. 3 vols. Phillipsburg, NJ: Presbyterian & Reformed, 1992–97.

VanDrunen, David. *A Biblical Case for Natural Law.* Studies in Christian Social Ethics and Economics 1. Grand Rapids: Action Institute, 2006.

———. "Calvin on the Church and Society." *Evangelium* 6 (2008) 10–13.

———. *Living in God's Two Kingdoms: A Biblical Vision for Christianity and Culture.* Wheaton, IL: Crossway, 2010.

———. *Natural Law and the Two Kingdoms: A Study in the Development of Reformed Social Thought.* Grand Rapids: Eerdmans, 2010.

———. *Politics after Christendom: Political Theology in a Fractured World.* Grand Rapids: Zondervan Academic, 2020.

———. "The Two Kingdoms: A Reassessment of the Transformationist Calvin." *Calvin Theological Journal* 40 (2005) 248–66.

———. "The Two Kingdoms and the Ordo Salutis: Life Beyond Judgment and the Question of a Dual Ethic." *Westminster Theological Journal* 70 (2008) 207–24.

Vangemeren, Willem. *The Progress of Redemption: The Story of Salvation from Creation to the New Jerusalem.* Grand Rapids: Baker, 1995.

Van Til, Cornelius. *Christian Apologetics.* Phillipsburg, NJ: Presbyterian & Reformed, 1976.

———. *Common Grace and the Gospel.* Phillipsburg, NJ: Presbyterian & Reformed, 1972.

———. *The Defense of Faith.* Phillipsburg, NJ: Presbyterian & Reformed, 1967.

———. *Introduction to Systematic Theology.* Phillipsburg, NJ: Presbyterian & Reformed, 1974.

———. *A Survey of Christian Epistemology.* Philadelphia: Presbyterian & Reformed, 1969.

Vos, Geerhardus. *Biblical Theology: Old and New Testaments.* Grand Rapids: Eerdmans, 1988.

———. *The Doctrine of the Covenant in Reformed Theology.* Ebook. 2012.

———. *The Eschatology of the Old Testament.* Edited by James T. Dennison Jr. Phillipsburg, NJ: Presbyterian & Reformed, 2001.

———. *Grace and Glory: Sermons Preached in the Chapel of Princeton Theological Seminary.* Carlisle, PA: Banner of Truth Trust, 1994.

———. *The Pauline Eschatology.* Grand Rapids: Eerdmans, 1953.

———. *Redemptive History and Biblical Interpretation: The Shorter Writings of Geerhardus Vos.* Edited by Richard B. Gaffin Jr. Phillipsburg, NJ: Presbyterian & Reformed, 1980.

———. *Reformed Dogmatics.* 5 vols. Bellingham, WA: Lexham, 2015.

———. *The Teaching of the Epistle to the Hebrews.* Edited by Johannes G. Vos. Phillipsburg, NJ: Presbyterian & Reformed, 1956.

———. *The Teaching of Jesus: Concerning the Kingdom of God and the Church.* Eugene, OR: Wipf & Stock, 1998.

Walsh, Brian J., and Richard J. Middleton. *The Transforming Vision: Shaping a Christian Worldview*. Downers Grove, IL: InterVarsity, 1984.

Waltke, Bruce K. *An Old Testament Theology: An Exegetical, Canonical, and Thematic Approach*. Grand Rapids: Zondervan, 2007.

Westburg, Daniel. "The Reformed Tradition and Natural Law." In *A Preserving Grace: Protestants, Catholics, and Natural Law*, edited by Michael Cromartie, 103–17. Grand Rapids: Eerdmans, 1997.

Westerholm, Stephen. *Israel's Law and the Church's Faith: Paul and the Recent Interpreters*. Grand Rapids: Eerdmans, 1988.

———. *Perspectives Old and New on Paul: the "Lutheran" Paul and His Critics*. Grand Rapids: Eerdmans, 2004.

The Westminster Standards: An Original Fascimile. Original English ed., 1648. Princeton, NJ: Old Paths, 1997.

Williams, Michael D. *Far as the Curse Is Found: The Covenant Story of Redemption*. Phillipsburg, NJ: Presbyterian & Reformed, 2005.

Williamson, Paul R. *Sealed with an Oath: Covenant in God's Unfolding Purpose*. NSBT 23. Downers Grove, IL: InterVarsity, 2007.

Wolters, Albert M. *Creation Regained: Biblical Basics for a Reformational Worldview*. Grand Rapids: Eerdmans, 1985.

Wright, N. T. *The Climax of the Covenant: Christ and the Law in Pauline Theology*. Minneapolis: Fortress, 1991.

———. *New Testament and People of God*. Minneapolis: Fortress, 1992.

———. *Paul and the Faithfulness of God*. Minneapolis: Fortress, 2013.

———. "The Paul of History and the Apostle of Faith." *Tyndale Bulletin* 29 (1978) 61–88.

———. *The Resurrection of the Son of God*. Minneapolis: Fortress, 2003.

———. *Surprised by Hope: Rethinking Heaven, the Resurrection, and the Mission of the Church*. New York: HarperOne, 2008.

———. *What Saint Paul Really Said*. Grand Rapids: Eerdmans, 1997.

Wright, William J. *Martin Luther's Understanding of God's Two Kingdoms: A Response to the Challenge of Skepticism*. Grand Rapids: Baker Academic, 2010.